From Gloucester to Philadelphia in 1790

*Observations, anecdotes, and thoughts
from the 18th-century letters of*

Judith Sargent Murray

Bonnie Hurd Smith

*"My pen, through life, has continued to me a never failing
reassurance, a never failing consolation — when nearly
overwhelmed with sorrow, I have seized this powerful little
instrument, which like some magick wand has dissipated
the glooms that enveloped my faculties, and I have
arisen from my writing desk, calm if not happy...."*

—Judith Sargent Murray,
from a letter dated March 15, 1817, Letter Book 19

Judith Sargent Murray Society
Cambridge, Massachusetts, 1998

Published by the
Judith Sargent Murray Society
Cambridge, Massachusetts
and
The Curious Traveller Press
a divison of
The Pressroom Printers, Incorporated
32 Blackburn Center
Gloucester, Massachusetts 01930

1998 © Bonnie Smith
1st Edition
ISBN 1-892839-00-8

Book design: Bonnie Smith, HurdSmith Communications
Map illustrations: Linda Bryant

Published with permission from the
Mississippi Department of Archives and History,
Archives and Library Division, Jackson, Mississippi.

ACKNOWLEDGEMENTS
For their unique interest and partnership in this endeavor, my
warmest thanks to the Reverend Gordon J. Gibson, Michael Hennen
and John Turner Sargent; for their friendship, perspective, and ready
ear: Westin Boer, Joanne Ciccarello, Sheldon Cohen, Martin David
Connor, Laurie Crumpacker, Joe and Helen Garland, Leslie B.G.
Goldberg, Polly Welts Kaufman, Martin Krugman, Polly Longsworth,
David McArdle, David A. Mersky, James Orr, Susan Porter, Mary Smoyer,
Susan Wilson, and Anne Teschner; for their invaluable research
assistance and advice: Ellen Nelson of the Cape Ann Historical
Association, Warren Little of the Cambridge Historical Society,
Sally Pierce of The Boston Athenaeum, Mary Ray of Gloucester City
Archives, Paula Richter of the Peabody Essex Museum, Doug Southard
of The Bostonian Society/Old State House, Chris Steele of the
Massachusetts Historical Society, Andrea Ashby of the Independence
National Historical Park, and Lydia Dufour of the Frick Art Reference
Library; for support far beyond the call of duty: Laurie Carter Noble;
special thanks to the Yearwood family, and especially to my parents,
Lydia Averell Hurd Smith and Alan A. Smith, and my sister, Lucinda
Bradford Smith, for understanding the importance of this project.

Cover: Judith Sargent Stevens (Murray), at age 19,
by John Singleton Copley. Courtesy of the Frick Art
Reference Library, New York, and the owner.
Background: Scan from microfilm of Letter 783, Letter Book 8.

DEDICATED TO THE
REVEREND GORDON J. GIBSON
AND TO THE MEMORY OF MY ANCESTORS

Fragment of the page from Letter Book 8 showing the
beginning of Letter 742, the first letter Judith Sargent Murray
wrote about her 1790 journey.

CONTENTS

*quoted from Letter 909, Letter Book 11, November 25, 1800,
written to author Sally Wood of York, Massachusetts, now Maine

"...a person whom we consider as one of the greatest,
and most happy instruments which God in his mercy
hath been pleased to send forth, to explain, and
unfold the sacred mysteries of the blessed gospel...."
(from Letter 803)

Reverend John Murray (1741-1815). Artist Unknown.
Courtesy of The Bostonian Society/Old State House.

INTRODUCTION

One early spring morning in 1790, Judith Sargent Murray and her husband, Reverend John Murray, boarded the horse-drawn stage from the busy seaport of Gloucester, Massachusetts bound for the neighboring port of Salem. It was their first stop on a six-month journey that would take the couple far from their home in Gloucester. Over sometimes treacherous roads, often by moonlight, they would slowly make their way through uncultivated lands and forests, small villages and towns, trading ports, and early centers of commerce to reach their destination — Philadelphia — where the first convention of Universalists was to take place.

Growing in popularity and number of established congregations, followers of this emerging liberal protestant religion determined to meet collectively and discuss their common destiny and individual interests. English-born John Murray, the first Universalist preacher in America, would play a prominent role in this convention spending over two weeks in Philadelphia helping to shape Universalist doctrine and government. "To unite them in one common, and glorious Cause, hath been the wish of his soul,"[1] Judith would later explain.

In many of the towns and cities they visited on their way to Philadelphia (and on the way home) John preached to crowds of up to two thousand listeners. By the time he returned to Gloucester, his notoriety as a charismatic orator and passionate promulgator of Universalism would forever establish his place as a national public figure and a leader in the cause for religious freedom.

Throughout their journey, Judith Sargent Murray wrote letters home to Gloucester relating in great detail what she and her husband saw and whom they met. The natural beauty of the New England countryside overwhelmed Judith and she described, with a sense of awe, both the wild and cultivated lands she saw. She also observed how populated areas were constructed and managed — that Worcester and Springfield, Massachusetts were promising centers of trade "in embryo," how the streets of New York were paved and easy to walk with their raised sidewalks, that Philadelphia was lit all night with elegant street lanterns, and that Bethlehem, Pennsylvania had constructed an indoor plumbing system at its famous female academy.

Often, the Murrays stayed with friends in elegant "mansions," as Judith called them, and she described the furnishings, works of art, and gardens of these private homes. She also introduced her readers to the families themselves, and discussed their daily routines and practices of formal entertaining. Some of these families owned slaves, an institution the Universalists at the Philadelphia convention voted that year to condemn — among the earliest public stands taken against slavery. Strongly opposed to this injustice, Judith relates in one letter with pleasure seeing a free black man attend one of her husband's outdoor preachings. He was, it seems, struck by John's message of universal salvation, based on the inherent equality of all souls.

When they did not stay with friends, Judith and John lodged at inns on the main roads. There, they met colorful strangers, heard interesting stories, and ate "sumptuous" meals. Roadside inns varied in cleanliness and safety, and there were unanticipated adventures to be had at each one.

Judith and John visited dozens of "curiosities" during their journey — the Skuylkill Gardens in Pennsylvania and the Federal Ship moored there, Charles W. Peale's museum and artist's studio, the Philadelphia hospital, mental ward, poor house, and employment service. In New York, then the home of the new federal government and the elegant Federal Building, Judith and John sat through a session of congress and witnessed the signing of the first treaty with the Creek nation. Of this event, Judith would write to her parents how justly, how amicably, the two sides had reached an agreement — one that would surely secure a lasting, peaceful coexistence. She credited George Washington with this diplomatic feat and described with what respect the leaders of the Creek nation were treated by their new neighbors, and with what honorable friendship they reciprocated.

Judith and John were presented at the "American court" in New York on their return trip, and they dined with President and Mrs. Washington and their granddaughter, Eleanor Custis. The President sat Judith on his left, and she would never forget the graciousness of the man she, and most Americans, revered above all others. In turn, George Washington probably never forgot hearing John Murray preach and was, according to Judith, moved by his words. Martha Washington and Judith immediately struck up a lasting friendship, and young Eleanor Custis would become a regular correspondent of Judith's.

The Murrays visited Vice President and Mrs. Adams in New York as well, with whom John had long been acquainted. Judith had met them in Braintree in 1788, and was delighted to find them still modest and unchanged by their elevated status in New York.

In Philadelphia, the Murrays met Sarah Bache, daughter of the recently-deceased and much-revered Benjamin Franklin. There, they heard first-person accounts of Franklin's frugality and brilliance — as well as his adherence to Universalist doctrine — and they were allowed to peruse Franklin's vast library as his daughter now resided in his home. In these, and in many of the places where they stayed, Judith and John were received with much affection and feted with great admiration.

They met Peter Pond, an explorer and trader who had recently returned from the Pacific coast with fossils, shells, and amazing stories. They saw David Rittenhaus's botanical gardens and "peeped" through his telescope at the moon. They marvelled at the inventions of "Mr. Ramsay," who had developed a mill and new kind of river ferry boat. They attended a July 4th celebration in Philadelphia, thrilled by the fireworks and exuberant crowds. They sat through commencement exercises at the University of Pennsylvania and the College of Philadelphia. Examples of fascinating characters and experiences abound, and Judith was delighted with each new adventure.

But there were many hours of loneliness and sadness along the way as well. Less than a year earlier, the Murrays' only child, Fitz Winthrop, had died in childbirth — stillborn, and pulled from his mother's body with 18th-century birthing instruments. For almost 20 years, through her first marriage to Captain John Stevens, and one year of marriage to John Murray, Judith had longed for children. This loss was agonizing for her, and the birthing process nearly cost her her life. At age 38, she was convinced she would never become a mother. For John Murray, this was the second infant he had lost. His first wife and baby had died in childbirth in England before he came to America. Ironically, neither John nor Judith could have known that one year later — she at age 40, he at age 50 — Judith would give birth to a daughter, Julia Maria, who would survive to adulthood. But in 1790, on this trip, Judith and John marked the one-year anniversary of their infant son's death and they mourned for their loss. It was difficult, sometimes, when they met or stayed with large families with healthy, happy children.

For Judith, who was extremely attached to her family, leaving Gloucester behind for six months often left her feeling quite lonely. Mail was slow, inefficient, and costly. If they travelled the Post Road from town to town, Judith would eventually arrive at a destination where letters could be received and sent and they could apprise family members of their changing travel plans. But often times small roads took them far away from the main road, and weeks would go by before Judith knew if her sister-in-law, Anna, had given birth and survived, if her brother, Fitz William, had returned safely from his trade voyage to England, if her mother's fragile health had worsened or improved. Her parents were aging, and she was particularly worried about their well-being. And sometimes, letters were simply lost along the way and news was even more delayed.

The couple also had to contend with John's exhaustion. As with most public figures, he drove himself hard. He rarely refused a request to preach or to meet with "adherents" if it meant spreading the "glad tidings" of Universalism. With the exception of their two-week residence in Philadelphia, their travel schedule was tiring even by modern standards. Even before the trip, John had frequent bouts of illness. This trip was a strain on him, and on their return trip — in Hartford, Connecticut — he collapsed and was bedridden for days. His followers filled the house where he lay ill, waiting for news of his restored health. Judith was frightened — far from home, childless, possibly losing her beloved husband. Luckily, John recovered, but it was an anxious time for both of them.

Judith, however, was made of strong, colonial stuff. That, and her unshakable faith in God's ever-present guiding hand sustained her. It was something she thought and wrote about as part of her daily consciousness. John could not have married someone with a deeper faith than Judith's. As often as despair filled her mind, eventually the emptiness and fear would pass. Her trust in God would prevail, and she would again be thankful for her many blessings. She would return to enjoying her present-day adventures, and be "zested" with the wonders each new day would bring.

Deep feelings of faith and loss, thoughts on politics and public policy, observations on the people and curiosities she encountered — very little escaped the attention of Judith Sargent Murray's pen as she spent many late evenings, by candlelight, writing home to her family in Gloucester. The letters presented here are an intimate window into a time long since past. They give voice to a woman who witnessed both the extraordinary and the ordinary in 1790. Never before read or published in their entirety, they are only the beginning of what we have to learn from Judith Sargent Murray.

[1]From Letter 803, see page 317.

STATES, CITIES, AND TOWNS
OF THE 1790 JOURNEY

Note: The names and spelling Judith Sargent Murray used when describing cities and towns have been maintained.

*This part of Massachusetts became the State of Maine in 1820.

MASSACHUSETTS, CONNECTICUT, AND RHODE ISLAND

"We were received at the [Worcester] public house,
into a decent parlour — a neat little Girl threw upon
the breakfast table an elegant damask cloth, and hyson
tea of a superior quality, with sweet bread and butter,
furnished us a most delicious repast...."
(from Letter 743)

"Perhaps no part of the United States, can produce
a greater variety of beautiful prospects, than fascinate
the eye upon Connecticut River — Nature is here most
luxuriantly diversified — The Grove top[p]ed Mountains,
the verdant Plains, the rich meadows, orchards,
variegated fields, and commodious dwellings, most
delightfully interspersed, altogether constitute
a chain of imagery, which is truly pleasing...."
(from Letter 743)

NEW YORK, NEW JERSEY, AND PENNSYLVANIA

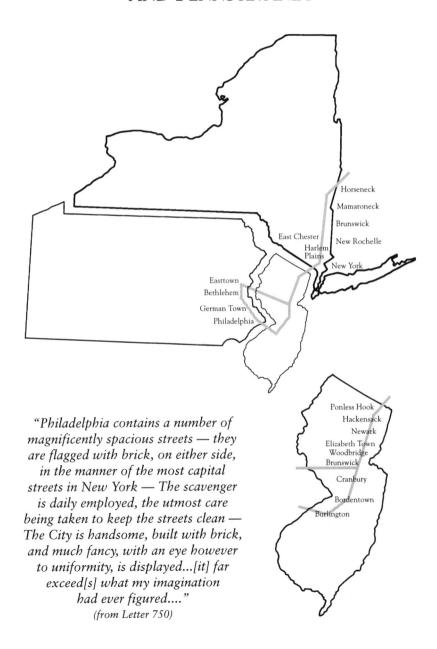

Horseneck
Mamaroneck
Brunswick
East Chester
New Rochelle
Harlem
Plains
New York

Easttown
Bethlehem
German Town
Philadelphia

Ponless Hook
Hackensack
Newark
Elizabeth Town
Woodbridge
Brunswick
Cranbury
Bordentown
Burlington

"Philadelphia contains a number of magnificently spacious streets — they are flagged with brick, on either side, in the manner of the most capital streets in New York — The scavenger is daily employed, the utmost care being taken to keep the streets clean — The City is handsome, built with brick, and much fancy, with an eye however to uniformity, is displayed...[it] far exceed[s] what my imagination had ever figured...."
(from Letter 750)

About the Letters

In 1984, a Unitarian Universalist minister named Reverend Gordon Gibson was serving a parish near Natchez, Mississippi where Judith Sargent Murray died in 1820. Like most UU ministers, he had read John Murray's autobiography, noticed that his wife had completed it after his death, and wondered what kind of person Judith was in her own right. Reverend Gibson began looking for research materials, but there was very little information to find — no biography, no personal papers, nothing of real substance.

Like others of us who have conducted research on Judith over the years, Reverend Gibson read Richard Eddy's *Universalism in Gloucester* which includes a footnote about Judith that reads: "At her death she left a large and valuable collection of manuscripts...these papers...were stored in an unoccupied house on her son-in-law's plantation, and...were found to be utterly rotted and spoiled by the mildew." Later, Reverend Gibson read another reference to these papers suggesting that a family Bible might still exist — in Natchez.

Puzzled by these discrepancies, Reverend Gibson decided to investigate. He searched out descendants of the son-in-law's family and, eventually, found the 20 letter books into which Judith Sargent Murray had copied her outgoing correspondence from 1765 to 1818, from ages 14 to 67.

Reverend Gibson brought the letter books to the very capable Michael Hennen at the Mississippi Department of Archives. He, in turn, sent the documents to the Northeast Document Conservation Center in North Andover, Massachusetts, under a grant from the National Endowment for the Humanities. Northeast Document preserved and microfilmed the letter books, returning them to Mississippi where they remain under Hennen's watchful eye.

Excerpts from the letters published in this book are transcribed from a copy of the microfilm. The 1790 journey letters are taken from Judith's Letter Book 8. Those letters have been reproduced in their entirety to give readers a contextual sense of the 18th-century genre of letter writing, including the obligatory salutations and closings that followed custom. Some are lengthy, meandering, and stream-of-consciousness. Others are punchy, filled with anecdotes and important historical information. Each letter, therefore, is preceded by a brief paragraph explaining its key content and to whom it is addressed.

The condition of the original documents made it impossible to decipher every word of every letter. The paper pages of the letter books are fragile and years of hot Mississippi summers stained their appearance with dark blotches of mildew. In many cases, ink shows through from page to page, and Judith's handwriting is not always legible. Where I simply could not read a word nor determine its meaning, I indicated such gaps with "...". Where I could not read a word but chose to insert a word based on her intended meaning, I did so using [ ].

Judith's punctuation will look unusual to contemporary eyes. She used either a comma, long dash, or nothing at all to end a sentence, and used commas liberally throughout her writing. I did not alter her punctuation except where a sentence ender was needed to guide the reader. These are indicated with [—].

Judith Sargent Murray's vocabulary is exquisitely rich and contains many words no longer in use. Her spelling is inconsistent and predates current rules of grammar. She rarely used paragraph breaks. Instead, because paper was so expensive, she filled her pages as densely as possible. And yet, here they are: a never-before-read collection of letters that offer an eyewitness account of a journey from Gloucester to Philadelphia in 1790.

—B.H.S.

I have committed to the flames, nearly all my letters, written previous to the year one thousand, seven hundred, and seventy-four, preserving only two or three, for the purpose of comparing myself — with myself — The letters which I have destroyed contained a kind of history of my juvenile life — Perhaps, it may be observed, it would have been well if I had made my conflagration more general — Yet, if those who may survive me, possess as much curiosity relative to me as I have experienced respecting those individuals of my kindred, who have lived before me, every thing I have written will be read by my posterity, should I be blest with descendants, with interest and avidity — Some of my letters I have purposely involved in ambiguity — let no one seek to lift the veil — every thing relative to me as an individual, I have endeavoured to render clear and unembarrassed, but when remarking upon the communications of others, I possess no right to be thus explicit — Upon the whole, I commend these volumes of letters to affectionate posterity, and, thus patronized, I am assured I have little to fear.

Judith Sargent Murray

Judith began her first Letter Book with this statement to future generations.
Her signature is traced from the deed of sale of her home in Gloucester.

"*Gloucester possesses for me superior charms —
My warmest affections hover round the asylum of my youth —
There resideth the indulgently venerable forms of my tender,
and ever honoured Parents, there dwelleth individuals whom
I sincerely love...In that spot rests the ashes of my Ancestors —
There too sleeps the cold gray tenement of...the little form,
which for a season, partook my sufferings...*" (from Letter 766)

*A Correct View of the Town and outer Harbour of Gloucester, and the appearance
of the Sea Serpent as was Seen on the 14th August 1817 — from the Original sketch
of Capt John Beach Jr.* Courtesy of the Cape Ann Historical Society.

"I am Jealous for the Honour of Our Sex"
Introducing
Judith Sargent Murray

Note to the Reader: *The information contained here is incomplete. The copies Judith Sargent Murray kept of her letters, written between ages 14 and 67, have not been read, analyzed, and interpreted in their entirety. Judith destroyed letters written before the age of 14, and saved only very few from her young adult years. To date, we have not found documents left behind by members of her family who might have written about her early development. For each stage of her life, the best we can do is piece together what we do know from what have. This biographical overview reflects this author's best knowledge of her letters and published work. —B.H.S.*

Gloucester in 1751 was a busy seaport in the vast British empire — its citizens hard-working and independent-minded, its character defined by the unforgiving waters and winds that brought both sustenance and tragedy. One hundred and twenty-eight years had already passed since Gloucester's first settlers had arrived from England. In 1751, her population was about 2,800. There were five parishes and no schools. Some families, in Gloucester for several generations, had achieved wealth and influence through their ability to import and export valuable commodities.

Judith Sargent was born into such a family on May 5, 1751 — the firstborn child of Winthrop Sargent (1727-1793) and Judith Saunders Sargent (1731-1793). Out of a total of eight Sargent children, three others survived: Winthrop (1753-1820), Esther (1755-1811) and FitzWilliam (1768-1822). Judith and her brothers and sister were the fifth generation of Sargents in America since their ancestors, William Sargent and Mary Epes Sargent, left England in the late 1600s to make their mark in the American colonies. On her mother's side Judith was descended from the great sea captain Andrew Robinson, who is credited with building a vessel that "schooned" and thus creating the term "schooner." Judith's Gloucester roots ran deep. Throughout her life, she would always consider the town her "dear native place."

Judith was raised in an elegant mansion in the Middle Street area of town, overlooking the family wharves and sailing vessels and surrounded by loving members of her extended family. Her uncles, Epes Sargent (1721-1779) and Daniel Sargent (1731-1806), were also successful members of the merchant class, their ships sailing regularly to the British West Indies and England. Judith's aunt, Catherine Osborne Sargent (1722-1788), Epes's wife, was an integral part of her husband's business dealings and of her niece's life. Mary Turner Sargent (?-1814), Daniel's wife, was another important influence for young Judith and would become the close confidant she nicknamed "Maria." Because trading brought the Sargents in regular contact with places and people far beyond their native shores, they considered themselves citizens of the world. They were enlightened thinkers, bringing books and ideas home to Gloucester. Judith's family home contained a family library — probably a rarity in Gloucester — and the Sargents believed wholeheartedly in education. Their sons were tutored at home to prepare them for Harvard College; their daughters were taught the rudimentary skills of reading, writing, and domestic work that were typical of upper class female education at the time.

There was a boldness to the Sargent family — an ability to lead, make tough decisions, and play a public role when necessary. They were politically active, first within the established colonial government and then as American patriots. As federalists, the Sargents at first believed that separation from England would harm the financial interests of the colonists. But as colonial rule became increasingly intolerable, they supported the creation of an independent nation and were very much a part of its founding days. In Gloucester, Judith's father served as General George Washington's purchasing agent during the war. In 1779, Winthrop and Epes Sargent were delegates to the state Constitutional Convention. Judith's brother, Winthrop, served as an officer in Washington's continental army, going on to appointments as governor of the Ohio and Mississippi Territories. The Sargent family self-confidence, courage, sense of honor and duty, were not, however, the province of its male members. These were defining aspects of young Judith's character as well.

Judith's was also a loving home. She was devoted to her parents — "the authors of my being," she called them — and very close to her brothers and sister. There were occasional disagreements, of course, but there was a prevailing, affectionate bond among the Sargent children that lasted throughout their lives. As yet, no surviving documents detailing Judith's girlhood have been found. But years later, as her family extended and Judith became a mother, aunt, and older cousin to numerous children, her loving nature and active participation in their upbringing suggest that her own was happy and supportive.

In such a home, Judith's developing mind must have been bored learning basic literacy and domestic skills — especially since her brother, Winthrop, was being taught so much more. Judith quickly outgrew her "ill taught Preceptress," and turned to the family library to continue her education. There, on her own, she took her reading and writing skills far beyond what was expected of her. Clearly, she was successful in her intellectual journey. But the vast and inexplicable difference between male and female education haunted her for life, and would become a principal subject of her work. Years later she would write to Winthrop, "I have, through life, mourned the want of early instruction...."[1]

Judith's earliest writing was poetry, which would always remain her first love. Her father, apparently, shared her work with family members making no secret of his pride in her ability. Father and daughter were very close, and he would always serve as an inspiration to her. Judith also began writing letters at a young age. At age 14, she decided to start keeping copies of her outgoing correspondence in "letter books" — indexed, sequentially numbered letters copied into matching leather journals. The first letter, in the first volume, was written in 1765 to her "dear Pappa" who was away from Gloucester on business. Earlier letters, Judith wrote in the introduction to Letter Book 1, she committed "to the flames" deeming them unworthy of saving.[2]

What Judith read during her early years is as yet unknown. Certainly, she read the Bible and the early Universalist writings her father brought home. However, we do know that at age 16 she inscribed "the best book that ever was written" in *The Oeconomy of Human Life In Two Parts; Translated from an Indian manuscript, written by an ancient BRAMIN*.[3]

Marriage, the War Years, and the Arrival of John Murray

When she was 18, Judith married John Stevens, the son of a prominent Gloucester family who had ties of blood and friendship to the Sargents. Like Winthrop Sargent, John was a merchant and he and his family were wealthy. Since marrying well was the singular expectation of young women of Judith's station, theirs was a suitable match although not based on love. Judith's letters from this period of time do not discuss their courtship, marriage, her parents' opinion, or domestic arrangements. "Mr Stevens," as she referred to him in her letters, simply begins to appear in passing conversation in 1769.

The Stevens' marriage lasted for 18 years and produced no children. During these years (from 1769 to 1787) Judith's world changed completely, as it did for every member of the British empire. The Boston Massacre took place in 1770. "Indians" dumped tea into Boston Harbor in 1773. Boston was filled with British troops, her harbor shut tight to force acquiescence to King George's will. "Minutemen" in Lexington and Concord resisted British attempts to destroy arms and supplies in 1775. The "shot heard 'round the world" was fired, and the American colonies, one by one, joined the fight for American independence.

The coming war was not all-consuming, however, and Judith's personal and spiritual life changed forever in 1774. A Universalist minister named John Murray had accepted Winthrop Sargent's invitation to preach in Gloucester to a small but dedicated gathering of adherents to the emerging liberal faith. John Murray (1741-1815), born in Alton, England, to a strict, even cruel, Calvinist Methodist father, had at first followed his father's faith unquestioningly feeling called to the service of God. He was a talented speaker and educator, especially with young people. After his father passed away, while John was still a young man, he encountered James Relly and the "good news" of Universalism. Relly's interpretation of scripture was based on a God who loved his "children" — all of his children — and offered universal salvation through faith. A God of love — not of damnation or "hellfire and brimstone" — made sense to John intellectually and spiritually. He became a student of Relly's and a preacher of the new faith. He also married, in the late 1760s, a woman named Eliza Neale. Soon after, however, John lost his wife and baby son in childbirth. He became distraught, close to financial ruin, and, he felt, a failure to God. John decided he no longer wished to live and so, not wanting to become a burden to his family, he decided to make his way to America and live out what was left of his life.

In 1770, John Murray boarded the *Hand-in-Hand* bound for New York. The ship ran aground off the coast of New Jersey, however, and John was forced to go ashore. There, he met Thomas Potter who kindly looked after him. Mr. Potter told John he had recently built a church, and that he had been waiting for a preacher to bring more tolerant religious views to its pulpit. His conversations with John quickly revealed John's past calling, and Mr. Potter urged him to preach. John declined. That part of his life was over. He had failed God, and failed himself. But Mr. Potter was persistent, telling John the wind would not change direction, and his ship would not sail, until he preached. Days went by, and no wind. Finally, John relented, and Mr. Potter gathered a sizeable crowd in his grove. A second time, John's calling to the service of God was made clear to him. His thunderous voice, his warmth, magnetism, and conviction in his chosen faith, earned John many friends in that place and the beginning of a new life.

The wind changed, and the *Hand-in-Hand* finished its journey to New York. By the time John arrived, Mr. Potter had already written to friends in that city about John. He was received with acclaim and affection, and spent the next few years travelling up and down the Eastern seaboard and preaching Universalist doctrine. In 1774, he accepted Winthrop Sargent's invitation to preach in Gloucester. In his autobiography, he later wrote:

November 3d, I repaired to Gloucester, and was received by a very few warm-hearted Christians. The mansion-house — the heart, of the then head of the Sargent family, with his highly accomplished, and most exemplary lady, were open to receive me. I had travelled from Maryland to New Hampshire, without meeting a single individual, who appeared to have the smallest idea of what I esteemed the truth, as it is in Jesus; but to my great astonishment, there were a few persons, dwellers in that remote place, upon whom the light of the gospel had more than dawned. The writings of Mr. Relly were not only in their hands but in their hearts.[4]

One of the "persons" John met was 23-year-old Judith Sargent — then, Mrs. John Stevens. She was ten years his junior, exceptional in intellect and beauty. Clearly, the first encounter between Judith and John Murray was electric. She had found an intellectual equal, mentor, spiritual teacher, and friend. She wrote to him on November 14 that they would, "with the strictest propriety, mingle souls upon paper"[5] and thus began a 14-year intimate correspondence between two friends who would eventually marry. The next month, in December, John visited Gloucester again and decided to stay. He wrote, "Here my God grants me rest from my toils, here I have a taste of heaven."[6]

Gloucester might have been a taste of heaven in some senses, but it was also entering a war. A major trading port, Gloucester was not isolated from the events taking place to the south in Boston. Rather, "Gloucester was in dire fear of an attack from the sea at any hour."[7] If that happened, Gloucestermen would be "at the mercy of the mightiest navy in the world."[8] Gloucester had voted to support efforts in Boston, its sister port, to boycott tea. They were also prepared to march to Lexington and Concord if need be. Now, they kept watch over their own harbor, waiting, their "nerves stretched."[9]

In June and July, the British passed restraining acts that further curtailed trade at sea — and the financial security of Gloucesterians. They had also passed acts banning unauthorized assembly and elections. British vessels patrolled the waters off Gloucester to enforce these regulations, and in July Gloucesterians saw British sails approaching their harbor. Judith described the scene on Middle Street for John Murray as the *Hope* came into view:

You wish for some particulars relative to our publick affairs, and indeed they have somewhat varied since you left us — Upon the day of your departure, the arrival of a schooner belonging to his Britannick Majesty, threw our people into great alarm — Immediately the drums beat to arms, the bells sounded portentously, and the streets were filled with the goods of the terrified inhabitants

— Females running up and down, throwing abroad their hands, the most heart affecting distress visible in their almost frantic gestures, when to heighten the misery of the scene, the Captain of the schooner dispatched a special messenger to the family of the Sargents, soliciting permission to visit them, and begging that some fresh provision may be sent on board, for which he will make ample payment, and disavowing at the same time all intention of hostility — "No, no, no" was the purport of the answer, worded in as strong terms as language could embody [—] We continued in a state of distressing suspense, through the whole of friday, saturday and sunday — all our men bearing arms even to their place of worship...[seeing] maneuvers on board the schooner, it was believed the war was coming up to the landing, Words are inadequate to describe the panic which took possession of the bosoms of the more timid sex, while our Men bravely prepared for opposition....[10]

In August, the British chased a daring trading vessel into Gloucester Harbor and again the alarm bell rang out from the Middle Street meetinghouse. Gloucester's men rushed to the waterfront, guns in hand, and successfully drove *Falcon* from their harbor — but only after one cannonball had lodged itself in Daniel Sargent's home on Spring Street and another across Middle Street, in the meetinghouse tower. Indeed, the war was just outside Judith's door.[11]

The war was all too present for John Murray as well. In 1775, General George Washington appointed him to serve as chaplain for two Rhode Island regiments stationed in Massachusetts. Outraged that Washington would choose a heretic for this post, members of the established clergy protested. Washington was furious, and made John chaplain of all the regiments from Rhode Island. John assumed his position but soon had to return to Gloucester due to ill health. There, he was instrumental in raising money for the citizens of Gloucester who were suffering from the effects of British blockades.

For Judith, the late 1770s were lonely and fearful while John Stevens was away from home and her brother, Winthrop, was fighting in the war. In a letter to John Murray, Judith wrote: "Mr Stevens alas! is far away, and I set alone in this forsaken and dreary Mansion!"[12] Winthrop, who by 1778 had been commissioned Aide de Camp to General Howe, received many letters from his sister in which she praised his patriotism and prayed for his safe return. In one letter, she wrote:

The brave are always humane and my brother adorns the valour of the intrepid soldier, with every gentler Virtue...May heaven send you safely to your native place, may discord hasten from our globe, and benign peace, reassuming the reigns of government give our youthful Warriors, to repose once more, under the dear covert of the paternal shade....[13]

Along with the British threat, Gloucester was overrun with small pox during the war years. Dozens of residents fled to the safety of the countryside, including members of Judith's family. But not all escaped the dreadful "hydra." Two years earlier, in the spring of 1776, Judith had been inoculated with small pox. She had seen too many people die — carted off to quarantined "pest houses" where they received no care. Inoculation was dangerous, but she could not bear to lose any members of her family — especially her politically active father, who journeyed regularly to pox-infected areas. If inoculation meant Judith could help her family by nursing them to health, she would take the risk. She did so — successfully. And, indeed, Judith was needed later on to bring family members through the disease — including her father.

A New Addition to the Household

By 1780, war activities had quieted down in Gloucester but Judith's life was as full as ever. One of John Stevens's sisters had just died, along with her husband, leaving five orphaned daughters. Their relatives in York were unable to care for the girls, so two came to Gloucester — Anna and Mary. Judith, now 21, took in Anna to raise as her own daughter. She described Anna's arrival, and her hopes for her young charge, in this letter to John Murray:

> Well, dear Sir, my little Girl is at length come and an idea of the importance of the charge disposed upon me, absorbs every faculty of my soul, I wish my cares could have commenced earlier, it is difficult building upon the foundation of another. I should be glad the mind which I have to form, might be unbiased by prejudice. I wish — in short I hardly know what I wish — Heigh! Ho! — ah! me — would I were in any other character — But peace my soul, and give me, O! thou God of consolation to pursue unrepining the path pointed out by providence — At an early hour, last evening, the little Anna was presented, my sister and her husband were with me — I met her, at the door, and taking her hand, led her into the parlour — you are welcome, my dear to this house, and to this heart — a tear, as I hope of sensibility stole down her cheek [—] I marked it with peculiar pleasure, and I introduced her to my friends — The poor child appeared exceedingly awkward, I endeavoured, by encouraging smiles, and complacency to create a decent measure of confidence and my sister on taking her departure requested my Anna to view her as a friend and obligingly hoped she would often be

allowed to visit her — This morning I conducted my little charge into my chamber, and seating her by my side addressed her — you are now my dear girl, to consider yourself as one of this family — your Uncle and myself expect you will reside with us until providence shall place you in a house of your own, and, from this moment it is my wish you should view me as a Mother — it is true my years are too few to entitle me to that revered claim, from an individual of your age — but as that power who always decreeth wisely, hath thought fit to deprive you of the guards of your youth, and to place your Uncle, and myself, in their stead, we have a right to demand your duteous confidence, and it is in the maternal character which I assume with pleasure, that I would care only for your future conduct — you do not enter this house as a servant, you are, my dear, to consider yourself rather as a daughter — The Girl who lives with me as a domestic, is visited by many persons of her own rank, I am not averse to rendering her life as happy as she can, a state of servitude is at best but barely tolerable, and it has a claim to every possible alleviation — but I shall be shocked to see you, Anna, taking up your abode in the kitchen. I shall expect you will esteem it a privilege to associate with me, and with my circle of friends — believe me, you will learn much from my friends — yet I would not wish you should assume a haughty deportment, with those who are placed in an inferior station — let sweet, and condescending benignity ever illume your countenance and manners, and always remember the distinctions now existing will e'er long exist no more, that we are hastening to that world, where the probability is, we shall reassume primeval equality...The dear Girl...modestly courtseyed, hoped to render herself in all things acceptable to me, and, with my permission withdrew — Thus much for a beginning —[14]

Throughout their time together, Judith would encourage Anna to seize every opportunity that came her way. Whatever intellectual ideas Judith had about female education, she now had the responsibility of raising a young girl and the chance to guide her young mind. Later, she took in Anna's sister, Mary, as well. Judith took her new role very seriously, as shown in this letter to Anna:

...you are, my Love, apprized that your prospects in life, are not the most eligible — An Orphan, and destitute of those advantages to be derived from fortune[,] it is incumbent upon you to seize every opportunity which presents for improvement — I do not, my dear Girl, speak this to wound your feelings, but merely to stimulate your efforts — While your dear Uncle and myself live, and possess ability, we shall aim at alleviating, as far as is in our power, all those evils which generally attend the happiest life....[15]

Christmas of that same year (1780) saw the dedication of Gloucester's new Universalist meeting house — the first Universalist church in America. John Murray, its pastor, oversaw the ceremony. Unfortunately, Judith was in Boston caring for her sick father. So many arrangements had been made, the dedication could not be postponed. Winthrop Sargent regretted missing the culmination of his hard work and Judith wished she could have been there as well, but her signature appears in the church's founding document.

In 1781, the Sargents and John Murray brought suit against Gloucester's Committee of Safety. Refusing to pay taxes to the First Parish Church — a church they no longer supported — the Universalists instead wished to support their own minister and their own church. At a time when church and town were one and the same, this act of defiance led the Committee of Safety to seize articles belonging to the Sargent family to pay the taxes. The Committee also wanted John to leave their town — immediately — refusing to acknowledge the legitimacy of his ministry or the Universalist church. Defying custom and their social standing, the Sargents, John Murray, and other noted Gloucesterians, took their case to the Supreme Judicial Court represented by James Sullivan, Esq. The favorable decision came down in 1785. The Universalists had won — for now.

During this time, John Stevens was building a new house on Middle Street and in 1782 Judith, John Stevens, Anna, and their servant girl took up residence in what Judith always referred to as her "narrow house." That same year, in Portsmouth, New Hampshire, she published privately and anonymously her Universalist catechism — a personal declaration of her faith. She was among the first women to do so, and explains how the project came about in this letter to a friend in London:

> If my little Catechism meets your approbation, it will possess a claim to my esteem, of which it hath hitherto been destitute — The story of its birth, and introduction to a censorious world, the preface truly gives — I am not my dear Madam a Parent — My years are not greatly multiplied — yet I have had the presumption to take upon me the charge of two orphan Girls — My task is arduous, and perhaps the tenderness of a Mother is requisite, to support the mind, and to render tolerable, the difficulties which too often spring up in the path of Education — My memory, standing in need of an assistant, I was induced to write — my friends earnestly requesting, I was induced to publish — Mr Murray was then in Philadelphia — but, upon his return he approved, he could not but approve, the

sentiments he had instilled [—] Thus the history of my little offspring
in short, and trifling as it appears, it is however the production of a
heart, glowing with gratitude and humble adoration, as it
contemplates the beautiful Order established by the Great, First
Cause — the tender care of paternal Deity[16]

Judith's faith was organic. God's love and guiding hand were a
reassuring presence in her life — never far from her thoughts.
In particular, faith buoyed Judith's spirits during dark times. When death
took her loved ones, she knew they would be reunited in the next world.
When things happened she did not understand, she knew, one day, God
would reveal His divine plan. Judith believed, completely, in Universalist
theology and in John Murray. Her conviction in his calling to serve as
God's messenger equalled John's. This, along with Judith's inability to
play a passive role in important issues, made her an early and
defining voice in the Universalist religion — long before she became
Mrs. John Murray. In the years just to come, Judith would need every
ounce of faith to sustain her.

Widowed and Poor, but Judith Begins to Publish

Sadly, like so many other merchants who made their living at sea, John
Stevens found himself unable to recover from the financial distress
caused by years of trade embargos and economic instability during the
war. His debts mounted rapidly, and he knew his inability to satisfy
creditors would eventually sentence him to debtors prison. In vain, Judith
wrote letter after letter asking local merchants to extend their credit
and offer her husband greater leniency. Judith was humiliated and
frightened. She had no financial recourse save her husband's earnings
and it was unclear what would happen to him. Would she, too, become
a destitute widow like so many other women? If it weren't for her
father's generosity, this could easily happen. And it was a lesson in
economic self-sufficiency Judith never forgot — one that became a
recurring theme in her writing.

Perhaps Judith's financial distress led to her first professional
publication. She had been writing privately for years, sharing her poetry
with family and friends. At age 33, she was finally beginning to have a
sense of her own voice and a desire to use it publicly and contribute to
national debates. Her relationship with John Murray, and their endless
conversations on political and intellectual subjects, no doubt drew out
her literary aspirations. As a woman in the 1780s, there were very few
ways to earn money — especially for women of her class. But she could
write under assumed names. She could voice her opinions *and* earn
money — and no one would know. In October of 1784, Judith published

"Desultory Thoughts Upon the Utility of Encouraging a Degree of Complacency in the Female Bosom" in the *Gentleman and Lady's Town and Country Magazine* using the pen name "Constantia." She would use this name regularly both for her published writing and in her letters, as an affectionate name reserved for her closest friends. "Desultory Thoughts" was an achievement in feminist thinking, and just the beginning of much more to come.

In 1786, John Stevens left Gloucester for St. Eustacius in the West Indies to avoid debtors prison. He saw no other solution but to leave, earn money elsewhere, and slowly make reparations back home. In March, he boarded a vessel owned by Judith's father and set sail. In a letter to her brother, Winthrop, Judith wrote:

> My heart, I confess, consents not to this arrangement yet it is countenanced by every friend — My opposition has been strong and although I am now silenced, I am not, however, convinced of its viability. It is supposed we shall be able to make restitution with our claimants, when they shall know my husband is beyond their reach, and the poor man flatters himself, that in the course of a few months, he shall be able to return blest with liberty and competency.[17]

Harassed by creditors, depressed, and in failing health, Judith decided to leave town for a lengthy trip down the Eastern coast through southern Massachusetts and Connecticut. She took Anna with her, and they spent some delightful summer months visiting friends and restoring their spirits.

But soon, back in Gloucester, Judith's life would take another sudden turn. On March 8, 1787, Judith woke suddenly from a deep sleep. It was 11:00 in the evening — dark, and cold. A vision had aroused her, even frightened her. The image of her estranged husband had appeared — so lifelike. In a letter to Winthrop, she wrote:

> ...such was my dream, and strong was the impression which it made upon my soul and quitting my bed I inserted in my memorandum book — Thursday night eleven o-clock — eighth of March 1787 [—] It was the first time I had been thus influenced by a dream — but such was the agitation of my mind, that I regarded it as the passage of some most favourable event...But alas! the middle of the month of April, produced Captain Webber from St Eustacia — We inquired, and we learned that on thursday night eleven o-clock eighth of March 1787th Mr Stevens expired!! and thus is finished, thus forever closed, the melancholy scene.[18]

Judith secluded herself in her home — sad, weary, unable to look toward the future. In a letter to Winthrop, she wrote, "Retirement is necessary to heal the wounds made by adversity."[19] The same day, she told her aunt, Mary Turner Sargent, who wanted Judith to visit her in Boston, "I yet find it difficult to leave home...."[20]

Elsewhere in the country, peace was finally at hand and the new American government was taking shape. The Articles of Confederation had been passed in 1781. England's Lord North was forced from office in 1782, and treaties with Britain were signed in 1783. The last British troops left New York in November. Thomas Jefferson drafted the separation of church and state legislation in 1786. The Ohio Territory was opening up and Judith's brother, Winthrop, was appointed its Secretary under Arthur St. Clair. Dr. Benjamin Rush's landmark *Thoughts Upon Female Education* was published, and the American Constitution was being drafted.

In Gloucester, John Murray was ill again and finding it difficult to work. Judith offered to help with his correspondence, and this lifted her spirits and helped restore his health. But the Committee of Safety had initiated a new challenge to John's ministry, this time declaring any marriage ceremony he had performed null and void. John's congregation was furious. Again, they called on their friend, James Sullivan, to take their appeal to the legislature. They wanted the legal and doctrinal legitimacy of John's ministry — and that of any other new ministry — upheld. While the ruling was discussed at the state level, Gloucester was not a safe place for John. Taking with him a letter of safe passage written by Judith's father, uncle, and their friend, David Plummer, John Murray returned to his native England in March where he waited for word of the legal ruling.

Before he left, John penned a letter to Judith in which he finally revealed his love for her. Now that she was widowed, John no longer thought such a declaration would be improper. They might never see each other again, and he wanted her to know what was in his heart. He left the letter for Judith to read in his absence. Judith was inexpressibly sad to lose another person from her life, and one to whom she had become so close. Her response to him:

> ...upwards of thirteen years have elapsed, since your first visit to this then happy Village, and in all that period, three successive weeks have not revolved, without bringing us letters, acquainting us with your movements, your well being, your hopes, and your fears — Now alas! what a long and dreary season is before us — The great waters are between us, suspense corrodes our peace, our comfortless spirits sicken at uncertainty, and the last charming beam of hope we are but too ready to yield — your letters penned when last in

Boston harbour, dear pledges of virtuous friendship, affectionately, and delicately conceived, are calculated to soothe my soul — Soft and gentle in their language, and most humane was the purpose of their Writer — Often have I wet them with my tears...I have thrown my eyes around this deserted apartment — It is shockingly wild — its very atmosphere seems impregnated with melancholy — My books, they cease to amuse — My pen, it is not now productive of pleasure — This despondency will not, however, continue — nature, quite exhausted, will either sink in the struggle, or my mind asserting itself, will rise superior to the dense clouds, in which it is at present enveloped — Excuse me dear Sir — if this paper meets your eye — excuse your friend [—] she is this day uncommonly low and you must tolerate her complaints....[21]

As the legislature mulled over the Universalists' latest petition, Judith kept John apprised of the news. His congregation had decided to continue meeting in his absence, showing town officials that John's forced departure would not close their church doors. Still, they longed for the return of their pastor. Judith wrote to him, "...you know not my dear Sir how deeply your friends are affected — a kind of solemn gloom takes possession of every countenance...."[22] Finally, the Legislature ruled in favor of the Universalists and religious freedom, as Judith wrote:

The event is happy, full indemnification is obtained — the majority in our favour in both houses of assembly, was prodigious, and an act is now in agitation, which, if passed, will establish that equality, among the various sects, in this our new World....[23]

To John, she reported:

...the general government hath referred to the next session, the consideration of an act, which will invest you, and Clergymen of every denomination, with privileges sufficiently e x t e n s i v e...My wish for you, Sir, is, that your heart may never be experimentally able to judge, of that anguish, which hath corroded the bosoms of your friends since your departure — But it is past — Blessed be God that I can say it is past, yes the sorrows of the past four months shall no more return...Of your ill health I dare not speak, I am struggling with apprehension, it is a precipice to which despair is momently pointing, but I fly from the mournful view, taking shelter in the bosom of hope — yes, you may be in health — yes, you may return and I may live to see it — What then — Why then, I will be truly grateful — discontent shall be no more, and I shall possess the blessings of tranquility....[24]

When Judith received word from John that he would return in the fall, she responded:

> I now hold the pen, with very different sensations from those which have heretofore agitated my bosom — My dear, my protecting friend is returning, there is no longer a necessity for his banishment, and I shall be — I shall be — in short I shall be very happy — a thousand times a day, do I whisper the tidings to my soul, My heart, my fond heart, throbs with esteem, and gratitude, hourly augmenting, and the pleasing perturbation of the little flutterer seems to render it too big for its enclosure...I will unwaringly believe that I shall pass with him, e'er yet I depart the World of spirits some tranquil days... I cannot write, a kind of pleasing tumult takes possession of my soul, destroying that composure, which is necessary for the purpose of arranging my thoughts...Yet I ought to write, and this letter is intended to meet you in Boston — welcome, then my dearest friend — thou art right welcome to the soul of thy Constantia....[25]

A New Marriage, Motherhood, and a Literary Career

John returned to Gloucester in September of 1788, sharing his passage with John and Abigail Adams who would become lifelong friends. When he arrived home, John asked Judith to marry him and she accepted. Winthrop and Esther, Judith's brother and sister, were not pleased. They did not consider John Murray a suitable match for their sister. He was not of their station, showed little hope of earning a decent living, and he could, it seemed, be emotional. These things were of secondary importance to Judith. She was in love, and on October 5 Judith and John quietly left Gloucester to be married. She told her parents:

> I go then, my beloved parents, with the early dawn I shall commence my journey — and I go happily in the assurance of your approbation, and greatly enriched by your parental blessings — It is true the presence of the Authors of my Being, during the important solemnity which I have in mind would inexplicably support and comfort me, but the unaccountable, and unreasonable prejudices, which my brother, and my sister, have thought proper to conceive against Mr Murray, is a bar to my wishes in this respect....[26]

Judith and John were married in Salem, Massachusetts on October 6. In another letter to her parents, she informed them:

> The solemn transaction to which with a degree of fearful apprehension I have for some time looked forward, is at length

passed, and the interest, the fame, the wishes, the hopes and the fears of Mr Murray, and your daughter, are henceforward inseparably united....[27]

In this marriage, Judith was happy, as she confessed to her aunt, Mary Turner Sargent:

I was early, very early, united in marriage to a worthy Man. His virtues were many, and I justly esteemed the husband which fate had given me...Yet, though greatly sensible of his worth, my ungovernable heart refused to acknowledge the softer emotions. I believed myself incapable of love as traced by the pencil of the Poet...In the misfortunes of Mr Stevens, I took my full share, and I lamented with the deepest agony the melancholy catastrophe of his life. But my serenity returned, and, as I had often thought and frequently expressed my sentiments, that after having worn the nuptial chain, and providence had sundered the bond, a subsequent life of retirement and freedom was most proper...But the event which bannished Mr Murray from America effectively removed the vale. I was solicitous to yield in person that relief which the balm of sacred friendship might supply, and that I was denied the privilege of sympathizing with a Man, whom I so much esteemed and revered was to be an agonizing consideration...In short, I could no longer deceive myself, my soul became a scene of tumult, and upon every rising thought was stamped too sure a confirmation that I had in fact become a slave to the most impetuous of all passions, of which I had, erroneously, considered myself incapable."[28]

Judith and John stayed with their friends the Plummers in Salem until the following week, when they departed for a long journey through southern Massachusetts and Rhode Island. One of their first stops was in Braintree, where they enjoyed the hospitality of John and Abigail Adams in their new home — the "illustrious Patriot and his truly amiable Lady," Judith called them. She further told her parents:

In the countenance of Mr Adams, the most pleasing benevolence inmingles with the marks of deep thinking and you immediately conclude the q[u]alities which constitute the sage, the philosopher, the politician, and the man of unbending integrity, are happily associated with the more social virtues...His Lady hath visited Courts — European Writers have ably penned her eulogy — I have not the Vanity to suppose that my praise can bestow one additional ray, yes, I may be allowed to say by way of supplement, that it is evident the domestic as well as the more brilliant virtues are all her own — We were soon grouped in familiar chat — It was with [difficulty] I remembered they were not friends of ancient date....[29]

John preached several times during their trip and Judith had a glimpse, perhaps for the first time, of how highly and widely her husband was regarded and to what extent they would both become public figures. They returned home for Christmas, where they found John's Universalist "friends" prepared to renew his ordination and prevent any further legal challenges. On Christmas Day, 1788, the Reverend John Murray was ordained Pastor of the Independent Christian Church of Gloucester. His response: "I now again, with humble gratitude to my divine Master, and grateful affection for you, my long tried and faithful Christian friends and brethren, most cordially accept of this call."[30]

Judith and John began married life in her elegant home on Middle Street. Before long, after a childless first marriage, Judith was elated to find herself pregnant at the age of 38. But as the days drew near to her delivery, her health quickly deteriorated. Turning to her poetry as a solace (as Judith did throughout her life), she wrote "Invocation to Hope!" which the *Massachusetts Magazine* published in July.

In August, a stillborn baby boy was pulled from Judith's body, its lifeless form her only contact with the son they had planned to call Fitz Winthrop. Her health worsened, and she lay close to death. John was in anguish, having lost his first wife and child in the same manner. For months Judith suffered. In a letter to her cousin, Paul Dudley Sargent, John wrote:

> The first Saturday in August our suffering Friend was taken ill. She continued to suffer more than any language can describe till the wednesday night the following. She was then, with the assistance of Dr Plummer, and his instruments delivered of a Male child weighing near fifteen pounds, whose spirit returned to the God who gave it, a few hours before it was born. We now flattered ourselves the worst was over, but, alas, never did woman suffer more than she has suffered since. Near three weeks we were obliged to have three nurses, and four weeks we were obliged to have two. I am not able to make you acquainted with her complaints. Sufficient to say, that for many weeks her life was despaired of, and day and night she suffered the most excruciating tortures. She is not yet able to sit on any seat but one which she is often obliged to use. With great difficulty she can walk from there to her bed which she can neither enter nor leave without assistance, and pain, and God only knows whither she will ever be well. However I am incoraged to hope...All these sufferings, however, she could have borne with more patience if her infant had been spared....[31]

By November, Judith was improving and able to resume her correspondence. John was away from home — preaching, as was regularly the case. In her first letter to him since the death of their son, Judith wrote:

> How many melancholy days, weeks, and months have passed since I last addressed, in this way, my best, my dearest friend — How exquisite have been my sufferings, and how are my maternal expectations buried in the grave with my first born son — yet let me not, by dwelling upon unavailing regrets still more deeply lacerate the bosom of him, from whose tearful eye, I would hide, by the interposing veil of tranquility, every sorrow — I write at my Father's, converged hither yesterday, in the carriage, and the rain coming on suddenly prevented my return — I hope you have obtained relief from your disposition, or that you will make it an object to attend to yourself...your absence is at all times a source of regret — and that I so much value your society, as not to be perfectly at ease without it....[32]

Judith turned again to poetry to help with her loss. The *Massachusetts Magazine* published her "PHILANDER, A Pastoral Elegy" in September, the heartwrenching "LINES, occasioned by the DEATH of an INFANT" in February of 1790, and "Lines to Euphelia" in the same issue.

The *Magazine* also published an essay Judith had submitted earlier: "On the Equality of the Sexes." The essay appeared under the name "Constantia" at the head of the March and April issues and it was a triumph. The *Magazine* also published her poem, "Lines to Philenia," (the pen name of poet Sarah Wentworth Appleton Morton) and Judith's essay, "On the Domestic Education of Children" in April.

John returned home to find his wife's health restored, and they began to plan a lengthy trip to Philadelphia. After 20 years of spreading Universalist doctrine up and down the Eastern seaboard, dozens of independent Universalist gatherings, societies, and congregations had been formed. By 1790, leaders of the faith agreed to hold a convention at which they would discuss both their individual agendas and common purpose. It was hoped the convention would produce a document that would affirm the truths of their faith and determine their future governance. John Murray was expected to play a leading role in the convention's proceedings, and it was essential for him to go. Judith, his champion and dedicated Universalist, wanted to lend her support. She also wanted to see more of the country and meet its leading citizens.

The trip took six months, and introduced Judith to President Washington (who had recently taken the oath of office), Congress and New York, Philadelphia, Connecticut, Rhode Island, and the environs of her native state. Judith was enamored of Philadelphia, its simple manners, architectural grandeur, Quaker-derived humanity, and opportunities for wealth. John was offered increasingly large sums of money to stay and lead the Philadelphia church. But Gloucester was Judith's home, and separation from her family was out of the question. All told, it was a thrilling experience for her and Judith filled detailed accounts written to her parents with anecdotes, thoughts and observations. It was, however, difficult to be so far from home for such a length of time and the loss of her son still weighed heavily.

They returned home to Gloucester in October where John resumed his parish duties and Judith her writing. In its January 1791 issue, the editors of the *Massachusetts Magazine* declared "Constantia" among their ablest writers. And, at age 40, Judith was pregnant again. She longed for a safe delivery, and this time she was rewarded. On August 22, she gave birth to Julia Maria. In September, safely recovered from the ordeal, Judith wrote to her mother:

> Well my Mamma — how good is the God with whom we have to do — hardly for a single moment did I dare to indulge a hope of the blessing which is now in my possession — I stand amazed at the event which hath taken place — at times I can hardly believe myself awake, and I am fearful that the coming moment will arouse me from my dream of happiness — yet when I press my child to my bosom — when her infant form is with each returning morning presented to my view — surely I cry this is substantial enjoyment — surely, this is real felicity — my wishes are at length crowned with fruition, and I am now indeed a happy Mother....[33]

To mark the event, Judith wrote the poem "LINES written by rocking a cradle," although it was not published until 1802 by the *Boston Weekly Magazine* under the name "Honora Martesia."

Judith was indeed happy, but her health would always be frail. Julia Maria, too, was sickly throughout her girlhood, suffering from recurring bouts of her "throat disorder" (which we know today as diphtheria or scarlet fever). Judith rarely travelled after Julia Maria was born and then only short distances. With John away from home so frequently, mother and daughter became very close and Judith delighted in her daughter's "prattling" and her inquisitive, outgoing nature. She was smart, strong-willed, and very beautiful — like her mother.

Elsewhere in America, the Bill of Rights had been ratified, adding the second founding document to the new American nation. Thomas Jefferson's anti-federalist efforts increased and he began using the term "republican party" — creating factions in what federalists believed should have been a sound centralized government. Mary Wollstonecraft's

Vindication of the Rights of Woman was published in England and found an audience in America as well. It was radical, controversial, and would forever be a benchmark in feminist history. Judith admired its content, despite her discomfort with the author's outspoken style. Years later, however, when Mary Wollstonecraft's character came under assassination, Judith defended her unequivocally.[34]

"The Gleaner" Champions Female Equality and More

While John continued to travel, Judith learned how to juggle baby, young Anna, domestic responsibilities, and work. Like other women of her station, Judith had domestic help — young girls from Gloucester who assisted with the myriad of domestic chores required to maintain a merchant class household. While Julia Maria slept and the household was running smoothly, Judith turned to serious essay writing — keeping up her correspondence as well, often late into the evening. She decided to develop a regular column in the *Massachusetts Magazine* in which she could address any subject she chose. Using a male persona, she thought, would engage readers and prevent them from dismissing a female point of view. And Judith had a lot to say. "The Gleaner" series began appearing in the February 1792 issue of the *Massachusetts Magazine*. Judith began her more reflective series, "The Repository," in the *Magazine* in September. Both series ran until December of 1794, when new editors chose not to continue publishing her work.

"The Gleaner" was a great success — much talked about, and few people knew "his" real identity. "The Gleaner" employed a variety of literary devices to entertain readers — from direct, reasoned political essays to writing short novels or "recounting" anecdotes Judith created to make a point. In particular, "The Gleaner" dismissed the notion that women's minds were inferior to men's. Rather, Judith argued, it was due to their lack of education that women seemed less able. She called on her vast knowledge of western history to argue her case, citing examples of women's accomplishments in Sparta, Rome, Hungary, Elizabethan England, and more. She challenged the biblical "Fall of Eve" myth, which had formed the basis of views on women for so many years. She had, in fact, been forming this argument since as early as 1777 when she wrote to her cousin, Catherine Goldthwaite:

> That Eve was the weaker vessel, I boldly take upon me to deny. Nay, it should seem that she was abundantly the stronger vessel since all the deep laid Art, of the most subtle fiend that inhabited the infernal regions, was requisite to draw her from his allegiance, while Adam was overcome by the softer passions, merely by his attachment to a female....[35]

And sometimes, she simply stated that women and men were equals:

> The idea of the incapability of women is, we conceive, in this enlightened age, totally inadmissible...To argue against facts, is indeed contending with both wind and tide; and, borne down by accumulating examples, conviction of the utility of the present plans will pervade the public mind, and not a dissenting voice will be heard.[36]

Judith challenged the notion that women should be economically dependent upon men. The war had produced hundreds of destitute widows, unable to earn a living or legally manage their affairs. In October of 1793, "The Gleaner" wrote:

> Was I the father of a family...I would give my daughters every accomplishment which I thought proper; and, to crown all, I would early accustom them to habits of industry and order...they should be enabled to procure for themselves the necessities of life; independence should be placed within their grasp; and I would teach them to *reverence themselves.*[37]

As bleak as opportunities for women were at that time Judith was, however, optimistic that change was in the air — that the hard-won ideals behind the Revolution would apply to everyone:

> Yes, in this younger world, "the Rights of Women" begin to be understood; we seem, at length, determined to do justice to THE SEX; and...we are ready to contend for the *quantity*, as well as the *quality*, of mind...I may be accused of enthusiasm; but such is my confidence in THE SEX, that I expect to see our young women forming a new era in female history...The noble expansion conferred by a liberal education will...give them a glance of those vast tracts of knowledge which they can never explore, until they are accommodated with far other powers than those at present assigned them....[38]

Calling again on her own past experience, Judith tackled the institution of marriage as it existed in the late 18th century:

> Marriage should not be regarded as a certain or even necessary event; [females] should learn to respect a single life, and even to regard it as the most eligible, except a warm, mutual, and judicious attachment....[39]

Mutual esteem, mutual friendship, mutual confidence, these are the necessary requisites of the matrimonial career...Be not afraid to come to the test. Look well to your individual thoughts; forbear to emblazon your virtues...if your long cherished attachment experiences abatement — shrink not from the voice of public censure— you are still at liberty — other pursuits yet open themselves before you.[40]

Good parenting, too, was of critical importance, Judith believed. She agreed with the concept of Republican Motherhood — that women should be educated to better raise future American citizens:

Much in this momentous department, depends on female administrations; and the mother, or the woman to whom she may delegate her office, will imprint on the opening mind, characters, ideas and conclusions, which time, in all its variety of vicissitudes, will never be able to erase. Surely then it is politic to bestow upon the education of girls the most exact attention.[41]

But Judith added a feminist twist to the Republican Motherhood argument, claiming that women deserved a quality education for their own sakes in order to achieve economic independence and self-worth. Judith Sargent Murray was among the first to take this feminist position and, as a result, became a defining voice in the progress of women.

Along with being a champion for women's rights, "The Gleaner" was a federalist patriot — a supporter of Washington and Adams and a critic of the "party faction" that arose under Jefferson. "The Gleaner" was a promoter of virtue, hard work, and self-reliance. Judith finally had a strong public voice. She used it well, and enjoyed it.

Two Deaths in the Family, and the Move to "The Metropolis"

Unfortunately, more change — and tragedy — lay ahead for Judith in 1793. Her beloved mother, whose health had always been fragile, passed away on June 27 at age 62. Judith had long feared this eventuality, remembering a letter she had written to her parents three years earlier:

I shudder at the approach of a Catastrophe, which may be awfully near! — I cannot bear the idea of a separation, a final of separation, from my parents — I have no children to supply the void which will then remain in my bosom — May they be continued in the present state of existence, until I also bid adieu to mortality — nor is there any thing so very irrational in this wish — The daughter of their youth, our years are nearly the same — Well then, I will hope the best....[42]

Judith, who had been in Boston when her mother died, rushed to Gloucester to care for her father bringing two-year-old Julia Maria with her. Winthrop Sargent's health was failing and, as with so many married couples, Judith's father passed away in December at age 66 leaving his daughter in despair. The "authors of her being" were gone. Their passing created a lonely emptiness for Judith that would never fully disappear. As much as a year later, she wrote to a friend in England:

> Yes, dear Lady, these eyes have marked the exit of the Authors of their Being!..Ah! Madam, It is in truth the Survivor who dies — Matchless were the Parents whom I have lost — The anguish of that separating moment was indeed inutterable — Their deaths, so rapidly succeeding each other — the agonies of my soul were too surely immeasurable: and my spirit well near died within me...many returning months have since revolved, bearing with them their apportioned good, and evil, and still I am continued the sport of contingencies, still I am continued to witness how joyless return those hours once illumed by a Father's presence, once devoted to a Mother's tenderness — to feel how desolate the being, when thus bereaved, who for the space of forty two years, hath been indulged and patronized by all the energy, all the wisdom, and by every blessing, which completes the aggregate of parental affection...My daughter, that inestimable treasure, sent me by a compassionate Creator, to soothe my hours of sorrow — is, I bless His holy and reverent name — every thing, which at her age, the most sanguine Mother could wish....[36]

Tragedy struck elsewhere as well. In France, King Louis XVI and his queen, Marie Antoinette, were beheaded. The bloody reign of terror began and many Americans, including Judith, responded with horror and condemnation. President Washington took a position of neutrality, hoping to preserve trade agreements. American ships were being seized by the British to curtail American trade in the West Indies. War with England was imminent, and the Indian Wars back home were escalating — Judith's brother, Winthrop, playing a leading role in the military. Judith, as the federalist "Gleaner," responded to all of these events in the *Massachusetts Magazine*.

In Boston, Universalism was growing in popularity and John was a frequent visitor to the church on Bennet Street. On October 23, while Judith was in Gloucester, John was installed at the church and began dividing his time between congregations in Boston and Gloucester. This eventually proved difficult, and in September of 1794 the Murray family moved to Boston. Anna stayed behind in Gloucester.

The Murrays took up residence at No. 5 Franklin Place, the Tontine Crescent, built by Boston architect Charles Bulfinch. His first townhouse design, Franklin Place was the height of elegance. The center of the building, over its gracious arch, housed Boston's public library and the Massachusetts Historical Society. It was walking distance from the Federal Street Theatre, Fanueil Hall, the (old) State House, Old South Meeting House, and the fashionable residences and shops on Corn Hill and Court Street. Judith would be close to her aunt, Mary Turner Sargent, and uncle, Daniel Sargent, who had moved to Long Wharf. Other friends and relatives were sprinkled throughout Boston as well. Gloucester would forever remain Judith's "dear native place," but Boston — the Metropolis — was an exciting center of political and cultural activity. Upon arriving, Judith wrote to her cousin-in-law in Gloucester, Dorcas Babson Sargent:

> For me, I have to say that beds, tables, chairs, looking glasses, pictures etc etc having all received their respective stations...Our situation is pleasing, and even rural, our apartments are convenient, and we shall enjoy every privilege with a higher zest if we can be permitted to partake them with our friends....[43]

A leading Boston newspaper, *The Federal Orrery*, soon became another outlet for Judith's writing. In October, she submitted a series of columns using the name "The Reaper" in which she discussed moral lessons learned from daily life. Unfortunately, the editor of the *Orrery* saw fit to edit Judith's work extensively. Apparently, he also suggested that John's hand was behind her literary success — not the first time this comment would be made. Angered, she pulled the series after only five essays had appeared and sent this letter to the editor, Thomas Paine:

> Sir
>
> The inclosed were written for the Orrery before the publication of the second Reaper, but the many alterations which you judged it necessary to make in that piece, dampened the ardor of my wishes for presentment. I do not expect that I shall ever rank with that elevated class of Writers, among which Mr Paine has secured his stand — but however moderate my pretensions ought to be, I have in my composition that decent kind of pride, which will not permit me to array myself— or to submit to be arrayed — in borrowed plumage. Rosseau in one of his publications, foolishly enough asserts, that whenever a female draws the pen — it is well known that some man of letters sits behind the curtain to guide her hand: and the audacity of this unmannerly Pedant, is one reason why I do not

permit any little thing which I design for the press, to pass under
the eye of the dearest of my friends....[44]

In April of 1793, the ban on theatrical entertainment in Boston
had been lifted. Long an admirer of this powerful literary and visual
form of communication, Judith tried her hand at playwrighting and her
first play, *The Medium: or, Happy Tea-Party*, (later renamed *The Medium,
or Virtue Triumphant*) was performed at the theatre on Federal Street in
February and March of 1795. This was quite a feat for an American
writer — male or female. At the time, American literary works, of any
genre, were ridiculed (even by Americans) as infantile attempts. Judith's
satirical play, which addressed class structure and morality, was
unfavorably reviewed in *The Federal Orrery* by the same Thomas Paine
who had criticized "The Reaper."

Undaunted, Judith submitted another play to her friends the Powells
at the Federal Street Theatre. *The Traveller Returned* ran in March of
1796. Thomas Paine's promotional piece in the March 2 issue of the
Federal Orrery described *The Traveller Returned* as "the joint production
of Mr. and Mrs. MURRAY." In the following issue of the *Orrery*, John
published a letter to the editor in which he defended his wife's literary
abilities:

> MR. PAINE,
> The communication, which you received, and which you have
> handed to the public, in Monday's Orrery, is unauthorized and false,
> and I declare, in the most solemn manner, that I never saw a single
> sentence, line, or word of the comedy, performed on Monday
> evening, until I saw it, precisely in the state, in which it was, on
> that evening, presented to the public, nor was I, until the completion
> of the design, apprized, that even an idea of writing said comedy
> had been formed. Let, therefore, its merits, or demerits, remain
> with the real author— the fact is, that neither the one, nor the
> other, directly or indirectly belong, to
> JOHN MURRAY[45]

At home, Judith had a very sick little girl on her hands. Just before
her fourth birthday, Julia Maria's throat disorder became quite serious,
as Judith told her sister-in-law, Anna:

> My child is at this moment stricken with a very severe attack of her
> throat disorder — it assumes a more alarming appearance than usual,
> for she is much swelled externally, as well as internally — and her
> natural voice is wholly lost! This circumstance, operating with the
> extreme heat of the season, and the general prevalence of the throat

distemper, implants in my bosom the most corroding apprehension — Oh! My Sister! should I be called to part with this child, where shall I find fortitude to submit with becoming resignation to a blow, which will at one stroke prostrate all those maternal hopes, which fond expectation, with genial influence, hath caused to bloom so fair, and to shed over my most melancholy hours the luminous beams of anticipation [—] To consign to the gloomy mansion of the grave an only child [—] yet I shall receive her again from the hands of that God who fashioned and endowed her — and we shall be ever with the Lord — Next Saturday she will have completed her fourth year, and we are preparing to celebrate this approaching anniversary — but there are yet four days to that era, and who shall say what those four days may produce!!! But the Father of mercies hath often rebuked her disorder — he may again rebuke it — and thus upon that day fill my mouth with the language of gratitude....[46]

John was having health difficulties as well. His rheumatism flared regularly, and he was exhausted from travel and the demands on his time. The contagious fever that had affected Julia Maria took the lives of many other children in Boston that year. That, and the recurring small pox, kept John in constant service to his congregation, friends, and family.

But when the family was in good health, living in Boston gave Judith the opportunity to enjoy cultural activities and witness important events. In July, she watched the grand ceremony of thirteen white horses and hundreds of military troops lay the corner stone of the new state house Charles Bulfinch had designed. She celebrated the election of her friend John Adams to the presidency in 1796, and attended the birthday gala for George Washington where she met the Marquis de Lafayette and his son, Washington. She attended the theatre regularly, having been given a box seat, attended concerts, visited the new museum, and took tea with dozens of friends. Periodically, young nieces or nephews would be sent from New Hampshire or Mississippi to visit their Aunt Murray for weeks at a time, and she enjoyed supplementing their education with all Boston had to offer.

Though Julia Maria's fragile health ruled out lengthy trips, mother and daughter made day trips or short-term excursions to Fresh Pond in Watertown, to Cambridge, and to Hampstead, New Hampshire, where her cousin, Epes Sargent, had moved with his large family. They visited family and friends in Portsmouth, York, and, of course, Gloucester. Judith wrote dozens of letters documenting these visits, describing landscapes, cultural activities, private homes, sumptuous meals, or public pageantry — whatever would entertain her readers, many of whom were young relatives.

At the close of 1795, Judith received a surprising letter from her brother, Winthrop, who was now living in Cincinnati and serving as acting governor of the Ohio Territory. Stricken with his recurring gout, Winthrop had been bedridden and required constant nursing. His nurse, Sarah Chappese, a married woman, had just given birth to their illegitimate daughter, Caroline Augusta. Judith, in typical style, feared for the life this unfortunate girl was about to face and wanted to help. Eager to do what was best for his daughter, Winthrop and Judith agreed that Caroline Augusta would be better off raised and schooled in Boston. But years of abuse and custody battles would go by instead, and Judith's loving, guiding hand was denied the "little blossom" who probably would have thrived as Judith's adopted daughter and Julia Maria's sister.

And Julia Maria wanted a sister or a brother. Now five years old, she wished she had young companionship as Judith explained to her sister-in-law whose home (and children) they had recently visited:

> Julia Maria has at last attained the age of regret, and the tear hath been frequently upon her cheek for the loss of her little Companions — "Mamma what do you think Winthrop is doing now? Where is Judy? O dear I wish I had a Brother or a sister to live with me as other little girls have" [—] these are her questions, and her complaints, so early do we learn the language of discontent....[47]

Julia Maria's "Mamma" was, of course, devoted to her daughter and attentive to her early education. Although they never met, Judith wrote letters regularly to Julia Maria's paternal grandmother — John's mother, who lived in London — reassuring her of Julia Maria's proper upbringing. Judith was always aware of her financial obligation to her daughter as well, and her duty to secure for Julia Maria a comfortable future. A champion of female education and economic independence, devoutly religious, Judith raised her daughter accordingly as she "sketched" for Mrs. Murray:

> We are solicitous to lay up for our child a sum, which may enable her, with her own persevering industry, when we shall be called hence, to preserve a kind of independence, and we confess also, that we are desirous of bestowing upon her that kind of education, which shall fit her to make a respectable figure in society, these, dear Madam are our views, and yet our means are scanty, the articles of living are very high, the price demanded in this Country for the instruction of young people is extravagant, with the life of her Father as our income will then cease, every human resource will be cut off from our child, and we are therefore naturally anxious to secure her, at least the means of information — she has never yet been a day at

school, but lest your maternal solicitude, taking the alarm, should lead you to fear that the mind of your little granddaughter is wholly uncultivated, I will sketch for you our present arrangements — the twenty second day of last August she completed her fifth year, and as the bed on which we repose is one third larger than common beds, she still sleeps in our bosoms — when returning morn unseals her lovely eyes, which are of a soft cerulean hue, she is accustomed to repeat with a solemn voice, and devout attitude, the Lords prayr and a morning hymn — it is many months since these, with a variety of little pieces, have been perfectly committed to memory — she then quits her bed, and her washing, and dressing, is always the work of my own hands, she next reads, spells, and repeats her grammar — the eleven first questions in Webster's grammar she can answer without the smallest hesitation; she knows the points and can call them by name wherever she sees them, she can read without spelling any lesson however difficult, after having studied it a while, and she has attained so perfect an idea of the sound of the letters, that she will spell out of a book any word if we can only give each syllable its proper and distinct tone — the words laugh, cough, and all of this description she also knows, and the sweet creature waked herself up last night, spelling a word, which she had pronounced in the course of the day very hard to learn. With regard to her needle, she can sew a plain seam, or hem, equally as well as I can myself — these rudiments of the lower branches of education she can receive from me, but the higher, and more expensive, should she be spared to us, await her added years....[48]

The Gleaner: A Literary and Political Triumph

It would take money to "preserve" Julia Maria's independence, and John's earnings as a minister were never substantial. That, and her desire to publish, kept Judith writing. The *Massachusetts Magazine* was no longer interested in her work, and new publication outlets were not immediately forthcoming. In April of 1796, Judith told her brother, Winthrop, she had decided to self-publish a book she would call *The Gleaner* — a three volume collection of her "Gleaner" essays (including some unpublished works) and her two plays.

She wrote to President Adams, asking permission to dedicate the book to him. He consented. She then determined the specifications of the book and its cost, and wrote to her many friends and relatives asking them to subscribe — a smart move on her part as she would explain years later to a publisher in Boston:

Our country does not regard with benignity the literary adventurer, and, against indigenous productions, a few instances excepted, her prejudices are strongly pointed. It is my opinion, I should have suffered in my pecuniary circumstances, by the Gleaner, if I had not, previous to its publication obtained a sufficient number of Subscribers, to secure, not only my expenses, but a handsome remuneration....[49]

All told, 759 people subscribed to *The Gleaner* before its publication, 859 sets were printed, and Judith grossed $2,475. Much to her great annoyance, the printers neglected to incorporate her final edits:

...in the course of my literary progress...while the proof sheet was in my hand, the whole impression has been struck off, and I have been disappointed, and mortified, by the appearance of those very identical errors, which I had carefully erased....[50]

Still, *The Gleaner* was Judith's masterpiece — read both in America and across the Atlantic by leading citizens and opinion makers. Her audience had now grown far beyond the reaches of the *Massachusetts Magazine*. And, in *The Gleaner*, Judith revealed her identity and forever established her place as a learned intellectual, a political analyst, and a champion of female equality, education, and economic independence. What's more, now everyone knew that this writing came from a female mind. Once *The Gleaner* was published, Judith spent months distributing copies and sending personal notes of thanks to subscribers.

At the same time, Judith began a steady correspondence with her four young nephews who were attending school in nearby Billerica, Massachusetts and Exeter, New Hampshire. "The boys" were Winthrop's sons, William Fitz Winthrop Sargent and George Washington Sargent, and Winthrop's stepsons from his wife's first marriage, David and James Williams. "Aunt Murray" encouraged letter writing as a way to supplement their education. Good writing, she felt, was an essential skill. Through letter writing, she could encourage their literary efforts, correct their grammar, and contribute to their moral development at the same time. Her own letter writing could set an example. In this letter to 11-year-old William Fitz Winthrop (called William), she shares with him her thoughts on the subject:

My beloved youth

You complain of incapability as a letter writer; I do assure you, my dear, I am charmed with this new specimen of your abilities in this line, and I do believe, that this elegant species of composition, is a treat which you may pursue, to great advantage, yet, I repeat, that I still conceive, facility in this art, can only be acquired by practice, and I have thought that the beauty, and perfection of this accomplishment, rested more, with the frequent exercise of the requisite talents, than almost any other literary pursuit. Judicious critics have determined, that an easy, rather than a splendid diction, is proper to an epistolary intercourse, but without giving an opinion upon this subject, it is not hazarding any thing to pronounce, that correctness is indispensable, and that a Writer who can command a common dictionary, will not be indulged in false orthography; spelling depends much upon memory, and memory is often treacherous....[51]

Family Illness, and a Great Loss for the Nation

Judith was no doubt thinking about her next writing project when, suddenly, John developed a painful tumor in his side. All through April and May he lay close to death, having barely survived an invasive operation she described to her cousin, Epes Sargent:

My Dear Sir

The illness of Mr Murray throws a gloom over this abode, which can only be dissipated by his returning health, and, what deeply points our distress, is the knowledge that the period of his restoration, should it ever arrive, is probably at a great distance: through succeeding weeks, he has been confined to his chamber, and almost wholly to his bed, upon the last fast day, and the two preceding sabbaths, he was unable to attend public worship, last sunday he was carried to church in a close carriage, from whence he returned to his chamber, and to his bed. He hath been a long time struggling with repeated, and heavy colds, the effects of these he hath, however, surmounted, but he is now exquisitely tortured by a large tumor under his left arm, the anguish of which is almost intolerable: his nights, particularly, are nights of agony, and his days are marked by langour and imbecility. His physician can neither discuss this afflicting tumor, nor promote suppuration; relief is, in his opinion, remote — he recommends patience, and in the meantime the swelling encreases in size, and is hard, and prominent — I have, for many days been agonized in the fear of scirilus...but from the [appearance] that the tumor this day assumes, Doctor Warren pronounces, decisively, that it is not of the scirilus kind, and the weight of a mountain is removed from my bosom....[52]

While John was bedridden, young John James, Epes Sargent's son, came for a lengthy visit to Franklin Place making himself indispensable to Judith during this difficult time. Never one to play favorites with her young relatives, John James, however, held a special place in her heart. By June, John was recovering, although slowly, as she explained to John James's father:

> ...it is at length reserved to me, to announce the more agreeable tidings of returning health, and peace. Mr Murray has got abroad, his spirits charmingly restored, and although he has now an open wound nearly three inches in his side, as this wound is at length in a state of healing, past sorrows has taught us to regard this as a very inconsiderable evil....[53]

At the end of the year, Judith — and the nation — experienced a painful loss when George Washington died. Everyone mourned the passing of their beloved chief, and Boston's reaction was swift and deeply felt as Judith told her sister:

> ...the deep mouthed bells have this day, in solemn, and aweful peels, uttered their melancholy responses — thus pointing, by the lengthened and soul afflicting knell, those exquisite sorrows, which at this moment assail, the keenest feelings of a bereaved Nation — Washington the brave — the great — the good — Washington the Patriot — the Father of his Country — Washington unrivalled in the annals of fame, and rich in deeds of peerless worth — This man of the people — whose name was a host in war, and who rendered us celebrious in peace — even he, is numbered with the dead! and Columbia, orphanaged, and stripped of her brightest hope, cannot but deeply feel the desolating calamity — Combining millions swell the voice of anguish, their lamentations are borne upon the heavy gale...The calamitous tidings reached us this morning and the effect produced, was instantaneous, and universal — a general consternation took place — the same spirit seemed to pervade the bosom of every individual, the shops were immediately closed — Business observed a solemn pause — the bells commenced their agonizing peels — the theatre, and museum, were shut, balls, festive assemblies, and amusements of every description, are suspended, ships in the harbour display the insignia of mourning, and a day of solemn humiliation, and prayr, in every place of public worship, in this Town, is contemplated....[54]

John presided over services for Washington at the Universalist church in Boston, which Judith also described for Esther:

[O]n entering the broad aisle — awed, and softened, by the solemnity of the scene, I melted into tears, my emotions were spontaneous, and nearly ungovernable, and it was with difficulty that I suppressed their audible manifestation [—] Mr Murray asayed to sketch the life of the departed Chief, but, overwhelmed by his feelings, he was necessitated to say, "And the noble acts which he did, and his greatness, they are not, and cannot be written, for they were very many["] — Mr Murray preserves a strong sense of the favours which, as an individual, he hath received from the beatified deceased — and the confidence reposed in him by the then Commander in Chief, when he appointed him the ecclesiastical guide to three regiments, while other Clergymen were confined to one, can never be forgotten....[55]

A Passing Illness and New Endeavors

Meanwhile, Judith's own health was failing. She was so ill, for so long, she believed she was dying. She had to make plans for Julia Maria's future and she asked her cousin, Epes Sargent, to serve as Julia Maria's guardian. She expected John would remarry, and that guardianship of Julia Maria should remain within the Sargent family. Epes had a large family, lived in the countryside, had the financial means and like-minded values to raise Julia Maria properly. This was the best plan, she told Esther:

> I have been induced to consider myself on the verge of my own dissolution, some circumstances attended my illness, which I conceived very alarming, and although I am not at present relieved, reason assures me, I must soon expect the messenger of death, and in the event of my removal, my principal concern, naturally rests upon my daughter — her youth, her volatile disposition, the plans which I have formed for her, and which I am most solicitous to execute, these all harrass my mind, and it is in vain that I search for a situation, in which to place her, that would in every particular correspond with my own views — I could confide her to your tenderness, but the children of your daughter are amply sufficient to fill your mind, and you have, besides, no school, which is adequate to my wishes — To a boarding school education I have...objections and should Mr Murray continue a house keeper...this house, when I am gone, will not be a suitable place for her, should he give her a second Mother, if he consults his own peace, the happiness of his child, or that of his wife, he will not hazard their continuance together — Viewing the subject in various lights, I have, after much deliberation, thought best to direct, that my daughter may be

boarded, during the four next ensuing years of her life, with Mr Epes Sargent of Hampstead, the salubrity of the country air will establish her health, she will be confirmed in the religion of my choice, she will be taught morals, needle work, industry, and economy; she will be taught the english, french, and latin languages; she will learn arithmetic, geography, and astronomy; she will acquire a taste for natural philosophy, and the belles lettres, and her music, dancing, and drawing, must be obtained afterward — I trust my dear in the event of my demise — that you will, from time to time, afford her your advice by letters, and I pray you to transfer to her, all that tenderness, which hath, through life, been most grateful to the heart of your sister — I may live to the full completion of my maternal duties, but the breaches made in my constitution, and the present impaired state of my health, do not invest this expectation with probability....[56]

In time, Judith recovered and was able to fulfill her "maternal duties." She also soon learned what effect *The Gleaner* was having on aspiring American writers as it continued to circulate. As an avowed champion of "indigenous productions," two writers in particular paid tribute to Judith in 1800. A local writer, Henry Sherburne, praised her throughout the lengthy preface to his *The Oriental Philanthropist*, writing:

...happy talents, Constantia, are confessedly thine! How sweetly pleads thy pen in virtue's sacred cause! with sentiments ennobling, pathetic and sublime, winning each selfish heart to charity and love! Columbia's sons and daughters, whose virtues are her glory, shall never cease to bless thee! future ages shall grateful own thy worth....[57]

In the novel *Julia,* Sally Sayward Barrell Keating Wood of York wrote:

I have seldom met with a woman who converses more sensibly or with more propriety upon every subject, than Mrs. Murray; she has lately published the Gleaner, a periodical work, in three volumes, that does great honor both to her head and heart; this production is not half so much praised and encouraged as it ought to be, and I believe that a little mean envy prevents its being admired according to its merits, and am persuaded that thirty years hence, when the admirable author sleeps in dust, when her heart has ceased to vibrate at the praise of virtue, or recoil at the idea of vice, the Gleaner will be universally read and admired, as the works of our Addison, and will be a very able competitor to the spectator. I have dined with this lady, and was charmed with my entertainment, and pleased to find that her literary pursuits did not interfere with her domestic virtues; she is a most excellent wife, and one of the best of mothers, and the perfect order and arrangement of her house-hold, declare her a complete house-wife; she employs every hour usefully, and her employments do not interfere with her conversation, which is always sensible, lively and instructive, and let the subject be what it will, she always renders it interesting. I have but seldom known any one so pleased with the praises of others, or so willing to commend sister excellence, and defend an injured and absent person: I am much pleased with her poetry, and join many of her friends in wishing she would consent to give a few volumes to the public.[58]

Kind words, but Sally Wood criticizes "female politicians" in *Julia* and Judith responded as we would expect:

My Dear Mrs W—

Since the receipt of your very flattering epistle to me, a multiplicity of little vexatious incidents, all of them singly, perhaps, lighter than vanity, but sufficiently formidable in the aggregate have rapidly succeeded each other, rendering it absolutely impossible for me, to pen those responses, which, however, glowed at my heart, and were frequently upon my lips...Your work is generally interesting, it seized irresistibly upon my faculties, and I did not relinquish the volume, until I had devoured every line....

I have, in truth, a very formidable accusation to profer against you. In your preface, you positively declare, that you have ever hated female politicians! — Surely you will, upon reflection, confess that you have expressed yourself rather too strongly, nor can I forbear acknowledging an opinion, that the passage in question concedes abundantly too much. May not a female be so circumstanced, as to render a correct, and even profound knowledge of politicks, the pride and glory of her character? How egregiously deficient would that woman appear, who, succeeding, by the constituted authority of her country, to sovereign power, should be unable to investigate, to direct, and to balance the various views, and interests of her subjects...can knowledge even as it relates to common life, ever become burdensome? and what is a knowledge of politicks, but a capability of distinguishing that which will probably advance the real interest of the Community, and ought a female to become odious, or even to be subject to censure, merely because she happens to understand what would best conduce to the prosperity of her Country? Are not women equally concerned with men in the public weal?...Yes indeed, all the relative duties, every philanthropic, every patriotic virtue, are proper to women — if we concede one point, we throw down the barriers, and it will not be easy to determine where they may again be erected....[59]

Judith's Role as Family Educator Expands

In 1801, Judith welcomed another young relative into her household who had journeyed from Natchez to Boston to pursue her education. Anna Williams, the daughter of Winthrop's wife and sister to David and James, settled in at 5 Franklin Place and became like a sister to Julia Maria. Anna and Julia Maria (who was now 10) attended Mrs. Payne's Federal Street Academy as well as music and dancing schools. Judith had purchased a piano forte for their home, which the girls used to practice. Outgoing and articulate for her age, Julia Maria became quite well versed in recitations and dramatic performances. John James, who studied and played music with the girls, had recently returned home to Hampstead after contracting an illness in Boston. Judith wrote many letters to John James and his father, praying for the recovery of her favorite cousin. But, sadly, John James passed away at the end of the summer. He was 20 years old. Judith wrote to Epes:

> ...the letter which announced the demise of that excellent young Man, whom she so unceasingly mourns, was perused by me with unutterable sorrow of heart....[60]

John James's death saddened her terribly, and surviving nieces, nephews, and young cousins in Gloucester, Newburyport, Billerica, Hampstead, and Exeter received even more letters from their Aunt Murray. Especially for Winthrop's sons and stepsons, she knew the distance from their parents in Natchez was painful — something she could appreciate only too well — and she made every effort to write or visit to alleviate their loneliness, as shown in this letter to William:

> Doubtless, my dear Boy, you are at present a child of suffering — a separation from such parents as yours, and from home, abounding with every gratification, which it has been in the power of affectionate indulgence to procure for you, must unavoidably be productive of this place — but as you possess as much natural good sense, as any little boy of your age, that I have ever known, I am persuaded that you will command your feelings, and calm the agitations of your mind by some reflections as the following — "It is absolutely necessary I should receive instruction I cannot obtain, in my native place, those advantages which are indispensably requisite, to my future advancements; I will occupy my mind in those pursuits that are pointed out to me; the more industrious,

and studious I am, the sooner I shall return to the bosom of my friends — I will endeavour to evince my affections, and duty to them, by making a rapid progress in all those branches of learning, to which my attention is required — This separation is as painful to my parents, as to me; they, however, submit to it for my benefit — they expect much from me— I will not disappoint them — they deserve everything — I will invariably seek to promote their happiness, and in order to do this, so desirable an end, I will endeavour to be all they wish me — I am as well situated as, while absent from my pleasant home, I can possibly be..." It is probable that, upon the night immediately succeeding the departure of your father your pillow was wet with your tears, the next night they did not flow so copiously — and perhaps you have now ceased to weep — but your regrets are still continued — yet, trust me my Love — they will almost momently lessen, you will become more, and more, reconciled to arrangements, which you will see to be unavoidable, until only those emotions will remain, that are, and ought to be, inseparable from the affectionate heart of a good, and dutiful child — You know, my dear, I speak from experience — I have frequently been separated from very dear parents, until at length they have ascended to heaven, and yet my mind has ever yielded to the necessity of injurious circumstances...I shall always devoutly wish that you may rapidly advance, both in the useful, and ornamental parts of your education — I shall supplicate heaven that your virtues may be exemplary and your benevolence uniform — that you may always be found in the paths of rectitude — In one word — that you may be an honour to the name you bear — a name venerable in my estimation, and precious to my soul, from having been borne by my dear and honoured Father, and my beloved brother, men, whom impartiality will consider, as reflecting a lustre upon human nature....[61]

Judith's concern for early education and moral development was well known, especially among her family. At home in 1803, Julia Maria began studying at the academy on Bury Street, a short walk from Franklin Place, and Judith corresponded regularly with her daughter's preceptors. She monitored Julia Maria's progress closely, and spent hours with her at home supporting her studies. Later that year Judith's cousin, Judith Saunders, moved from Gloucester to Dorchester where she and her friend, Clementine Beach, had decided to open that town's first academy for girls. Judith consented to let them use her name to generate interest in their endeavor, and she helped draft their business plan, write and place advertisements, find and purchase property, and recruit students. The "Academy at Dorchester" promised:

Reading, English, Grammar, Writing, Arithmetic, the French Language, Geography including the use of the Globes, needle work in all its branches, painting, and hair work upon ivory, and [Mrs Saunders and Miss Beach] pledge themselves to pay the most scrupulous attention to the health, manners, and morals of the young Ladies, who may be entrusted to their care....[62]

Judith was publishing poetry again as well in the *Boston Weekly Magazine*. She was busy, and enjoyed all the children in her life but she missed her husband and his long absences. John's inspirational appearances were still very much in demand and, as long as his health held out and his responsibilities in Boston allowed, he travelled. His was a restless spirit, which Judith had always known. But still, the loneliness was painful. "The absence of Mr Murray renders this place a comparative solitude," she wrote to her sister-in-law, Anna, in 1803 — a feeling she shared regularly with her female relatives.[63]

The Gleaner Continues to Cause a Stir

While Judith was overseeing the children, boarding young relatives, or visiting their schools, *The Gleaner* was still being discussed in literary and political circles and in the daily newspapers. Mercy Otis Warren had just published her lengthy history of the American Revolution, and perhaps "indigenous productions" — even those by women — were becoming more acceptable. Judith thought highly of Mercy Warren's monumental effort, writing to her:

Respected Madam

It was with pride and pleasure that I received your prospectives — Pride, that my name was still found written in the volume of your memory; and Pleasure, that you had at length determined to endow the world with a production it had long wished to see issue from the press, with a production on which anticipation hath delighted to dwell, and which has been considered as a fund in reserve, containing historical and biographical information, moral truths, and elevated sentiments, cloathed in habiliments of substantial texture — in habiliments wove by the strong hand of judgment; rendered brilliant by the abundant resources and verigated powers of fancy and receiving a beautiful finishing, and last gloss, from the fashioning fingers of taste, and elegance. May your volumes obtain the celebrity, to which merit is entitled, and may your publication look with a benign aspect, upon the evening of your useful, and distinguished career...I have the honor to reciprocate those sentiments of amity, which constitute the conclusion of your letter, and I am with affectionate admiration — Madam, your most obedient etc etc J.S.M.[64]

In June of 1806, Judith gave permission to Reverend Robert Redding of England to republish *The Gleaner*, writing:

Certainly, my dear Sir, I not only consent to your publishing The Gleaner in England, but your proposal meets my warmest approbation, and I do grant unto you The Reverend Robert Redding of Truro, in Cornwall, full liberty to reprint said Volumes....[65]

Judith did, however, insist on correcting the typographical errors left in place by her first publisher.

Unfortunately, in Boston, Judith's cousin, Lucius Manlius Sargent, took it upon himself to publicly criticize *The Gleaner* in the *Columbian Centinel*, a local newspaper. He even went so far as to strew torn pages from the book on Judith's doorstep — behavior that left her baffled, angry, and hurt. Perhaps he acted out of jealousy, as he was having difficulty publishing his own work. In a letter to him, Judith challenged:

Although I know not what action of my life can have rendered you so confirmed and inveterate a foe to me, yet I shall bear, and forbear with all the calmness I can command...Well Sir — Go on, continue to imbibe poison from whatever plant shall stand in your way, but know, that the day of retribution will at length arrive....[66]

To the editor of the *Centinel*, she wrote:

When we find an enemy among our nearest surviving kindred, the circumstance is particularly painful. I have for many years been harrassed, and mortified, by a variety of vexatious incidents — yet nothing like a regular criticism, upon any thing I have written, has appeared. The Malevolence in force toward me, has been exemplified by cutting up the pages of the Gleaner and strewing them upon the steps of my door, previously inscribing the margins with insulting remarks — by smut, and ribalrdy, in the public prints, and by a forged letter, designed to perplex, and ridicule me. What can have excited, and rendered so uncommonly active, the rancour of Mr Lucius Manlius Sargent I am yet to learn— Our immediate Fathers were Brothers, and from his first breath, I have omitted no opportunity of evincing toward him uniform tenderness....[67]

Judith and the *Centinel* were corresponding on another matter as well. Apparently, someone had sent work to the newspaper using the pen name "Honora" but making clear the author was, in fact, Judith. Judith used the name "Honora Martesia" in the *Boston Weekly Magazine* to publish her poetry, and this would be an easy mistake for readers. Judith responded with rightful outrage to the editor:

> ...what, at this moment, particularly afflicts me, is a report handed me, by respectable authority, that it is believed I myself have written the lines which appeared in the Centinel of wednesday last!!! The idea of setting down deliberately to pen my own panegyric, is such a glaring outrage to propriety, and so torturing to my feelings, that I could never enjoy a moment's peace, if I were conscious of being guilty of such a ridiculous indecorum — My object in writing to you yesterday, was, if possible, to obtain some clue, by which I might trace the author of the lines in question designing, if I succeeded, to solicit permission to give, in your paper, the real name, thus removing myself an odium, so completely abhorent to every sentiment of delicacy — But I have no knowledge of the hand writing you have so obligingly inclosed...God knows — so much of deception has been practised toward me, that I can hardly tell what to credit...If any expedient should occur to you, by which you can take off from the minds of those who attend to such baggatelle, the impression that I am the Honora of the Centinel, you would relieve me from a pressure, which absolutely renders me nearly wretched — For myself, I am so embarrassed, that I can determine upon nothing — I pray you, Sir, to think for me, and be assured of the...gratitude of J.S.M.[68]

That summer, Esther's husband, John Stevens Ellery, passed away and Esther moved to 3 Franklin Place — next door to Judith — where the two sisters could share their lives. That fall, Judith began work on her third play, *The African*, corresponding regularly with her friends the Powells about possible actors and dialogue. It was "brought forward" in Mr Powell's theater in early 1807, but was criticized in the papers and closed after one performance. To date, no one knows what this play addressed. We can surmise, given other statements Judith made on the subject of slavery and the Universalists' early condemnation of that institution, that her play contained an abolitionist message. Years later, sending the play to a friend, she wrote:

> The African was performed once upon our boards...it afterwards received a mortal stab, from the gall steeped pen of Mr Pollard. It was denied a second hearing, and its resuscitation became impossible....[69]

Judith had also heard that an American editor wished to showcase American writing by publishing a volume of indigenous works. She sent him a copy of *The Gleaner,* with an explanation of how it had been received in some circles years earlier:

Sir

I am informed that you have requested American Writers to forward [you] their publications, for the purpose of candid Criticism, and I am advised to put the Gleaner into your hands. Through the medium of a young person whom I have accidentally met, and who appears interested for me, I tender my volumes to your acceptance. The Gleaner has been both lavishly praised, and severely censured, while my self partiality, is ready to pronounce, that my feelings as an author have been unnecessarily, and too pointedly wounded — yet, not a single observation that bears the most remote affinity to genuine criticism has hitherto met my eye...Repeated attempts have been made to prejudice the public mind against my production, and I have potent reasons for believing, a systematic plan for its distribution has long since been in operation — I cannot be persuaded that what Washington, Adams, Ramsay, Belknap, Clark, Harris, with a long list of names, distinguished in the literary annals of our country, have condescended to approve, can be wholly destitute of merit, and from the celebrity of your character, correct judgement, and acknowledged rectitude, I indulge the most sanguine hope — I do not shrink from criticism — far from it — I rather invite it. I ask only justice, but I would lodge my appeal in the bosom of benevolence, associating judgment, good taste, and strict equity...A second edition of these volumes would reform the abuses which have so unfortunately obtained [from the first printing], but my present prospects admit no hope of such a remedy — From a man of integrity I would gladly receive, and accede to, almost any proposal which might effectuate a purpose so desirable...your most obedient very humble servant   J.S.M.[70]

The fall of that year, in 1807, brought the Murrays to Philadelphia with their now 16-year-old daughter. It was Julia Maria's first lengthy journey with her famous parents and, according to Judith, she "mark[ed] every pleasing novelty with all the wonder of young applause. She keeps a circumstantial account, of whatever she considers worthy of observation...."[71]

More Young Relatives Arrive in Boston

When the Murrays arrived home in Boston, it was time for Anna Williams to return home to Natchez — a sad event for the small family. At the same time, friends of Judith's brother, Winthrop, had asked Judith to help oversee the education of their son, Adam Louis Bingaman, who planned to attend Harvard College in Cambridge. Thinking he would make a fine brother for Julia Maria and fill the empty space left by Anna's departure, Judith agreed to take him into her home. By early fall, 14-year-old Adam had joined the Murray household. He was exceptionally bright and engaging, and the two young people became very close as Judith described in a letter to Winthrop:

> ...it cannot be denied, that a very strong, and mutual attachment, glows in the bosoms of Adam Bingaman and my daughter — but this attachment is as pure, as the visions of a slumbering Cherub. Julia Maria, on her part, declared, that she devoutly wishes heaven had given her such a brother...Julia Maria is naturally an admirer of Genius, and she has been delighted to meet in the bosom of an associate, an inmate — They take their lessons in musick together, they paint in the same style, they sing, they read together; their tastes are similar; they are fond of conversing upon the languages, upon the fine arts, to which they are passionately devoted, and the homage which they render to superiority of intellect, amounts adoration. Adam addresses to my Girl, the poetical effusions of his leisure moments, he regards her as the most perfect, and the most accomplished of human beings; while the idea of sexual distinctions, seems never to have obtained in their minds, or to be banished from their recollection...Should this mutual, and I will own very tender esteem, changing its aspect, assume the face of love, although that love will indeed be nobly based, yet, for me, it will be most unhappy, for my lips can never sanction any connexion, that shall in the decline of my life, remove my daughter from my presence. Yet events have seemed beyond my controul — Providence placed this youth in my family and he has conducted in a manner calculated to command our affection, and our esteem. If, when he first distinguished our child, we had removed him from our dwelling, it is my opinion, so ardent are young attachments, that a procedure so violent would have augmented the evil and remarks prejudicial to the delicacy of female reputation might have been made. I judged it best to constitute myself a party....[72]

Judith's nephew, William Fitz Winthrop, had also moved into 5 Franklin Place after graduating from preparatory school. He was sent to Boston to study with tutors to prepare him for early admission to

Harvard. The money Judith received from her brother and the Bingaman family to support the two boys in her household helped with finances, but the Murrays were having increasing difficulty making ends meet.

John's Stroke, and Financial Distress

In the fall of 1809 came a real blow. Years of exhaustive travel and regular bouts of ill health took their toll on John. At age 68, he suffered a stroke that left him bedridden and helpless although, thankfully, his mind remained alert. Judith was utterly distraught:

> There is, my long, and tenderly beloved sister, nothing to be done for the restoration of my husband, for which I so ardently wish, as once more to see my poor, afflicted, suffering brothers, and their very meritorious wives. If the scattered individuals of our family were once more collected, where they might reciprocally console and aid each other, I think I could bear the rude buffetting of time, I think I could submit to the storms which assail the winter of my life, nor would my composure, my firmness, be thus prostrated. But, when I view one Brother distanced near three thousand miles, and the other as effectively removed from my sight, as if he too were a dweller in the Mississippi Territory, when I view my distressed husband, helpless as an infant! I will confess to you, my sister, that my mind is shaken as by a mighty tempest[,] that the waves of affliction nearly overwhelm me, and that there are times, when I am ready to sink beneath the burden of existence...I bless God that the mind of my husband invariably reposeth upon the rock of his salvation, or, if a murmur at any moment escapes his lips, it originates in the disappointment he has experienced, relative to a speedy departure out of time...It is nearly seven weeks since the poor sufferer has been able to raise a finger on his left hand, he could not change his position in his bed a single inch, if he might thereby obtain the Universe! Yet in the whole of his left side although totally useless, so exquisitely sensible to the touch, that during the operation of moving him, his anguish is greatly augmented....[73]

Finances continued to deteriorate. John was unable to work, of course, and the Universalist Society he had led kept lowering their support payments due to their own lack of funds. America was soon to become involved in another war — the War of 1812. In Boston that meant trade embargos, threats of British invasion, and the consequential failure of businesses, banks, and investment institutions — dividends from which were the Murrays' main source of income. In 1809 Judith was 58, in poor health, and tired. In a letter to a member of the Universalist Society, in which she asked for the money she felt they were due, she wrote:

> I accumulate years, and my health is broken, while the whole weight of our domestick arrangements rests solely upon me....[74]

In October Adam went off to college, taking up residence on Harvard's campus. Judith had been authorized by his parents to serve as his guardian in any matters that might arise. Life at home for Judith revolved around caring for Julia Maria, whose regular bouts of throat disorder and fevers continued, with rambunctious William — "too great a Lover of Play"[75]— and with her invalid husband whose left side remained paralyzed. John required a live-in nurse and up to four men to move his substantial frame from his bed to a window seat or out to their carriage for journeys to the countryside. Judith made regular trips to Gloucester as well to care for Esther and their brother, Fitz William who were both regularly ill. Winthrop wrote to her from Natchez about his severe pains from the gout. His health, too, was fragile and Judith greatly feared losing any of her precious siblings.

On one of her visits to Gloucester, Judith received a letter from John — most likely dictated to a friend — in which he expressed his sorrow for the difficulty his illness had brought into her life. Judith responded:

> My Dear, my beloved, my venerable sufferer
>
> Who says that you have not been made to me an instrument of great good? Who says that you ought to be second to any in my gratitude, in my affection? Was it not by your mouth that our God, and Father, thought best to show me the way of life more perfectly, and is there not many a denunciation, which being found in holy writ, would have harrowed up my affrighted soul, had not thy irradiated mind, by dispersing the clouds, produced the luminous comment repleat with peace, life, and happiness? Are you not the Father of my child? Is there, can there be a more excellent thing, do I not in her enjoy that desideration for which my soul long languished, and which I have hailed as heav[e]n's best gift? Away then with every recurrence to accidental evils, to the thorn in the flesh, to human frailties, from which no mortal is exempt. What are the fading evils of time, to the substantial felicity in possession, and reversion, of which you have been made to me the beloved medium. Talk not of forgiveness, of offences, or of pardon, but let us mutually bear, and forbear, and let us hand in hand pursue the rugged path, which yet remains, until we arrive at that beatified

state, where sin nor sorrow will no more invade, and where we shall be completely blessed. I am happy to find your approbation of your child so unreserved, she does indeed merit every effort which we can make in her favour, and I persuade myself you will, in every particular, discharge to her the whole duty of a Father. I rejoice your airing in the carriage was so refreshing, and I trust my poor, way worn sufferer, will find many resting places on the road, in which he can sincerely say it is good for me to be here...May God forever bless you [—] I am truly your faithful and affectionate Wife[76]

In November of 1811, Judith lost her sister, Esther, who breathed her last with her sister by her side. Judith was tired of illness and death, but had to tell Winthrop the sad news:

Alas! Alas! my brother you have now but one sister! — I have seen the open graves of my Father, of my Mother, and now of the only sister of my blood, and yet I survive to communicate the intelligence...Three melancholy night[s] I watched alone by her bed side, and, Great, and Good God, I witnessed her last gasp...There was no struggle, no apparent sufferings...Her children are inconsolable, our loss is irreparable....[77]

Later that month, Judith published a moving tribute to her sister in the *Columbian Centinel*.

More Publishing, and Judith Welcomes Her First Grandchild
As the spring of 1812 approached, Judith and John published John's *Letters and Sketches of Sermons* — in two volumes, by advance subscription, just as she had published *The Gleaner* years before. They hoped this endeavor would bring them additional income since, as she explained to the book's publisher:

It is true a pecuniary compensation has not been our first object, but we are not rich, our income is diminished nearly one half, and our expenses are greatly accumulated....[78]

In May, Winthrop's second son, George Washington Sargent — named, of course, for Winthrop's friend the president — came to live at 5 Franklin Place. Adam Bingaman, who had graduated from Harvard College the previous fall, was planning to move home to Natchez. Over the past four years, his relationship with Julia Maria had deepened and the two were now very much in love. The thought of leaving Julia Maria behind made him grief-stricken, and he worried that his very beautiful friend would find a new suitor. To reassure him of her love, Adam asked Julia Maria to marry him in secret. He would tell his parents in Natchez about their marriage, return to Boston, tell Julia Maria's parents, and then go through a proper marriage ceremony. Knowing her parents approved of Adam, and wanting to prevent unnecessary pain, Julia Maria agreed. Months later, Judith explained the circumstances to Winthrop:

> Thus did she yield to the ardent solicitations of her lover every thing which a delicate female, over whose conduct discretion and propriety are unremitting, and vigilant guardians, could yield, and a few days previous to Adam's departure, won by his example, and softened by a mutual tenderness, mutual regrets, and mutual despondence, she exchanged with him, without my knowledge, the most solemn, and sacred vows....[79]

Adam left Boston in August. Julia Maria, who had never before concealed information from her mother, found her present situation distressing. Her illnesses continued, and by January she finally had to tell her mother about her marriage. Julia Maria was pregnant, Judith told her sister-in-law:

> My poor Girl, totally inexperienced, was unconscious of her situation until January, when with deep contrition she revealed to me the only secret she had ever concealed from me....[80]

Judith decided to keep the marriage out of the newspapers until a ceremony could take place. As much as she cared for Adam, Judith prayed her daughter had not made a hasty decision. They were both very young, and there was little recourse if the marriage failed. But, as she wrote to Winthrop, "...time only can determine whether this connexion be a blessing, or the reverse...."[81]

In May, William moved out of 5 Franklin Place to begin his studies at Harvard. Meanwhile, months went by with no word from Adam and Judith began to think the worst — that he had lost interest in her daughter. But he did return to Boston in time for the birth of his daughter, Charlotte, Judith's first grandchild. Not surprisingly, it was a very difficult birth for fragile Julia Maria:

> My daughters hours of peril were most distressing, and uncommonly multiplied. Forty eight hours she continued in indescribable agonies, when she gave into my bosom a lovely female infant, for whom, as we have not the power of providing, we entertain a thousand apprehensions. She will probably be the heiress of my misfortunes,

and of my dependence, My daughter continues extremely feeble, but God I trust will completely restore her....[82]

Adam left four months later for Natchez. His wife and baby daughter stayed behind in Judith's care. Illness continued to loom over the household and debts increased as John's book did not produce the revenue they had expected. Judith spent the last night of her aunt Mary Turner Sargent's life at her bedside on September 13, mourning the loss of her friend and confidant of so many years. That winter, though, she received word that Anna Williams, who had lived at 5 Franklin Place for several years, was to marry a Mr. Thompson. Anna had written to Judith with the happy news, telling her she had recently reread *The Gleaner* and had taken to heart Judith's views on marriage. Judith was pleased, responding to Anna:

> Marriage is the highest state of friendship — let your husband enjoy your undivided, unreserved confidence...The married pair should never be rivals, they should be friends. Husband and Wife should not be considered as terms synonimous with Master and Slave — Equality should be the motto of wedded life...although sixteen long years have passed by since I published that work, I have not yet found reason to retract a single opinion — nay years have rather established my sentiments....[83]

The Approaching War and a Wayward Nephew

That summer, Judith had John Murray's will drafted and, with great difficulty, he was able to sign it. Everything would go to her, they decided, and then to Julia Maria upon her death. They were all so ill, all the time, it seemed only right to make final plans. By September, Julia Maria was so "shockingly wasted"[78] Judith feared for her daughter's life. Breast-feeding, in particular, was draining what little strength Julia Maria had. Adam had been silent, and Judith had to remind him to write to his wife:

> ...a letter of consolation from a husband on whom she doats, will enable her to meet with tranquility the solitary hours of adversity, to which she is condemned....[84]

Whatever difficulties lay within the walls of 5 Franklin Place, outside was also precarious. On October 1, 1814, Judith wrote to Winthrop:

> Our town is converted into a Garrison. Soldiers are night and day patroling our streets, and martial musick is every where resounding

— Thousands are flocking to our protection — The fortifications are momently acquiring additional strength, all Classes of Citizens volunteer their services....[85]

As trade was halted, banks foreclosed, and the economy devastated, Judith wrote to a friend:

This war spreads almost universal desolation, and consequent gloom...Peace alone, by the revival of commerce, can restore our prospects....[86]

Luckily, later that month, Judith was also able to write, "Our fears of an attack from the British begin to subside...."[87]

Judith adored her granddaughter, as she told one of her aunts: "Our little Charlotte is...the life, the treasure, the idol of the house...."[88] But across the river in Cambridge, William was not behaving like a treasure. Far away from his strict father since he was quite young and now on his own among older students, William was about to be expelled from Harvard. He was missing classes, drinking, smoking cigars, and borrowing large sums of money to pay for his amusements. Not interested in finishing college, he thought he might take up privateering and seek his fortune at sea. In vain, Judith spoke with Harvard's "government" on his behalf, arranged for tutors, and tried to guide him down a wiser path. Each time, he seemed to comply with her (and his father's) wishes only to go off again on jaunts to the city with friends. In December, he outright disappeared and Judith had to dispatch her cousin, Lucius Manlius Sargent, to find the boy. Lucius Manlius eventually found him heading for a privateering ship out of Portland, and returned him to 5 Franklin Place. "Manlius" was enormously helpful to Judith with William, and she forgave his earlier condemnation of The Gleaner.

But the worst of William's behavior was yet to come. Back in Boston, he became demanding and even violent. He insisted on more money from Judith, threatened her, and showed no sign of respect for her authority. One morning in January he became particularly uncontrollable. His younger brother tried to intervene, but Judith sent him to school fearing for his safety. Judith refused to let William leave the house until they had settled matters, hiding his cloak and hat. William threw stones through the windows to retaliate. Judith sent for a doctor and for Lucius Manlius. William locked himself in his room. Lucius Manlius was convinced that William should be sent home to his father immediately but it was winter, travel was difficult, and Judith did not want to disappoint her brother.

She spent the next year finding more tutors for William far away from Boston, to whom she gave strict rules not to let him return without notifying her first. William wrote to her expressing his great remorse, and Judith never lost hope that he would settle down some day, resume his studies, and reinstate his place at Harvard. In one particularly exasperated moment, she asked him:

> William have you no ambition — no fear of public shame...Will nothing satisfy you except you can infix indelible disgrace upon your kindred?...Did you mean nothing by your promise of future good conduct[?]....[89]

The Preacher Meets His Redeemer

In February, another peace treaty with Britain was signed. Bells rang everywhere in the city of Boston. At 5 Franklin Place, they finally heard word from Adam who, it turned out, had joined the war and fought in New Orleans. He was now studying law, with no plans to return to Boston nor send for his wife and child. In August, Anna Williams's new husband, Mr. Thompson, arrived in Boston for an extended stay in Judith's home while he conducted business in the city. Judith was tired, rarely writing letters any more except on business or for necessary family obligations. And that fall, her beloved husband of 27 years passed away. He had longed for the peace of death — longed to meet his Redeemer and be free from pain. John finally had his wish, but it was an agonizing loss for his wife and daughter:

> My beloved my sympathizing my brother
>
> Many weeks, in the estimation of calamity years, have passed on since I last addressed you. During this period I have watched the expiring moments of my long suffering, my venerable, my now beatified husband. His demise took place on Lord's day morning 3d instant, at 6 oclock, and as the interment of his precious remains, could not be delayed, he was entombed on the following monday evening 4th instant, with all the...arrangements, and honours, which his now mourning and deeply penetrated congregation, could bestow. My respectable husband died as he had lived, bearing uneqivocal testimony to the grand, and fundamental truths of revelation...his character has been elevated to no common height, his patient, and uncomplaining endurance of suffering, his unwavering faith has stamped his testimony with the seal of integrity, and given that confirmation to his confidence in his own views of sacred writ, which will rejoice in the heart of the christian. His capacious, and lucid intellect, was, two days previous to his demise, decidedly deranged, yet even then, his hard pressed mind, seemed a

noble edifice, shook by an overwhelming storm, the duration of which would be transient...and thus have been laid in the grave a Man, to whom from sentiment and from principle, my heart, my soul was engaged, and thus is your sister once more a widow — A Widow — desolate sound — but I too shall soon lift my head on high, for my deliverer, my Redeemer still lives, and the time of my emancipation draweth nigh...I will yield to the remonstrances of an aching heart, a swimming head, and trembling fingers, which are momently stimulating me to relinquish my pen [—] I am, most devotedly, your affectionate and deeply affected sister [90]

John Murray was interred in Boston's Granary Burial Ground, only a few blocks from Franklin Place. Two services were held for the great preacher — one in Gloucester, the other in Boston, which began with a long procession from his home to the Universalist meeting house and on to the burial ground. The notice of his funeral which appeared in the *Columbian Centinel* included the words:

> Many are the witnesses of his labors of love...and many can seal to the truth and happy effects of his ministry. He rests from his labors, and his works follow him...free inquiry in an eminent degree has been advanced by [his] unwearied researches....[91]

John had made Judith the executor of his will, giving her all decision-making powers. Judith's finances, however, would only worsen during the next few years. The Bingaman family still owed her money, and Adam's long silences were worrisome. Her brother, Winthrop, was by now virtually supporting her.

By the end of September, Judith had been approached by several of her husband's followers to publish the autobiography he had been writing. In fact, it was a promise she had made to John before he died. He had left behind hundreds of pages of a detailed account of his life up to 1774. Their friend, Reverend Edward Mitchell, who had recently moved from Boston to New York, offered to help Judith complete the story and prepare the manuscript for publishing. Reverend Mitchell wrote to various friends in New York, Philadelphia, and other places who could provide anecdotes about John, and he provided a character sketch of his friend for Judith to use. Judith began to edit the work and 1,100 copies were published in a few months, in one large volume, by Messieurs Francis and Munroe. It sold for $1.50. (Sadly, because Judith, not John, completed the work, the history of their relationship, what she meant to John and to Universalism, are left out. Judith was too modest, or felt it too inappropriate, for her to presume to write this content.) Before the book's publication, Reverend Mitchell was instrumental in selling advance subscriptions and, after it was published, copies of the actual publication. He was, in deed, a good friend and, as a minister, second only to John in Judith's estimation.

October was spent visiting the troubled William at his new tutor's home in Norton, Massachusetts. His behavior seemed to be improving, but in November he ran away to the home of his former tutor who, by all accounts, was less puritanical. He began running up more debts, however, and Judith's exasperation was growing. She had no money to send, she told him. When will he stop his "career of folly?"[92] His father, the strict and unyielding Winthrop, was annoyed with his sister. Take a firmer hand, he told her. Part of this was her fault, to which she responded:

> My brother I am old, I am feeble, I am a woman — my health is broken, my mind is depressed — I am unequal to any uncommon exertion....[93]

Privately, Judith was convinced that William was insane.

Preparing for Her Final Days and Julia Maria's Future

Winthrop had urged Judith to move to his home in Natchez rather than having to continue supporting his sister and her household in Boston. Winthrop did not approve of Julia Maria's marriage, however, nor of Adam and his family whom he "abhorred" and Judith could not contemplate a separation from her daughter:

> My daughter, and her infant, are still more endeared to me, since the demise of their Father, they are all that is left of him...I cannot voluntarily separate myself from them, and the improper conduct of my son in law, is a bar to their residence in your family....[94]

As for his condemnation of Julia Maria, Judith explained the circumstances — again — reminding him that she and Adam had, in deed, completed the marriage ceremony and registered their union in the state of Massachusetts. Julia Maria had acted out of love, in the full knowledge of her parents' affection for Adam. She had come forward in time to have the marriage known before the birth of her child.

> This is the height of her offences — they do not, in my opinion, constitute her a criminal — All who know my daughter sincerely love her, you do not know her — you once hated her Father...[but] you relented toward him, and possibly you may relent toward this unfortunate child....[95]

Judith's greatest fear at this time was that seemingly indifferent Adam could at any time send for his wife and child. Legally, Julia Maria would have no choice but to obey. Judith dreaded this outcome:

> I am afraid of A.L.B. because the Law has placed the destiny of my only child, and now of my darling grand child, in his power — he can, if he pleases, remove them forever from my view — is not this fact enough to fill me with the most dreadful apprehension? God only knows how much the fear of a separation from my children, harrows up my soul....[96]

In June, Adam did write that he wanted Julia Maria and Charlotte to travel south as soon as he had sufficient funds. Judith thought:

> ...our only hope is that we may be able to soothe him to our wishes...all her friends are extremely opposed to her removal, she is much beloved here, God grant she may be permitted to continue in her native place — One thing is certain, wherever she goes, her Mother must be her Companion — added to my maternal feelings, which are perhaps as strong as ever glowed in the bosom of a Mother, I throw my eyes upon her pallid Countenance, I remember her slender health, and every hour I painfully recollect, that she is all that is left of her dear departed Father, I should be miserable, most miserable, in a state of separation from this child....[97]

What should she do?

> If he comes, she must go, and can I allow her to depart without me? and yet can I leave this consecrated Mansion, the ashes of my husband, the ashes of my parents, and now in the winter of my days perform a journey of more than three thousand miles...[and] surrender comparative independence, for an uncertain dependence, upon persons and things, of whom I can form no idea....[98]

Judith wished to remain in Boston. She hoped to live out her last days in the home where John had died, and be buried next to him. Meanwhile, she travelled to nearby Newton regularly to visit her ailing brother, Fitz William, who, like Winthrop, suffered dreadfully from gout. Winthrop wrote of his plans to visit Boston in June to tend to his troubled son. Judith also welcomed David Urquhart (son of her niece, Mary Williams, who had visited her years earlier), and Winthrop Sargent Harding into her home to oversee the education of yet two more young men.

Seeing her brother again after so many years of separation was a joy. Winthrop was ill, however, and bedridden for much of his visit. When he was well enough, he was contending with William. Winthrop stayed in Judith's home for several weeks and then purchased a house in Cambridge, near Harvard, where he resided until September. By the time he left, William had been reinstated at Harvard and Winthrop took his son, Washington, home with him to Mississippi.

Judith continued her efforts to pay off debts and make arrangements for her daughter's future. Since John's death, she had had to contend with tax collectors for the first time. While John was alive, his position as a member of the clergy had exempted him from paying taxes. This consideration did not extend to his widow, however, which Judith found utterly unreasonable. Over the next two years, she sold land in the Ohio Territory she had inherited from her father, sold her shares in the Gloucester bank, continued trying to sell John's books (in America, England, and Ireland), but was still largely dependent on Winthrop. Even so, she was determined there would be something left for her daughter. Both she and John had carefully worded their wills to prevent Adam from controlling their money through his wife:

> It seems to me it would not consist with the kindness, to which she is entitled, to render her during her whole life powerless...were her husband worthy of confidence, I should be comparatively happy....[99]

She also knew she had to prepare Julia Maria for losing her mother. They had always been close:

> When the time shall come, and come it quickly will, that I shall sleep quietly in the narrow house, comfort yourself, my daughter, with this indubitable truth, that you have been to me the greatest blessing, which heaven, through a long protracted life, has vouchsafed to bestow upon me — Some jars there have been, but the most brilliant sky is occasionally checquered by clouds, and you, my Love, have always emerged with tenfold brightness....[100]

Judith was still having a long distance quarrel with the Bingaman family over money. Numerous letters went back and forth, Winthrop tried to intervene down in Natchez, but the Bingamans insisted Judith was trying to cheat them and they were slow in paying. Judith had kept detailed receipts, of course, and the debt was eventually paid off. These transactions, however, only served to sour the relationship between the two families still further. As it was, Winthrop refused to accept Adam in his home and the Bingamans, who had wanted their son to marry a wealthy Southern woman who would bring more slaves to the family plantation, were no doubt dismayed to learn of their son's marriage to a relatively poor daughter of a liberal clergyman who condemned slavery. They probably regarded feminist, outspoken Judith with skepticism, wondering what ideas she had implanted in the mind of her daughter.

How and where Judith would spend her final days remained uppermost in her mind. She was receiving offers for her townhouse which was badly in need of repair before it could be sold. She could not, however, make these kinds of decisions until Adam was clear about his wishes. Increasingly, Judith realized it was important for her to be near a minister she respected and Hosea Ballou, now serving her husband's church, was not that minister. Theirs had always been a turbulent relationship, since Gloucester, and both she and John disapproved of his theological views. Occasionally, Judith still attended church in Boston as it was proper for her to do, but her opinion of Ballou never changed. Facing her final days, she went so far as to inquire of her friend Reverend Mitchell in New York about living in that city:

> It is my wish to be in the vicinity of a minister of the reconciliation, and that my dying hours should be solaced by the soothings of a preacher of glad tidings — I believe in imputed Righteousness — or rather in an inheritance by union with the great head of every Man, in the atonement, in God the Saviour — I know no other God — He says "I am God the Saviour, and beside me there is no other["] — I believe in a judgement to come — that God hath appointed a day, in which He will judge the World....[101]

In the early months of 1817, Judith struck up a new friendship with the Russian Consul, Alexis Eustaphieve, who asked to purchase *The Gleaner*. Judith sent him this work, along with her last play, *The African*, and the two exchanged letters about books they had read or borrowed from each other. It was the coldest winter they had had in 30 years, and Judith complained, "It is so extremely cold, that my chilled fingers seem to refuse their office...."[102]

By March, she wrote to Mrs. Leonard, John's former nurse, that her eyesight was rapidly failing:

> My pen, through life, has continued to me a never failing reassurance, a never failing consolation — when nearly overwhelmed with sorrow, I have seized this powerful little instrument, which like some magick wand has dissipated the glooms that enveloped my faculties, and I have arisen from my writing desk, calm if not happy [—] but alas! alas! this indulgence is now greatly abridged — My sight is so much impaired, as to put it out of my power to write a single line in the evening, and you know the evenings, and the mornings, have

been for forty years of my life, my seasons of Harvest, from the wintry morning I am cut off, by the finger, and even heart chilling influence of this inclement season, wood is a prodigious article, and economy frequently keeps me in bed — but I ought not to complain, I am now sixty five years of age, and during this long period of protracted life, my eyes have rendered me good service, for which benefit gratitude should be found in my heart and dwell upon my tongue....[103]

Judith also received word that month that the Universalists planned to build a new church in Boston. She thought, how fitting it would be to call it the Murraytanian Church and perhaps Reverend Mitchell would return to Boston to serve. More than anything, she wanted to keep alive the memory of her husband: "...my love for the name of the deceased, induces the strongest complacency in whatever may rescue it from oblivion..."[104] she told Reverend Mitchell. She was infuriated when the church was consecrated in October without a single mention of John by Hosea Ballou, and only a brief — and nameless — nod from Thomas Jones, "a Man at this moment reaping the fruits of my husbands patronage...."[105] How ungrateful, she thought.

Both David Urquhart and Winthrop Harding were excelling in school, and had grown very dear to Judith. As with her other young guests, she corresponded regularly with their parents about their progress and expenses. In one amusing interchange, Judith had to explain her domestic arrangements to Mr. Harding who was concerned that his son's chamber was not warm at all times. She responded:

> I am 66 years of age, and I have never yet had a fire in my chamber, except when confined by illness — I do not see the utility of this plan — a short winter morning is barely sufficient to dress, breakfast, and be in time for Doctor Gardiner — from Doctor Gardiner Winthrop proceeds to Mr Webb, and he does not return home until one o-clock, The fire then, would only serve to dress by, which were he my own son, I should consider as rendering him too delicate....[106]

Judith's solution was to set aside a room for the boys upstairs which she kept heated and lit. There, they could study in comfort before retiring to their bed chambers. In addition, she could not afford to hire a man servant to prepare fires and unattended fireplaces in the chambers of sleeping children could lead to disaster.

That winter, Julia Maria contracted a deadly fever:

> My daughter has been a great sufferer during the past winter, she has been brought, by an inflamatory fever, to the gates of the grave — her agonies were beyond description — for nine successive days,

she swallowed every twenty four hours, three hundred drops of laudanum, and even this prodigious quantity, did not always mitigate her pangs....[107]

Julia Maria continued an invalid for many months while little Charlotte, not quite four years old, continued to grow and delight everyone in the household:

> Our little Charlotte can read in any english book, without spelling. Taking up the News Paper she calls out — "Grandmamma do you want to buy any superfine flour? here is some to be sold" — she already spells out of books, all those little words, which sound the same but are of dissimilar orthography [—] she sent by Mrs Williams, a very fine cambrick handkerchief to her Father, of her own hemming....[108]

Julia Maria was still so ill in May that Judith considered taking her to the healing waters of the Saratoga Springs. Julia Maria was hesitant to travel a great distance without her husband, thinking it improper. Instead, Judith took her to Newport, Rhode Island in June with Charlotte and David Urquhart. Before they left, they received word that Adam was coming to Boston to collect his wife and daughter.

What happened next is not entirely clear. Judith penned her last letter from 5 Franklin Place on August 14 to her sister-in-law, Mary Williams Sargent, Winthrop's wife. She discussed plans she and other relatives had made to care for their unkempt family plot in Gloucester and erect a marble marker in honor of their ancestors. She had arranged for a local tradesman to build a sideboard and bureau of the finest quality for Winthrop. After that, the letter books end.

We can be certain that Judith left the young people in her care in good hands, that she sold her townhouse and took care of other financial arrangements. We do know that Judith accompanied her daughter to Natchez and settled there on the Fatherland plantation. How long the journey took, how quickly Judith's health deteriorated, and how much of life in Natchez she enjoyed, no one knows.

On June 9, 1820, Judith Sargent Murray died at Oak Point in Natchez and was buried in the Bingaman family plot at Fatherland — three thousand miles away from John Murray. Julia Maria engraved on her mother's grave stone, "Dear Spirit, the monumental stone can never speak thy worth." Judith died just six days after her brother, Winthrop, had passed away. Later that September, seven-year-old Charlotte also died. Julia Maria gave birth to a son, Adam Louis Bingaman, Jr. in 1821, but in 1822 her health finally failed and Julia Maria died. Julia Maria and Charlotte are buried with Judith at Fatherland.

Julia Maria's son, Adam Jr., grew up to marry and father a daughter, named for his mother. She died, childless, of consumption in 1865 at the age of 24. There are no direct descendants of Judith Sargent and John Murray.

As for others closest to Judith, Fitz William Sargent died in 1822 at his home in Newton. Her cousin and confidant, Catherine Goldthwaite, died in 1830. Cousins Epes Sargent died in 1822, Daniel Sargent in 1842, and Lucius Manlius Sargent in 1867.

But dozens of children, dearly loved by their "Aunt Murray," remained to thrive and have children of their own. Hundreds of their descendants are spread today throughout the United States and beyond, carrying surnames like Sargent, Saunders, Goldthwaite, Plummer, Allen, Urquhart, Williams, Hough, Ellery, Stevens, Rogers, Turner, Osborne, and Binney — all of whom carry with them a piece of Judith's legacy.

Judith also left behind a written record of a life lived — an account of both the ordinary and extraordinary. She left essays, poems, and plays which entertain and inform.

But in a larger sense, Judith Sargent Murray left behind her courage and wisdom. The words and actions of the people who formed the American nation survive and inform long after their passing. We are still learning to appreciate Judith's role in those defining days, and her effect on succeeding generations. In a sense, we are all her spiritual descendents — certainly, her beneficiaries.

End Notes

[1]   Letter to Winthrop Sargent (her brother), Sept. 26 1808.
[2]   See p. 17.
[3]   This book is owned by the Sargent-Murray-Gilman-Hough House Association, Gloucester, and is housed in The Sargent House Museum collection.
[4]   *Life of John Murray*, p. 203.
[5]   Letter to John Murray, Nov. 14, 1774.
[6]   *Life of John Murray*, p. 211.
[7]   *Guns off Gloucester*, p. 83.
[8]   Ibid.
[9]   *Guns off Gloucester*, p. 81.
[10]   Letter to John Murray, July 28, 1775.
[11]   *Guns off Gloucester*, pp. 105-114.
[12]   Letter to John Murray, July 28, 1778.
[13]   Letter to Winthrop Sargent, Feb. 25, 1778.

14 Letter to John Murray, Dec. 2, 1780.
15 Letter to Anna, the orphanned Stevens relative, June 16, 1782.
16 Letter to Mrs. Pilgrim of London, Oct. 31, 1784.
17 Letter to Winthrop Sargent, April 21, 1786.
18 Letter to Winthrop Sargent, May 5, 1787; I do not know if the memorandum book referred in this letter still exists.
19 Letter to Winthrop Sargent, June 5, 1787.
20 Letter to Mary Turner (Mrs. Daniel) Sargent, June 5, 1787.
21 Letter to John Murray, Jan. 18, 1788.
22 Ibi d.
23 Letter to Mrs. Gardiner, April 4, 1788.
24 Letter to John Murray, May 8, 1788.
25 Letter to John Murray, May 18, 1788.
26 Letter to Winthrop and Judith Saunders Sargent (her parents), Oct. 5, 1788.
27 Letter to her parents, Oct. 12, 1788.
28 Letter to Mary Turner Sargent, April 15, 1788.
29 Letter to her parents, Oct. 12, 1788.
30 *Life of John Murray*, p. 233.
31 Letter from John Murray to Paul Dudley Sargent, Oct. 1, 1789; from *The Dolphin*, newsletter of The Sargent House Museum, Spring 1994.
32 Letter to John Murray, Nov. 29, 1789.
33 Letter to her mother, Sept. 22, 1791.
34 Letter to Sally Wood, April 21, 1802.
35 Letter to Catherine Goldthwaite, June 6, 1777; see Harris, p. xxv.
36 *The Gleaner*, No. LXXXVII (the numbering of the *Gleaner* essays in the *Massachusetts Magazine* and the book, *The Gleaner*, do not correspond. I have used the book's numbering to enable readers to find the essays more easily.
37 *The Gleaner*, No. XVII.
38 *The Gleaner*, No. LXXXVII.
39 *The Gleaner*, No. VII.
40 *The Gleaner*, No. XIII.
41 *The Gleaner*, No. XXXV.
42 Letter to her parents, Sept. 18, 1790 (see p. 297).
43 Letter to Mrs P— of Hampstead, England, Nov. 15, 1794.
44 Letter to Dorcas Babson (Mrs. Epes) Sargent, Sept. 19, 1794.
45 Letter to Thomas Paine, Nov. 11, 1794.
46 Letter to the Editor by John Murray, *Federal Orrery*, March 2, 1796.
47 Letter to Anna Parsons Sargent, August 17, 1795.
48 Letter to Mrs. Murray in London (John's mother) Oct. 10, 1796.
49 Letter dated June 7, 1806, recipient unknown.
50 Letter to Messieurs Belcher and Armstrong, June 7, 1806.
51 Letter to William Fitz Winthrop Sargent, March 29, 1799.
52 Letter to Epes Sargent, May 3, 1799.
53 Letter to Epes Sargent, June 13, 1799.
54 Letter to Esther Sargent Ellery (her sister), Dec. 23, 1799.
55 Letter to Esther Sargent Ellery, Jan. 18, 1800.
56 Letter to Esther Sargent Ellery, Dec. 23, 1799.
57 *The Oriental Philanthropist*, preface.
58 *Julia*, pp. 21-22.
59 Letter to Sally Wood, Nov. 25, 1800.
60 Letter to Epes Sargent, Sept. 21, 1801.

61 Letter to William Fitz Winthrop Sargent, Sept. 18, 1802.
62 Letter to Judith Saunders, Nov. 29, 1802.
63 Letter to Anna Parsons Sargent, May 7, 1803.
64 Letter to Mercy Otis Warren, June, 1805.
65 Letter to Rev. Robert Redding, June 4, 1806. I have yet to determine
    if *The Gleaner* was, indeed, published in England.
66 Letter to Lucius Manlius Sargent, August, 1806.
67 Letter to the editor of *The Columbian Centinel*, August 29, 1806.
68 Ibid.
69 Letter to Alexis Eustaphieve, Russian Consul, Oct. 4, 1806.
70 Letter dated Oct. 4, 1806, recipient unknown.
71 Letter to Mrs. Sargent (unclear which one), Nov. 11, 1806.
    As yet, we do not know if Julia Maria's journal survived.
72 Letter to Winthrop Sargent, Sept. 26, 1808.
73 Letter to Esther Sargent Ellery, Nov. 27, 1809.
74 Letter to a member of the committee that governed the Boston
    Universalist church, August 5, 1809.
75 Letter to Winthrop Sargent, Oct. 1, 1809.
76 Letter to John Murray, Oct. 9, 1810.
77 Letter to Winthrop Sargent, Dec. 1, 1811.
78 Letter to Messieurs Francis and Munroe, April 11, 1812.
79 Letter to Winthrop Sargent, Dec. 7, 1813.
80 Letter to Anna Parsons Sargent, May 3, 1813.
81 Letter to Winthrop Sargent, March 8, 1813.
82 Letter to Winthrop Sargent, June 22, 1813.
83 Letter to Anna Williams (Thompson), Feb. 14, 1814.
84 Letter to Adam Louis Bingaman, Sept. 8, 1814.
85 Letter dated Oct. 1, 1814, recipient unknown.
86 Letter dated Oct. 17, 1814, recipient unknown.
87 Letter dated Oct. 17 1814, recipient unknown.
88 Letter to an aunt, Oct., 1814.
89 Letter to William Fitz Winthrop Sargent, Feb. 4, 1815.
90 Letter to Winthrop Sargent, Sept. 11, 1815.
91 *Columbian Centinel*, September, 1815.
92 Letter to Rev. Mr. Clark, Nov. 2, 1815.
93 Letter to Winthrop Sargent, Nov. 16, 1815.
94 Ibid.
95 Letter to Winthrop Sargent, Sept. 23, 1817.
96 Letter to Winthrop Sargent, Jan. 27, 1816.
97 Letter to Winthrop Sargent, April 8, 1817.
98 Letter to Winthrop Sargent, Oct. 23, 1817.
99 Letter to Winthrop Sargent, Dec. 31, 1815.
100 Letter to Julia Maria Murray, July 22, 1816.
101 Letter to Rev. Edward Mitchell, May 7, 1817.
102 Letter to an aunt, Feb. 16, 1816.
103 Letter to Mrs. Leonard, March 15, 1817.
104 Letter to Rev. Edward Mitchell, Oct. 22, 1817.
105 Ibid.
106 Letter to Mr. Harding, Oct. 20, 1817.
107 Letter to Mr. Harding, Jan. 17, 1818.
108 Letter to an aunt, March 23, 1817.

"Upon Tuesday morning...we quitted Gloucester —
It was the fourth of May; the morning was fine,
and I was enriched with a Father's blessing...."
(from Letter 742)

"I purpose, my ever honoured friends, making it a rule
to address you upon the close of every week...I shall,
with pleasure recount occurences as they take place...."
(from Letter 743)

Judith Sargent Murray and Reverend John Murray lived here,
in Gloucester, from 1788-1794. The house was built in 1782.
Photo by Bonnie Smith.

The Letters

THROUGH PROSPEROUS MASSACHUSETTS TO "VERDANT," "EQUAL" CONNECTICUT

Letter 742 To my Father & Mother Boston May 7th 1790

In the first letter, written by Judith to her parents in Gloucester, she details the trip (by stage) she and John took to Salem and Boston. The "Orphan" mentioned in the letter is Anna, her first husband's niece. Anna lost her parents at a young age, and Judith and her family looked after her. "Aunt Allen" is Sarah Sargent Allen (1729-1792) who married Nathaniel Allen of Gloucester. "Mr and Mrs Saunders" are Judith's maternal aunt and uncle. The "family of my Uncle" refers to her uncle, Daniel Sargent, and his wife, Mary Turner Sargent, who lived on Long Wharf, Boston.

Doubt not, my beloved and ever honoured Parents, that I shall, agreeably to your request, as often as time and opportunity may serve, be very circumstantial in my accounts to you — My addresses to such a Father — to such a Mother, will be prompted both by duty, and inclination, and so well doth my heart know, the tender solicitude of real affection — so well is it acquainted with the corroding agonies of suspense, that it will, upon every occasion, seek to spare, as much as may be possible, the feelings of those whom it so sincerely venerates, and loves. My purpose is, to transmit to you a detail of the progress we make, taking it for granted, that you will impart to such friends, as may take an interest in our proceedings, whatever communication you may judge proper, and I must request you to preserve all the lines which you may receive — For we may possibly wish to recur to the particulars of our journey, and I shall not have leisure to make copies — Here then my honoured friends, commenceth a journal, which your parental affection will render strongly interesting — Upon Tuesday morning, as you know, we quitted Gloucester — It was the fourth of May; the morning was fine, and I was enriched with a Father's blessing — My sister too — Dear Girl, the tear was in her eye — she came to bid me adieu — this was very good of her, and I shall not easily forget it — My poor disconsolate Orphan — her ill health distresses me — she looked more than language can express — I commend her solemnly, to the kindness of my Father, and Mother, and to that of my beloved sister — We came on, the badness of the road considered, tolerably well, and we reached Salem about 2 o clock in the afternoon, finding the family of Doctor Plummer, much distressed — where, however we dined, drank tea, and lodged — Wednesday morning, after calling upon Mr & Mrs Saunders, and breakfast with Mr Cleaveland, we left Salem, about nine O clock — The weather was not quite so propitious as upon the preceding day — it was rather wet yet we did not receive much injury, and we reached Boston just as the hungry bell had began to clamour — Here we were received with accustomed kindness and I had the pleasure of congratulating the family of my Uncle upon his perfect restoration to health — yesterday was so tempestuous, that we could not go abroad, but this morning's sun hath risen with fair presagement — I yesterday put on mourning for my unknown sister, and I shall probably make upon this day, many visits — On monday next we calculate to commence our journey, and the first conveyance shall furnish you with its continuation [—] Please to present my regards to all friends, particularly to my Aunt Allen, and her children — May God forever bless my revered Parents, and may they ever remember with pleasure their truly, and gratefully affectionate Daughter

"...we reached Boston just as the hungry bell had began to clamour...." (from Letter 742)

Southeast prospect of Boston, from the *Massachusetts Magazine*, November 1790. Courtesy of The Bostonian Society/Old State House.

Letter 743 To the Same Saturday Evening Hartford
May 15th 1790

Letter 743 marks the trip along the Boston Post Road, through western Massachusetts and into Connecticut. Of particular interest is Judith's description of Worcester, the "Embryo of a great City," including the inn where they stayed and the meals they enjoyed. Judith loved the countryside in the Connecticut River Valley, and describes the town of Suffield, Connecticut in detail. John has been asked to preach in Hartford on Sunday, so they will stay here for two days. Judith has just celebrated her thirty-ninth birthday (on May 5) and she pays loving tribute to her parents. The "sister Ellery" mentioned is her sister, Esther Sargent Ellery, who was four years younger than Judith. "Mr Ellery" is Esther's husband, John Stevens Ellery, and "Sally" is their daughter, Sarah, who was 13 years old in 1790. Judith's "sister Anna" is her sister-in-law, Anna Parsons Sargent, who was married to Judith's youngest brother, Fitz William.

I purpose, my ever honoured friends, making it a rule to address you upon the close of every week — Saturday evening, unless prevented by some unavoidable accident, shall, during the continuance of my journey, be invariably devoted to Parents, who are so tenderly anxious for my well being — I shall, with pleasure recount occurences as they take place, and however my letters may be delayed on their way to you — assure yourselves, that they will, in due time, be presented — Agreeably to our intention we quitted Boston on Monday last, about three O clock in the afternoon — The tear was upon my cheek — Accustomed, in that seat of hospitality, and amity, to the most unequivocal marks of indulgent, and tender friendship, my bosom, when leaving it, is always agitated by the sigh of regret [—] we took a cup of tea at the house of a friend in Newton, and reached Weston on Monday evening — There also we were accommodated at the dwelling of an acquaintance, but, as Mr Murray hath not frequented the western Road, which is now chosen for dispatch, we have since made our stages at public houses — We have not, however, as yet been furnished with the smallest cause of complaint — Our Inns have hitherto supplied us with every requisite — The weather on Monday and Tuesday was intensely hot, but this only seemed to enhance the value of those delightful breezes, which we have since most gratefully enjoyed — Tuesday evening produced us at Shrewsbury, which we left on wednesday morning, purchasing an appetite for breakfast, at the very moderate rate of an enchanting ride of eight miles, over a beautiful tract of ground, which brought us to Worcester — Worcester is a County Town [—] superior, and inferior, Courts, are held there, it wears a face of industry, and is probably the Embryo of a great City — Its situation is truly pleasing, and its present appearance authorizes the most sanguine hopes — We were received at the public house, into a decent parlour — a neat little Girl threw upon the breakfast table an elegant damask cloth, and hyson tea of a superior quality, with sweet bread and butter, furnished us a most delicious repast — Indeed Hyson tea is a luxury with which we have been indulged, at every stage one only excepted, and then the place was supplied by excellent souchong — [those who] recollect how extremely grateful this article is upon a journey, especially to a female Traveller, will not be surprised to find it thus particularly noted, and I take this opportunity earnestly to recommend it to all persons, passing through the good inns of Worcester, that they fail not to stop at the very excellent Tavern — That is, I mean, if they have occasion — opposite Thomas' printing office — known by the name of Patch's Tavern — Leaving Worcester, we ascended the town of Leicester, and, not having the same reason, we were not with the...sufficiently impassioned to conceive any degree of magic in the letters, which [constrict] a name — Yet we were not a little pleased with having passed a considerably stint of rough road — Leicester boasts an Academy, which is established in the seat of the late Mr Lopez, a merchant of Jewish extract, and of great eminence, and far [advanc]ed integrity — this Mansion house was purchased by the present Proprietors, for the laudable purpose of founding a Seminary, for the instruction of youth — Leicester Academy is however upon decline — Wednesday night we lodged at Spencer, and being much fatigued, tasted with particular satisfaction, the sombre pleasures of the pillow — Thursday also, after ascending, and descending, a number of activities, and declivities, for this is indeed a land of hills, and Vallies, well wooded, and watered, prepared us for a similar enjoyment on thursday night at Palmer, four miles this side of which, we surmounted the principal difficulty we shall have to encounter, from the road, until we pass New Haven — We came on over what are termed Springfield Plains — but which if I held the pen of description, I should be induced to entitle Vistas — over a fine level road, cut through thick Groves of trees, forming on either hand, a lofty and most agreeable shade, for an extent of many miles, and reached Springfield about ten O clock [—] The morning was divine, and we breakfasted in a most luxurious style — Springfield makes a very respectable appearance, it presents a num[ber] of decent dwellings, and is perhaps another of our large trading Cities, yet in its infancy — About twelve O clock we crossed Connecticut River — This River, in many places, separates the state of Connecticut from that of Massachusetts to which state, Massachusetts, we shortly after bid adieu — a temporary adieu as we trust — It contains many persons, very dear to us, and our best affections centre there — Perhaps no part of the United States, can produce a greater variety of beautiful prospects, than fascinate the eye upon Connecticut River — Nature is here most luxuriantly diversified — The Grove toped Mountains, the verdant Plains, the rich meadows, orchards, variegated fields, and commodious dwellings, most delightfully interspersed, altogether constitute a chain of imagery, which is truly pleasing — Amid these charming scenes, presenting in beautiful, and enchanting succession one hour before sunset, we reached the paradisical Village of Suffield — We had promised ourselves merely a shelter for the night, but upon our entering this rural retreat, which if sylvan desties there be, is very proper for their resort — the house of entertainment was in full view — It is kept by a venerable pair — but if we except their own individual figures, nothing about them, hath the appearance of an inequity — The house is just completed, it is in an elegant style, and every thing wears the Order of neatness — In addition to a convenient number of apartments, what they term their stoop, is ample, and pleasing — It is inclosed by a handsome Chinese railing, and fitted up with seats painted, and adorned, for the reception of the traveller, who may upon some fine day, or serene evening, prefer this airy shade, to the confinement of a parlour, or chamber — In a retired parlour we took our seats — Just under our window a fertile spot was prettily and tastefully laid out, keeping from the beds of which, was all that variety of vegitation, which is generally cultivated in an American garden to which, as I trust, the summer months will give perfection — Beyond the garden was an extensive view of the Village, most delightfully opening — It is built upon a direct line[,] the commodious dwellings erected upon the right, and the left, skirting a spacious, and handsome street — Upon a gentle occlivity, in an airy situation towers with modest dignity, the snow white Frame which Edifice, is sacred to the God of Christians — It is finished in a pleasing style and does much honour to the good people of Suffield — May that order, innocence and tranquility of which the hue it has received as an expressive emblem, and which ought to distinguish every Christian Society, at all times encircle its respectable Founders — at Suffield, apparently the abode of health, and happiness, we tarried last night, and this morning passing through Windsor, a cultivated, compact, and pretty Town, we came on to Hartford — Hartford I have heretofore aimed at sketching — Perhaps if Connecticut hath a Metropolis, the annual election, or inauguration of the Governor being declared, and performed in Hartford, entitles it to that distinction. Mr Murray had intended to have passed on to Weathersfield this evening, but being much solicited to officiate here, upon the ensuing sunday, we do not proceed upon our journey until Monday Morning — Doth my Father, and Mother, recollect, that on this same, ensuing Lord's day, their eldest daughter will have completed the thirty ninth year of her age? How apprehensive was the mind of my

dear Mother, upon the afternoon of this day, thirty nine years back —
How agitated was the manly bosom of my Father, but joy came in the
morning — With what rapture did you alternately press the little stranger
to your bosoms — she was your first born, much was her appearance
desired, and she first originated in your minds, the sweet sensations
created by parental love — your regrets, your sorrows, for a little moment
they excited not — Oh! that I still possessed the power to [send] them
far away[,] to extinguish from your revered bosoms, every pain, every of
those evils, with which the present scene abounds — But cheer up —
my honoured Friends — To a night of tears, succeeds the refulgent
morning, and the period is not very distant, when we shall assemble in
the house of our common Father — You will be so obliging as to
remember me to all inquiring friends — especially to my sisters Ellery
and Sargent, Mr Ellery, and Sally, my Anna, and every individual who
make a part of your family — When I meet Philadelphia I shall address
my friends severally — but I cannot write, while upon my journey, with
my accustomed felicity — I trust in the God of all consolation, that I
shall meet you, upon my return, in possession of at least as much health
as when I quitted Gloucester, and I pray that the present mild season,
may conduce to the restoration of my Mother, and consequently to the
pleasures of my Father — Mr Murray will speak for himself — and I am,
with the best affections of my soul, ever yours ———

Letter 744 to Mrs Sargent Hartford May 16— 1790— Sunday Morning

*"Mrs Sargent" is Judith's aunt, Mary Turner Sargent, who was married
to her uncle, Daniel Sargent, and lived in Boston. The two women
were very close friends. In this letter, Judith describes some touching
moments she shared with her husband, and the Murrays' mutual love
of nature. Judith's use of the word "Art" refers to human intervention.
"Turner" and "the Boys" are Mrs. Sargent's sons. "Mrs Powell" is
Catherine Goldthwaite Gardiner Powell, Judith's first cousin. Known
popularly as "Madame Powell," she lived in Boston.*

Just thirty nine years this very day, have I been a daughter of
this scene of Vicissitudes — Fruitful of changes hath it been to me —
yet I have enjoyed much, Friendship zested by sentiment, hath been
mine, and with encreasing confidence I reproof, that I rank among the
first of my acquisitions, the attachment by which you have distinguished
me, and which, with most benign influence, hath warmed your gentle
bosom — Our journey is at length commenced — A sketch of the first
week of our excursion, I have hastily penned for my Father, and Mother.

The Country is at this season particularly charming, The earth is cloathed in most beautiful verdure — the trees are in full foliage, and we add, the pleasures of anticipation to those we already possess — We reached Palmer on thursday — I took up my pen — Mr Murray drew me to the window — see my Love, you are losing a most charming scene — I instantly obeyed the summons — It was all of Nature — Art had not presumed to embelish[,] not a single dwelling was in perspective, but the setting sun, throwing over the Landscape its embelishing and most beautifying radiance, rendered it indeed divine — Mr Murray took my hand and we passed down the activity together — A serpentine River meandered by — its Banks were enchantingly diversified — its surface was brushed by the curling zephyr, and yielded by the parting rays of the setting luminary — The River romantically presenting through a variety of openings, here jutting out and in an ample bend, and there terminating to a point, seemed to lose itself in groves, which apparently intersected its progress, until again gushing out in a number of little rills, it sweetly murmured along the grass grown carpet — In the background a venerable mountain seemed to reach the clouds — and out spread beneath — Thick woods, Vallies, and spacious meadows, were alternately displayed — At a distance a tall tree, single, and independent, seemed stationed the sovereign of the Grove — The tufted Oak, the verdant Pine, the trembling Aspin, and the weeping Willow conspired to variegate, and beautify the scene — The Birds in the branches melodiously chanted their Vespers — the sky was magnificently serene — none but lucid clouds were fliting there — The Mind of Mr Murray is constituted to enjoy, with high wrought satisfaction, the beauties of Nature — Not a songster which spreadeth the party coloured wing, not a flower which blooms but seems capable of inspiring him with an enthusiastic kind of rapture — The surrounding views were well calculated for his meridian, he gathered a bouquet composed of the wild flowers, which adorn the woods, and presented it to me, with a well turned compliment, descriptive of the gladness, and devotion of his soul — he pointed out the names[,] qualities and ability of the objects before me — he expatiated upon the variety and harmony of Nature, and he led my attention from Nature, up to Nature's God — In short the promenade altogether was most delightful — your presence, my friend, would have greatly heightened those pleasures, which we indulged, until the evening shadows warned us to hasten for shelter, to our commodious, and well furnished inn. I flatter myself I shall hear from you either at New York, or Philadelphia — you will please to remember our affectionate regards to my Uncle, and to the young gentlemen — Turner I suppose is returned e'er this [—] We kiss our hands to the dear Boys, breathing for them the salutations of tender love — you will be kind enough to remember me to Mrs Powell — and say to her that if I must with any thing which I can conceive worthy her attention, I will avail myself of her obliging permission to write — till when she will please to accept my acknowledgements, and regards, Mrs— alas! alas! adieu my beloved friend adieu — I am ever yours ———

Letter 745 to my Father & Mother Horseneck May 22d 1790 Saturday Evening

In Horseneck, Connecticut, the Murrays stayed in the home of Mr. Branch, whose business involved supplying the markets in New York with agricultural products. Judith describes the trip along the way, including their stay in Hartford where they met Daniel Webster and where John preached and was urged to remain permanently. Lengthy accounts of Stratford, Fairfield, and Norwalk are given, including observations on the destruction by the British during the "recent conflagration." Here, and in later letters, Judith notices the prevalent "equality" in Connecticut. By that, she means both evenhanded civic and urban development, and a less noticeable class system compared to that of Massachusetts. She observes, with dismay, the disarray of Stamford's burial grounds, makes note of the rough terrain, and reports that they have, for the time being, escaped the "Influenza" whose deadly effects had seized hold of the towns through which they had travelled. Finally, Judith reassures her parents that she is healthy. Having lost a child in childbirth less that a year earlier, and her own health severely threatened as a result, Judith's parents would naturally be concerned for her safety during the rigors of travel. (Note: "Green Farms" is the historic name for Westport.)

One hour before sunset we reached this Place, we are in the hospitable Mansion of a Mr Branch, who is happy in a numerous and amiable family, consisting of his lady, five sons, and six daughters — They seem gratified by our abode with them, and solicitous to prolong our stay [—] We are however soon to depart. We entered the avenue, which leads to this commodious seat, shaded by a row of tall locusts, planted upon a straight line upon the right, and the left, in beautiful Order — The Mansion is erected upon the banks of a river, the oppostite side of which is pleasingly variegated, by thick groves, verdant plains, and fertile fields [—] Convenient quays are built upon this river, which hath its source in the Ocean — and Horseneck supplies, by this passage, the market at New York (from which City, it is distant about 37 miles) with a variety of articles, such as beef, butter, poultry, pork, and a variety of vegetables — The full freighted vessels are wafted a few rods from this door, and the ships of the generous Master of this domain, spread their white sails to enrich him — The River is before him and in the back ground, and upon the right and the left, an extensive, and fertile country is displayed, thus pleasingly uniting the blessings of the earth, and the sea — But I am to take up my account from Hartford — To a large, and attentive audience, Mr Murray, upon the last Lord's day, held forth the words of life. Many friends united to press his immediately fixing among them, and they were very liberal, in their promises of a large, and ample support — We passed some time at Hartford with Mr Webster— Author of the institutes etc etc[,] he hath lately united himself to a Lady of Boston, a pretty agreeable Woman, and, he heath become a regular Citizen In this same Mr Webster I am most pleasantly disappointed, I had figured him a dogmatic, and arrogant Pedant — but in his manners, he is easy, and unassuming, In one word, altogether the Gentleman — Wallingford is twenty eight miles from Hartford, and we came on through Weathersfield, and Worthington[,] pleasant and thriving Villages, early tea time producing us there — Wallingford you already know — Mr Murray, unable to resist the solicitations of his friends, abode in Wallingford one day, meeting his adherents in their place of worship, upon the evening of his arrival, and at four O'clock the ensuing afternoon — Tears, joyful tears were shed upon the occasion — one good old Lady, pressing my hand, congratulated me upon what she termed my happy, happy lot — Wednesday morning we passed on through North, to New Haven, where detained on thursday by the rains, which fell in copious showers — our day was pleasantly appropriated, to our very affectionate friends, Col. and Mrs. Drake — of New Haven — my beloved Parents, will recollect I have already attempted a view — We left it on friday morning, and passing through Milford, a promising little Town, took our way to Stratford ferry — which crossing, we proceeded on through to Stratford Village, neat and well built, most hospitably situated, and surrounded by views truly enchanting — It hath an episcopalian Church, highly elegant, a meeting house in a good taste, and a well finished brick school house — These all situated in the eye almost in a direct line, and produce a very pleasing effect [—] a gentleman in the medical line, with whom Mr Murray was wholly unacquainted, having never stopped in that place, came up to the Carriage, and introducing himself, earnestly entreated him to abide there, at least during a short space [—] he was, he said, authorized to write the supplicating voice of his neighbors, and he would not allow us to proceed, until he had extorted a promise, that he should be gratified on our return — There is it appears to me, a a greater semblance of equality in the state of Connecticut, than in Massachusetts, and if it cannot boast a capital, in a style of such decided superiority, perhaps it displays a greater number of handsome well built towns, which seem amicably to rival each other, the flourishing and thrifty appearance of which add much to the pleasure of the Traveller — Our last night's stage was at Fairfield; Fairfield was once the seat of elegance, and industry, but being wafted by the Ocean, and contiguous to the scene of action, during the late hostilities, its principal dwellings, in the course of the contest, were, by the hand of vindictive power, laid in ashes, and it hath not yet recovered its positive beauty — The burning of Fairfield hath occasioned some beautiful, and affecting stanzas, from the pen of Colonel Humphrys which, with that elegant Writer's other productions, will long claim the admiration of the American Reader [—] Fairfield however, although its disrobed chimneys, still give it an air of melancholy, is in many instances rebuilt — We were accommodated much to our satisfaction, at Penfield's Tavern, a pretty landscape was in view, and a glassy pond before the door, the border of which was ornamented by trees, in full and fragrant blow — beyond is a range of woods, and plains, and upon the right hand, the temple sacred to public worship, with a number of decent dwellings, thrown around it — behind this house a fine garden, well cultivated, and very productive, and the traveller is obligingly furnished with every requisite — as you, my dear Sir, contemplate a tour this way, I am the more solicitous to note these particulars — At sun rise this morning, from Fairfield, [we] came on through Green Farms, Norwalk, and Stamford to this Place — The vestiges of cultivation are every where displayed — Propriety is in many instances visible, and, to the inquiring eye, the buddings of elegance stand confest — The remains of the conflagration lighted up by the British, during the late struggle, are still but too conspicuous in Norwalk — while its pensive state remind the Passenger, of the high price at which we have purchased the pompous title of Sovereign, and Independent States — Yet Norwalk hath its charms, and we were particularly pleased, with a beautiful fall of water — at Stamford we met with an agreeable family by the name of Jervice, which we have engaged to visit on our return — I have made one observation, shocking, I confess to my feelings — However [critical] it may be, I cannot witness without pain, any failures in a proper attention, to the remains of the deceased — The burial grounds are in many places left without the smallest inclosaries, in one instance we saw a number of graves, promiscuously scattered, upon the margin of a salt water Creek, which had run up into the road, which we passed a second time through the midst of them! — The high post road in Stamford is directly through the grave yard — The sepulchral stones rise upon either hand, and not even the slightest railing interposes between them and the Passenger!! The face of the Country over Horseneck is rough, and scarcely passable — Hardly doth a view of the surrounding woods and plains[,] although now in their most gaudy attire[,] recompense the risk which the traveller runs — Yet I think I have passed even worse roads than Horseneck — I could give a list of fatiques[,] of frights and of fears, of hair breadth scapes but I do not wish to keep a calender of grievances — We have met the Influenza wherever we have sojourned — It hath passed through every Town and Village and almost every dwelling and it hath been in many instances fatal — Hitherto we have escaped this contagious and afflicting disorder and we indulge a hope that our continued exercise and change of air will secure us from its attacks — We pray you to remember us to our friends — particularly to Mr & Mrs Ellery[,] Miss S.S. Ellery[,] Mrs Anna Sargent[,] my Anna etc etc

      You command me to transmit to you an exact account of my health and feelings but perhaps the necessity of being circumstantial may be obviated when I assure you as with the strictest truth I can — and I do hereby certify to all whom it may concern that I am actually and bonafide precisely the same both mentally and corporally as when I left Gloucester [—] this authentic fact being established I flatter my self it will be superfluous to add that my heart beats with warm attachment for my friends and that I am with tender affection ever most cordially and dutifully yours

Letter 746 To Mrs Sargent Maroneck May 23d 1790

Written to her aunt, Mary Turner Sargent, from Maroneck, New York (now Mamaroneck), Judith meets a blind girl and reflects on her own good fortune despite her momentary "gloom." She notes with delight the "flowering footsteps" of spring.

She is blind — totally blind — said the good Girl, and she had a tear in her eye as she gave the information — "Lack a day" said the inquirer, ["]what can have produced so great a misfortune?" — We cannot tell, rejoined the tender hearted female — But this very day twelve months, she could see as well as either you, or I — I entered the Tavern in a kind of pensive gloominess — a train of melancholy reflections had enwrapped me — Mr Murray was giving directions respecting his horse, and I had seated myself mournfully by the window, my head bent upon my hand, The parlour door stood open, and from the bar room, the above Confab caught my ear — when starting up I exclaimed — Good God how strong is the principle of ingratitude in this heart of mine — I possess almost all my wishes, and yet, because I cannot in this transient, this fleeting abode, ingraft complete felicity a croud of regrets are collecting, in a thick phalanx they are approaching, and they have already well near routed every better feeling of my soul — suppose, like this poor woman, I had no eyes for the ten thousand beauties which surround me — suppose — but I will suppose no more — I will learn to enjoy with thankfulness the present moment, and to confide in sovereign goodness for futurity — Oh! my beloved friend, if we could more frequently take a view of the suffering sons and daughters of adversity, although the humane heart would deeply feel for the unfortunate, yet, think you, that a kind of tranquility would not result from the comparison, which would at least teach, that species of acquiescence which originates contentment — I take leave to inclose you the progress of our journey — We meet, as we advance, the flowering footsteps of the spring — this fine season is now enwreathed in vernal beauty, and every breathing gale richly perfumed is indeed odiferous — The trees in their variety are now all in full bloom — and, perhaps, the pleasures derived from a view of budding Nature are not surpassed by those which the harvest yields — Upon the birth day of the year, imagination dilates [—] Fancy throws her brightest colours upon perspective scenes — no matter how high the finishing, anticipation will bear her out — How are you my lovely friend — How are your charming children — Forget not, I pray you to transmit us the most speedy information — kiss the sweet Boys for me, and present me suitably to all

NEW YORK: THE SEAT
OF THE AMERICAN GOVERNMENT

Letter 747 To my Father and Mother Brunswick
May 29th 1790 Saturday Evening

Of great historical significance in this letter is Judith's description of New York, showing her keen interest in architecture and engineering and her ability to recount minute detail. In New York, Judith and John sat through a "debate of Congress" — from the upper gallery, where women were admitted. At first, she was overwhelmed by the "august" importance of the occasion, but then disappointed by the seeming disregard with which legislators took their responsibility. She notes that part of the debate involved whether or not the "seat of government" should be moved to Philadelphia — which we know it did, until the capitol city was constructed. Judith observes the "royal" atmosphere present in New York's federal buildings, and explains how President and Mrs. Washington held their "levee days" — the one day a week citizens were presented to the President and his Lady. Judith describes New York's burial customs, which she found unusually elaborate compared to those of Gloucester.

Before reaching New York, Judith and John spent time in
New Rochelle where John had lived years earlier. Their hosts, the
Bartow family, received them in a manner that became typical of later
visits — with joyful affection for their old friend John. Judith describes
at length the Bartow's home and gardens, possessions, and family life.
She notes that the Bartows kept no slaves, but hired both black and
white servants. In 1790, in Philadelphia, the Universalists condemned
the institution of slavery in the defining document they published.

The Traveller shall come — he shall inquire for me — but I
shall not be found — My place shall remain — But I shall be no more,
and only the Gray Stone will rise to my remembrance — It hath been,
from the commencement of this journey, a favourite object with my
husband, to devote this evening, and the ensuing sunday, to an old, and
worthy friend in this City — here he had often sojourned, here he had
found a home, and here, he persuaded himself the hospitable Man —
the Christian waited to receive him — Flushed with the most pleasing
hopes he came on, you know he hath a heart warm and affectionate, as
sincerity, and friendship can render it — But alas! Mr Dunham sleepeth
in the chambers appointed for all living — his earthly tenement, more
properly speaking, is consigned to the narrow house — and five months
since, his enlarged spirit winged its trackless way, whither we are swiftly
hastening — It is true his companion, and his children remain — it is
true they received us with the utmost tenderness, and it is true they are
making every effort to contribute to our happiness — yet, selfish as we
are, the knowledge of this event, hath given to this week a melancholy
close — a train of mournful ideas rush upon my mind — almost a
complete month hath elapsed, since a single sentence from home, hath
reached my ear! and considering the precarious state of changeful time,
what revolutions may not have succeeded! But it is painful to reflect, it
is necessary to my peace to believe that my indulgent Parents, and those
friends who share so largely, in my best affections, still exist — that
they exist upon this globe, and that they exist in tolerable tranquility
— Let me then endeavour to chase corroding apprehension from my
bosom. If my memory be not treacherous I parted with you at Horseneck
— The Country, as I said, was rough, but crossing a Brook, disguised by
the name Biram River, which brook or River, separates the state of
Connecticut from the state of New York, we advanced through Rye,
and Maroneck to New Rochelle — From New Rochelle Mr Murray
expected some happy hours — It was formerly, for a considerable length
of time, the place of his residence, and a Clergyman of the Church of
England, was to be his host — I confess, that from these out lines, I did
not expect much — but my husband was better informed — Mr & Mrs
Bartow were the friends of his youth — he had successfully pleaded to

the paternal ear, the cause of their early loves, and he had been the prime instrument of uniting them, or of obtaining the parental sanction to their union — We arrived at the seat of Mr Bartow, just as the shades of evening began to prevail — Mr Murray had not visited these friends for many years — and he remembered the instability of Man. We had came forward over a frightful road, and we were much fatigued — We entered a spacious inclosure, which seemed to wear the appearance of a court yard; the home was plain, and neat, and it had received my favourite hue — a covered Piazza furnished with seats, gave a most commodious appearance to the front and it was filled with smiling boys — we stopped, "Is Mr Bartow at home["] — No Sir — "Is Mrs Bartow within?" No Sir, they are both gone to visit a sick person, but we expect them momently — Some of the children, when Mr Murray was last here, had not received a being, and the rest were infants [—] the servants were entirely changed, and of course we were wholly unknown but observe a proof of the general hospitality to which this family was accustomed — a black Man — not a slave — Mr Bartow keeps no slaves — approached. "Shall I put up your horse Sir?" — yes, replied my husband, and immediately leaped from the Carriage — Come, my dear, step in — With my eyes I remonstrated — but the dear Man is sometimes absolute, and our baggage was expeditiously placed in the Hall — As I entered the parlour, every thing struck me with surprise — China jars, urns, and Vases of the richest texture, and filled with natural flowers, adorned the Chimney — The floor was elegantly carpeted, superb silver candlesticks, with tall wax tapers and every piece of furniture, in a style of corresponding elegance — For a family in such taste, I was not prepared — I seated myself, however, in the window — A young Lady held in her arms a beautiful baby, apparently about three months old, he was habited in white muslin, and he startingly accepted my salutations — Sweet innocent, thought I — not yet initiated with the previous forms, deemed requisite to a social intercourse, your smiles are those of Nature, and they are pleasingly, and unartificially bestowed — Mr Murray addressed the children (who had now, with looks of decent inquiry, took their seats around the spacious parlour) with great affection, assuring them he should have recognized them, wherever he had met them from the strong resemblance they bore to their parents — at length, with much hesitation, originating in his apprehension for the reply, my husband requested some account of an ancient Lady [—] she is living — she resides entirely with Mr Bartow, and is now in her chamber — I will call her if you please — she arose instantly, and the alacrity of her movements, evinced her wishes for the Ecclairusement, which she calculated must now take place — The remarkable Matron descended — the dignity of age was hers — and presenting her hand, she said I should know you, sir — but my sight is dim, and all my faculties are decaying "Have you thus forgotten your friend Murray?" — Murray, she repeated — Heaven forbid — O welcome — most welcome — a soft and unequivocal expression of satisfaction now whispered through the little assembly — it was a name familiar to their ears, often had they heard it repeated, and never unaccompanied by expressions of virtue — Curiosity now gave place to a solicitude to please, and the boys acquitted themselves in a manner which evinced their naturally obliging dispositions, improved both by example, and ...My feelings were in a measure relieved, but when I reflected how nearly youth, and extreme age, approximated to the endearing kindness of unadulurated Nature, I was not entirely at ease — Mr Bartow's carriage however now entered the court yard, and they were immediately in the Hall [—] Mr Murray advanced, his Constantia in his hand — "Is it possible — exclaimed Mrs Bartow — is it can it be possible, and she stretched out her arms to embrace him, and folding me also, to her bosom she kissed my cheek, with all the fervour of a sister — Mr Bartow's manifestations were less impassioned, but they were equally unequivocal — he also extended a hand to my husband, and imprinted upon my cheek a fraternal kiss — Mr Bartow is a genteel, elegant figure, and there is benignity in his aspect, which cannot fail of being, to the physiognomist, a letter of recommendation — He is, as I said an Episcopalian Clergyman, and he inherits from his Lady, a competency, which hath put him in possession of a degree of independence — His fine, extensive, and flourishing fields furnish him every year, with a super abundance of grain, in all its varieties — his gardens prepare for him a large supply of every vegetable, the sheep of his own pastures yield cloathing, and much milk, butter, and cheese, a large number of these plentifully accommodate him — Bacon, and pork, Poultry etc etc these are all of course, and neither he nor his, can know a want to which he hath not the means of administering — Mrs Bartow is a native of New York, of dutch extract, a good family, and as you have seen, of considerable property — her manners are prepossessing, and she often reminds me of my amiable friend the Lady of Doctor Plummer — They have seven sons, but no daughter [—] they have buried two promising females, and one male infant, and they have the care of an orphan Niece, the young Lady we saw at our entrance, who is no doubt happy in their protection — They retain in their family as Preceptor to their children, a young gentleman whose easy and engaging deportment, is in no sort descriptive of the pedagogue — They have two white maid servants — One white Man, who with a black Man and Woman, constitute the whole of their household, and of the veneration of every individual Mrs Abrams is in full possession — While in one grateful Circle the rising sun, and the condescending evening, collects this happy family — They untie in harmony the praises of a preserving God, and after attending a portion from the sacred Oracles of truth, they prostrate themselves in adoration to the Creator of the Universe — I am free to own I consider the custom of kneeling, when addressing the Deity, but decent, and becoming and I would gladly see it adopted by that sect, whose opinions it is my consolation that I have embraced — The morning succeeding our arrival, displayed to our view a truly enchanting scene — The house, as I said, is neat, and the sun, that universal beautifier[,] rose majestically over the surrounding views — a clean gravel walk borders the Piazza adjoining to which appears upon a well shorn grass flat, a variety of fruit trees, yielding, at this time, all the pleasures of anticipation — the fine flower garden is elegantly enclosed and at this season, the snowdrop, and the lilack form a most pleasing combination — Every blow which enriches the month of May, composes in this garden of Mr Bartow, to gratify the eye while the lily of the valley, than which perhaps there is not a more delicate, or sweet scented flower, as if not satisfied with decorating the parlour, borne from its modest bed, diffused from the surrounding vases its rich embosomed sweets — Beyond the flower garden, is an ample level tract which nature hath handsomely disposed [—] it is ornamented with a variety of beautiful trees, and further on, the land and water, romantically intersect each other — High grounds bound the prospect upon the left, which grounds are crowned by thick groves, of umbrageous shade and diversified hue, and upon the right, rolls the sound, over which full in view, vessels are constantly passing, and repassing too and from New York —

The stranger, riding post through new Rochelle, will remain unconscious of the beauty of the environs, but the seat of Mr Bartow, is not the only little Eden, which it hath to boast — The french were its first European Settlers [—] they fled from a religious persecution at Rochelle, hence the name of the Village New Rochelle — But very few of the descendants of those Religious remain — New Rochelle hath a small stone Church, the members of which are Episcopalians to whom Mr Bartow officiates — New Rochelle suffered greatly in the course of the late troubles — It was alternately possessed by the Britons and Americans — Our old Lady, whose veracity is not to be questioned, related to me a tale of horror — her children, in conformity to the entreaties, and commands of their parents, had fled the place — her husband was in the agonies of death, and she herself bowed down by years, and misfortunes — Thus was she circumstanced when a Banditt — authorized by no party, under the banner of the most savage rapine, entered her house, and stripped her of every thing valuable which she possessed!! — Nor was this enough, they audaciously demanded her money — With more fortitude than commonly fall to the share of humanity, she refused to consent to total ruin, when they proceeded to threats of a very serious nature — but observing that she preserved her firmness, they outrageously seized, and dragged her to a tree, and proceeded to fit a thong to her neck, with which they prepared to suspend her in the air — Once more however, they thought proper to question her, when to the following effect she most heroically replied — My husband is even now in the arms of death, and for the remnant of life, which might remain for me, it is of little consequence — My children, I bless God are removed from your power, neither they, nor I, have given the smallest cause of offence — We have never taken an active part in the present contest — we have wished for peace — you have robbed us of every thing within your grasp — My children will want what I have, with their knowledge, concealed [—] I will not, for the sake of a momentary existence consign them to poverty — you may take my life — I am not afraid to enter into the presence of my Maker — I know you not — but to God you stand confessed — His all seeing eye is upon you and depend upon this fact — the Almighty will assuredly make requisition for innocent blood — The Savages trembled, as she spoke, the thing fell from the enervated hand of the murderers, and, as if enraged to be thus under the influence of any feelings proper to humanity they violently thrust her from them — It was in the depth of winter, and slipping upon the Ice, she received a contusion upon her shoulder, which confined her during many weeks, and upon the evening of this memorable, and eventful day, the father of her children, and the loved Companion of a length of years breathed his last!! This Lady had been educated in the lap of tenderness, affluence, and ease — she was born, and has lived during the prime of her life, in the City of New York — But some time, previous to the commencement of the late struggle, she accompanied her family to New Rochelle, expecting to close the scene in a peaceful, and elegant retirement, which had been prepared for them — On Tuesday morning we quitted New Rochelle, coming on through East Chester, crossing Knight Bridge, and passing over Harlem Plains, to New York — The country round New York is mountainous, and the traveller is amused with all the charms of variety [—] a few elegant seats are scattered near the City, and we entered through a fine airy space, known by the name of the Bowery, and bordered by neatly finished, and convenient dwellings — The ground upon which New York is built, was originally very unequal, but, with incesant labour, and industry, the hills have been thrown in to the Vallies, and it is now a fine extensive tract, nearly level — Everything in the City of New York, seems upon a larger scale, than in the Town of Boston — and I am told it covers a full third more ground — The streets are longer and more capacious, and [there] is an air of thriftyness, as well as elegance about the buildings far surpassing any thing I have ever yet seen — The streets of New York are paved with more exactness than those of Boston, many of them are arched and to obviate the inconvenience of pavements, to

*"...in the presence of Almighty God, and in view of
a numerous Concourse of people, the illustrious,
and immortal Washington, took his oath of office...."*
(from Letter 747)

President George Washington's inauguration.
Federal Hall, the Seat of Congress, New York, April 30, 1789,
Amos Doolittle engraving, 1790. Print collection of the
Miriam and Ira D. Wallach Division of Art, Prints and Photographs.
Courtesy of The New York Public Library.

the stranger, they are generally raised on each side, several inches above the surface, and smoothly laid with brick over which you may pursue your way, with much ease — The houses are principally of Brick and Broadway presents a pile of buildings, in the centre of which, the President resides, which are in deed truly magnificent — The Citizens of New York have erected many public buildings, no less than twenty Churches, among which are Episcopalians, presbyterians, Quakers, dutch institutions, Roman Catholics, and Jews [—] The Columbian University is a spacious structure, presenting in Front no less than sixty windows — The Hospital, Bridewell and Work house, figure respectably, and I am told are under excellent regulations — St Paul's Church towers with mingling elegance, and grandeur, and is fronted by a Monument, sacred to the memory of General Montgomery, adorned with military insignia etc etc — But my attention was principally attracted by the federal edifice — Its very air majestically descriptive, seems to designate it consecrated to National purposes, and it is of course interesting to every genuine American — Almost entirely unacquainted with the terms of Art, the attempt to delineate, may draw upon me an accusation of arrogance yet I will nevertheless hazard a slight sketch [—] Its situation is pronounced ill judged — It is however erected at the head of broad street, of which it commands a complete view — an elegant church is nearby finished upon its right, and upon its left, a good street of a thrifty appearance winds its way — The Federal structure is magnificently pleasing and sufficiently spacious — Four large pillars in front, support an equal number of columns, with their pediment — A large gallery also, presents, in which in the presence of Almighty God, and in view of a numerous Concourse of people, the illustrious, and immortal Washington, took his oath of office, being thus solemnly inaugurated, and cloathed with powers, which we doubt not he will continue to exercise, with augmenting celebrity to himself, as well as for the public weal — Thirteen Stars, the American Arms, crested with the spread eagle, with other insignia in the pediment, tablets over each window, which tablits are filled with the thirteen arrows, surrounded with an olive branch, are among the principal ornaments which emblematically adorn, and beautify the front of the Federal Edifice — The entrance introduces into a square room, which is paved with stone, from which we pass on to the Vestibule in the centre of the pile — This Vestibule is lofty, it is floored with marble, and highly finished, with a handsome iron Gallery, and a sky light richly adorned — From this Vestibule we proceed to the floor of the Representatives' Room, and through arches on either side, by a public staircase on the left, and a private one on the right, to the senate Chamber, and other apartments — The room appropriated to the Representatives is spacious, and elegant — It is worthy the respectable assembly now convened there — It is sixty one feet deep — fifty eight feet wide, and thirty six feet high [—] its ceiling is arched and I should have called its form Oval, but I believe the technical term is octangular — four of its sides are rounded in the manner of arches which adds much to its beauty, and gracefulness — the windows are large, and wainscoted below, interrupted only by stoves, which I think are four in number — above are columns, and pilasters, with entablatures variously disposed, and in the pannels between the windows, trophies are carved, and the letters U.S. surrounded with laurel — The Chair of the Speaker is opposite the principal door — and it is elevated three steps, the chairs of the members form around it a semicircle — a writing stand properly furnished, is placed before every chair. In one piece a number of these stands are connected, which piece forms a segment of a circle — upon the right and left of the speaker, are semicircular compartments, in which are tables for the accommodation of the Clerks — Over the great door, and fronting the Speaker two Galleries are erected — The lower Gallery projects considerably — This is commonly, during the Sessions of the Assembly, filled by gentlemen, and the upper Gallery is appropriated to Ladies — Besides these galleries, a space upon the floor, separated by a bar, may be occasionally occupied by visiting individuals — This apartment is furnished with three doors, exclusive of the principal entrance, all of which are conveniently disposed — The chairs, curtains, and hangings in this room, are of light blue harateen, fringed and tasselled, and the floor is elegantly carpeted — We have received many civilities from Mr Goodhue, who introduced us into the upper Gallery, where we attended the debates of Congress, for near four hours — the scene was truly august, and as I threw my eyes around, taking a view of the delegates of America thus convened, a solemn air pervaded my bosom — a new, and undefinable sensation originated a hand of enraptured veneration, and I prepared to listen with most profound attention — But I shall own a truth — Let it be better said in a whisper — my reverential feelings considerably abated, as I observed the apparent negligence, of many of the members — a question of much importance was agitated, and investigated by several speakers — and that with a warmth, and energy, which would have done honour to a Demasthenes, or a Cicero, while, with all imaginable sang froid, gentlemen were walking to, and fro — their hats occasionally on, or off — Reading the News papers — lolling upon their writing stands — picking their nails, biting the heads of their canes, examining the beauty of their shoe Buckles, ogling the Gallery etc etc [—] yet we were fortunate enough to hear some of the best Speakers, among them Mr Maddison, Mr Ames, Mr Sedgwick, Mr Jackson, and Mr Vinning — From the stairs upon the left hand of the Vestibule, we reach a Lobby that communicates with the Iron Gallery, which leads on one hand to the door of the representatives Room, and on the other to the senate

Chamber — The senate Chambers is pleasingly decorated — the pilasters etc are highly ornamented, and amid the foliage of the Capitals, a splendid star makes its appearance, surrounded with rays, while a small medallion is suspended by a piece of drapery, with the interesting letters U.S. in a cypher — The ceiling presents a sun, and thirteen Stars, which appear in its centre — The Chimnies are finished with American Marble, said to be equal for the beauty of its shades, and high polish, to any found in Europe — The Presidential chair is, of course, stationary in the upper end of the senate chamber — It is elevated several steps from the floor, and placed under a superb canopy of crimson damask — The chairs arranged semicircularly, as in the room of the Representatives, with the window curtains, and hangings are also of crimson damask, and the floor is richly carpeted — From the throne, or chair of state, his highness, the Protector of the Union, delivers a speech at the opening, and close of a Session which doth not much vary either in form, or manner, from those delivered by a british Sovereign, we differ essentially in nothing, but in name, and it is possible the time is not far distant which may invest us with royal dignities — There are in the Federal edifice, many other apartments, besides those of which I have attempted a sketch, guard rooms, Committee Rooms, and a handsome library — In the room of audience, we were shown portraits of the reigning King, and Queen of France, which are very fine Paintings — One side of the Federal edifice is furnished with a Platform railed in with iron, which affords an agreeable Walk, and the cupola is in good taste, highly ornamental, producing a very pleasing effect, and summing to give a finishing to the whole — An elegant statue of Lord Chatham once distinguished a principal street in New York, and in a spacious square, majestically towered an equestrian figure of George the third King of Great Britain — But alas! such hath been the ascendancy, shall I say of Gothic animocity, as to procure their destruction – New York exhibits no promenade, equal to the mall in Boston — But we intend visiting the orangery, and the seats on the north river, on our way home, and we already know this River abounds with beautiful imagery [—] The North or Hudson's River, rolls its waters along its Banks — the sound divides it from Long Island — Straton Island is in view with many other less considerable Islands — Thus variously are the Land, and water prospects displayed — New York, however suffers in the lack of good water — Every family not residing in the Bowery, being obliged to purchase tea water etc etc [—] New York is undoubtedly a populace, and opulent City; many of the streets remind me of the picturesque views, which we have so often admired upon paper, at present the seat of Government, it may be considered as the Metropolis of America, but it is probable it will not retain this distinction — During our attendance in the federal Edifice, a removal was proposed, seconded, and laid upon the table

[—] Philadelphia, and New York are rival Cities — the Southern chambers are for convening in Philadelphia, the question hath been frequently agitated, until it has become annexed to the most important National concerns — I am told there is an agreement between the Southern, and Eastern Members — If the Eastern delegates give their voices in favour of one question, the Southern Gentlemen, will aid them in another! If this information be correct, will not that august Body depart (while engaged in this kind of dangerous, and unbecoming traffic, much from their dignity? [)] Is it not bartering for public weal? — Yet Members of Congress are but Men — General Washington hath consecrated one day in the week his levee day upon which gentlemen visit him without ceremony, passing in and out at pleasure — Mrs Washington's Levee is upon friday — the General is always present — Ladies then pay their Compliments, and strangers, having an acquaintance with any of Mrs Washington's familiar friends, are properly introduced — Had we tarried long enough in New York, we should have been presented — We have that honour in prospect, upon our return — Lady Temple hath also her Levee days — The whispers of malevolence and ingratitude against our illustrious Chief, are already afloat! He is accused of favouritism if I may so express myself, and the name of Colonel Humphrys is repeated, with a jealous kind of Acrimony — But enough of dignities — Massachusetts may almost be said to be in the neighborhood of New York — yet, strange to tell, there is very little similarity in their customs — for example — the habiting [of] a dead body, and the ceremonies attending an interment — To a shroud made in New York, the Gloucesterians would be at a loss for a name — An elegant Sachenet Muslin is chosen, the purchase of this muslin doth not always consult [an] income [—] three yards is not more than sufficient — It is laid in double folds, and fitted to the waist — the sleeves are separate, and the shroud is cut around to the bosom, in which fashionable Tucks is plaited — A broad sash confines the folds round the waist — The head is elegantly draped, and white silk gloves, and hose, are drawn on [—] When the Corse, thus arrayed, is laid in a mahogany coffin[,] is richly ornamented and lined with muslin, and a flounce of the same, of the depth of the Coffin, is folded thick, and fastened upon the upper edge of this last receptacle — the bottom of which flounce, being out spread, forms a covering for the body — The Corse is placed in the great hall, or entry, and every passenger is at liberty to view it. Eight Pall Holders are selected, all of whom, together with the officiating Physician, and Minister, are not only presented with gloves, but with fine holland scarfs, one of these scarfs will take three yards and three quarters of linen, and it is folded and tied upon the shoulder, and at the side, with six yards of broad black ribbon, much in the manner, in which our little Masters have been accustomed to wear their sashes.

The good Woman who ties the scarfs, and she who dresses the Body, receives also of the same white lining, the full length of a scarf, together with gloves — These scarfs are worn at the funeral, and upon the sabbath next ensuing — the Pall holders and Physician, attending at the church, in which the deceased had been accustomed to worship — No Female, not even the nearest relation, who forms the smallest pretensions to fashion, ever attends a funeral, except, upon the demise of a young Lady — When the Pall is borne by eight maidens, dressed in snowy white garments and wearing white plain lawn hoods, and scarfs, made in the manner of the black hoods, and scarfs, worn some years since [—] These hood and scarfs, with ribbons, gloves and fans, are given by the relatives, and the females make their appearance upon the Lord's day next succeeding, at the house in which their lost companion, was wont to worship — Every person who attends a funeral, both within, and with out doors, is previous to the interment plentifully served with wine of the finest quality, a waiter is appointed to every apartment, who is very attentive [—] Large quantities of liquor is often swallowed — ten gallons of prime Maderia, has been recently expended for a single funeral — You will forgive me, my dear, and honoured Parents, for being thus circumstantial — Keeping no other journal, and taking no copies of my letters, these papers must be considered as my memoras Lumis —

On the morning of this day, the sun rose majestically, when passing the Ponless hook, Hackinsack, and second River, we reached the Jersey Shore, and came on to Newark — Newark is a pleasant Village, where we passed an hour most agreeably with Mr and Mrs Smith, Parents of the Gentleman, whose letters upon Universalism you have read — They are situated in a romantick little retirement, and the serenity of years is in their possession — Our road this day, has been for the most part charming, it seemed a level path, and through gardened lawns, and umbrageous Groves, but to describe the variety of prospects land, and water, enchantingly diversified — hills, and Vallies, woods, and plains — ploughed Land, and interjacent meadows — To give I say a picture of the ten thousand rural, and pleasing views with which the Jersies abound, would fill a Volume, and having already so unreasonably swelled my letter I shall only say, that we took in at our eyes large draughts of pleasure [—] Elizabeth Town through which our road lay, is a pretty compact spot — Rahway and Woodbridge, are more scattered, and crossing the Rariton we arrived, as I said, at this place — Brunswick — These accounts may possibly amuse my tenderly anxious parents, and, I repeat, I may one day be fond of retracing, by the aid of these items scenes which I have so highly enjoyed — We have reason to be very grateful for a state of health, not materially interrupted — in the midst too of great mortality [—] During our abode in New York, not less than five persons were, in the course of a single evening, interd in one Vault

"Philadelphia is indeed the Metropolis of the American World and, it is advancing forward to a state of high perfection...." (from Letter 765)

Arch Street, with the Second Presbyterian Church, Philadelphia, ca. 1799, by Thomas Birch. Courtesy of Independence National Historical Park, Philadelphia.

[—] Yet we continue to the full as well as usual — May the angel of health watch over those we love, and protect them from every evil — I do not now write particularly to my Friends — You will please to assure them of my hearts affection — If they take a sufficient interest in our movements, to wish a regular detail you are authorized to show them my letters — and when they consider the circumstances and fatigues under which they are throw[n] together, their attachment to the Writer, may induce them to read with a degree of pleasure — This is my fourth letter since I left home, I breathe a fervent wish that they may reach your hands — Mr Murray alway[s] unites with me in expressions of the tenderest and most grateful remembrance — May the peace of Heaven be with you all —— We are ever yours ——

PHILADELPHIA AND ITS "CURIOSITIES"

Letter 748 To the Same Philadelphia Arch Street
June 5 1790 — Saturday evening

This letter gives a vivid sense of the hazards of 18th-century travel by stage and by private coach. On their way to Philadelphia, Judith and John decided to make a side trip to Bethlehem, Pennsylvania to visit the famed Bethlehem Academy. But off the post road, travel was rough and isolated. They did not see another person for many miles. The first tavern they reached, late at night, had no food or beds they could use. The second lodging they approached, the following afternoon, seemed equally dismal but turned out to be more than suitable. Here, they feasted on a wonderful meal and met other travellers who were also on their way to Bethlehem. Another obstacle to travel in this area, for the Murrays, was language. Dutch, or Germanic languages, were more prevalent here than English.

Earlier, on their arrival in Philadelphia, Judith again notes John's enormous popularity and how strongly he was urged to make Philadelphia his home. He was offered a free residence and a considerable sum of money. Judith tells us that had her family not lived so far away, she would have agreed to stay. They "lodged" with Captain Duncan, whose wife had recently died in childbirth — something with which Judith was all too familiar. In Philadelphia, she met the "son of Dr. Franklin." The renowned Benjamin Franklin had only recently passed away, and Judith and John witnessed the outpouring of sentiment for him. They became friends with Franklin's son and with his daughter, Sarah Bache.

In this letter, as in so many others, Judith reminds us how long it took for letters to be delivered. They had now been travelling for a full month, with no word from home.

At length your Travellers are set down in Philadelphia and to remove the anxious inquietude of the tenderest of Parents they gratefully say they have enjoyed much, are in possession of continued health, and that their progress hath not been impeded by any uncommon event — We are at present lodged in the house of Captain Duncan, the widowed husband of the lady, whom you know by the name of Lear — The beauteous female, who would have received us with open arms hath joined her sister angels — Captain Duncan is a sincere Mourner — Her departure out of time took place last August, and his eye is yet humid for her loss — His garb is the livery of sadness and the cypress weed still betokens his undiminished sorrow [—] His infant daughter, whom to usher into being, his fair Companion yielded up her own life — is his only consolation — she is indeed a lovely Babe. The Mother of Mrs Duncan resides in the family, of which she hath the care — She was one of Mr Murray's first friends in this City and she received, and embraced us as a daughter — Indeed I am already the sister, and the daughter, of a hundred worthy hearts — Mr Murray's connexions croud around me — nothing can exceed their congratulations, and their manifestations of pleasure, at his presence — One of the principal characters in this City, hath offered him a genteel house, for a residence rent free during life, if he will continue here, Previous to his arrival, his friends entered into an agreement to guarantee unto him, two hundred pounds per annum, besides a number of prerequisites, which they assure him a number of prerequisites will be never failing appendages — Many respectable characters are in the list of my husband's favourers, among whom, the son of Doctor Franklin is the foremost — Could I remove those I so entirely love I could very cheerfully bid adieu to the State of Massachusetts, but strong are the bands which bind my soul, they are indeed interwoven with my existence

On Monday morning last, we departed from Brunswick — It is a small City but one of the most ancient in America — It hath three religious societies, and a Seminary, which takes the name of Queen's College — We passed the Sunday agreeably in the family of Mrs Dunham, her children are some of them advantageously established, and she indulges for the rest, the most rational, and pleasing expectations — She parted with one daughter, whose residence is twenty eight miles from Brunswick, while we continued under her roof — She parted with her with many tears, but she resigned her to a worthy, tender, and manly Protector — Another daughter is destined to New York for her education, her eldest son is the principal Physician in Brunswick, and she hath another son, a student in Queen's College — Her family is numerous, consisting of five sons, and three daughters, I admire them all, they are a family of love, sensible, polite, and benevolent, they will always hover round my most pleasing recollections — But it is the Wife of her Son, the Lady of Doctor Dunham, whom, as I believe, this without much hazard, although upon so short and limited a knowledge, ranks among the most amiable of Women — Lovely, gentle, tender, and sympathizing, Female may peace surround thy dwelling, and may thy little family, which with such judicious care thou art leading to the practice of every Virtue, render into thy maternal bosom, a full harvest of enjoyment — thus crowning with glad fruition thy setting life — Forgive, my beloved friends, forgive I entreat you, this apostrophe — It is designed as a means unto my own soul, for deep upon the tablets of my heart is inscribed the name of this charming Woman. Hither to we had pursued the great post road — but, urged by curiosity — and in pursuit of information, we now set our faces toward Bethlehem — This was quite an eccentric movement, it was many miles out of our way and we came over much rough road, yet we were obliged to confess ourselves amply compensated, for every fatigue — we recrossed the Rariton, pursuing our route along its Banks the margin of which was adorned by the most luxuriant foliage, and taking our way through woods of an amazing content, and beautiful growth — Tall oaks, chestnuts, and cedars, lifting their heads, between the exactly proportioned branches of which, the beautiful azure, of a serene sky, enchantingly presented — Interjacent plains, diversified by water pieces, given us by the pencil of Nature — elegant scenes, which Mr Murray declared wanted only to be stocked with deer, to exhibit an exact picture, of the Park of an english gentleman — such were the views which for a time arrested our delighted attention — But our difficulties soon commenced — Passing Somerset Court house the situation of which is lofty and commanding, and which once served as an encampment for General Green, a dreary road opened before us, it was solitary, and frightfully rough it was a way we had never travelled, and but for the small log houses in a ruinous situation, which were scattered at the distance of many miles, not a vestige of the human footstep could have been traced — We sat in momently fear of the destruction of the vehicle in which we travelled, and uncertain of our way, our minds were constantly, and fatiguingly engaged — it was a wearisome day, when worn by toil, we hoped we should be indulged with a decent resting place, at night — at length the shades of evening gathering round, the expected Tavern appeared — but alas! it could furnish us no refreshment [—] a small inconvenient room, which opened into the high road, served us as a bed chamber, and to have made an impression upon the bed was impossible — At early dawn on tuesday morning we departed, hoping to be better accommodated as we proceeded, and after advancing ten miles onward, over rocks, hills, sands, and wet clay, We arrived at another log house, [hardly] a tavern — its appearance was dismal and my heart sickened as we approached — Yet, fainting for lack of sustenance, and worn by fatigue, we were necessitated to alight — we entered the house, when to our great surprise, the doors of the several apartments being flung open, four little neat rooms were displayed, the plump, and well made beds, with snow white sheets, and pillow cases, bearing testimony to the good housekeeping of the Land Lady, and what was better still, our then situation considered, a large breakfast table, surrounded by Ladies, displayed tea, Coffee, toast, bread, and butter, radishes, and thinly sliced beef — The Ladies were strangers to me — I saw they were travellers, and decency directed my steps to a vacant apartment — But a female voice in obliging accents, vibrated most delightfully upon my ear "Will it be agreeable to you Ma'am to breakfast with us?" To judge in what manner I was affected by their civility, you must have been exactly situated as I was, Mr Murray approached, and I need not say the invitation was accepted, with many acknowledgements — but I add, we breakfasted most deliciously — During the repast, I chanced to address my husband by his name — "Bless me," said the female who had in the first instance so politely accosted me — "Can this be Mr and Mrs Murray?" We bowed ascentingly — "Why Madam I have a letter for you, but I calculated upon meeting you in Bethlehem, ["] —

The daughters of the Ladies with whom we so fortunately breakfasted, had been sent to Bethlehem for their education, which, being completed, they were proceeding to the stage to take them from thence, and the letter which she mentioned, was addressed to me, by a gentleman with whom I had formed an acquaintance in New York, and whose daughter was also at Bethlehem — It was indeed to introduce the amiable bearer, and to assure me she had it in her power, to be very advantageous to me at that place — Thus relieved from our anxieties respecting the Road, and many other disagreeable suggestions, we set forward with the stage being able to accompany it quite to Bethlehem — For a great length of way, we gained a gradual ascent, when passing rapidly down, an amazing steep mountain, some pleasing views, and a few dwellings were thusly scattered, until reaching the Banks of the Delaware, we crossed the river, and first set our feet upon Pennsylvania ground and passing on to Easttown, which is a pretty little Village, built principally of stone, and inhabited almost entirely by the Dutch, We reached Bethlehem on Tuesday evening — But as this same Bethlehem, is properly an Episode in our journey, I shall give it a place in some future letter — On Thursday Morning, crossing the Lehigh, we pursued a road extremely solitary, and very rough — Few dwellings except the houses of entertainment met the eye, and you may travel an extent of seventy miles in this part of our Country, and not meet a single person unless a traveller should cross your path — whose language you can understand — The people generally conversing in Dutch, or in an unintelligible land of jargon — At the public houses, which are tolerable, we some times found it difficult to make the Inn Keeper, comprehend as much English, as was necessary to his administering to our necessities — but on thursday night a family in a more informed style, were our hosts, and commencing out Friday's route, we were most agreeably affected, to find ourselves once more in the great road [—]While the milk white stone, opportunity lifting its head, informed us it was just thirty miles to Philadelphia — The Country now exhibited a very high state of cultivation — Our way was plain before us, and we came on to German town felicitating ourselves upon the fast approaching period of our journey — German Town is large, handsome, and well built — It is said to be one of the oldest Towns in Pennsylvania — the major part of the dwellings are of stone — you will recollect German town, was the scene of that fatal morning, upon which the Americans, mistaking each other for Britons, made such dreadful havoc among their brethren! We reached this City about four O clock yesterday afternoon, and this day we have appropriated to rest.

My next letter shall be in continuation — I confess I am much surprised at obtaining no letters from my friends, I trust your communications are delayed by accident, and not by misfortune — You will please to accept our hearts respectful love and tender Duty —

Letter 749 To Mrs Sargent Philadelphia Arch Street June 6 1790

Here, Judith expresses her anguish over the lack of communication from home. She urges her aunt to write. The two boys mentioned are Mary Turner Sargent's sons.

In closing my journal for your perusal it may seem strange — I do not see that additions are superfluous, yet fond of every opportunity, which can furnish a pretense for reiterating expressions of regard to my amiable friend, I seize with avidity the pen — hazarding the danger of tautology, of fatiguing you, and a thousand other disagreeables [—] I confess I am rather hurt by not meeting you upon paper, in this City — Trembling for my interest in the hearts of one I so truly love, the suggestions of jealousy officiously obtrude — But a confidence in your attachment, asserts its unyielding powers, and sweet expectation is reinstated in my bosom — Perhaps the post of this day, may confirm my hopes, banishing every idea derogatory to that undying amity, which we have vowed — God grant you may not be prevented from writing by illness — May health, and tranquility shed over the coming days, their balmy influence — If you have not already written, I beseech you in the name of all that is tender, do not delay a single moment, after the receipt of this letter — I will be grateful for a single line, and if it assures me of your welfare, and that of your children, I will rejoice — This is the third packet I have forwarded to you, please to let me know if you have received them in their Order, Apologies would be unworthy of our mutual friendship, your tenderness for me will, I repeat, give you an interest in my movements — Adieu — Remember me to those whom you believe wish a place in my heart — Fitz Winthrop, and Lucius Manlius, will always take the lead — I am, you know I am, devoted to yours —

Letter 750 To my Father & Mother Philadelphia Arch street June 12— 1790 Saturday

Philadelphia astounded Judith. It "far exceeded what [her] imagination had ever figured" and she believed Philadelphia, not New York, should serve as the American capitol city. In this letter, she gives a wonderfully rich account of Philadelphia's architecture and design, its "order" (which she loved), its public buildings, city streets, watchmen and chiming bells. She discusses the prevalence of Quakers, and their influence on making Philadelphia tastes plain and modest. She enumerates the many contents of Philadelphia's enormous market, marveling at the variety and quality. Finally, she expresses concern for her sister-in-law's approaching "hour of danger" — meaning, that Anna was due to give birth.

We have been in this City nine days — We were a full month upon our journey, and not a single line have we yet received from any of our friends — How, my beloved parents, can we account for this — Inattention from those we greatly love, cannot fail to wound — yet I had rather desire your silence from this source, than from a still more afflicting cause [—] It is indeed very strange — but I forbear to reflect

You will expect from me some account of this great City — but depressed by disappointment, and apprehension, can it be imagined I should proceed with my accustomed spirit? — Boston, New York, and Philadelphia, may be considered as a Climax, of which Philadelphia is the ascendant — It is a large, populace, opulent, and beautiful city, and ought undoubtedly to be considered as the Metropolis of America — It extends between the River Delaware and the Schuylkill — The Delaware washes its eastern Borders, and the Schuylkill its Western — The City rises in a gradual ascent from these rivers, to the centre — it abounds with springs, and although an island City, it is commodiously situated for navigation — The streets run parallel with the rivers, and they are croped at right angles — Many object to Philadelphia, on account of its uniformity, but I confess my self so great a Lover of order, as to be enamoured of its beauties in whatever shape they may strike my admiring gaze — yes, to the charms of regularity, every faculty of my soul delights to do homage — I would trace her in every walk, she should lead my steps, adorn my bosom, and grace my life — nor do I believe regularity exceeds variety — for surely order may shape, and discipline the numerous train of Versatility — Philadelphia contains a number of magnificently spacious streets — they are flagged with brick, on either side, in the manner of the most capital streets in New York —

The scavenger is daily employed, the utmost care being taken to keep the streets clean — The City is handsome, built with brick, and much fancy, with an eye however to uniformity, is displayed — Many of the houses are uncommonly lofty — The eye is pained in measuring their summit, and they far exceed what my imagination had ever figured — Streets of three miles long are compactly built — Elevated, and elegant structures rise upon either hand, and as the dwellings are all exactly upon a line, the prospect is beautifully extensive — The State House, the Court House, the Academy, the Philosophical academy, and the Library, form, in one range a stately group — The State House is augustly magnificent — The front of the library presents a Niche, which is to be distinguished by a statue of the venerable and illustrious Franklin — Behind the State House a public wall or garden is tastefully, and elegantly arranged, the whole being disposed in enchanting, and various order — the gravel walks are, alternately, in a direct line, or pursue a serpentine course — they are roled with much care, have a red hue, and are exactly smooth , Interjacent Lawns delight the eye, a great variety of well pruned trees shade, and beautify, and the white palisade octagonally set inclose the most attractive and rare shrubbery — These walks, and the surrounding views, are indeed charming, and perhaps they want only to be more spacious to equal any, prominades which our globe can exhibit — From a window of an upper apartment of the philosophical Academy, we are presented with one of the most enchanting prospects, that my eyes ever beheld — the Country, in the highest, and most beautiful cultivation — grounds nearly level, extended by Nature, and richly embelished by Art — Beautifully diversified by Groves, plains and superb Edifices, which, in regular succession, arrest, and complete the view — from another window, in the same apartment, we are shown the library, and a number of other elegant structures, and from a third, the delightful walks above sketched — This City contains a variety of public buildings, valuable paintings, and other curiosities, which, during my abode here I shall probably visit, and possibly, with my usual temerity, I may attempt these outlines — Twenty six congregations assemble in this City, under the banners of Christianity, but the majority of the Citizens, and those too of the highest consideration, are Quakers — The Founder of Pennsylvania was, as you know, the immortal Penn — There is a remarkable plainness in the manners, and habiliments, even of those who are not of the society of friends, at least as far as I have seen, no doubt there are a class of people, of another description — yet I believe the whims and caprices of fashion, or the extravagances of disipation, are not prevalent, in an equal degree, to what may be witnessed in the Metropolis of our State, I am informed, however, that Philadelphia is losing much of its ancient simplicity, and the probability is, if the seat of government should ultimately be established here, it will not be behind, in the career of — What shall I say — I want a word — so e'en let it pass — At present the dissimilarity is sufficiently conspicuous — In Boston, the passing carriage, nay every genteel street, or walk, presents you with the full dressed Lady, here, such an appearance is extremely rare, and the close white satin Bonnet, obtains a decided preference — Mr Murray numbers among his established friends, a gentleman whose annual income amounts to upwards of a thousand pounds sterling — he is not, nor ever was a quaker, he is a confirmed Universalist, and, by the way, zealous in his efforts to detain us in this City — yet the garb of this gentleman seems fashioned by the hand of simplicity, and his Lady's muslin mob, is close fitted to her head, her bonnet is the modest quaker cut, and her brown satin [gown] her highest dress — The Market in Philadelphia is prodigious, it is said to exceed any single market in the Island of Great Britain — it extends in a long range through the middle of one of the principal streets, to which it has given name — Its roof is arested, and plastered upon the inside, and supported by one hundred, and forty seven [massive] brick pillars — It is floored with brick, and it is every day regularly purified — It is divided into three parts, and in the intervals, are displayed a variety of articles of cloathing, ornamental trinkets, etc etc [—] The other morning, invited by the beauty of the weather, I accompanied a Lady, through the Market — The scene was to me novel, and extraordinary — The Market produced all kinds of Butcher's meat in great abundance, sufficient to yield a large supply to thousands, and every thing seemed of the best quality [—] Powdering tubs filled with salted beef, pork, hams, smoaked, and green tongues etc etc and all in perfect order — Poultry of every description — milk, cream, butter, eggs and cheese, in astonishing quantities — These articles lined the Shambles — Vegetables in all their variety, were on one side neatly displayed — lettuce, asparagus — green peas, which have been abundant during the three past weeks, and are still in high perfection, cucumbers, radishes, new potatoes etc etc etc — The fruit market next drew our attention, such cherries, and such strawberries, but I do not intend an exact inventory [—] Every thing is in the greatest plenty, and the strawberries are equal in size, to a robin's egg [—] twenty five hundred bushels of green peas, are disposed of in one day, in this market, and although the quantity of provision deposited at early dawn, is really astonishing — yet before ten o clock it is entirely distributed — The wheat Market is upon the out side, where you may be accommodated with any quantity — Purchasers may be supplied with a single pound of meat, and upwards — The Market is not so well supplied with fish — yet it is not wholly destitute of this Commodity — but if I be thus circumstantial, there will be no end of my scribbles* — I pass on to say, that the streets of this City are lighted every night, and that the lamps continue burning, until the return of morning, renders them no longer necessary, and the order, and regularity of this beautiful illumination, produce a fine effect — Watchmen patrol the streets, and the announcement of half past twelve O clock, reminds me of the description of a night in London. Be not anxious about my health, I am in the house of a lady, who exercises for me, in every respect, the tenderness of a parent — She is blessed with experience as well as humanity, she is Mistress of true politeness, and she knows to pity, to soothe, and to encourage — May God preserve my friends — Oh may the hour of danger, approaching my sister Anna, be happy — Dear Timid Fair One, May her expected offspring, in perfect form, and beauty, soon fill her arms — She is not, I trust, doomed to embrace a lifeless Corse — Enviable is the lot of that Mother, whose smiling infant draws from her gentle bosom, the salubrious stream, and who is allowed to rear to maturity, the creature of her bounty and affection — Fare well — you are all in possession of my hearts love —

*One article which agreeably ornaments the market, should not be omitted — It is supplied with an elegant variety of natural flowers — here Ladies furnish their Vases, and upon entering the walk perfumes of the most odiferous kind are inhaled. Persons of all descriptions, whether from necessity, convenience, or curiosity mingle in the Market, and we are under the necessity of literally shouldering each other ——

Letter 751 To my Sister Philadelphia Arch street June 14th— 1790

Again, Judith laments that she has not heard from her family in this letter to her sister, Esther. None of her current enjoyments equal the relationships in Gloucester she treasures. Judith and John are staying at the home of Mrs. Woodrow, whose husband is deceased. One of

Mrs. Woodrow's daughters has recently died, leaving a grandchild in her care. Two daughters remain — Mrs. Binney and Mrs. Jackson — and Judith befriends them both. Judith describes Mrs. Woodrow's financial difficulties after the war which were not uncommon. She mentions her favorable impressions of the Bethlehem Academy, which she details extensively later on. With almost half of Philadelphia Universalist, John is "courted" regularly to make the city his permanent home and his talks are widely attended. Theatre, in Philadelphia, was shunned by society and Judith was discouraged from attending. An admirer of the theatre, Judith regretted this obligatory bow to social custom. Judith has met educator and physician Benjamin Rush.

Although I conceive that in writing so circumstantially to our beloved Parents, I transmit to my very dear sister, every particular — Yet I cannot deny myself the pleasure, of addressing a separate page to her — Do you not know my dear, that more than a month hath elapsed since we parted from home, and that we see now, as I believe, distant more than four hundred miles, while we have not received the smallest information from you, since the morning upon which your humid eye, confessed your regrets at our approaching separation — Had I not the most indulgent of friends, I should be ready to deem their silence, in the highest degree unkind — but my yielding mind imputes the apparent neglect, to some of those casualties, which mark humanity, and render us the spirit of contingencies — It is true a sucession of worthy, and affectionate beings, claim my attention, but accustomed, from the commencement of our existence, to certain attachments, few events can compensate for the loss of natural connexions — The Lady with whom I at present reside, performs in every respect, the part of a Mother but I am not readily her daughter, and I sigh to behold the faces, the beautifully venerable faces of my real parents. I smile upon social pleasures, and for the affectionate attentions which I receive, I am truly grateful — but I would press to my bosom a real sister, and when I consider that only a few days beyond a month, a little month, hath passed since I left Gloucester, I can scarcely believe that I am right in my calculations, and imagination would persuade me, that swift footed time, hath certainly made a panic in his career — I have not yet visited the curiosities of this City, otherwise it might be in my power to make a selection for your amusement — I admire the Philadelphians to whom I have been introduced — you were pleased with Mrs Binney, and Mrs Lear, and I am sure, you would be equally charmed, with the other branches of their family at least as far as I have seen them, I risk little in pronouncing them amiable — We are lodged with the Mother of those ladies — Their Father paid the great debt of nature several years since — Nothing can exceed the tenderness with which we are treated, and my heart would be most perverse, were it not sensibly, and gratefully affected — Mrs Woodrow hath been a daughter of affliction — yea even in the severest sense of the word — Of thirteen Sons, and daughters, whom she hath borne, only two females now remain — yet they all bid fair for maturity, her husband, as I said, is no more, and her parents are laid in the narrow house — By the late fraudulent, and fluctuating times, she hath been stripped of an ample fortune — To her Town, and Country house she hath been accustomed, and her style of living was elegant — Upon the death of Woodrow, her estates consisting of houses, and lands, were estimated at the lowest compensation, to be worth ten thousand pounds sterling — But a division being necessary, and the heirs not agreeing, the property was disposed of at public auction, and the late continental currency was received as payment! The consequences were such as might have been expected — From the wreck of her more exalted hopes, she hath however substantiated what her economy renders a competency, and she swells no sigh, but for the departure of her friends — The death of Mrs Lear attended with most agonizing circumstances sits heavy upon her soul — yet she supports herself with genuine Christian fortitude, and heroically girding up the loins of her mind, she awaits her passage to a better World — The infant bequested her by her expiring daughter, is her peculiar care, the idol of her affection, and it is indeed, a most beautiful Babe — she hath devised to this child, with the full approbation of her surviving daughter, the whole of her remaining property, and the little orphan will possess, at her grandmother's death, as much as discreet management will need — Her children are amply provided for — Mrs Binney is in very easy circumstances, and her Eliza, who hath taken the name of Jackson, is well married — you would be delighted with the conduct of Mrs Binney, in her family, she hath two sons, and two daughters, her eldest son is placed at an Academy, in Burdentown — her youngest son, who was born a beautiful infant, hath been subjected to agonies so exquisite, as to stamp upon his little figure irremediable deformity — yet his countenance is pleasingly expressive, and nature hath liberally endowed his mind — If Mrs Binney discovers any partiality, it is for this child — Her girls are both charming, the youngest is almost an infant — The eldest, who is twelve years of age, hath received great advantages, having been constantly attended, for a considerable length of time, by no less than five Preceptors, and, it appears, that her improvements are fully equal to her opportunities. I have never seen a Girl of her years, more accomplished — Speaking of education, I am reminded of our excursion to Bethlehem, I wish you had been of our party to that Village — Were your daughter a few years younger, I should use my influence to have her placed at the Seminary in Bethlehem — but she is now too far advanced toward Womanhood, for such an arrangement — Had I a daughter, and could obtain the means of defraying the expenses which would accrue, she should absolutely assume the Bethlehem Cap, & the hallowed walls of that sanctuary, should shield the pretty innocent — The second daughter of Mrs Woodrow, Mrs Jackson, is a beautiful and truly amiable Woman, she hath two fine children, and is hourly expecting the birth of a third — Were I altogether under the guidance of prudence, could I divest myself of those natural ties, which bind my soul, I might, in the City of Philadelphia, be invested with ease, elegance, and even affluence

The gifts of fortune in this Metropolis court our acceptance — but Mr Murray is indulgent, he will be influenced by my feelings — we shall reject them, and a life of independence, and embarassment, will terminate in a death of humble poverty — Upon our first arrival in this City, a genteel house, rent free, for life, and two hundred pounds sterling per annum was proferred us, which sum is now augmented to two hundred and fifty pounds, and many persons assure us, that in the course of one year, it would amount to five hundred pounds, Mrs Woodrow is earnest in her solicitations, since the death of Mrs Lear, or rather Mrs Duncan — Universalism is so prevalent in Philadelphia, that it is judged one half the City either privately or avowedly have embraced the sentiment — Clergymen of all persuasions attend Mr Murray's investigations of truth, and the religion of benevolence, seems to be rapidly gaining ground, yet, I observe with much surprise, ideas altogether repugnant to a liberal, and rational spirit, take place — For example, the theatre is open, and the most approved pieces are performing, yet we find it impossible, except we would wound the feelings of a very large majority, to attend — Doctor Rush, the celebrated Doctor Rush, who provides the female Academy, established in this City, who is a man of letters, a Philosopher, a Writer, and to crown all a sincere, and valuable Convert to the Christian faith, even Doctor Rush hath not, for twenty years, been found in the theatre, and thus tacitly, as well as by an explicit declaration of his sentiments, is Doctor Rush censured, of the frequent use of the theatre — It is in vain that we urge the morality of a good Play, and the advantage to be derived from reducing a system of ethics to practice, and adorning them with all that impressive action, and elegance of language, of which stage personification is susceptible — The reply is uniform — "The Play house is a school for vice. The lives of performers are generally infamous, and by taking a seat at the theatre we countenance, as far as in our power, idleness and debauchery — ["] It is said the Southern, and middle States, are, in many respects, at least a Century behind the Eastern World, particularly in that polite taste, and elegant polish, which is the result of expanded, and unprejudiced reflection — Whether the above fact, may be considered as a proof of this assertion, I pretend not to determine, but I am sure, it operates much against my arrangements, for an attendance upon dramatic exhibitions, was one of the pleasure which I contemplated in this journey — you will have the goodness to remember me affectionately to your husband, and your daughter, and I pray you always to believe me, most tenderly yours —

Letter 752 To Anna Philadelphia Arch Street June 15th 1790

In this letter to her "Orphan Girl," Judith assures her of her continuing concern for her wellbeing. She paints a vibrant picture for Anna of her visit to Harrongate, famed for its "medicinal springs" for invalids. She describes gardens, lawns, "Chinese houses," and concerts given twice a week by lantern light. John has been asked to preach in Maryland, but probably will not go that far out of his way on this trip. John joins Judith in reminding Anna to watch her manners while she is a guest in other people's homes.

Although during my absence, I have denied myself the pleasure of chatting particularly with my beloved Girl, taking it for granted that the general letters which I have addressed my parents, have been communicated to her — yet she is nevertheless the constant object of my care, the ward of my continued hopes, and the sweet Orphan for whom to the Great Disposer of events, the fervid wishes of my soul, daily ascend — She rises with me in the morning, she takes a place with me upon my pillow, and the unceasing desire of my heart is, to present her an amiable Woman, possessing an improved mind, regulated passions, and those uniformly correct manners, which cannot fail to please — you doubtless know the route, manner and conclusion of our journey hither, and you are apprized of our being in a circle of pleasant and respectable friends, who are studious to furnish and to zest our enjoyments —

This morning hath completed one of the plans which originated in their polite attention — The weather is divine, and we have enjoyed it most delightfully by a pleasant ride to Harrongate, where we have breakfasted in high style, uniting the rich and refined repast, of a sentimental hour — Harrongate is distant from this City, up in the road to Frankfort, about four miles [—] We pursue our course through Kensington, along the skirts of the Delaware River, which River is navigable for large ships, upwards of two hundred miles, and for small craft more than three hundred — The Country is highly cultivated, and beautifully variegated — Harrongate is an enchanting recess, fitted up for the accommodation of invalids, or those who wish to inhale the salutary breezes of a clear, and salubrious air — Four miles as I said, from this City, a few rods from the road, upon the left, we enter a neat, and commodious airy, shaded on either hand, at the extremity of which an elegant seat seems to add a finishing to the scene — The rural beauties of Harrongate are multiplied, and enchanting — Figure to yourself an extensive green, exactly level, and smoothly shorn, upon this Green, place two dwelling houses, of a neat and thrifty appearance, only not adjoining — Let your Court yard be railed in with white palisades, and entered by an arched gate upon the left of the Avenue — through which you pass — place an Orchestra, conveniently furnished — Range upon your Lawn Chinese summer houses, romantic arbours, oblong tables, shaded seats, umbragious groves, and a variety of fruit trees — Behind your dwellings, let imagination throw a delightful garden, flowers, and shrubs displayed in the best taste, a gravel walk cut though the midst two bathing houses, at the extremity, in which you may drink the Harrongate waters, or receive with great security, and convenience, the shower and plunging Baths — Place at small distances a number of little ornamented pillars, with Lamps attached, indicative of the artificial day, which, at the commencement of evening, will be lighted up — Let Nature be cloathed in her richest, and most ornamental garb, adorned with all the varieties of verdure, and many of those party colored beauties, which gaily enamel the mead, and grace the garden, and, as a most attractive combination, let your buildings etc be painted white — If you can imagine all this, you will form a good idea of the romantic view, with which we were this morning beyond expression charmed — Harrongate is famed for three medicinal springs, and great benefit is said to accrue from the use of its waters [—] It is if course, the resort of all those who wish to drink of these streams or try the efficacy of the baths — Harrongate is frequented by much genteel company — it is a delightful morning's ride, and every Monday, and Friday evening, it is splendidly illuminated, when a concert of vocal, and instrumental musick, is performed — Gentlemen, and Ladies, are accommodated in the best possible manner, every method being in requisition to allure an endless succession of company — Of its two dwellings above mentioned, one is the residence of the Proprietor, where every thing is prepared for the refreshment of the guests, and the other is wholly devoted to their reception — The apartments are small but commodious, fancifully decorated, and furnished with the rural charms of Nature, and we are expeditiously supplied with every thing which the season can afford — Rules, an exact conformity to which is required, are conspicuously posted, an[d] it is in our option to take our repast in the house, in either of the chinese boxes, which are thrown up and down the green, or in any of the arbors, in which seats and tables, in an oblong direction, are pleasingly displayed — The best attendance is provided, and there is an pleasingly displayed — The best attendance is provided, and there is an evident solicitude to give satisfaction — Of the expenses consequent upon this very high, and complicated entertainment, not being allowed to discharge our own bill, we cannot give an account — A smiling little Girl presented me, at my departure, with a bouquet of richly perfumed flowers, and we returned to town, with the finest feelings which gratitude, replete with fervant thanks to a benificent Creator can inspire — We wonder much that we have not heard from you, since our departure Did you know that a line, under cover to the Fitzgerauld, would have found its way to me — Mr Murray is solicited to visit Maryland — If he goes I shall accompany him — but I rather believe his engagements will not allow a compliance with the importunities of his friends. I hope these summer months prove favourable to your health — I hope you have enjoyed much and I trust we shall spend a tranquil winter together — Exercise, and change of air, as you know, hath always been friendly to me — I have a fine appetite, and increase in size, more than I could wish — I am, however, doomed, as I have too much reason to fear, to suffer through life, from the management to which I was once so infatuated as to submit [—] Not a day dawns, but actual pain, cruelly reminds me of the past, and I live to mourn the sacrifice made to ignorance, and arrogance — Had I been in this City — but reflections are unavailing — Yes, I feel it is a melancholy truth that regrets are indeed useless. Adieu, my Dear Girl, my mind having taken this gloomy turn, it would be painful both to you and to myself to add — I am, my Love, with sincere affection your Maternal Friend

Mr Murray bids me say, that he reiterates most tender regards — We hope you so conduct, as to obtain the approbation of the honoured, and indulgent friends with whom you reside — We hope, and we pleasingly believe, you will embrace every opportunity of rendering them those kind of services, which will preclude the idea of your being considered as a burden — Let discretion be your guide — Suppress the risings of your spirit, when stimulating you to wound, or to detract — but give free, and full scope to the ebullitions of your soul, when they impel you to exercise candour, and to communicate pleasure —

Letter 753 To my sister Anna— Philadelphia Arch Street June 16— 1790

Judith's sister-in-law, Anna, is due to give birth any day. Judith offers her love and concern, and hopes her brother, Fitz William, has returned from his latest voyage to witness the birth of his first child. Judith imagines the happy scene, wishing she could be present.

Before this paper can have the honour to kiss your hands, I trust, my dear Anna, that you will have very essentially added to the obligations, which the Writer is under, to love, and to esteem you — At the moment of your reading this letter, your painful hour will, if I have calculated correctly, have passed over, and you, I fondly hope will be amply compensated for every suffering — Indulge me, I pray you for a moment, and I will pursue the interesting subject — Fitz William is returned — for fancy would not, in any consideration, omit from her group, so capital a portrait — Well the beauteous little stranger, whose infant form, replete with loveliness, personifies the birth of innocence — is placed on the lap of good Mrs Odel — The sweetly blushing, the modestly tender, and now thrice happy parent, is confined to her maternal bed, and, with smiles of sweet complacency, with silent, and corrected transport, the charming Mother regards the scene — Fitz William — how enraptured is the youthful Father — The feelings, the big emotions of his full soul, he wants words to express — What then let the eye of observation trace his honest countenance, and the glow of satisfaction, delineated there, the manly pleasure which sparkles in his fine eye, flushes his cheek, and animates every feature, will be sufficiently expressive — In a reclined posture he stands, one hand perhaps is in his bosom, and the other significantly extended — Now, glad attentions dwell upon the Cherub stranger, anon it glances upon his beloved Anna, until at length, in joyful extacy, he clasps the pretty creature in his paternal arms, bearing it triumphantly to her, who so large[ly] constitutes, and who so fully shares his happiness — But the new sensations — the ten thousand pleasures, the sweet augmenting tenderness, which surprise the bosoms, and play about the hearts, of the young parental Pair [—] what tongue can describe, or what pen depicture — Your Mamma all the Matron's dignity, is hers, and she looks around her, with becoming and chastized enjoyment — your Maria, her fine face is moulded by sweet expression, and, upon this occasion, every feature is replete with the tender joy of her delighted bosom —
My Father, and Mother — their revered countenances are cloathed in smiles, and they exultingly behold their children, tasting those transports which they, themselves, at so early a period experienced — For my sister — she contemplates with serene happiness the objects

which surround, and her beauteous cheek flushes a yet higher bloom — your eldest sister is, I presume, in Boston — I too am absent — but do you imagine that we will be denied our share in such a scene — No certainly — For myself — during the reverie of the moment, I too step forward — upon the benign, and complacent countenances of my parents, I gaze transported, I embrace my Fitz William — and I imprint upon the lips of my sweet Anna, the kiss of love, when, seizing from her bosom her charming infant, I press it to a heart, which beats for it, with warm affection — Often, again, and again, I reiterate my congratulations, and my soul is absorbed in pleasing contemplation — Is Fancy premature in her representations — and are you still held in durance? Accept then, these effusions, as a prelude to the coming joy, and doubt not the bliss is but suspended — Let not undue apprehension depress the mind of my lovely sister — every agonized moment, will but enhance the felicity of that contemplation, which probably awaits — If Fitz William be not yet returned, a little time will no doubt restore him — if your infant doth not yet fill your arms, the period is but postponed, and, as I believe, gratulations will yet be proper — When you meet my brother — say to him for me, every [thing] that is tender — trust me, dear Girl, the feelings of my heart will abundantly justify you — Assure him of my fond affection, and let him know that wishes, warm from my bosom, are hourly wafted for his felicity — When you embrace your child, think of the share which Nature hath given me in the little Being, and let it learn to attach itself to her, who will always cherish for it the dearest interest — May you, my dear, from every circumstance derive eventual enjoyment — May tranquil pleasures be ever yours, and may you never know a dimination of your attachment to her, who is most affectionately your sister, and your friend —

Letter 754 to my Aunt Allen — Philadelphia Arch Street June 16— 1790

Still, the "doors of fame and fortune [are] thrown open" to John, Judith tells her aunt, Sarah Sargent Allen (1729-1792), and he is repeatedly urged to stay in Philadelphia. Their trip has already been delayed due to his popularity and the multiplying requests for him to speak. Judith describes her frustration with the Philadelphians' disapproval of the theatre, wishing she could attend. She inquires after her Aunt Allen's health, knowing that their last meeting might have been their last. In fact, her aunt died less than two years later.

I assure my self, my dear Lady, that a line from me will give you pleasure, I know too, that it is my duty, and I feel it to be my inclination, to contribute as far as may be in my power, to your enjoyments — We flatter ourselves, that your children will not be displeased to receive intelligence from us — The tranquil feature of my Cousin I— will, as we believe, wear an added complacency — In the countenance of your son Winthrop, the smile of assured affection will triumph, and the glowing cheeks of my Cousin Mary, will flush a yet more animated bloom — Nor will I allow these ideas to be the growth of Vanity — Certainly not — I rather dignify them with the name of a firm, and unsuspecting confidence in your distinguishing, and continued partiality — Know then, my indulgent friend that we possess, in a good degree, the blessings of health — that the season is uncommonly mild — for at this moment — even in the City of Philadelphia, although the summer is so far advanced, we are fanned by the salutary breezes of a temperate morning, the heat of the meritorious day is not intense, and the evening is divinely serene. Know that we have every where been received with the most marked attention — Candor, and liberality have advanced to meet us, reason and reflection have stood suspended, until we have, by friendship, and esteem been cordially embraced — Mr Murray is warmly solicited to reside in this City, and very handsome proposals are made to him — Many of the first character are in the list of his friends and he may command a genteel competency — Our progress to this place hath continued a full month — The rough roads, the weather often unpropitious and, above all, the pressing solicitations of friends upon whom we were necessitated to call, have unavoidably delayed us — yes, although our movements have been slow, our pleasures have not been the less pointed [—] a thousand pleasant circumstances have succeeded each other — Nature hath been cloathed in her most beautiful garb our prospects have been enchantingly diversified, and, with the richest, and most grateful perfume the vernal gales have been impregnated — If you wish for a more circumstantial account of our journey, my Mother will delight to gratify you, and you may thus be enabled to trace our every step — I wish earnestly to see my friends, of whose present situation, I am totally ignorant — I have not received a single line from Gloucester, nor even a message, during my abode in Boston, since my departure from home, which was upon the morning of the fourth of May!! I trust, my dear madam, that you enjoy more than your accustomed health — you have certainly been a great, although a patient sufferer, and whenever I reflect upon the inroads, which the wasting complaint from which you have so long suffered, is making in your constitution, my spirits sink, and the sigh of apprehension swells my bosom — Retrospection often wanders — to the last time I filled a seat in your social parlour — After some endearing manifestations of your affection, pressing my hand, with more than your wonted tenderness — you impressively said — "I may never see you more — God forever bless —" tears arresting the unfinished benediction, you were silent — but there was in that silence, an undescribable expression — I do not wish to indulge melancholy anticipations, I would rather look forward to future hours of calm enjoyment — I am pleased, as often as I reflect upon the little establishment which your eldest son hath obtained — Its emoluments I know are small, but any thing which engages the mind, and which, with economy, will yield a support, is undoubtedly preferable, to that Ennui consequent upon a life of inactivity — To Winthrop I most sincerely wish the greatest prosperity — he is really a worthy young Man, may domestic happiness bless and reward his life, Mary is a charming Girl — she hath ever possessed a warm place in my bosom, and I rejoice that the morning of her days, opens so serenely — May her pleasing prospects multiply, May her career be tranquil, and may it be terminated with innocence, and honour — I am happy that my beloved Aunt hath thus collected her young folks around her, and that their deportment is so discreet, and so proper, so respectful to her, and so honourable to themselves; have the goodness to assure them jointly, and severally, of my tender, and unabating regards — and if there are any among the social party, which so frequently collects in your hospitable parlour[,] persons who honour us by this remembrance, I pray you to tender unto them, our grateful compliments. The gentlemen of the Drama particularly engage our esteem, while recollection fondly presents the sentimental scenes of the past winter [—] The Theatre in this City, is now open and a company which we are told possess great abilities, is employed in performing first rate pieces, but so rigid are the prejudices of a large proportion of our connexions here, that we cannot[,] consistent with prudence, take seats in the Play House — It is strange, but it is nevertheless true, that opinions the most obsolete seem, in this large, populace, opulent, and enlightened City, to be in strong force, and every where more or less prevalent — No doubt the preponderance of quakerism, during succeeding years, has greatly contributed to preserving the simplicity of manners, which in many instances, distinguish the people — To all which can be said in favour of moral exhibitions, under proper regulations, the disposable lives of Performers, furnish, and is considered, an unanswerable objection — Be this as it may, I am free to own that I am rather disappointed — I had promised myself much pleasure at the Theatre, nor can I see the indelicacy, or impropriety of witnessing a chaste, moral, well written piece — yet the most polished, and respectable characters in this city are anti-Dramatists, and the Universalists are first in the opposition — ["]Mr & Mrs Murray at a play! Impossible — they will never conduct thus improperly" — you know who said, that if even taking meat, would offend a weak brother, he would abstain — This is enough, it is proper we should become all things which we consistently can, unto all Men, and it is just that we should submit — It is impossible for us to say when we shall return — Were Mr Murray disengaged, and did not the ties of blood, and friendship, bind with tenfold cords, this heart of mine, Philadelphia would become our permanent residence — The doors of fame, and fortune, are thrown open to us in this City, and our religious inducements are multiplied — Accept, dear Lady, my hearts affection, and my unabating Duty, and believe me ever yours —

Letter 755— To my Aunt Prentiss— Philadelphia Arch street June 16th— 1790

This letter recounts two anecdotes told to Judith by John Jay, former Secretary of Foreign Affairs and diplomat, whom Judith admired as a man of peerless integrity. At age 18, Jay suffered from extreme illness and depression and, apparently, actually died. It was winter, and his mother, refusing to inter the body, kept her son at home in a very cold room. A day and a half later, he awoke and retained vivid memories of his "glimpse of the other world." In another story, Jay's spirit visits the home of a dear friend as Jay lay dying and needed to see him. Judith's use of the term "clay built tenement" refers to the human body. She still misses her home and family terribly. Still no letters.

Few of my friends are entitled to more of my consideration than, the tender and sympathizing relative, to whom I now employ my pen — It is many weeks since I left home — shall I own a truth — In the admeasurement of my own mind, at least as many months seem to have revolved — I lift my eye, my mental eye toward Boston — toward Gloucester — reflection magnifies the distance, they become painfully remote, whole Continents seem to rise between, and the retrospective eye, can hardly fix a point whereon to place them — Are not our connexions a little unkind — Can you, my dear Aunt yield at Credence — I have not received a single line, or message, from home, since my departure! Surely every one I love cannot have ceased to exist, and I am happy enough to hope the best — Measures are taken to induce Mr Murray to fix his abode in this City — he hath, I do assure you, had very handsome offers, and ease, and affluence seem to await him here — But this is a subject, upon which I would not interfere, and with which I dare not trust myself — Of the extent, and opulence of Philadelphia, I had formed no adequate idea — The magnificent air of the buildings, the length, regularity, and capaciousness, of the streets — the number of public edifices, and the multitude of its inhabitants, greatly exceed what my imagination in its utmost latitude had led me to expect — Our journey hither was very pleasant, and since our abode in this City, nothing has been left unassayed, which it was conceived would contribute to our happiness — yet it is a fact, I have not enjoyed so much, from any source, as from an afternoon devoted to Mr Jay — Of Mr Jay, if my memory be correct, you have already heard, Mr Murray, as I believe, at a very early period of our acquaintance, narrated to you, a very extraordinary circumstance, relative to this peculiar favourite of heaven — I am not however quite as certain — and, whether or not, I feel assured, my dear Aunt, that it will be pleasing to you, to have among your treasures, a succinct account, of a supernatural event, which seems too well established, to admit of doubt — I had the privilege of setting full three hours by the side of Mr Jay, and there is, it appears to me, an expression in his countenance, which would become that of an angel of God — He is bowed down by years, and his head is white as snow, his life hath been a uniform example of benevolence, and he is now, with calm resignation, waiting the passport, which shall admit him to the realms of blessedness — I received from the lips of Mr Jay, the substance of the following relation — Mr Jay was bred a Quaker, and his youth was exemplary — With <u>avidity</u>, with <u>fear</u>, and with <u>trembling</u>, he <u>worked out</u> his own <u>salvation</u> — <u>He indeed worked it out</u> — To him the son of God was of little consequence, for with sparks of his own kindling, he was seeking, to encompass himself about — and in the robe of his own righteousness, it was his choice to be adorned — The powers of his mind were, by Nature, strong — and he partook not the smallest tincture of enthusiasm — his system might have been the result of heathen morality, and in the truths of rectitude, humanly speaking — He continued his career, until he had completed his eighteenth year — when his soul was exercised in a most remarkable manner — The sorrows of his heart were, for two complete years, beyond description. Duly impressed with an idea, that he was destined to everlasting perdition — peace was a stranger to his bosom — Tears of agony rolled down his youthful cheek — at the throne of grace he was almost constantly prostrated, and reiterated were his supplications for mercy — a gleam of light would occasionally pierce the dun obscure, but ten fold darkness would next enwrap him round in comfortless despair — He was, during these struggles nearly wanted to a skeleton — and to the act of suicide, he was often strongly, and almost irresistably impelled, after he had continued in this melancholy way, for the term of two complete years — It happened, that a destructive pleurisy raged in this City; it was generally fatal, and with this disorder, young Jay was violently seized — a Physician was called in, and he was pronounced in iminent danger [—] The sufferings of his body were indeed great, but the wounds of his spirit, were abundantly more insupportable — his case grew every hour more desperate, and the Doctor gave it as his opinion, that he would not survive the third day — Dreadful was his situation, for thick darkness enveloped his mind "I go, my parents" he exclaimed — "horrid truth, I go, and I shall meet a God armed for my destruction!" "Oh my son" returned the agonized Mother "If such will be of your fate, you who have lived a life of innocence and Virtue, wholly exempt from blame, where will the guilty World be found?" — He continued under these terrific apprehensions, until the fifth day of his illness — His sufferings still augmenting, and his exit momently expected — With tears of agony, and trembling dread, he repeatedly requested a draught of those cooling waters, the assuaging influence of which, would be denied him, in that World of liquid fire, whether he was so rapidly hastening — In this shocking situation he was unexpectedly continued until the afternoon of the ninth day of his indisposition, when without the smallest mitigation of his mental, or corporal pangs, he expired — The season was severely cold, and the demise not admitting of doubt, it was judged convenient, lest the body should too suddenly soften, to prepare it for interment — This, however, his Mother absolutely forbid — The Father and other friends remonstrated — He is unquestionably dead — why not then proceed to perform the last offices? To satisfy, or obviate, the objections of the Old Lady, the Doctor was summoned, he examined the body, having recourse to those experiments, usual upon doubtful occasions, and he pronounced the desolation certain— Yet, still the maternal mind refused acquiescence, and in compliance with what they believed a weakness, resulting from the depths of her sorrow, they consented the deceased should remain, for some time upon the bed of death — The residue of the afternoon, the ensuing evening, and through the whole of the long winter night, until the ensuing morning, the body continued an undoubted corse — when lo! to the astonishment of numbers, who waited the event, with a gentle sigh the heart stricken young Man once more opened his eyes, upon the fleeting scenes of time — The consequent amazement — the many questions, the prevalent confusion — the agitated transport of the Mother, the mingling joy, and glad surprise manifested in her every word, and action, every thing of this sort, will be more easily imagined than described — But it is the discoveries made to Mr Jay, which I cannot forbear regarding as an added revelation, and that will particularly interest every individual, in whose candid, and unprejudiced mind, the foregoing recital obtains credit — Had the fiery gasps been still delineated, which, upon the affrighted imagination of Mr Jay, had been so deeply imprinted, I should have rationally concluded, the view, no other, than a continuation of his dream but when prospects were opened, when truths were conveyed, of which, through his whole life, he had never formed the most remote idea, at the suggestion of which he would have been beyond expression shocked, what are the reflections which reason, open to conviction, will make? Mr Jay not finding himself in mind in a liquid sea of divine vengeance, or kept alive in a tartanean stream of fire, the fuel of which was sulpher and brimstone, was <u>comparatively</u> happy — Not, however, hav[ing] embraced the truth, <u>as it is in Jesus</u>, he could not take his seat among the elect number — yet he was cloathed in a white robe, and a celestial guide received him — The form of his body appeared as here to fore — but it was a spiritual body, and consequently light as air — Its movements were easy, and performed with the utmost alacrity — Nothing, he assured me, that his mortal eyes ever beheld, can in any sort, give an adequate idea, of the magnitude, solemnity, beauty, richness and grandeur of the scenes with which he was surrounded — An extensive plain was out spread, the horizon of which his eye could not reach, and its surface was cloathed with the most beautiful, and grateful verdure — It was diversified by glassy rivers, and meandering streams, and airs melodious beyond what expression, or even idea, can reach, were wafted all around — The divine symphony of those celestial sounds, yet vibrates, although faintly upon the ear of this distinguished saint — his tongue expatiates thereon, and with tears of joy, he assays to delineate its seraptic powers — Beings innumerable flitted before him, many more in possession of tranquility, but upon the brow of others, care, and deep anxiety were prevalent — Those upon whose spirits the peaceful morning had dawned, were cloathed in snow white Vestments while the spotted hue remained upon the garments of others — How happy are we, my beloved Aunt, who know that after the sealed are taken up, an innumerable company shall appear, who shall wash their robes, while in the blood of the Lamb — Mr Jay was unpleasurably affected, as he marked the traces of sorrow visible upon the features of the dejected countenance, but this guide informed him, the hour approached, when the angel of the Lord, should preach the everlasting gospel, when all evil should be done away, when pain should forever cease, and God Himself from every eye, should wipe off every tear — He saw, he heard, and his philanthropic soul rejoiced in redeeming love. He witnessed, during his absence from the body, the death of three individuals in this City — two white Men, and one Negro Man — One of the white Men, quitting his clay built tenement, received the spotted robe, with the attending inquietudes, while the black Man, who was ancient, and had suffered much, bounding from his enfeebled body was arrayed in white garments, and the joys of the emancipated spirit stood confessed — Mr Jay, upon his return to life, related the deaths of these persons — the exact time when — the particular streets, houses, apartments, and even situations from which they made their exit — With a number of circumstances, relative to the black Man, during the preparations made to visit the body — Enquiries were immediately made, at the several dwellings, and every requisite particular succeeded, precisely as he had related — These facts are corroborated by a number of respectable witnesses, and no doubt of their authenticity can reasonably be entertained — Mr Jay remarked that nothing impeded his progress — the thickest walls could not obstruct his view, and his passage was instantaneous — He beheld a separating veil, the transparency of which fully disclosed the Mansions of bliss, prepared to receive the immortal, made perfectly blessed, whose head is already crowned with everlasting joy — Through this veil, one of the individuals, whom he had seen expire, immediately passed — But this veil, when he assayed to penetrate — the further side of which, could he have attained, the probability is, he would have no more been doomed to an abode in mortality — he was again encircled by the body — The extatic vision was no more, the angelic notes were heard at a distance, or reiterated only by memory — the agonies of his disorder were returned, and most gladly welcomed, for he flattered him self they might be harbingers of <u>real demise</u> — Ardently he wished it were no sin to expedite his departure, and he would have rejoiced to have passed through the most excrutiating tortures, flames, and death, if he might thus have regained the World of Spirits — But his elevated, and enlightened intellect, soon possessed tranquility, his will became regulated, his passions all subdued, or corrected, and, with much submission, becoming acquiescence, and holy resignation, he hath from that period, awaited the mandate of his God — Through a length of years he hath been crowned with domestic enjoyments — happy — his marriage choice, and in a pleasant, and amiable family. The countenance of Mrs Jay is uncommonly open, and benign, but it is unnecessary to add, or even to attempt, description of her appearance, when I say she seems literally the counterpart, of the distinguished individual, to whom she is united — They possess, in the winter of their lives, unbroken tranquility, a divine expression beams from their eyes — urbanity gilds their actions, and by an opening heaven, their features seem already irradicated — The life of Mr Jay has exhibited a series of benevolence — to the mental, and corporate wants of his fellow creatures, so far as his power extends, he hath uniformly administered [—] to the bed of death he is frequently summoned, when, with energetic confidence, and a smile which would become an inhabitant of the celestial World, he preached peace to the dying, and despair flieth at his approach [—] The interest of the Widow, and the orphan, is committed to his charge, and integrity is the motto of his character — In the glimpse of the <u>other</u> world, with which he hath been favoured, he observed, that every individual received a *form*, similar to that with which the soul is arrayed, during its sojourn upon the globe, and he obtained his knowledge of...precisely as in the present world — yet the etherial texture, was beyond expression dignified, beautified, and adorned — In one word, "<u>it is raised a spiritual Body.</u> ["] The experience of Mr Jay, is replete with very extraordinary circumstances

— In addition to the above vision, he related many anecdotes, from which I take leave to select the following [—] He was, not long since, visited by a distressing illness, which it was believed would be his last, he remained, during many hours speechless, receiving no sustenance but what was administered in a teaspoon — through the whole of which period, his happy, his privileged spirit, was expatiating amid scenes, the magnificence, and beauty of which were inessable — He had a Friend, who resided several miles from this City — he felt an inclination to visit him, and instantly passing, in idea, through the window of his apartment, he was seated at the bed side of the Man he greatly loved — His friend saw the appearance, and addressing his Wife, assured her that Friend Jay had that night departed out of time — for he had seen him in his chamber — Early in the morning he quilled his home, and presented himself in Philadelphia, with an expectation of attending the funeral obsequies of the supposed deceased — My account of Mr Jay running to such a length, you will not, my dear Aunt, wish me to add, after I have assured you, that I am, with sincere and respectful affection, ever your etc etc

Letter 756 To Mrs Sargent Philadelphia Arch Street June 18— 1790

The weather is unbearably hot. Judith feels unwell and quite "dispirited" from the lengthy separation from her family. She takes to her bed. Suddenly, John enters her chamber and places letters from home in her hand. Her spirits are revived.

The winds at length propitious to my prayers, have wafted to me, indubitable proof, of the well being, and continued kindness of my dear, and tender friend — The heat of yesterday was intense, it encreased the langour of my soul — Dispirited, and only not lifeless, I retired to my chamber — In vain the dear, good Lady, with whom we reside, and who, in every thing a parent ought to be, assayed to dissipate the glooms, which although her well judged politeness would not permit her to note, her endearing efforts to soothe plainly evinced, that scarce a movement of my soul could escape her observation — unavailing, I say, were her benign regards — Fancifully melancholy the period of my absence from my friends, was unreasonably magnified. It looked, I imagined, as if all my former hopes, and fears, I must perforce relinquish — as if to all those invigorating amities, which for so long a period seemed interwoven with my idea of identity, now wholly lost to a new existence, to a new sense of things, and new connexions, I must unavoidably awaken — Say not, that no more than six weeks had elapsed, since I was clasped in the arms of my beloved, and faithful friends — These six weeks appeared in my contemplation, as many centuries and I sank under the gigantic form, which the distance, and the long, long period of absence, assumed — It was about eleven o clock on the seventeenth of June one thousand seven hundred and ninety — when Mr Murray entered my chamber — I heard him mount the staircase, I know he had been visiting among his friends, I knew he was much affected by the heat, and I expected to see him fatigued and debilitated — he entered, however, with one of the most benevolent smiles, and taking my hand — he pressed it with much affection to his lips — What will you say to a letter from your Father — from your friend? — I knew it was not post day, and I peevishly replied — Excuse me, my dear — I do not feel in a disposition to trifle — By way of answer to this saucy impatience, he placed your well known seals, together with a letter from my Father, upon my knee — The intense heat — I felt it no more — the genial gales of tender affection arose, and by their odiforous airs, my soul was refreshed, and, gently breathing hope, and sweet complacence, were once more mine — I seized the papers, with avidity, I read with transport, and the tear of many was upon my cheek — I proceeded on — it was a moment pregnant with delight, and my soul was in a situation to enjoy it — What were my sensations, with what eagerness I perused, and what big emotions swelled my bosom, you, loveliest of Women, will imagine, although my pen is greatly inadequate to their description — Again my heart is attuned to harmony, the pleasures of possession, the bliss of expectation, are again mine — Again the letters of friendship are before me, and once more with sweet composure, I prepare to pen my responses — The morning is divinely fair, and I am uncommonly tranquil, a kind of playfulness obtrudes, and contemptuously regarding that Jade Pandora — it suggests to my pen, against her name, and office, a thousand invectives — What can stimulate the Witch, thus to arm...against your repose — Let me see — Upon my honour, I believe I have made the discovery — This same Erysipelas seems to be her strong hold — if I mistake not, she unmasks her battery, directly in your face, and, urging with much malice, her envisioned shafts, she banishes for a time the lily, and the rose, robbing your sweet countenance, of some of its principal graces — Now this incendiary, this malignant, this desolating — no term of contamity can be extravagant, when designed to designate one, who enlists in her train every mischief, this peace destroying Pandora was, you know a celebrated beauty, and a notable Dame into the bargain — Fashioned by the decripted god, and beautifully endowed by all their Deity shape, she came forth a finished piece and, for a season, she was no doubt wonderfully careful — But that same principle of curiosity, or sexual obstinacy, yielded Disobedience [—] growing too strong for her reason, nothing could satisfy the Hussey, but rummaging to the very bottom of her contagious box! — It is probable when she found herself whelmed in a deluge of evils, which so copiously issued from their confinement, she mightily regretted, the consequences of the false step which she had so indiscreetly taken — Regrets frequently produce envy, Pandora became subject to this passion, and a very large proportion of this hydron ill, mingling with her constitution, suddenly incorporated therewith, becoming one with the despoiled Nymph — and, from that moment, down to the present era, the malicious trollop hath been particularly edged against every face, every figure, and every mind which bore the nearest resemblance to her pristine beauty, and thus I account for the rooted aversion which she seems to have conceived from my lovely friend — hence her unwearied pursuit, and having measured Hope, from the bottom of her urn, she cherishes the idea, of reducing to her own level every distinguished, every amiable Fair one — But seriously, I should not be thus in spirits, were it not evident, that you had arisen from her last assault, abundantly victorious.

I am astonished to learn that you have received no more than one letter from me, I have repeatedly written, but they will, as I trust, ultimately come safe to hand — Right happy am I, that my descriptions serve to amuse you — how abundantly would your flattering remarks compensate, if they had even been a work of labour — We have been fifteen days in this Metropolis — We have seen much, and we have much yet to see [—] I had intended, by this post, to have sketched for you a delineation of Schuylkill gardens, a place of public resort, four mile from this City — I am not so vain as to imagine that their enchanting beauties will live in my page, but I would, however, attempt at least a bird's eye view, did not engagements, which cannot be avoided, compel me to postpone my design — it is, however, but postponed and in my next letter, if nothing particular interferes it shall kiss your hands — The prattle of our dear Boys, possesseth a fascinating power over my soul — do not, I pray you, omit it — To Mrs Walker, and to Mrs Powell, I shall shortly write — To those Ladies, and to all inquiring friends, particularly to the individuals of your family, you will, with your accustomed kindness, have the goodness to remember me, precisely as you shall judge proper — Your reflections, upon my birth day, are like yourself — they are as sweet as incense, offered up at the shrine of Amity, and they do indeed soothe, and harmonize, the best feelings of which my bosom is susceptible — No, my friend, I do not believe Virtue to be so unduly rigid, as to interdict the sentimental intercourse of souls — under the auspices of rectitude, under the requisite regulations of Virtue, the finest feeling of humanity may be indulged — Holding the pen of correct, chaste, and holy friendship, the page of information may be given and received — at least, such are the dictates of my understanding, yet I know that prudence, and direction, should always be of our counsel, that circumstances alter cares — and that I ought to be silent — Yes, I do believe that a Great, First Cause — although invisible, produces, and governs all the events of our lives — and that as we are not invested with a controaling power, it is always wisdom, to submit implicitly, and without murmuring — Those are, as I believe, most happy, who practice upon this maxim, upon whose actions it is properly influential — upon whose lives it hath a rational effect — Adieu — I am interrupted — Once more I repeat — that I cannot be other than your affectionate and admiring friend ———

Letter 757 To my Father & Mother Philadelphia Arch Street June 19— 1790— Saturday

Judith is relieved to receive their letter, which reassured her that the family was in good health. Here, she reports on meeting "the family of Doctor Franklin," particularly his daughter, Sarah Bache, who tells them her father thought highly of Universalist theology. John is being treated with the great honor, and Judith describes in detail College Hall which was made at his disposal during his stay in Philadelphia. Judith describes her meeting with Doctor Benjamin Rush. Apparently, Dr. Rush had formed a negative opinion of John years before, swayed by public opinion. But after meeting him, and hearing him preach, Rush changed his mind and expressed his admiration for John's courage. The Murrays visited the "Alms house of Philadelphia" and its manager, Mr. Cummings. She describes the many "curiosities" in his home, including birds, fish, plants, and an extensive kitchen garden. She also explains how the alms house is managed, paid for, and what it was like to walk through. The experience made her extremely uncomfortable, but she admired the institution and its efficiency. She felt this was yet another example of the Philadelphians' humanity. "Sarah Sargent Ellery" is her niece, Sally.

Very long, and with much impatience did I wait for letters, from my friends, my soul sickened with apprehension, and I endeavoured to banish reflection from my bosom — Thursday last, however, presented me a line from my Father — it was short but it was expressive, it informed me that my beloved Circle enjoyed accustomed health, and it gave peace to my heart — I thank you, my dear Sir, very sincerely I thank you, for your benign intelligence — I am happy, my dear Mother, comparatively happy, to learn, that although indisposition still clouds your days, yet, that as you are not worse than common, your complaints do not gain ground — I am pleased that Sarah Sargent Ellery enjoyed enough of health, to accompany you, my Dear Sir to Boston, I am pleased that my

Anna was at Salem, and I rejoice in the felicity of every one — one more piece of information, would have added to my enjoyment — I am extremely anxious respecting my sister Anna, and I greatly regret that her name occurs not in the catalogue of my friends — I trust that no evil will betide my gentle sister — I regret also that I missed the packet of letters designed for me in Boston: They were no doubt replete with indulgent tenderness, and I commission you, my beloved Parents to return my acknowledgments to the Writers be they who they may — Well by way of continuing the cursory account which I have done myself the pleasure of transmitting to you, I am now to recollect the events of the past week, and so various hath been the scene, that I protest I hardly know where to begin — To tell you the numbers we have seen, the persons who have visited us, and whom we have visited, to describe their manners, and to enumerate their civilities, would take up more time than my present engagements will allow ——— The sentiments of the Universalist, are every day growing more respectable in this City They are adopted by the family of Doctor Franklin — Mrs Bache, the distinguished daughter of Doctor Franklin informs us, that it was her Father's opinion, that no system in the Christian World, was so effectually calculated to promote the interest of society, as that doctrine which exhibits a God, reconciling unto himself, a lapsed universe — The Philadelphians are, as I have said, exceedingly anxious to fix Mr Murray among them — At first, a genteel house, rent free for life, with a salary of two hundred pound sterling per annum, was proferred him — they next proposed two hundred and fifty, and finally, they add, if he will pledge his word, to return to them, so soon as he can adjust his affairs Eastward, they will insure him, exclusive of his house rent, an annual income of full four hundred pounds sterling — The Church, which is the property of the Universalists in this City, not being sufficiently spacious, to contain the numbers who flock to hear, application was made to the Reverend Doctor Smith Provost, or President of the College, and Academy, for the use of a building, belonging to and known by the name of The College Hall, when a special meeting of the Trustees was called, and unanimous consent of friend Doctor Smith requested Mr Murray's presence at his home, who, you will not doubt obeyed the summons — The President and Professors escorted the Universalist to the Hall waited upon him to the pulpit, stairs, and then took their seats in the Assembly — Mr Murray, after delivering a discourse, did not feel authorized to appoint a future lecture — The President immediately addressed him — "Sir, I expected you would have published other opportunities, for you are to know, the use of the Hall is yours, when, and as frequently as you please,["] and accordingly three times in the course of one week, large serious, and respectful audiences are collected in the Hall — Besides the President, the Reverend Messieurs Magaw, Rogers, Bend, Macdual and Andrews, regularly attend, and Mr Murray receives from those gentlemen, uniform and marked politeness — The College Hall is a large, and commodious building, an ample stage is raised several feet from the floor, upon which is erected the reading desk, or pulpit, and a number of convenient and elegant seats, are ranged upon the right, and left — the remaining space is filled with benches, and there is a large Gallery in Front, and upon each side [of] the pulpit — The Hall is adjacent to the College, which is a venerable Pile, and the Professors have their residence, in neat surrounding tenements — where I have had the pleasure of spending some agreeable hours with their Ladies — On sunday, Mr Murray collects his adherents at the Lodge, or Church of the Universalists — The Reverend Doctor Blair, is a confirmed convert to Universalism — Relly is his Oracle, although, as I was informed by Doctor Rush, he hath, in some particulars, gone beyond his favourite Author — reconciling difficulties, which Relly hath not attempted — Doctor Rush is a Man of sense, and letters — he is well known in the medical, and literary World — I am happy that I can name Doctor Rush, as an open, and avowed Professor of, and ornament to the Religion of Jesus — addressing my husband, this morning, he candidly said "Why, my dear Sir you have stood much alone, you have indeed buffeted the storm — What a torrent of traditional prejudice — malevolence, and calumny, you have had to encounter [—] Twenty years ago I heard your name — you were preaching in Bachelor's Hall — No consideration would have induced me to come within a mile of the place, and had I met you in the street, I should not have believed it had been you, except you had been distinguished by horns, and a cloven foot — But now peaceful, and blessed to myself, is the resolution — The Bible is a consistent book, containing every thing excellent — I was particularly charmed with the new pastorial account of your ordination — Never I believe was [there a] more beautiful piece of Oratory, than was exhibited — when pressing to your bosom the book of God, with the expression attending that elevated, and proper action" — Thus for Doctor Rush — Not keeping copies of my letters, I really forget what sketches of this City, I have given you — The plan of Philadelphia is not yet completed, although its magnitude, beauty, and regularity is astonishing, Doctor Kearsley, hath endowed a hospital for ancient Women of decayed fortunes, where they are received, accommodated, and supported, according to their several exigencies — upon the same line is erected a house of employment, and a hospital, upon a larger scale — Building which do honour to the genius, and humanity of the Philadelphians — The hospital we have yet to see, but we passed yesterday afternoon at the house of employment — It is a nobly liberal, and benign establishment — It is a well regulated community, and may be called the City of Refuge — The asylum of distress — The structure is lofty, and spacious — It is divided into two wings — upon the right wing, under the care of a Matron, are the female wards — upon the left are those of the Males and the whole is under the superintendence of a gentleman who, with his family, resides at the house — This manager is indeed a gentleman — his only daughter is the Wife of Doctor Dunlap, one of the principal Physicians in this City, from whom, and from his amicable Lady, I have received more than civility — gratitude hath inscribed their names upon the brightest page of Memory. Mr Cummings, the Manager, is a Man of taste — quite a Vitriol, and his collection of curiosities, is respectable — We were entertained with a view of the gold, and silver fish, in their varieties — With birds of numerous kinds, among which are the Barbary Dove, the Carolina indigo bird, and a pigeon, which if not as famous as the pigeon of Massachusetts, possesseth the art of communicating intelligence, altogether as well — Mr Cummings hath a method of apparently imersing his birds in a little Ocean, where they seem to feed, hop, or fly, much at their ease, while all around the gold, and silver fish divine, in various directions, their watery way — The description is perfect, nor can we fathom it, except it be explained — It is produced by a double glass globe, and its effect is fine — Mr Cummings exhibits the Guinea hen, Guinea Pig, Peacock etc etc [—] His collection of plants, flowers and shrubs is extreme, and beautiful, they are arranged with great order, and taste, and he hath the largest, and best regulated kitchen garden, I have ever seen — we were handsomely regaled with strawberries of the richest kind — prodigious fine cherries, fresh raisons, and almonds, and the evening presented tea, coffe[e], bread and butter, cakes etc etc —

But you will ask, are the destitute persons under this gentleman's care, thus deliciously fed, and if not, what is all this to the purpose? Certainly, it would not be good policy, to render the abodes destined, as the dernier resort of poverty, too alluring, as the fascinating prospect might then slacken the sinners of industry — But a Man who unites humanity, with elegant taste, and manners, who is fond of regulating his ideas, and his actions by the beauty of order, will, as I believe, discharge with uniform consistency every duty — This benign institution owes its birth to voluntary subscriptions, but it is now supported by a public tax — Distress is a sufficient recommendation to the house of employment, and every effort is made to improve the Vagrant — Five hundred persons are relieved at one time, and in the different wards, the greatest order, and cleanliness is preserved — If the individual is able, he, or she, must perform an allotted task. Every thing worn by these Out casts of fortune with their beds, bedding, table linen etc being manufactured within their walls — But for the sick exigencies, is generally made — We passed into their kitchen, and dining room, which

were both highly descriptive of the excellency of the establishment —
Their meals are good and regularly served — eight persons set down at
a table — They have their Chapel [where] they [daily] assemble for
devotional exercises — In short, perhaps the World cannot produce a
better ordered, or more liberally endowed plan, for the relief of the
wretched, than is exhibited, in the Alms house of Philadelphia — yet,
from a view of these sons and daughters of adversity, my very soul
recoiled. Imagination traced in their woe begone countenances, the
series of misfortunes, which had conducted them to this last resort of
the miserable — Here the meagre form, with sharp and piercing [eyes]
then glided by — there forlorn, and trembling age, tottered along —
Here a group of little wretches, who seemed the offspring of disease,
and misery, hung upon the homely garments of their abashed Mother,
and there, discontent sat triumphant, in the faces of those, whose youth,
and firm health, seemed to entitle them to a more reputable, and
independent life — a few of those sons, and daughters, of misfortune
passed me with an indifference, which seemed the result of apathy, others
appeared to aim at a kind of superiority — Indignant and lowered upon
the brow of some — grief was pourtrayed upon the faces of others, and,
from the gaze if inquiring modesty assayed to retire — and, said my
whispering Monitor — These are haunts which idle curiosity possesseth
no right to penetrate — If spectators cannot mitigate their misery, they
but do implant a fresh, and perhaps the most barbed arrow, in the bosom
already but too often, and too deeply wounded — I heard the guardian
Angel — I stood corrected, and I hastened from the apartments of
Adversity — We have visited Schuylkill gardens, and we have drank
the Harrongate waters, and we have been every where highly gratified
— With good Mr Jay, I have passed a happy afternoon — from his own
lips I received an account of his transition to the World of spirits, and,
from corroboratin[g] circumstances, I cannot doubt its authenticity, its
supernatural, and celestial verity. Expect a continuation in my next
letter — and believe me ever dutifully, and affectionately yours —

P.S. If I except two or three days, which have indeed been extremely
hot, the weather hath been mildly temperate — Please to furnish me
with the earliest possible intelligence of the arrival of Fitz William, and
let me know what you learn of my eldest Brother —

Letter 758 to Miss S.S.E. Philadelphia Arch Street
June 21— 1790

*Judith wrote Letter 758 to her 13-year-old niece, Sarah Sargent Ellery,
her sister Esther's daughter. It is typical of many Judith wrote to her*

*young relatives, taking an active and loving interest in their moral
upbringing and education. In this letter, she tells Sally how much she
loves her, and gives her advice on how a young lady in her position
should behave — with quiet dignity and virtue. She tells her "real
worth" is what makes a person of value, not his last name. She wants
Sally to appreciate the good fortune she has in her family and her
education, and not to look down on those less fortunate. Finally,
Judith cautions her about prejudice. She wants Sally to form her own
opinions. She counsels her to "give ear to simple truth only," and
make up her own mind.*

With much pleasure, I set me down to pen this, my first Epistle,
to my sweet young friend — under what pleasing auspices does my dearest
Girl communicate the Career of life — Heaven grant that no portentous
cloud with baleful aspect may ever obscure the scene — So completely
are you guarded, so benignly sheltered, so loved, so cherished, and so
taught, that any one not immediately employed about you, may be judged
improperly arrogating, who officiously attempts to obtrude the finger of
direction, or the lesson of caution — yet, influenced by that charming
sensibility, which so often trembles in your eye, you will receive the
effusions of tenderness, with modest pleasure, and a pleasing kind of
satisfaction, will, I persuade myself, play about your heart — The Writer
of this letter, confidently believes, that she shall always take rank among
the first of your friends — she is the only surviving sister of your Mother
— We obtained existence from the same venerable source, upon the
same virtuous bosom we were soothed, supported, and lulled to repose
— "In infancy our hopes, and fears were one," and under the same benign
shade we together grew — I am conscious, that I experience for you, my
dear, a very strong affection, and in preferring my claim to answering
regards, I plead the rights of nature — while my strong wishes for a
place in your youthful bosom, are excited by your sweet, and amiable
disposition, by your endearing manners, and uniform docility — These
have meliorated the common feelings of affinity, into a binding and
improving attachment — an attachment which I have been ready to
think as it originates in a higher source, resting only upon real merit as
it partakes less of individuality, and is more abstracted from selfish
considerations, than the feelings consequent upon lies of consanguinity,
as it is, I say more of soul, and less of body, I have been induced to
suppose it superior to the claims of kindred blood, It is, however most
happy, when natural affection combines esteem, and when we can boast
that our own family, presents objects, best entitled, from their intrinsic
worth, to our most distinguishing approbation — I persuade myself, my
Love, Nature having cast your mind in the softest mould, that the
complacent smiles of your observing friends will always attend your steps

— I know that humanity is subject to error, and that the wisdom, and caution of experience, is requisite for the youthful Voyager — but you will never intentionally offend, and the task of directing your way will be easy — attended up the eventual sleep, by a tender, indulgent, and judicious Mother — sheltered by the paternal wing, privileged by a view of the animating countenance of delighted, and admiring Grand Parents — already considerably cultivated, and improved, auxiliary aid must, I repeat, be deemed superfluous — yet, stimulated by my feelings, and in some measure authorized, by the kindred glow which swells at my heart, I shall, presuming as I am, reserve to my self the liberty occasionally to applaud, caution or direct — I know that a solicitude to please will always be a conspicuous trait in your character, but you must take care that this same solicitude, never betrays you into undue concession — Many a young Creature, whose elegant, and improved Mind, hath been the seat of candour, hath been induced by that mild disposition, which would not allow her to utter a contradiction, to join with the declaimer, probably in blasting the reputation of a friend, or, at least, loaning her sanction to a slanderer — It is true, that at your time of life, silence is generally the most becoming — Yet, my dear, you may give a language even to silence, and there are times, when, should you not firmly, and audibly oppose, you would not only be censurable, but even criminal — To malice, and malevolence, I would never even tacitly assent — The barbarous traducer should never be honoured with my smile, and it will always be in your power, to evince a proper resentment, by quitting a party, engaged in murdering the fame of a fellow creature — I will, my dear, take leave to caution you, against Prejudice, at your age, Prejudice easily usurps dominion in the unsuspecting bosom, and when once it seizes the crown of approbation, it erects itself into a Despot, and we are ready to believe, every idea, which would make head against its imperious sway, in actual rebellion — Prejudice is too frequently the bane of social life, it is often a bar to investigation, and consequent improvement, and it excludes from our esteem, and confidence, the very persons, from whom probably we might derive the greatest advantage — There is, my sweet Girl, one sentiment, which I would indelibly inscribe upon the tablets of your heart, it should form the basis of all your plans, it should mingle with every idea, swell, and fashion every thought, and stand prominent in every arrangement — Virtue, in all its varieties, I will approve — Vice whatever its modification, I will eternally detest — It is true, if a good action be performed by any one, to whom I am particularly attached, I shall, of course, experience superior pleasure [—] But if rectitude brightens the character of those, whom I myself, or my parents, have deemed unworthy I will not, however, with hold my esteem — An individual, a family, may for a time appear cloathed in the garb of distance, and reserve, Perhaps misrepresentations have been afloat — real facts may have received false Hopes, and circumstances may have strangely conspired, to create unpleasant ideas — Well, what is the consequence — Prejudice, armed [beast], steps in — it infixeth its envenomed fangs, and it is ten to one but the hydra Monster may extend his malign influence, to generations yet unborn — Now, what I wish for my beloved Niece, is that her opening mind, which I know is by nature innocent, ingenuous, and good, should, as much as possible, be continued unadulterated — Of family distinction an American should not boast — real worth is at present, the only Coronet, which can encircle the brow of a Columbian — Learning is indeed a gem, but we are not to ridicule those, who being denied opportunities of improvement, of acquiring knowledge in early life, appear in the rough state of Nature, without that polish, which judicious lapidary might have bestowed — Prejudice, in such instances should never be tolerated — Hath a series of disobligation, for a length of time, succeeded — how difficult to bar the encroachments of prejudice — I tremble for my Girl, yet I would assay to guard her bosom, against the inroads of the fiend and while I left her open to conviction, to equitable decision, I would exclude all undue warmth, leaving her an unbiased judgment, at liberty to make her own election — What of ill offices have been done — What of actual offence hath been given, and Envy or misapprehension, have, for a time been triumphant — yet the present is a changeful scene — we are rapidly passing on, the minds of Men and Women are fluctuating, Enmity may be exchanged for cool indifference, and indifference may be converted into friendship, and attachment — Well, would it not be in the highest degree absurd, to refuse the proffered good, because previous evil had heretofore been manifestly prevalent? My whole view in this tedious, as you may possibly deem it harangue, is to suggest to you the propriety of giving ear to simple truth only, of preserving your reason, unclouded by a Prejudice or delaying to make up your mind, and of possessing yourself of that kind of plausibility, which, to those who would pursue the walks of rectitude, the mutability of human Nature, hath rendered absolutely requisite — Implacability is the offspring of Prejudice — but a female possesseth one advantage, gentleness is ornamental to her character, and there are few offences, which she ought not to forgive — To acquire friends is a very capital object — Arduous however is the pursuit — Yet a friend, is a kind of Phenix, sometimes raised by the luminous action of Reason, from the ashes of an enemy — But to add unnecessary — your beloved Mother is your instructress, and she is fully adequate to a task so pleasurable — your Mother my dear is your proper Advisor, Protectress, and, allow me to say, your only proper confidant — yet I trust you will always know as your maternal Aunt, your affectionate and sincere friend etc etc

Letter 759 to Madam Walker Philadelphia Arch Street
June 21st. 1790

Judith apologizes to her cousin for not having written sooner. She explains that her social obligations keep her busy, and that she hopes to visit her on their return trip to Boston when she will be "Mistress of [herself]." She shares her thoughts about the passage of time, and about life "this side of mortality."

Could I, my dear Madam, address you as often, as imagination presents you, the accusation of negligence would never rest upon me — nor would you be furnished with reason for complaining of my silence — But, continually changing the scene, and reduced to the necessity of yielding as large a proportion of my time to strangers, whose obliging [entrea]ties entitle them to my grateful attention, indeed, whose magnificent marks of regard, at most give them rank, in the venerable Circle of old, and approved friends — Thus circumstanced, I say, and necessitated to furnish for my parents, a succinct account of my movements, I confess I have hardly a moment at my command — Yet, I cannot be denied the privilege of presenting my self before you, as a Candidate for your continued esteem, and of assuring you, that you have not distinguished a person, whose heart can be ungratefully forgetful — I had intended calling upon you previous to leaving Boston, but I was extremely embarrassed by my momentary abode in that place, and by the many claims produced upon me there — your experience, my dear Madam, will I doubt not in form you, that we may be so seduced as to render it impossible, or improper to obtain what we may, however, very sincerely wish the best [—] human beings are too often subject to prejudices — These prejudices, it may sometimes be incumbent upon us to venerate; at least to obey, and if we are rendered unhappy by a caprice, which we cannot subdue — Discretion will teach us, to veil thereto, or at all events, it will inculcate submission — When, however, I return to our Metropolis, I may have more leisure, and be more Mistress of myself, and, in the interim I am persuaded it will be pleasing to you, to learn that our journey has been pleasant, that we have in many instances been highly gratified, and that I enjoy as much health of body, and mind, as I expect will fall to my share, this side immortality — I trust the serene prospects which seemed opening to you, when I had the pleasure of visiting you in your little apartment, are continued, and that you will enjoy, with the good matrons with whom you reside, a peaceful retreat — Tenants of a moment, Reason would teach us, not to be over solicitous, respecting our accommodations if we can enlist the tranquility it will give to surrounding objects an air of cheerfulness, and we shall perhaps enjoy as much, as was designed for mortality   So various are the dispositions, and inclinations, which actuate the Denizon of time, that we have need of much complacence, great pliability, and an equal quantum, of what may be termed condescension, if we would preserve, during our peregrination, tolerable serenity — But what am I doing — sententiously remarking, to a Lady, whose various opportunities, and observations, must have furnished her with every idea, which, upon such a subject, can possibly occur — Blushing at my temerity, I resign the officious pen, and only take leave to add, that I am, with due affection, and respect, yours etc etc

Letter 760— To Mrs E.S. Philadelphia Arch Street June 22d. 1790

This letter is written to Dorcas Babson Sargent (1749-1836), the wife of Judith's first cousin, Epes Sargent (1748-1822). Judith was very close to this family and their numerous children, particularly to Epes who she called her "brother of affection." Years later, when the Epes Sargents moved from Gloucester to Hampstead, New Hampshire, Judith was a regular visitor and correspondent with Epes and his children and they, in turn, visited their "Aunt Murray" in Boston.

Given Dorcas Sargent's interest in raising children, Judith paints for her a richly detailed account of the Bethlehem Academy. Run by a community of Moravians, the Academy (which still exists) was open primarily to girls, from ages 7 to 14. Boys could attend up to age 7, when they were sent to the neighboring Nazareth Academy. Judith describes the Bethlehem Academy's grounds, buildings, and the marvel of indoor plumbing. She enumerates the many trades practiced onsite, their weaving and embroidery, the inn and shop — with all of which she was "beyond expression charmed." She explains the daily routine of the community and the students, including religious exercises, meals, and clothing. She lists what was included in the curriculum, reporting that if she had a daughter she would not hesitate to send her to Bethlehem. (In fact, years later, when Judith faced the decision about where to educate her daughter, Julia Maria, Judith kept her in Boston where she could watch over her frail health.) Finally, Judith describes the burial practices of the Moravians, a subject that was always of interest to her.

Having, from the melancholy period, which deprived us of our maternal friend, been distinguished by you, my dear Mrs Sargent, with obliging and [tender] sisterly regard, you very naturally supply, in some measure, the void, which her demise had left in my heart — That I love you very sincerely, and that I esteem and respect the propriety, and discretion of your character you will never, I flatter myself, doubt — The beautiful little group who gather round you, possess my very best wishes, and Mr Sargent is the brother of my affection — My feelings thus impelled, you will, I pleasingly believe, permit, and indulge their effusions — for during so long an absence, I cannot deny myself the pleasure of making my appearance by letter, in a family, of whose domestic enjoyments, I have so often sat an admiring spectator — Various are the scenes which have been presented, and many worthy persons we have seen, yet, however novel, or pleasant the succession of ideas, they have not been able to obliterate the sweet remembrances of home felt good — I have this morning been endeavouring to summons before me, the several events of our journey, for the purpose of selecting for you, something which may be calculated for your amusement, and as you are so usefully engaged, in forming the opening mind, I think I cannot do better, than to make for you a little sketch of our Bethlehem tour — We were drawn thither, by the fame of that Seminary, and high as our expectations were raised, we are obliged to acknowledge them far surpassed — Bethlehem is in the State of Pennsylvania, situated fifty four miles North of Philadelphia — It is a beautiful Village, which may, without the smallest enthusiasm, be pronounced a terrestrial Paradise — It is true, we do not wander through Orange, and through Citron Groves, but nature hath shaped the most enchanting walks, embowering shades, meadows, hills, and dales greet the eye, with most refreshing Variety — Parallel rivers pursue their glassy course — the margins of which are planted by the most flourishing and highly perfumed locusts, Cedars, Chestnuts and a variety of trees bearing in their season, the most delicious fruit — Now the fertilizing stream murmurs along, in a direct line now indented, or projecting, its Borders still ornamented by the richest foliage, its diversified meanderings exhibit the most pleasing, and romantic views — Upon an eminence in Bethlehem, the cultivated scene opens before us — a chain of verdant hills encircle it, and this little Eden, is embosomed in the midst — The Town, with a very few exceptions is built with stone, and the dwellings are generally planned upon a large scale — The house of the Brethren, that of the Sisterhood, the Asylum for widows, and the Seminary for young Ladies, are uncommonly elevated and capacious, and there is an air of dignified simplicity remarkably exemplified, through the several structures — The greatest Order, and unanimity, is preserved in Bethlehem, even their water works are characteristic — the inhabitants are supplied from one spring, a cistern conveys it to their kitchens, by the aid of a pump, worked by a water Machine, the cedar pipes receive it, and the ready spout issues at pleasure, the purifying stream in every dwelling — The Town was originally founded by Germans — Many natives of Europe now reside there, and they preserve their ancient customs with much exactness — A great variety of Arts, and manufactures, are carried to high perfection in Bethlehem, among which is the business of the Tanner, Clothier, stocker[,] Weaver, Tin Works, Blacksmith, Gold and silver smith, saw and sythe Maker, Wheel Wright, and Chaise and harness maker — Grist Mills are fashioned upon the best plan, and they have a Brewery after the English model, Printing, and book binding are said to be finished in the neatest manner — in short they exhibit, and encourage, all the common Crafts — Their Religion seems to be a system of Benevolence — its foundation is true Philanthropy, upon which broad base, is erected the super structure of Philanthropy — I admire, beyond expression, the regularity conspicuous in every department, and the Virgin Choir derive all the advantages, which the Cloistered Maiden can boast, without connecting her restraints — I inquired of one of the sisters, if it were in her power to quit her engagements — Our doors, Madam, replied the charming Recluse, are always open — but once relinquishing this retreat, a reentrance is very difficult — The Circle of Amiable Women dwell together in perfect Amity, every one cultivating and exercising her different talent, the profits arriving there from, constituting a <u>common fund</u> — Never did I see all kinds of needle work carried to higher perfection — every flower produced by prolific Nature, is exactly imitated, as to render it only not impossible to designate them — I never saw them surpassed, by any imported from Europe, and with the beauty, richness, and exquisite shading of their embroidery I was highly pleased — as we pass through the apartments, the tambour embroidery, flowers, etc etc are displayed for sale — I requested that their Value was beyond my reach — Neither is the Loom, or the distaff neglected — Cloths of a superior kind are manufactured in Bethlehem — and we were shown the art of spinning, without a wheel! — The sisterhood consists, at this time, of about one hundred Maidens, who after a night of such slumbers, as health, and innocence bestow, assemble in an elegant apartment which is a consecrated Chapel — This apartment is properly fixed up, it is furnished with an Organ, and Musick books, and upon the right, and the left, the following inscriptions, in beautiful capitals meet the eye. "God hath appointed us to obtain salvation, by our Lord Jesus Christ, who died for us, that whether we wake, or sleep, we should live together with Him. I will greatly rejoice in the Lord; my soul shall be joyful in my God, for He hath cloathed me with the garments of salvation, He hath covered me with the robe of righteousness" [—] In this Chapel the female Choir, at early dawn, and at closing evening, hymn the praises of the Redeeming God, and prostrating themselves in His presence, the most venerable individual among them, presents their united petitions, and thanksgivings, at the throne of Grace. At one board they are every day seated, and persons selected for the purpose, prepare their table. The

Wash house is at a considerable distance, where the apparel of the sisterhood, the Tutoress, and their pupils, is made fit for use, and in the best possible manner. The establishment of the brethren is of a similar kind, and a like institution in favour of widowed Matrons is admirably completed — They seem to have rectified all that was wrong in their system — Their Males and females, under the chaste auspices of the Marriage covenant, may now form for themselves this civil compact — It is true they must gait their respective refinements, but choosing a spot in Bethlehem, they may commence house keepers, continuing, if they please, their intercourse with, and attachment too their former Associates — This privilege is denied to any, but a Moravian — for although you may sojourn for a time in Bethlehem, yet if of any other persuasion, you cannot become a Free holder in that Place — Married people are not, as heretofore, separated [—] They live together much in the manner of the rest of the world, nor are they, as I observed, arbitrarily united, by the whim, or caprice of the brethren — Only one Inn is allowed in Bethlehem — but this is upon an extensive plain [—] Travellers are supplied with every article which the season will afford, and that in as fine order, as at a first rate table — Eighteen double beds are furnished and the emoluments accruing, augment the common stock [—] But it is a Seminary of Virtue, and every excellent quality of the heart, to which almost every embellishment is added, that these Elysium fields, will chiefly interest an enlightened, and judicious public [—] Place your daughter at Bethlehem, and, for a very moderate consideration, she will be taught a perfect knowledge of her Mother Tongue — she will be taught the French, and German languages, with the utmost elegance, and propriety — Reading, Writing, Composition, and Arithmetic, will be given her, in as high perfection, as she is capable of attaining them — She is furnished with an opportunity of acquiring Musick, painting, and geography, with the rudiments of Astronomy, and the strictest attention will be paid to her health, and to the purity of her morals — It is, however, in your option, to omit, for your Girl, any of these branches of study — It is scarcely necessary to subjoin, that needle work, in all its varieties, is taught in Bethlehem — An early habit of Order and regularity, without which I sincerely believe, no one important object was ever yet obtained — will also be secured — The pretty Candidate for excellence, is summoned by a bell from her pillow — she must rise at a certain hour, wash and comb, and, neatly apparelled she must attend prayrs — Breakfast succeeds, after which the several employments and amusements of the day take place — By the way, these morning and evening prayrs are playing on their guitars, which they join with their voices, chanting some divine Poem to the praise of the Saviour of sinners — These devotional exercises are performed in a little consecrated chapel, which makes a part of the school building, and into which no male ever enters. Six O clock is the hour of rising, and eight, of retiring to rest — A lamp continues burning throughout the night, and the students are often lulled to sleep, by the soft sounds of vocal, and instrumental Musick — The school is divided into a number of apartments, each apartment, to its dimensions, contains a smaller, or larger number of Ladies, Every division hath its particular intendant, or tutoress, and over all there is a Superior [—] The Lodging Room is on a separate story, in a lofty situation, and accommodated with a ventilator — The Culinary apartment is under the ground floor, and the diet is wholesome and sufficiently varied — Twice in the course of a year, they pass a public examination at which the Reverend teacher of the Bethlehem society presides, and every sunday collects the whole Congregation [—] Men, Women, and children, in the great, or common Chapel, which exhibits some very affecting selections from scriptures — Performances upon a very fine Organ, accompanied by a Violin, and bass viol, constitute a very delightful part of public Worship in Bethlehem — Singing you know is among the essential Rites of the Moravian Religion, and their music is next to divine — Church service is performed alternately in English, and German, and its matter is rational, and instructive — The young ladies are much accustomed to walking, and Bethlehem abounds with delightfully Romantic promenades — Every fine evening, guarded by one or other of the Governantees, without whom they never make an excursion, they pursue the pleasingly salutary exercise — Regular stages from Elizabeth Town, Lancaster, and Philadelphia, to this Seminary, have recently been appointed — This produces the children who have friends in the Towns from which the stages set out, or in, those through which they pass, upon a post evening, in the great road — We were so fortunate as to accompany the stage to Bethlehem [—] a happy concurrence of events, brought us acquainted with its passengers, who were three Ladies going thither for the purpose of taking home their daughters — but the Girls were strangers to their design, Two miles from the town, we met the smiling train — It was indeed the most lovely group, my eyes had ever beheld — a very large proportion of the school were drawn out — The hope of bundles, letters, or messages from their friends, had winged their steps — The Girls, whose parents the Carriage contained approached — for a complete year they had not seen them — They caught a glimpse — they looked again, with charming rapture they clasped their hands — O! my Mamma, my Mamma, the gushing tear finished the exclamation, and they stood enwrapped in all the extacy of innocent, affectionate, and joyful surprise — yet, mingling regrets soon balanced the bliss of the moment, and they could not, without perturbed emotions, behold the approach of that [day] on which they must quit a society, where dwelleth chastened indulgence, serenity, and love. A Lady belonging to New York, had placed her only daughter in this Seminary, for her education — after an absence of twelve months she visited her — Stopping at the Inn, she sent for her child [—] But impatient to embrace her, she set out to shorten the return of her Messenger — The child appeared, but the growth she had obtained, and the alteration of her head dress, prevented her Mother from distinguishing her, until the pretty creature taking her hand, pressed it with soft, and duteous affection to her lips — The Lady, bursting into tears, would then with impassioned emotion, have clasped her to her bosom — but so exactly regulated were the feelings of the sweet Cherub, that with direct and correct affection she requested — "Be composed my Mother, consider we are in the street, and let me attend you to the Inn, which is just in view["] — Upon reaching the house, the Lady observed — My Dear there are schools in York — In consenting to this separation, great is the sacrifice made by your Father, and myself — Consider, you are our only child, and if your improvements be not far beyond those which you can make in your nature City, we enjoin it upon you to return [—] O! My Mamma, replied the young sentamentalist, excuse your daughter — do not, I pray you, think of such a step, but let us rather be grateful to that providence, which hath appointed for your Helena an Asylum, where she can receive every information, and at the same time be shielded from every Vice — Coercive manners are unknown in the school, and hence it is articled, that if a child prove of an uncommonly refractory disposition, she shall be returned to her Parents — I asked a student if they had any punishments, and of what Nature? — and she informed me, that advice, and gentle remonstrance, generally answered every purpose, and if these should prove ineffectual, the name of the incorrigible, with the Nature of her offence, would be recorded — but that in the annals of the Bethlehem school, only one solitary instance of such an event, had hitherto occured. — Recommended by the superior, and introduced by the above mentioned ladies, we had an opportunity of making many observations — We passed through the several divisions of the school, we examined the tambour, and embroidery, executed by the children never did I see any thing in that line to equal it — We attended to their painting and composition — upon these subjects it would be arrogant in me to decide — but I was beyond expression charmed — We listened with solemn pleasure, as they played and sang in Concert —

"Peace on earth, good will to Men,
Now with us our God is seen,
Glory be to God above
Who is infinite in love."

Do you not think the tears gushed in the eyes of our Murray — Do you not believe that my heart swelled with transport? Every thing was admirable — But, I must repeat, the exact order and punctuality, to which the students are accustomed, will probably be the coevals of and produce upon their future lives, the finest effect — Not satisfied with designating three hours, their clock striking even the quarters, regulates, with wonderful precision, every movement — Hither to I have thought, had heaven blessed me with a daughter, from my own guardian care, I would never surrender her — but I am now free to own, it would be the height of my ambition to place her, at the age of seven years, at Bethlehem, and to continue her there, until she was fourteen — It is amazing what erronious conceptions are formed of this Seminary — Even at New York, I heard the Gentleman, and the Man of letters, exclaim — "What, immure your Girl with in the Cloistered walls of Bethlehem? Surely then you do not intend her for society["] — yet, it is true, that there is no undue confinement, nor restraint — Even the sisterhood make frequent excursions to the adjacent Villages — I have heard much of the awkwardness, and the [immature] heart of the Bethlehem scholar, but I could not trace it in a single instance, and there absolutely is, in their manners an elegant care, and simplicity, which is enchantingly prepossessing — Indeed, dwelling there together, they are constantly accustomed to society, and, it is a fact, that Bethlehem is the resort of the genteelest strangers — It is true dancing is not taught in Bethlehem — but if it be taught proper dancing may be a subsequent acquirement, and a young Lady, designed for the great World, may be very soon initiated into its customs — Mean time, at Bethlehem, she [acquires in her] early days, a good foundation — she will imbibe the chastest system of morals, with a fund of benevolence[,] her mind will be stored, and she will receive almost every embellishment

An exact uniformity in dress is not required — It is a request made to parents, and guardians, that all excess may be avoided, and they are fond of seeing the children in white — The Cap, however, is, if I may be allowed the expression, an insignia of their order — all the young Ladies put it on — it is made of Cambrick, received a narrow border of Lawn, sets close to the head, and is fastened under the chin, with a pink ribbon — It is of pure white, indeed all the Bethlehem linen is uncommonly white, and although, upon a cursory view, we are induced to think, this same cap could only suit a handsome face — yet, however they manage it, I protest there was not one of the Girls, to whom it did not seem to add a charm — The fashion of the cap worn by the inhabitants, and which, for more than a Century, the Moravian Women have not changed, sets also close to the head but it is a different pattern, and not near so becoming — It is however assumed by every female, of every description — Maids, Wives, and Widows, and, by way of distinction it is fastened by the Maidens, with a red, or pink ribbon by Wives with a blue, and by widows with a white, and this knot of ribbon, is the only ornament worn by a Bethlamite female — I inquired if they did not wear black upon the demise of a friend — No, replied an old Lady, in whose composition the milk of human kindness seemed the prevalent ingredient — we judge the deceased are happy, so we do not put on black — In the Moravian manner of intering their dead, as observed in Bethlehem, and the ceremonies attendant therein, there is something, to me, singularly pleasing — So soon as the spirit is departed from whatever chair or whatever part of the Town — the body is cloathed in white linen, and if a female, the Cap received the Ribbon which designates the order — and the corse is borne to a small, neat chapel [designed] for this purpose, where it is deposited upon stands until the hour of interment — One of the brethren ascends the highest Edifice, which commands the whole Village, and proclaims the death, by means of a German Instrument of Musick, the name of which I could not learn, and he hath a method of conveying this intelligence, which ascertains the sex, age, and connexion of the deceased. When the hour of burial approaches, the brethren, the sisterhood, and the children of every description, are by a number of french horns, summoned to attend divine service, in the great chapel, where an exhortation is delivered, and the singing, and instrumental musick, produces a proper, and solemnizing effect — The Body is then borne from the chapel, and placed upon a stand on a beautiful green — the males ranging themselves on one side, and the females on the other — The Body is covered with a snow white Pall, which is ornamented with red, blue, or white ribbon, according to the station of the defunct — upon this Green, a divine anthem is performed, when the deceased is borne to the sepulchrs, instruments of music, resounding, the whole Village, ranging themselves in decent, and beautiful Order, join in the procession — at one of these funerals we attended and we entered the burial ground with a raised, chastized, and solemn kind of satisfaction — Religious exercises were performed at the grave, which being in German, we could not understand, when a sacred concert of vocal and instrumental music again resounding was continued during the interment, and until the Assembly had quitted the Grave yard. There is a regularity peculiarly pleasing, even in the burial ground at Bethlehem — It is a spacious level plain, decently walled in, exactly divided, and, on one side, are placed the Males, and on the other the females — The Graves are laid out upon a straight line, and we can walk between every one, with as much ease, as we could pursue our way along the gravel Walks of a parterre — The Gray stone is not raised, as with us, but from a modest tablet, which is generally shaded by the verdant grass, and which bears a concise inscription, we receive the necessary information. Thus, these Denizens of tranquility live — and thus their passage out of time is marked. But to return from a digression, which I assure myself will not displace — I have further to say, that I was much charmed by the Governantees of the Bethlehem seminary, there is a decent propriety in their manners, which I have rarely seen equalled — Their very gestures are particularly expressive — The French Preceptress cannot command a word of English, yet there was in her every movement, a kind of language — There is something romantic in her history; of an ancient, and noble Family in France, she made one in the suite of the Princess Louisa, and her education was consequently of the highest kind — Influenced by the example of her royal Mistress she took the veil — and continued, during twelve years, an acquiescing sister — But possessing a superior Mind, and being a Woman of information, reflection originated doubts — She had been invested with some dignities in the Cloister, and she questioned those whom she supposed capable of instructing her but her difficulties rather augmented — until at length, after encountering a series of misfortunes, she escaped, and relinquishing her family, and religious name, she took that of a rivulet over which she passed, which was Fontaine, and finding means to transport herself to Holland, the transition to Germany was easy — In Germany, embracing the Moravian faith, she received an account of the Bethlehem society, when obtaining strong recommendations to the Brethren, she crossed the Atlantic and was received by them, as a valuable acquisition to the school, of which she now constitutes a principal ornament — By such a character, thus qualified, you will conclude the french language is taught with the utmost purity, and elegance — This Lady hath resided nearly two years in Bethlehem.

Boys are continued in Bethlehem, until they are seven years of age, when they are transplanted to Nazareth, a Village about ten miles distant, for the completion of their Education. In Nazareth the students — "Bless me," exclaims your husband — "What an Eternal scribbler is this Cousin of ours! Will the Woman never have done? Heavens shield us from her lognacity" — Cry your mercy, dear Sir, the regulations of Nazareth — especially as I was not there, I will leave you to conjecture, and I will intrude no longer, than to assure my dear Mrs Sargent, that I am very sincerely and affectionately her admiring Friend —

Letter 761 To Mrs Powell— Philadelphia Arch Street June 23d— 1790

Catherine Powell was apparently an admirer of "natural curiosities" and here Judith obliges. In this letter, she relates her visit with Peter Pond of Milford, Connecticut who told them stories about his lengthy journeys out west and to Canada. He traded with the "Aborigenes," saw unusual animals, fossils, skeletons, salt springs, and shells at the Pacific Ocean. He brought back with him many examples of these natural curiosities, and gave Judith and John some shells and a vial of salt to take home.

I am free to own, that I should regard an opportunity of contributing to the pleasures of my dear Mrs Powell, as a very fortunate circumstance, but so excellent hath been her life, as to render it improbable, that the common occurrences of a journey, can possess for her, that novelty, which might render them pleasing. Nature, however various, is in some sense the same — She generously furnishes her Landscapes with hills, and Vallies, fields and meadows — Mountains, and extensive plains. From her fertile bosom, thick forests arise — Groves Variegate the mead, and flowers gaily bloom [—] Rivers almost every where meander, and the spring always restores, and beautifies — Very tender must be the interest which we take in the Narrator, if from a detail originating in objects so familiar, we can derive any considerable degree of satisfaction, and perhaps the journalist, while self amused too often fatigues the reader — you are however, as I believe, an admirer of Natural curiosities, and, if so, I flatter myself that I am furnished with a little relation which may lay claim to momentary attention [—] Mr Murray hath not often pursued the Western Route to Philadelphia — his several friends having their residence in various parts of the Country, hath necessitated a circuitous progress. But, under obligation to reach the City, upon an appointed day, and intending upon his return, to proceed in his accustomed manner, he took the way, in his judgment most conducive to dispatch — A road, however frequented, must to a stranger, be in some sort solitary, at least it presents but few social enjoyments, and to obviate in some measure the inconvenience a friend offered us a letter of introduction, to Peter Pond Esquire of Milford; a kind of grateful decency, necessitated our acceptance, although, it must be confessed, from the same Mr Peter Pond, we did not expect much — yet we delivered our recommendatory introduction, and being ushered into a commodious apartment, we were not agreeably disappointed. The countenance of Mr Pond is expressive of penetration, and intelligence — his features, every line of his face, seem marked by information — But if this were all, he had not had the honour of being introduced to Mrs Powell, for she is not, at this period to be told, that Nature although embellished by art, is not, however, negligent of those traits, which serve as an index to a character.

Mr Pond himself, his age, and education considered, may perhaps not improperly be considered as a curiosity. He is a native of Milford in Connecticut, and after being sixteen years absent from his Wife, and family, during which period, they remained wholly ignorant of his fate, he hath returned, in every respect enriched, and improved, to set down with an easy competency for life — he hath travelled no less than fourteen hundred leagues, into the interior of the Country, beyond Canada which led him to the Borders of the pacific Ocean, and to the very edges of the river, the courses of which he pursued five hundred miles, where the justly celebrated Cook sailed, in the progress of his discoveries —

Mr Pond maintained a lucrative trade with the Aborigines, and he penetrated so far, as to receive the almost incredible price of twenty dollars, or rather their value, for one pint of New England Rum! His observations upon the savages, are circumstantial, and interesting, and if attended too, might probably throw some lights upon their origin — His opportunities, and means of information have been considerable, and, arguing from analogy, similarly, and in some instances perfect likeness, he forms conjectures truly rational — Various parts of the Country which he penetrated, abounded in quadrupedes, among which were the Reindeer, not commonly found in America, the horse and Buffalow, apparently of a different kind from those of the Western Territory. Our adventurer passed over an extensive tract of land, the soil of which consisted of a glutinous kind of Mare, or Bilumen, which possessed, in a high degree, the power of petrefaction — It was almost in a state of liquifaction, adhering to the feet of the Passenger — Its hue is a jetty black, and he brought with him a phial of it, which he submitted to our inspection — This Globe abounded with a variety of petrefactions, among which were many kind of shellfish, and fossils, with bones of animals, which we have been induced to believe inhabit only the deep, and, as this mould is found full five hundred leagues from any Ocean, the question is how came they deposited there? Mr Pond collected a number of Curiosities which he hath generously distributed, the Literati claiming the preference — yet, of a part of those which he returned, he was polite enough to make us a compliment. Mr Pond passed a number of salt springs, which continually throw from their bosoms, a mineral salt, which forms and covers, the surface of the earth, to a considerable depth, for an extent of thirty square miles yielding an abundance of salt, sufficient to load ships of the longest burden, and almost any number — Of this salt he furnished himself with a portion — tasted and found its flavour peculiarly agreeable — quite aromatic — and equal in whiteness to common salt — A share of this Curiosity we also obtained, which with our shells, etc etc we shall upon our return, take great pleasure in exhibiting — Then we passed, with Mr Pond, an hour of pleasing information, our reflections were thrown into a most interesting train; a copious field presented — the wilds of conjecture we assayed to penetrate, and we came on, originating a thousand ideas, which however fanciful, conduced nevertheless, much to our amusement — and, I pleasingly hope, I have derived at least one advantage, the power of complying, without fatiguing you, with the obliging request, you did me the honour to make, upon the evening previous to my leaving Boston. Mr Murray unites with me in tendering most respectful compliments to Mr Powell, and we have the pleasure to be, with esteem, and affection yours etc etc

Letter 762 To Mrs Sargent Philadelphia Arch Street June 26— 1790

A year ago at this time, Judith gave birth to her stillborn son, Fitz Winthrop, and nearly lost her own life as well. In this letter to her aunt, Mary Turner Sargent, she expresses her profound sadness over her loss, and believes she has "forever bid adieu" to motherhood. She will, she writes, adopt the "Virtues of Resignation" not knowing, of course, that she would give birth to a healthy daughter the following year.

Judith and John have visited the famed Schuylkill Gardens, taking Gray's ferry — a "floating bridge" — across the Schuylkill River. Judith gives her aunt a lengthy description of the Gardens including the "banqueting house" where the public is received, the indoor botanical gardens, outdoor trees, plants, walkways, arbours, "summer houses," covered seats, ice house and the food they were served. Judith tells us it was in the Gardens, at the Federal Temple, where the ratification of the Constitution was celebrated. There is a "transparent picture" of George Washington on the grounds, and the Federal Ship is moored nearby. On Tuesday and Saturday evenings, the Gardens were lit by 2,500 lanterns for the public's pleasure. Judith and John attended one of these evenings, and were treated to fireworks and an outdoor concert. Judith compares the experience to "Jay's Elysian Fields," meaning John Jay's early encounter with heaven (see Letter 755).

Once more I hold, to my very dear friend, the pen of sweetly familiar scribble, setting down quite at my ease, to chat with one, whom I am assured, by the charming consciousness which plays about my heart, will listen with indulgent, and unabating candour — I stand indebted upon the page of friendship for two letters, and I presume, with superior pleasure, to discharge the arrears — It was a happy thought, which bore you along, upon the wings of excursive fancy, the Companion of a journey, to the pleasure of which, you have thus largely contributed — Not a green bank, not a shady Grove, or a glassy rill, can now present, but immediately, like one of the daughters of paradise, — arrayed in spotless white, I place there by your beauteous image — in the arms of my imagination I clasp the lovely form, and it animates[,] cheers, and adds a richer colouring to all the glowing scene. If my cursory journal hath helped to illumine a solitary hour which would have otherwise have passed melancholy along — I shall esteem myself indeed fortunate — The departure of your son Turner, must have opened a new wound in your gentle bosom — May the path of the dear youth be made prosperous before him — May He, who holdeth the waters in the hollow of his hand, calm the surface of the waves, breathe the propitious gale, and crown with success the undertaking of his manly, and independent spirit — Do not write by candle light, I would not for the world be an accessory to your sufferings — No indeed, dear as every line of yours to me, I would not purchase these testimonies of your friendship, at the expense of the smallest increase of that alarming sensation, the aspect of which is already sufficiently formidable — I know the benevolence of your disposition, will lead you to find your enjoyment in the felicity of others, and of course, I do not consider your civilities to the S— party as problematical — It is indeed strange, what could originate the story of your son's matrimonial connexion — It was probably forged in the Wilds of conjecture, and the idea taking air, was, in the prolific imagination of the notable Dowager, blown up to an authenticated certainty — but, really, I think it is too early to match this little Girl, even in the fruitful brain of a Lady Blue Mantle, or of the Arbitrary Fabricator of unthought alliances — In regard to wearing black, I am free to own, I could wish this sable livery was only the appendage of real grief — when the heart is deeply lacerated, a correspondent hue, is proper, but, of course, I cannot but regret, when this decent memento, is prostituted to the purposes of hypocrisy — With respect to my health, you, who know the inmost reaches of my soul, know also, the state of the tenement in which it is lodged — My complaints are not of a nature to yield to change of air, objects, or exercise, to time only they must be submitted and what kind of a physician this same time may prove, we have yet to learn — I enjoy, however, a good proportion of the balmy blessing, and it is my wish to combine tranquility — sweet indeed were the expectations which swelled my bosom this time twelve month — richly did I enjoy them, and all the bliss of expectation was mine — but to such charming anticipation the probability is, that I have now forever bid adieu, and I will if I can bind to my bosom the becoming, and necessary Virtues of Resignation — your dream was possibly fanciful, and if I dared, I would attempt an interpretation, I could almost wish your little Girl had not so precipitately broken your slumbers, but we must conjecture the rest — The frequent commemorations, with which your family so frequently honour my birth day, are pleasingly flattering — May God bless my Fitz Winthrop, our Lucius Manlius, and their charming Mother — May the unmixed beverage which they quaff, stand as an expressive emblem, of the lasting, and unadulterated attachment, which they bear me — your quotation from his holiness, the Pope, I believe to be opposite, and my heart is inconsequently grateful. Let me see — what have I further to say? — Did I not promise you in my last a jaunt to the Schuylkill gardens? I did, you say — well then my mildly gentle friend, my sweet attendant spirit — borne on the wings of fancy, come along — The road is smooth before us — It is a beautiful level plain, and, on either hand — Lawns and Groves, fields of grain, and interjacent meadows, delightfully variegate the scene — Only four miles from Philadelphia, on the road to Maryland, lies our present Goal — To do justice to these Gardens, is beyond my power — to sketch them, these shall be the height of my ambition — Four miles, as I said, from Philadelphia, upon a floating Bridge we cross the Schuylkill upon the banks of which is erected the rural seat of a Mr Hamilton — which preferred strong claims upon our attention — while, from the view given us at Gray's ferry, we are not induced to anticipate much from our excursion. It is true the dwelling immediately attained, wears a thrifty appearance, but the attractions are little better, than what might be expected, from a decent tavern —

This, however, is only the house in which preparation is made for the guests, and ascending a flight of steps, which open upon the right, and which, with wonderful industry, are smoothly shaped out of solid rock, we reach a winding gravel walk, firm, and neatly rolled, and bordered on each side by the beautifully shorn grass — At this moment a view of the banqueting house unexpectedly breaks upon us — This banqueting house riseth upon the left hand, it is an elegant building formed of hewn stone, presenting in front, a superb Orchestra, supported by white columns, sufficiently ample, and ornamented by a portrait of the immortal Handle — The whole of the lower story of this building is thrown in to two apartments, the one a spacious Hall, elegantly finished — the Chimnies of rich American Marble, highly polished, and the Hall conveniently furnished, for the reception of company — Its form is oblong, and from the center of that ceiling, is suspended that very identical crown which the Philadelphian Youth, representing a Messenger from the celestial World, most unexpectedly produced, over the head of our beloved President, when, crossing the aforementioned Bridge, he was passing on his way, to take his seat at the head of government [—] By a well finished stair case in the Hall, we ascend the upper apartments, which apartments are neat, and commodious — the other Room upon the ground floor, is known by the name of the green Room, and when the wintry blasts are abroad, is a receptacle for the exotics which form, above form, in rows of painted inclosures, marshalled in Botanical Order, take their respective ranks [—] The upper end of this room is pierced with large openings, supplied with glass of prodigious size, and they are eleven panes deep — Indeed the windows, with very little interruption, constitute the whole of this side of the building, and, during the wintry season, a great proportion of heat is preserved, by the aid of multiplied Stoves. We will now, my sweet friend, if you please, step back to the first entrance of the Gardens — Upon the left you will recollect is this neat stone edifice, and upon the right a well fancied white pallisade is thrown along a bank, which is washed by the Schuylkill, several gravel walks present, the left leading to the house — We ascend the Glaces — five cozy steps in the first, and ten in the second, produce us in the area exactly before the door, and we then command a full view of a romantic summer house , in the front of which, is a full length transparent picture of Columbia's Illustrious Chief — Fame crowning him with laurel — The picture is as large as life, and it is said the likeness is happily preserved — This summer house, is the super structure of a convenient, and well planned ice house, and upon the right of the building, an oblong section of the garden, tastefully inclosed, and chiefly devoted to exotics, fancifully winds its way, lifting upon its fertilizing bosom, and in high perfection, whole rows of lemon trees, while the Orange tree, waits only the ripening influence of the advancing season, to attain its fullest growth, and richest pulp — The fruit upon the Almond tree is completely formed, and this too, asks but the patient aid, of that heat, which the intense rays of July, and August, will bestow, to crown it with maturity — The Pomegranate is now in full blossom — the blow of which is a superb scarlet, of a beautiful texture — Among the variety of plants found in this enclosure, are the numerous family of the Olois, and not less than thirty different species of the geranium, also the sensitive plant, fly trap etc etc — Seats are placed up, and down, upon the grass plats, and tall trees, of umbrag[eous] foliage form an ample shade — The serpentine gravel walks, which are irregularly regular, are although apparently pointing in various directions, terminate, however, in a common centre — Proceeding directly forward, we pass through an elegant arched gate which seems to be guarded by the figure of a satyr, extremely well painted — but this, as well, as the smaller avenues, all produce us in the wilderness into which we enter, passing over a neat Chinese Bridge and hastening forward to penetrate a recess so charming — It is indeed a wilderness of sweets, and the views are romantically enchanting — The sums every moment changing — now sidelong bends the path, then pursues its winding way — now in a strait line, next it is lost in a pleasing labyrinth, until again it breaks upon us, in every possible direction — we seem to ramble among thick Groves of Pines, Oaks, Wallnuts, Chestnuts, Mulberries etc etc [—] While at the same moment, we are surprised by deep borders of the richest, and most highly cultivated flowers, in the greatest variety, which we might be led to expect, even in a royal parterre — Every Gale comes forward loaded with perfumes, and by odiferous breezes, we are momently fanned. In the flower borders, the silver Pine, Turin Poplar, Bay Tree, and a variety of ever greens, are judiciously interspersed — The scene is apparently fashioned by the bounteous hand of Nature although we cannot so far admit the deception, as to exclude from our idea, the Handmaid art — On one hand the lowly Valley, richly shaded, is fancifully adorned — the mountain laurel condescending to flourish there — and on the other, grass grown Mounds variegate the scene — Here the excavated Cavern gives a degree of wildness to the prospect, and there the tall woods, with there enfolding branches, insensibly disposeth the wind, to all the pleasures of contemplation — while the bending river, breaking through the trees, largely contributes to beautify the whole — suddenly, however, we reach an open plain, and are presented with a pleasing horizon — but, as suddenly, thick trees again intervene — until at the extremity of the walks, a mill, and a natural cascade terminates the prospect.

Shaded seats are artfully contrived at every turn, and the grounds abound with arbours, Alcoves, and summer houses, which are handsomely adorned with odiferous flowers — among these summer houses the little Federal Temple, arrests our principal attention — It is the very Edifice, which upon the celebration of the ratification of the constitution, was carried in triumphant Procession, through the streets of the Metropolis, and upon a gentle Activity, infixed upon the summit of a green Mound, it hath now obtained a base — It is a Rotunda, its cupola is supported by thirteen pillars, handsomely finished, upon the several bases of which, is to be inscribed the Cyphr of the State, designed to be represented — a stone is placed upon every capital, and the Top is crowned with the figure of Plenty grasping the Cornucopia and other insignia, The ascent to this Temple is easy, and it is grained by semicircular steps, neatly turfed — The views from this enchanting little building, are truly beautiful — Before us is the Lawn smoothly shorn, further on the Schuylkill, which displays a number of interjacent points of land, extending their verdant angles so far, as to deceive the eye, by wearing the appearance of parallel rivers, and, beyond, an advantageous prospect of the City of Philadelphia unexpectedly breaks upon you. On the left hand winds the Country, in a high state of cultivation, and at this season, in its most delightfully becoming garb to which the back ground exhibits a counterpart, and the prospect in this direction is terminated by tall thick woods — upon the right the extensive meanderings of the Schuylkill are continued, with a sketch of the waters of the Delaware, and a most pleasing view of the Jersey Shore — But, to give a regular description, I should have written upon the spot — My Memory is not tenacious, so, my sweet friend, we will note beauties, as they occur, rather than confine ourselves to that method, which, however we would glad possibly attain. The Federal Ship is now moored in the Schuylkill, It is a well constructed miniature, and is, upon the evenings of exhibition, a prominent addition to the interest of the scene — I was much pleased with a little building, which romantically makes its appearance, upon a living spring, where, through the intense heat of the summer months, every kind of provision is preserved, equally cool, as in the depths of winter.

To give a list of the variety of plants, flowers, and fruits, which lend their aid to beautify, and to regale, I ought to have passed whole days in the gardens — They are tastefully, and judiciously displayed, and effectually guarded, by a brass tablet, which, at every turn, elevated upon a small pillar, respectfully requests Ladies, and gentlemen, walking over the grounds, not to injure the shrub trees, and flowers, as a hope is entertained of preserving, and beautifying the collection — The whole improvements, including the kitchen garden, contains about ten acres of ground, and every tuesday, and saturday evening, these gardens are splendidly illuminated, by no less than two thousand, five hundred lamps — The illuminations abound with imagery, festoons, stars[,] pyramids, etc etc but the manner of the display is constantly varying, and the Lamps are so artfully disposed among the trees, as to render it impossible to discover, by what means they are suspended, and we are almost ready to conclude the whole the effect of magic — The illumination of the cascade, Mill, Federal ship, and the transparent picture of our immortal President, had, upon the evening we passed there, a particularly fine effect, while an exhibition of fire works, from the federal ship, added highly to the grandeur of the scene — ["]The top sail shivers in the wind" was melodiously chanted on board this same Federal ship — The admittance into these gardens, upon public days, is by a ticket, for which three sixteenths of a dollar is demanded, and we then take our seats in the banqueting house, in any of the summer houses, arbours, or covered seats — or walk over the grounds at pleasure — Whatever we wish, in the greatest variety which the season will afford, is...immediately furnished — the liquors are all iced and the little prints of butter, are served up neatly decorated with this transparent, and, at this season, very agreeable substance — All this is, however, a separate expense, yet the charges are moderate, and the tea, Coffee, Sugar, bread, and butter etc are all of the best quality. We requested some fruit, and were given our choice of Mulberries, strawberries, Cherries, Oranges, or Pine Apples — The Waiters are habited like gentlemen, and seem to possess all that kind of attentive Alacrity, which I have heard attributed to European servants — The company often order their refreshments to the seats, arbours, or summer houses, scattered over the grounds — To prevent comparison, if we wish to pass out by the stone steps, mentioned in the beginning of this account, we receive a gratis ticket, from the Porter, which we return upon our reentrance — Persons are often induced to pass this arched, and foliage crowned gate to ascend, by the aid of a winding rock, shaped by nature into commodious steps of lofty convenience, which commands a captivating view of the Country — An individual, making a decent appearance, may enjoy the pleasure, of walking in the Gardens, free of all expense, upon any day, tuesdays and saturdays excepted

Upon the evenings of these public days, a concert of Vocal, and instrumental musick is performed, and these convivial seasons, often, as I am told, produce in the gardens, as many as a thousand Votaries of taste — The evening however, which we so highly enjoyed in this terrestrial paradise, was much less crouded than usual — Many well dressed, and genteel persons were nevertheless present, and, as I marked the different parties pursuing their way through the various walks, as inclination led, apparently unconnected with, and totally inattentive to surrounding Circles — as I saw this, and as I Listened to the sounds wafted from the Orchestra, I declare I almost fancied myself in Jay's Elysian Fields.

Amid these Walks upon a divine morning, after making a delicious breakfast at Gray's, upon fruit, and Hyson tea, we have contemplatively wandered — the branches of the trees were then filled with Woodland songsters, and we had an opportunity of making the comparison, between the pleasures derived from Artificial lights, and crouded scenes, and those which are reaped, from the retirement, generally attached to rural haunts, the musick of the groves, and the influence of yonder Orb, that universal enlivener of Nature, and her grateful children — The Schuylkill gardens have been called the American Vaux hall — They are certainly a little Eden, for which Nature hath done every thing, and art has made most wonderful additions — Great merit is undoubtedly due to Mr Gray, who is decidedly a Man of taste — He is daily making improvements, and he receives with gratitude every suggestion — we visited Harrongate, previous to our view of this charming recess — It certainly cannot be compared with Gray's Garden — yet the medicinal Springs, and commodiously adjoining bathing houses will secure to Harrongate a share of attention —— Well, my sweet friend — I fancy you will now readily dismiss the Scribbler — Adieu then and continue I pray you to love your Correspondent

Letter 763 To my Father and Mother Philadelphia Arch Street June 26th— 1790

Not having heard recently from Gloucester, Judith is worried about her mother's health and about Anna's approaching delivery. In the Woodrow home (where she and John are staying), Judith has helped deliver the baby of Mrs. Woodrow's daughter, Mrs. Jackson. Only a year earlier, Mrs. Woodrow had lost another daughter in childbirth. This time, everything went well but Judith must have had difficulty reliving her own experience and her tragic loss.

Judith and John have visited painter John Trumbull's gallery, and she describes his works depicting great moments in the Revolution and the formation of the new government. They have visited David Rittenhouse's home where they took "a peep at the Moon" through his telescope. "Language is inadequate" to describe her feelings, she tells her parents. Judith recounts an anecdote she has been told about an early lesson in frugality learned by Benjamin Franklin, whose memory is still "highly revered" in Philadelphia. Rhode Island has ratified the Constitution, bringing the "Federal List" to thirteen states.

Thus the weeks roll on, while, with superior pleasure, I hail these returning days a part, of which, I have consecrated sacred to my beloved Parents — I have written to several of my friends, the next Mail will convey my letters to Boston, and I trust that our multiplied packets, will come to hand in due order [—] In the well being of that Circle, in which you, beloved, and honoured parents, must ever be to me, the most prominent figures, I am anxiously interested — It is indeed a long period since I have heard from Gloucester, and the feeble tenor of my Mother's health, with the approaching difficulty of my sister Anna, set heavy upon my mind — This morning hath shed its brightest beams upon this family — Mrs Jackson is safe in bed with a fine daughter — she hath had a most happy hour, no persons present but her Mother, her sister, and myself, her sufferings were indeed light, but the joys of Mrs Woodrow, are not unmired — her lost daughter riseth to her view — Ten Months since Mrs Lear expired, in this very rock of Nature, after enduring agonies not to be described, or even imagined — yet thus gently hath her sister passed the ordeal — God give our sweet Anna a period as propitious — The calls upon Mr Murray daily encrease, and new inquiries press upon him — The Convention is nearly closed, Mr Murray will inclose you a printed copy of the result of their proceedings, and every occurence in this line, I surrender to his pen — Amid the promiscuous Circles which I have seen in this City, I have, as I believe, formed some valuable connexions, and my heart is truly grateful — The Hospital, and Mansion, with many other etceteras, I have not yet seen — but these are pleasures still in prospect — We have visited Mr Trumball's room — his paintings are not many — at least his present exhibition is small, but they do him honour — A view of the late siege, and relief of Gibralter, he hath delineated so expressively, as to lead you to fancy your self upon the spot — Many of the figures are taken from life, and General Elliot, you will not doubt, is the principal personage — The Members, who constituted the Congress, which signed our Independence, live upon his Canvass — he hath grouped them most successfully, and he hath, it is said, preserved exact likenesses — I imagine this piece, will be truly acceptable to posterity — Our Countrymen are in the very act of deliberation — One of their Associates is declaiming, and attention swells the features of every face — Mr Adams, now Vice President, is a prominent figure in the piece, and the venerable shade of Doctor Franklin, conspicuously introduced, seems to sanction the Assembly. The present Governor of Massachusetts, as you will recollect, at that time filled the chair, and consequently now appears in his place [—] In short, it is undoubtedly a most valuable painting — Mr Trumball has given from his admirable pencil, the transaction at York Town, of which day General Lincoln was the Hero — These pieces, with the reduction of Prince Town, where our illustrious Washington more particularly presided, are the principal paintings, in the present collection of the artist — Mr Trumball is allowed by connoisseurs in this indeed fine art to possess in the line of his election, uncommon zest, and every lover of excellence, will wish him success — We have taken a peep at the Moon — of Mr Rittenhouse you have often heard, he will unquestionably be mentioned with applause, so long as science shall possess sufficient charms, to captivate the Man of letters — We regretted that his Orrery being separated, we lost the opportunity of admiring, and profiting by its elusidating powers — Mr Rittenhouse is in a great measure, as I am told self taught, but he possesses all the excellent qualities of the Philosopher — his improvements are well known, and, as I believe duly appreciated — yet he is humble as innocence, affable, and easy of access — he is happy in his matrimonial connexion, his Lady being a very superior character, and, as I have heard, a confirmed Universalist — Mr Rittenhouse hath two daughters, the eldest of whom hath taken the name of Sargent, and his granddaughter, Miss Sally Sargent, is now a Candidate for a place in the Bethlehem school — His younger daughter, Miss Rittenhouse entertained us with some excellent airs upon the Piano Forte, and we were shown, some beautiful paintings, which were the offspring of this young Lady's talents, and application — The Residence of Mr Rittenhouse is elegant, neatly finished, and furnished, and in the back ground, is a little improved spot, in a very high state of cultivation, exhibiting a most valuable collection of plants, and flowers, where the high scented lemon tree fragrantly blooms — little Groves of myrtle line the pallisade, and the english Jasmine, makes a very considerable figure in the parterre — Through a Piazza, shaded by honey suckle, or Woodbine, we passed a little Octagonal Edifice, which contains philosophical apparatus — where the telescope was elevated, and having never before looked through one of those glasses, the milder beauties of night's fair Empress, were all, that had hitherto met my eye — But great indeed was my astonishment, as this body, in all her borrowed charms, broke upon me — I was, and I am, at a loss for a comparison [—] stucco work illumined heavenly radiance — No it will never do, all imagery falls short of my ideas — the dark shades, apparently indented, the bright circles, the variegated splendor — but I will not assay to describe, language is inadequate, and recollection can only admire in silence

Mr Rittenhouse seems to be one of the few, whose merit, even in this undistinguished state of being, hath been crowned with those emoluments, and that applause, which are in some sort commensurate, with those pretensions, which he has a right to form— Happy in domestic life, and possessing a genteel competency, the pleasures of retirement are his — his days are passed in literary enjoyment, and his moments are questionless marked by wisdom — As I listened to the harmonious notes, drawn from his daughter's instrument, as I beheld the complacent countenance of Mr Rittenhouse, as I inhaled from the well arranged parterre, and from every flowering shrub, the odiferous perfume — as I passed on through the sweetly shaded walk, [it was] a most divine evening — when the "As if her head she bowed, oft stooped through a fleecy cloud" [—] Thus surrounded, as I took my way, to the little Octagon, sacred to the enjoyment of sentimental speculations, I could scarcely forbear, audibly exclaiming — Surely this is the abode of happiness, and these haunts are the recesses of tranquility — It is true the health of Mr Rittenhouse is apparently upon the decline — Complaints indicative of decay, are as the selfish will pronounce, but too manifold — yet his exit out of time, will be but his birth, into a new, and better mode of existence — It is but to open the cage, and let the Prisoner fly, and, if I may judge by report, and by appearances — it is only in future Worlds, that Mr Rittenhouse can know augmenting felicity. Anecdotes relative to Doctor Franklin, as is usually the case upon the demise of a great Man, are afloat — from the mouth of Miss Ellmore, many years a resident in his family, I select the following — Doctor Franklin is, as we know, a native of the Capital of New England, and it is storied that quitting Boston, for Philadelphia, his first Night's lodging, after he had crossed the Delaware, was in a Quaker meeting house, his purse not furnishing him with sufficient cash, to answer the demands of an Inn! Be this as it may — Miss Ellmore's account is from his own lips. Embarking for England, and arriving there, he engaged himself as a journeyman Printer — his gains were small, and his expenses greater than he wished; Accident brought him acquainted with an ancient female, the morning of whose life had been gilded by the bright sun of prosperity, but who, in the evening of her days, was reduced to the scanty pittance of only three pounds per annum — Her education, and some particular infirmities rendered it impossible for her to encrease her income by labour — and possessing a kind of decent Pride, which prevented the application to those, who might have relieved her, she contrived, by economy, so to manage her little sum, as to render it adequate to her necessities — Doctor Franklin was curious to know her plan of life, and she informed him, that her diet consisted entirely of oaten meal, which her coals prepared, without the smallest addition, except what it received from this same fire — This was her whole support, and this nourishment, appeared quite sufficient in the exigencies of her Nature — Her spirits considering her years, and her misfortunes, were good, and she was much in flesh — "Well, but" said young Franklin "although I would fain try this experiment, yet not living by myself — I have no means of preparing this frugal repast, for there is a kind of Necessity, for my accommodating myself, to those, with whom I associate["—] The good woman soon obviated with difficulty, by informing him, that as fire, and water, were the only additions which [t]he oaten meal received, if he would purchase that article, it would be easy for her to prepare it with her own — This expedient was eagerly accepted and for a great length of time, almost the whole of the young man's earning were redeemed — Thus did the frugality of youth lay a foundation of the ease, and affluence of succeeding life [—] Doctor Franklin was still more penurious of time, appropriating every moment to the best possible purpose — his character is, as I believe, deservedly respected — perhaps his Genius was as nearly universal as that of any mortal's who hath yet lived, his memory is highly revered in this City, and it seems to me, beyond a doubt, that he has deserved well of Mankind [—] Allow me to congratulate you upon the Accession of the State of Rhode Island, to the League of Amity [—] We are now, once again, the thirteen United States, and our Federal List, seems at length complete. The Rhode Islanders — but having reached the bottom of my paper — To introduce a reflection upon a Free Sovereign State, will be neither respectful, nor decorus — I will then, only add, that I am ever most dutifully yours

Letter 764 To Mrs Sargent Philadelphia Arch Street July 2d 1790

*This letter contains mostly family news. "Cousin E.S." is Epes Sargent;
"Captain I—" is Ignatius Sargent, the son of the Mrs. Sargent to whom
the letter is addressed (her aunt, Mary Turner Sargent).*
   *Judith reports that the weather undergoes extreme changes in
temperature where they are, and she relates a story about a wealthy
Quaker gentleman, living across the street, who supplied fuel one
winter to the poor.*

   Once more a pleasing sense of additional obligation, to my
friend, placeth in my hand the pen of acknowledgment — How often
am I necessitated to a confession of your labours, of your kind attention
— but it is a delightful necessity, and my heart is fond of dwelling upon
a theme so pleasing — yes indeed, you must have felt very severely,
when your desert proved, notwithstanding its size, and promising
appearance, a mere bagatelle — Nay worse — When, instead of being
refined, meliorated, and brought to perfection, by the genial sum of
meridian Friendship, it rather seemed the scanty produce of some
unpropitious soil, the manure of which had been unjudiciously collected,
from the ungrateful wilds of suspicion — yet, I have only to plead in my
defense, the undue influence, and tyrannical sway, which a kind of
constitutional impatience, frequently usurps in my bosom, and when
this Despot assumes the reins, it would annihilate every movement of
intervention, and instantly possess the object, which its tenderness, or
its caprice, had induced it to wish. Instigated by this bosom invader,
this foe to my tranquility, I yielded too hastily to the suggestions of
despondency, that some fatal accident, revolution, or — or — In short
I cannot tell what had occasioned your silence — I do not however
pretend to justify the unwarrantable effects of arbitrary rule,
I acknowledge I have been betrayed, into a deviation, from one of the
most rational, and solitary laws of amity, and I throw myself entirely
upon the mercy of the sweet Arbitress of my fate — A few consolatory
pages, I imagine will have found their way to you, before this my
confession, shall meet your eye and the truths they contain, when lodged
in the bosom of candour, will, I doubt not, powerfully advocate my Cause,
and, in a measure compensate for those regrets which my impetuosity
hath occasioned. To you, my sweet friend, I have hitherto been indebted
for accounts from Gloucester — one only letter from my Father, and
that in no sort circumstantial having reached me — The last mail, having
handed me a second letter from my Father, and a most flattering address
from my Cousin E.S. [—] Indeed I can with justice say, that from the
hour which summoned their departed mother, to the abodes of felicity,
the affectionate regard which both Mr and Mrs Sargent, have manifested

to me, have been in no respect short, of what I might have expected from the most Tender relative — But, from no pen have I heard a single syllable, of Ignatius or his Maria, although in a letter written from Boston, to my sister Anna, I was very particular in my expressions of that affection, which my heart acknowledgeth for them [—] Ignatius knows to value the unborn worth, and maternal virtues, of his beloved Mother — Maria is capable of distinguishing her many excellences — hence they cannot be other than decided favourites of my heart — May they enjoy that uninterrupted tranquility, they so decidedly merit and which they so well know to improve — If their felicity should be in proportion, to my wishes for their well being, their voyage through life will not be scanty of the most substantial pleasures — I drop a tear over the exit of Captain H— he was an upright Man, and firm in his attachment to the message, and Messenger of truth — I hope my Aunt D— will reap satisfaction from the presence of her son, and I trust that the return of Captain I— hath increased to my Uncle the means of enjoyment — your jaunt with Mrs M— was like yourself, benevolently good — It was rural, and pretty, and like every other proper action, was productive of proper honorable pleasure — Item — I should be fond of visiting Miss Etherton's retreat — I am pleased that Mrs T—'s health will allow the exercise of riding, and obliged by her remembrance of me — Fitz Winthrop's graceful bow is so strongly connected with his prepossessing figure, that they always rise together in my idea, and hovering round the little recess of mediation, I see him enter the door of your retirement, I listen to his endearing prattle, and, in imagination, I clasp him in the warmest embrace — I am happy to learn that he is under the care of Master L— from the character of that gentleman, I conceive him to be all which an individual ought to be, who undertakes to form the infant mind, to teach the young idea how to shoot — Mr Murray hath a high opinion of Master L— and the information that Fitz Winthrop is entrusted to him, must of course be to us, a very pleasing piece of intelligence — I believe almost every part of America can furnish Counterparts of your observations respecting the weather — The transition from heat, to cold, is indeed often instantaneous, and the wonder is how a machine so complicated, as is the human conformation, is not more frequently or more early wrecked upon a voyage so confessedly precarious — Pennsylvania experiences the rigours of heat, and cold, almost in their extremes, but the beauty of the Country, and the richness of the soil, abundantly compensates for every inconvenience — Mentioning the severities of the seasons reminds of an anecdote which this morning drew my attention, Directly opposite this abode of hospitality resides an opulent Quaker, his house is lofty, and it hath an air of elegance — upon its left is a luxuriant meadow in which one solitary Cow is seen to wander, and the back ground, as I am informed, exhibits a little garden, which, without a hyperbole may be termed a terrestrial paradise — But this same Quaker, is in every respect, a Miser of his joy, his front shutters are constantly, and unsociably closed — Four weeks, this day, have we had our abode with in call of his door, and not the smallest variation to the following order, have we observed — About five O clock in the morning, a maid servant throws open the windows, and airs, sweeps, and scrubs the apartments with all possible expedition, when this business is accomplished, the shutters are again closed, and they admit no ray of light, until the next morning returns the periodical hour — The inhospitable door of this Quaker, seldom turns upon its hinges, and hardly a foot is seen to pass his threshold — If the weather be prodigiously fine, a plain Chariot takes him, and his Lady, out for an airing, and in a kind of gloomy silence returns them, and this, I am told is their most excessive movement — This, much by way of exordium — The poor of Philadelphia suffered much during the past winter, in the want of fuel — This neighbour of ours, quitted his bed, one morning, uncommonly early — The cold was extreme and before his servant could enkindle his blazing hearth, the gloomy Master keenly felt the rigours of the day. The effect of this accident, was prodigious — It produced reflection — it produced sympathy. He summoned a principal Magistrate — "Are not many of our fellow creatures destitute, during that severe season of the means of mitigating its horrors?" Certainly they are — "Well then I have three hundred pounds in my closet — It is at present useless to myself — I dare not, it would be dreadful to with hold it [—] I pray thee take it, and distribute it, as thou shall see fit, among the necessitors — observing only that I exclude the friends from my share in this charity for I know that for them, ample provision is made." See, my lovely friend forth from the bosom of the flinty Rock, the universal Father, can at His pleasure command the most salubrious waters to issue — but to you, I leave the comment — The various reports of travellers are indeed strange even so strange as to destroy whatever measure of credibility, they may in fact, merit. The intelligence which with such sympathetic tenderness, and affectionate alacrity, you have transmitted to me, gives me real joy — Fitz William is certainly one of my treasures, and I rejoice that his little girl supports her spirits, during the melancholy period of expectation which is allotted her — May the protecting angel hover round the passage of young Rogers, warding from his head impending evil, I behold in the face of that young Man, the image of his Mother, and my heart spontaneously offers up for him, its fervant aspirations. The conduct of ———— is indeed intolerable — Pity that when an accommodating spirit is so indispensable, she has no means of commanding its aid — Poor Mrs — Fielding, painting a most amiable Clergyman, makes it a commanding trait in his character — that his tongue was never known to utter an invocative, and that the highest provocation, could never so far irritate him, as to extort any stronger exclamation, than "Poor soul! Poor soul!" In imitation of which I greatly admire, I repeat, Poor Mrs — Her ambiguities, and her insinuations, have absolutely put me beyond all Patience ———

Letter 765 To my Father and Mother Philadelphia Arch street July 3d. 1790 Saturday

In this letter, Judith continues her description of Philadelphia — the "Metropolis of the American World," as she called it. She describes its buildings, ease of travel, furnishings, and the Quaker language and customs. They have visited Charles Wilson Peale's museum which contained an eclectic collection of live and stuffed animals, insects, fossils, and birds, along with Peale's now famous portraits of Washington and other American leaders. Judith relates a story about the "Chicktaw" chief who was on his way to the delegation in New York to sign a treaty with Congress. The story is about the first meeting between this man and George Washington, and with what respect Washington treated him. Judith introduces her parents to more of her new friends, and gives a lengthy account of taking tea with Sarah Bache, Benjamin Franklin's daughter, who resided in her deceased father's home. Judith wrote that "language is inadequate" to describe how she felt standing in the great man's library — the largest she had seen outside of "Cambridge College" (now Harvard University). Judith repeats Sarah's description of her father's last days and the financial difficulties she had during the "late war." "St. Clair" is Arthur St. Clair, Governor of the Northwest Territory, under whom Judith's brother, Winthrop, was serving as Secretary of the Territory. In fact, Winthrop spent much of this time serving as acting governor during St. Clair's frequent absences. Years later, Winthrop petitioned Congress to be compensated for this work but was unsuccessful. He did, however, become Governor of the Mississippi Territory under the Adams administration, only to be removed from office by the anti-federalist president Thomas Jefferson.

A second letter from the paternal pen of my honoured Father, hath bestowed sweet serenity upon my bosom, and by assuring me that my efforts to communicate pleasure as successful, hath added a fresh motive for diligence — The probability is that the sufferings of my beloved Mother, will never cease but with the career of mortality [—] Right happy should I be could I render her precious life more tolerable — But submission is a lesson which however indocile we may chance to be, we are yet all intimately necessitated to learn — The intelligence from Fitz William, it must have given you a delicious moment. — Upon the far distant banks of the Delaware it hath afforded me a song of domestic joy — I trust your next letter will announce to me the birth of a little being, who will possess an undoubted claim to my affection. My Sister ought to have written, there is hardly any price within our reach, which we should consider too high to purchase intelligence from our friends, and we unitedly request, with sincere, and honest tenderness, to greet every relative for we can assure them, without equivocation, that they are indelibly engraven upon our hearts — I saw a gentleman, the other day, whose brother is one of St. Clair's party upon the river, he hath recently received a letter from Marietta, which letter informs him, that the Governor Secretary, etc were not expected until August, or September, and you will consequently cease to wonder, you have no late tidings from my brother — your letters, my dear Sir, speak the heart of a Father, can they want an additional recommendation — believe me they are received, with becoming gratitude, and they are indeed balm to the bosom of your daughter — I am pained to learn that fortune still continues to frown upon you, but the present scene will close, and beyond, the prospect of unfading bliss, is unclouded. The rapid growth of this City is wonderful — It is little more than a Century, since it was the residence of untutored Nature — The beautiful water of the Delaware, and its rich, and fertile banks, confessed only a savage Lord — Now, Arts, and Sciences, in all the variety of their improvements flourish here — Philadelphia is indeed the Metropolis of the American World and, it is advancing forward to a state of high perfection — There is, however, a whimsical kind of singularity, remarkable in the Majority of the inhabitants of this Capital — For example, an elegant Carriage, superbly finished, and ornamented in the height of the present taste drawn by beautiful horses, which are glittering with the richness of their trappings — which carriage is attended, by servants, its complete livery, approaches, while the Lady issuing therefrom, exhibits in her dress, a perfect pattern of simplicity — The Buildings, as I have observed, are highly elevated, and the ascent to them is, in many instances, by a flight of marble steps fancifully turned, and even polished — The furniture of the houses is in a rich, and highly ornamented style so that it is only by their personal habiliments, that the Quaker can now be distinguished. I call this peculiarly whimsical, because as it is not <u>uniform</u> in its operations, it seems to merit the charge of caprice — I confess there is elegance — in a plain garment to which the motley vagaries of fashion would in vain pretend — but when <u>plainness</u> is adopted in a <u>religious view</u>, should it not be consistent, should it not involve the several articles which come under our jurisdiction? The Quakers contend for their <u>Thee</u> , and their <u>Thou</u>, in a grammatical view, and I believe they are correct — The <u>frugality</u> of the Philadelphians hath been said to border upon <u>perniciousness</u> — and they have been accused as unsociable, and inhospitable — We have found them greatly the <u>reverse</u> — I asked a Lady, from whence an idea, apparently so foreign from the truth, could be derived? Perhaps her reply may be accepted as a real state of the case — "Philadelphia is a thorough fare — Multitudes are constantly passing, and repassing — Strangers — without an introduction — present themselves — they tarry for a night, and are gone — and receiving no particular attention, they pronounce us illiberal, and contracted — But were we to distinguish every transient Passenger, we should be engaged in a constant round of visiting, and it would surely be a frivolous kind of life, which should be hourly boding us to persons whom we never before saw, nor perhaps ever expected to meet again — But trust me, Madam the constant resident, or even the traveller, who taketh time to form connexions, will find the Philadelphians open, generous, affable, and humane. Monday last Mr Peale was obliging enough to present us with tickets of admission to his Museum — which gives us access at pleasure — This Museum contains a collection of curiosities from sea, earth, and air — Availing ourselves of the politeness of Mr Peale, we have repeatedly visited his Museum, and we have enjoyed an entertainment of the highest kind — The Museum is a spacious oblong room — It is pierced by a large opening at one end, and lighted horizontally at the other, a handsome arched ceiling, commences in the Centre, which is continued to the Further extremities of the room [—] The curiosities are judiciously, and tastefully displayed, and the Gallery is lined with portraits of the most illustrious Personages who have figured in the late Revolution — The American Hero, with many of his General Officers, the most respectable Presidents of the old Congress — Secretaries, and many distinguished Citizens — The train of French Worthies, such as the Marquis La Fayette, Count de Rochambeau, Lazerne, Gerrard etc etc [—] A cursory view will not admit an enumeration of the natural Curiosities — They consist of Marine substances, fossiles[,] fish of various kinds, insects, birds from the fabled Pelican, down to the smallest American Humming Bird, with a large collection of Quadrapedes — These animals are all exactly preserved, both in form, and beauty, and not a feather of the gayest plumage is faded, or in the least disordered — Their eyes indeed are <u>artificial</u> but they seem to beam with the expression of Nature, and the affect produced upon the mind, when considering ourselves surrounded by the associated inhabitants of every element is beyond description — Linneus reckons six classes of animals, and he places insects in the fifth, which he again subdivides into seven orders — These are exhibited in the Museum, through glasses, according to their succession, and the most scrupulous regularity is preserved — Many efforts of art are also shown in Peale's Museum, among which a knot of flowers, cut in paper, by a girl who was born without either hands, or arms, making use of her toes instead of fingers! with likenesses of the King, and queen of France, executed upon white sattin, and produced by a single spark of electricity, are not the least considerable — we are also shown an elegant manuscript copy of the Alcoran, written in Arabic, and neatly framed and glassed — A piece of the Bastile, that so recently formidable grave of the imprisoned, is also laid up here — But when I would assay the smallest sketch, such an infinite variety crouds upon me, that imagination, visiting this Cabinet of curiosities, is lost amid the multifarious collection — Mr P— exhibits several living animals among which is a number of the most beautiful birds — That curiosity of Nature the Opossum, and the Hyaena, confined in iron cages, are also to be seen here — Mr Peale is, you will judge, a virtuoso — he is too, a very respectable artist, and his moving pictures recently exhibited, were productive of the highest satisfaction They have been unfortunately injured but he is endeavouring to prepare them for a display previous to our departure — He was obliging enough to indulge us with a beautiful sample, the last morning we called upon him — It was a perspective view of a mill seat, near the falls of Schuylkill — The azure sky is out spread, and the distant prospects rise around — The glazing stream, gently glides in the trembling dam, when sucking down in a torrent, it forms a romantic Cascade, making its way through the Arches of a neat, well finished Bridge, in a copiously flowing, and beautifully natural manner — the view is ornamented by umbrageous trees, through which appear the mill house, with the water wheel performing with amazing velocity, its revolutions and dashing around its humid spray. By what machinery this wonderful effect is produced I know not, but certainly the delineation of nature, in perfect motion, must be confessed a surprising attainment of Art. At the entrance of the Museum is placed a wax figure of Mr Peale, which so near[l]y resembles life, as to be absolutely, by a late Indian Chief, mistaken for the Artist himself. This Aboriginie, had obtained among his tribe, the Chicktaws, the highest degree of honour — Having, for as many intrepid acts, received his tenth name of applause — beyond which distinction, he could never advance — he was upwards of eighty years old, when he was deputed by the Chicktaw, and Cherokee Indians, to lay their requisitions, relative to the fulfillment of a late treaty, before the Convention of the delegates of the United States, then setting for the purpose of forming a constitution, on the City of Philadelphia — The first article with which the Indian Warrior was careful [to] provide himself, was a wig, of which he was remarkably fond — to which he added a hat, and a walking stick, thus accommodating himself with a <u>weapon</u> of defense or as it might have happened, of offence [—] This Indian betrayed all the peculiarities of his Countrymen, and was of course grave, sententious, and respectable — He had not a word of English but his gestures were so expressive, and his observations so accurate, that it was easy to comprehend him, or to give him every necessary information — General Washington called upon him — the Hero of Nature was unfortunately absent; the General called a second time, but the delegate was again abroad — he however returned before the General had passed far from the Inn and, informed of the Visitor, by whom he had again been honoured, with surprising alacrity he speeded after him, a number of spectators were drawn to their doors, and windows, to witness this uncommon interview, thus destined to pass in the streets — The Indian advanced close to the General, then receding a few steps, placed his hat under his arm, pointing significantly to the heavens, and to the Earth, drew with his cane the figurative Circle, and after performing the most profound obeisance, presented his hand — for some time they seemed to confer, and the aged Chief returned to his Inn, much elated by his reception, giving his attendants to understand, that the Great Sachem had invited him to take wine with him, upon the ensuing day

      With the figure of Mr Peale, as I said this savage was greatly struck, and there was nothing he beheld, which appeared to him so utterly incomprehensible. I had intended to have sketched for you, the circle of connexions, which we have formed in this City but momently enlarging, the attempt is become of too great magnitude for a letter — I will however note, as a memento to myself, a few of the most prominent figures — I flatter myself that Mrs Woodrow, and her family, hath already obtained, in the bosom of my friends, a degree of consideration — I am too much indebted to Doctor Dunlap, and his Lady, not to have long since introduced their names — Mr & and Mrs Mackie are people of fortune, their manners are pleasingly interesting; they are generous, open, and hospitable, and they have bestowed us uncommon attention — Mrs Mackie is delicately feminine, she is a native of New York, highly accomplished, and truly elegant — She takes a deep and a very natural interest, in the truths promulgated by Mr Murray — her professions to me are sweetly soothing, and, if I would avail myself of her liberality, she would load me with pecuniary favours. Mr & Mrs Ball, I have, as I believe already mentioned — Mrs Wescot and Mrs Keppel are widow Ladies of immense fortunes, by whom we have been regarded with marked and flattering attention. With Marshall, a Quaker gentleman, we have enjoyed some delightful hours — he is an able advocate for Universalism, and I have been charmed with his manuscripts. He hath laid the Companion of his youth in her bed of death — but he is surrounded by a numerous family of children, and grand children, his house is neat, and decently furnished, and he hath a large, and well chosen library — We passed our time in this library until summoned to tea, and, as we listened to the white hour at sage, we could not but confess the moments marked by wisdom — I have already mentioned the family of Doctor Franklin — We yesterday, by appointment, attended the Levee of his daughter Mrs Bache — This Lady appears to be happy in her matrimonial connexion — the countenance of Mr Bache is agreeable, its manly expression is tempered by a prepossessing sweetness, his figure is good, and his character highly respectable — Mrs Bache is a most amiable Woman, easy of access, affable, and perfectly engaging, and there is in her every feature, an open frankness, which cannot fail of giving pleasure, she hath been well educated and consequently possesses a cultivated mind, and the social complacency of her manners, is descriptive of the woman thoroughly well bred, she hath a promising family of children, consisting of four sons, and three daughters — she now resides in the Mansion home of the late Doctor — It is, although in the very heart of the City, an elegant Retirement. We enter through an arched avenue, which immediately produces us in a square, seemingly detached from the noise, and confusion of the Town, although, in fact it is but a few paces from Market street — The building is in the Philadelphia manner, lofty and commodious — The furniture is neat, and the collection of pictures Capital, highly descriptive of the best Art —

We were shown Chinese figures, of rich Porcelain, superbly habited after the manner of their country, and their robes proclaimed them of no vulgar character — We were introduced into the Library of Doctor Franklin — the collection of Volumes is prodigious, I never saw it surpassed, except in the Cambridge University — The library is ornamented by the Bishop of St Asass and his family, and, as I surveyed these figures, the books, the writing desk, and considered myself in the favourite recess of the illustrious deceased, my sensations were — but language is inadequate to their description — We were entertained with vocal, and instrumental music, and no attempt to contribute to our amusement was left unessayed — upon a beautiful Lawn, embosomed by the willow, the weeping willow, and a rich variety of fruit trees, under the wide spreading shade of the Catolphin, now in full, and enchanting blow, the tea table, with a number of seats, was placed, and by the deliciously scented evening breeze, we were sweetly fanned — Mrs Bache speaks of her Father, in a manner becoming a daughter — Upon his patience, his equanimity, and his fortitude, she dwells with peculiar pleasure — His illness was tedious, and his agonies of the most peculiar kind — yet he was always Master of himself, and a smile of serenity constantly irradicated his countenance — Two days before his death he observed, to his daughter, that he did not recollect, in the course of his whole life, ever being for a single moment angry with her, and

Mrs Bache adds, that the whole tenor of his conduct, was most endearing — No pang, however severe, possessed the power to ruffle his temper, not the meanest servant could administer to his necessities, but it was exactly right — every thing prepared for him was delightful and to attend upon him, was thus rendered truly pleasurable; Mrs Bache, seems to have drank deeply from the fountain of Republicanism — she declares, had heaven given her any number of boys, they should every one be furnished with a mechanical Art — Her eldest Son hath completed his apprenticeship to a Printer, and she directed herself, with the effect which this circumstance had, upon a young coxcomb, passing on in the stage with young Bache, to a neighbouring City — The descendant of Franklin exhibited the marks of a gentleman, and the Fop inquired into the nature of his pursuits — "I am a Printer Sir—" What Sir, a Printer! and he instantly ordered into his features, the most contemptuous expression — observing, during the remainder of the journey, the most obstinate taciturnity. Mrs Bache suffered much during the late troubles — When the British advanced to Philadelphia, she had been no more than three days confined to her bed of maternity — Mr Bache was not in the City, he had accepted a post under Congress — Hard money she had none — for the family had loaned to government, immediately upon the commencement of the Contest, every farthing which they could command — Thus destitute of the means of support, when the English should take possession, and apprehensive of the treatment which she should receive, she was obliged to quit her home, and fly for safety, her first stage was distant thirteen miles, where believing herself in a state of temporary safety she abode three weeks, when she pursued her way across the Country thirty miles further, where she continued two years, enduring a variety of hardships — With the name of Doctor Rush, you are familiar, and my catalogue of etceteras, I must reserve, until I have the happiness of joining once more, our domestic Circle — When this period will be, I am unable to say, but you will do me the justice to believe, that no effort in my power shall be lacking, to accelerate its approach — I think we shall leave Philadelphia in a week, or two, but being necessitated to pay so many visits upon the road, our progress homeward will be but slow — yet, be assured, my ever honoured parents, that wherever we may be, we are unitedly, duteously, and affectionately yours — Item — At the Levee of Mrs Bache, we met the celebrated Mrs Henry, the present principal of the American company of Players, and Miss Henry, her daughter, a beautiful, and accomplished Girl, about thirteen years of age — Mrs Henry is personally acquainted with, and thus often played with the celebrated Mrs Siddons — Item [—] the Reverend Doctor Smith & Lady — The Reverend Mr Rogers & Lady with Mr & Mrs Davison, have shown us so many civilities, that gratitude impels us to give them a place, among my prominent figures —

Letter 766 To Mr E.S. Philadelphia Arch street
July 5th. 1790

In this letter, written to her cousin, Epes Sargent, Judith laments with him the loss of a close relative. She explains that she has less time to write now without the domestic help she is used to, and must spend more time caring for her husband. She reflects on the value of her friendship with Epes, which was one of the closest and lengthiest in her life — both intellectually and emotionally. She shares with him her thoughts about staying in Philadelphia, where she and John would most assuredly live out their days in affluence and fame. Had her child lived, she would have encouraged this decision as the most responsible for his future. Since he died, she has no desire to leave Gloucester and her parents, brother, sister, Epes and his family, the grave of her stillborn baby and the "ashes of her Ancestors." Still, she says, she will do what John wishes and knows that whatever place they inhabit is God's will. "Catherine" is Epes Sargent's 16-year-old daughter (1774-1852); his "angel Mother" is Catherine Osborne Sargent (1722-1788), Judith's beloved aunt, who had recently passed away. Catherine, who was married to Judith's uncle, also named Epes (1721-1779), was active in the business affairs of her wealthy husband and was no doubt an important influence on Judith. Along with Judith's father and other prominent citizens in Gloucester, Judith's uncle Epes was an early follower of the Universalist faith and an important champion of John Murray. Epes and Winthrop Sargent were centrally involved in challenging the established church's right to tax the Universalists who wished to support their own church. They refused to pay taxes and some of their possessions were seized by the town — including pieces of Epes Sargent's silver. But they won their case, and struck the first blow for freedom of religion. Even so, John Murray's ministry continued to be challenged, and Uncle Epes Sargent played an important role in securing John's safety. It is small wonder that Judith and his son, who were close in age, became dear friends.

Such a length of time hath elapsed, and such a variety of scenes hath take[n] place, since I recognized in the form of a letter to me, characters which were once so familiar, and which have always been dear to my heart, that it were vain for me to attempt a description of the mingling sensations, which surprised my soul, as I perused their elegant, and affectionate expression — yet the pleasingly grateful emotion, althoug[h] disdaining the vestments in which language would essay to cloathe them, will forever remain, traced in indelible inscriptions upon the tablets of my bosom — I think, my dear Sir, the loss of our maternal friend, must be regarded by us, as a source of regret — so long as the separating veil shall continue to intervene between our groser Men and the ever beauteous, the sweetly benign shade — Mortals may pretend to be so far disinterested, as to find their felicity in the enjoyment of those they love, even though divested of all participation therein, save what is bestowed by sympathy, yet I imagine, that while huma[n]s, we must feel as those who have had attained that perfection of being, which will endow them with the unclouded exercise of reason — I wish any partial Eulogist, during his fanciful excursion with his more humble Friend, could have invested her with that manly diction, that happy selection of language, charming succession of ideas, nervous arrangement, and elegant polish of style, which distinguishes his own magic page [—] could he, I say, have thus gratified her, thus indeed the Banks of the Hudson, and the Delaware, might have gladdened in her song, and its days thus strongly marked, would doubtless have been as immortal, as the floods of those rivers — But as it is, I do assure you, my intrigues with the muses have been greatly circumscribed, I am not so well situated for writing, as upon a former tour — then a duteous little girl was constantly at my elbow, cheerfully performing every little task, such as laying my paraphernalia in order, occasionally wielding the needle etc etc [—] Now, it is true my dignity may be considerably augmented, and my sentimental pleasures much advanced, yet, you who are blest with a companion so properly, and so unremitingly attentive, will readily conceive, that I am now to Mr Murray, in some sort, what, in our last excursion, my Anna was to me; and, of course, I have hitherto continued myself with a cursory account of my route, contained in the letters to my Parents — These letters, my dear Sir, if either you, or yours, express a wish to see, I have requested my Mother, to put into your hands. Yes, an intellectual attachment I pleasingly believe, can never expire, and the reflection that I have worn and that I still wear, with individuals whom I highly esteem, the silken bands of friendship, hath beamed a ray of benign light at...the darkest moments, which have shrouded the voyage of life — Friendship — blessed Friendship can indeed illumine the scene — Its powerful influence, piercing the dun obscure, often breaks upon the soul, in the mildly spreading dawn, or bursts upon it in all the glory of meridian day — and, it is not true, that although the tenement which enwraps these finer movements, may remotely wander, yet the mingling wishes, the kindred hopes, and fears of congenial minds, can annihilate distance, and anticipating the privileges of future immortality, can meet, and mark their hours by the dearest enjoyments — A removal from Gloucester is an event, which I have never yet realized — I will freely confess to you, my friend, I seriously believe, a residence in this City, would crown the Career of our Murray, with both fame, and fortune — But what are these bubbles — and what is their amount — Indeed if that infant, to whom I loaned so transient an existence, and who for a season enkindled in my bosom the brightest anticipation — had that infant been given to my bosom, I should have deemed it my indispensable duty, to have made every effort in my power, as far as rectitude would have authorized, to have promoted his interest — But as he is, I religiously believe, amply provided for, in the paradise of our God, and as I am couldly debared every rational prospect, of again reiterating those charming expectations, which once so delightfully winged my hopes, what remains, but that I hasten to the world of spirits, there to embrace his airy footsteps — The whole of my plans are now circumscribed, by a desire for a humble competency, and a resolution to pluck as many flowers, as I consistently can, on my way to that hour, which shall unite me to a being — who strange as it may seem, possesses my heart's best affections — Agreeably to this sentiment, I thus argue — Gloucester possesses for me superior charms — My warmest affections hover round the asylum of my youth — There resideth the indulgently venerable forms of my tender, and ever honoured Parents, there dwelleth individuals whom I sincerely love and there apparently stationed, is my select, my sentimental friend, his amiable Companion, and a beautiful little group, the individuals of which, I fondly believe, imbibe with their earliest growth, sentiments of affectionate esteem for her, who most devoutly wishes that for them the path of life may be strewed with the finest flowers, which can bloom in the garden of mortality — I might add, fanciful as it may seem [—] In that spot rests the ashes of my Ancestors — There too sleeps the cold gray tenement of your angel Mother, with many a friend laid low, and there is deposited the little form, which for a season, partook my sufferings — Yet, after all, decision rests not with me — My wishes ought to be formed by the inclinations of Mr Murray — as a Wife, it doth not become me to direct, and as a Christian, I ought rather to say — He who fixeth the bounds of our habitation, will take care to appoint for us a place — you will have the goodness to tender my affectionate regards to Mrs Sargent — I have written her, sometime since, a very long letter, with a very saucy conclusion — which letter, I hope came safe to hand — Poor Catherine — I grieve that the morning of her days is so enveloped in clouds — May meridian life brighten upon her, and may its evening close serenely — Give unto her, and the rest of the sweet boys, and Girls, my heart's love — The assurance of your continued and unfeigned regard, is to me, my dear Sir, a source of very much felicity and you will, I am confidant, believe, that I am most gratefully, and affectionately your highly obliged kinswoman —

Letter 767 To Mrs Sargent Philadelphia Arch Street
July 8th 1790

Judith apologizes to her aunt for not writing more frequently but "claims on her time" continue to grow in number. This is a very reflective letter, with thoughts about the presence of ancestors in their lives, about death and suicide. Judith has sent her parents the pamphlet from the Universalist convention which outlines their agreed upon Articles of Faith and Practice. John will present this document, along with an address, to President Washington during their return trip to New York. Judith expresses concern over a recent uprising on the island of Martinique, where one of Mrs. Sargent's sons is headed. She reports that she and John will attend the commencement exercises at the College in Philadelphia, now the University of Pennsylvania.

How unremitted are the attentions of my dear, obliging friend, and how sweetly doth she manage, to entwine a charm, with each revolving period — Potent is the magic influence, which binds me unalterably, and eternally hers — Engagements with their multifarious claims grow so fast upon me, that I have hardly an instant allowed me to acknowledge your letter of June 25 which came to hand soon after I made up my last communication — Yet, in the midst of hurry, I select a few moments, and said moments shall be consecrated to you — They shall assure you, that the vivid emotions of gratitude, and tenderness, are, in my devoted bosom as energetic as heretofore, and that I cannot cease to love, and to admire, you will learn from my journal, the occurrences of the week and I can only add, that a few days will perhaps remove us from the splendidly various scene, but as we are to pass some time in the Jerseys, if you still continue to enclose for me, in New York, your friendly pages will be carefully preserved, until my arrival there, which if our arrangements succeed, will be some time the last of this month ———— your conviction of the existence of Beings of ancestral order, whose movements not impeded by the heavy vehicles in which we are imprisoned, find means of communicating with the precipient Mind, must be, to you, a source of much pleasure — How delightful to conceive that the sacred shade of your honoured Mother, is guarding your hours, suggesting your actions, and breathing into the bosom of her lovely daughter, a portion of that fortitude, which so eminently distinguished her own life — How rich is the solace, which induces you to behold her pointing you to unclouded day — to that day, which exhaling the tear drop from your humid eye, shall render you completely blessed — I do assure you, my charming Friend considerations of this nature, are productive of my brightest moments — The whole of the scene you describe is before me, I fancy myself in your chamber — I hear, at that late hour of the night, the uncommon clamour of the knocker, the domestics crouding to the door — I imbibe your hopes, I am grateful, the source considered, for your fears — I am pierced by the shafts of suspence, and my perturbation encreases, until the letters are in your hand — Do not afflict yourself, for the mistake relative to the breaking the seals — Mr Murray uses different impressions, indiscriminately, and my Father is not critical, nor can the accident be attended, with the smallest unpleasant consequences, save the anxiety which it hath been productive to you — Pity that mischevious Genius, which no doubt hovers near, should so often counteract the benevolent designs of guardian spirits, should thus have availed itself of a circumstance, so trivial, and immaterial, should thus have tortured my friend — but I trust that its malevolent influence was transient, and that you have long since ceased to regret — My husband hath had an answer to the letter in question, and not the smallest notice has been taken of the seal — I sincerely wish you had read said letter, you would have found in it an account of the proceedings of the American Universalists, assembled by their delegates, in convention in this City — The printed Pamphlet with a copy of the articles of Faith, and Practice to which the Convention hath agreed, and which they recommend to their Constituents — Mr Murray, upon his way through New York, is to present the Articles with an address from the Universalists, to our liberal and impartial President — Were not those females, who thus unexpectedly finished their Career, rather to be envied than otherwise? At least as Christians, we ought to suppose the manner of their demise, the very best which could possibly have taken place, for it was allowed by that unerring Wisdom, who hath numbered the hours of our head — Was it the Greeks, or Romans, who esteemed sudden death a blessing? Do you not recollect the young Men, who for an act of filial Virtue, rendered, by attending circumstances, an uncommon exertion, were rewarded by receiving an immediate passport into the etherial World, through the instrumentality of a messenger winged upon the electrical flash of the forked Lightening? — The poor way worn Traveller, seizing with impatient hands, his small remains of life, is surely an object of commiseration — yet, I must confess, I cannot easily reconcile the act of suicide, with my ideas of resignation to that power, who made, upholds, directs, and hath the undoubted Right of disposal — although I am aware, even in this event, that the consistency of my creed, compels me to say, what hath been said a thousand times, before — "Whatever is — is right" I trust that the God of peace, will still the Riot, and calm the anarchy, which hath erected its hydra head, in Martinico — and this before the arrival of our young Adventurer — May the dear youth be guarded by the all protecting hand of Deity — May his path be made strait before him, and may he be returned in safety to your maternal bosom — I am this day to make one of the audiences, at the ceremonies attendant upon a commencement, and although so long a Resident in the neighbourhood of Cambridge, the day will yet furnish me with a Novel scene — Farewell, I must sacrifice at least half an hour, for the purpose of making my Toilet — My dearest love to our children — regards to all inquiring friends — Continue, I pray you, to know me as your unalterable Friend ———

Letter 768 To my Father and Mother Philadelphia Arch Street July 10 1790 — Saturday

Lengthy descriptions of events, people, and places are contained in this letter. John and Judith have attended the July 4 (Independence Day) celebrations at Christ Church over which Reverend Doctor Smith, President of the University of Pennsylvania, presided. Prominently featured in the ceremony were members of the Society of the Cincinnati, an association of General Washington's continental army officers which was formed in 1783 (at the close of the war) to support the widows and children of slain officers and to lobby the Continental Congress for unpaid wages. (Judith's brother, Winthrop, was a member of the Society.) Other celebratory events described here include a display of fireworks at the State House and elaborate demonstrations, music, and military parades at Schuylkill Gardens later that evening. The "throngs" at first demonstrated "boisterous manifestations of unbridled joy," but then "wild disorder" ensued and the Murrays had to make their escape through an underground tunnel. Later in the week, they visited friends including Mrs. Mackie who helped Judith disguise herself so she could attend the theatre! Not wanting to embarrass her husband or herself by committing an act that went against social propriety in Philadelphia, Judith donned a black shawl and bonnet and, "in coy," visited the Philadelphia "Play house" where she saw two short plays, a reenactment of a battle at sea, and a pantomime act. She describes the theatre in great detail, including its architecture, interior design, lighting, ventilation, scenery, music, and refreshments. Judith and John also attended the commencement exercises at the University of Pennsylvania, held in the "German reformed church" (which she details), and where they heard a humorous oration by William Bache, Benjamin Franklin's grandson. She was annoyed with a young man and woman flirting in front of her, wishing they had better manners. Finally, Judith describes for her parents the Philadelphia hospital and mental wards. She viewed the institution as another example of Philadelphia's prevalent "philanthropic spirit." Here, she wrote, "every method is taken...to mitigate the calamities of the sufferer."

Sunday last being the anniversary of Independence, and the Reverend Doctor Smith being requested to deliver a discourse, to the Gentlemen of the Cincinnati — Mr Murray omitted his morning service, that he might attend upon the Doctor, at Christ Church — and accordingly we presented ourselves in the great congregation — Christ Church is an elegant building. It hath three spacious openings — It is handsomely glazed, and neatly finished; the pulpit is in the best taste, it is richly ornamented, decorated with Cherubims and crested with a winged Dove — It riseth under a superb Arch, variously painted, and furnished upon the right, and the left, with a copy of the Decalogne, in beautiful gilt Capitals — Fronting the pulpit, is an Orchestra supplied with a magnificent Organ, and the galleries rest upon ample and uniform arches, which Arches are supported by many pillars, neatly fluted; Every thing was performed in honour of the day, which the observance due to holy time would allow — The Cincinnati, and other military marched in procession to the sound of solemn musick — The bells chimed most melodiously, and in the body of the church conspicuous pews were reserved for the Cincinnati — Doctor Smith chose his subject from Isaiah Chapter 52d Verse 10th "The Lord hath made bare his holy arm in the eyes of all the nations, and all the ends of the earth shall see the salvation of our God" [—] The Doctor's discourse was elegant, and animated — He was necessitated to accommodate himself to the day, as sacred time — to the day, as the anniversary of an event, which will no doubt continue memorable, to the latest posterity — It was incumbent upon him to unite the peculiar features of a sermon, with those of an Oration delivered to a particular Body of distinguished Citizens — yet, without embarrassment and with the most happy arrangement, and elegance of expression, he effected every necessary purpose — He opened his discourse with a beautifully sententious exordium in praise of the fundamental truths of our most holy Religion, with an energetic Euloquium upon the Messenger of Peace — upon such who bring glad tidings of good things and in a natural gradation, he proceeded to connect temporal blessings. The arm of the Lord had indeed been made bare, in favour of this Columbian World — It had been made bare, even in the sight of the Nations — He expatiated upon particular privileges, with which we, as Americans are endowed, and with nervous conciseness, he enumerated them.

The Cincinnati were handsomely complimented, and their virtues feelingly eulogized — He barely touched upon the apprehensions, with which the order had filled the people, and judiciously allowed our band of Heroes, the applause which they so justly merited, when instead of arming themselves with indignant pride, they evinced the benign aspect of their association, by revising, correcting, and pruning, and by attributing to a holy jealousy in their fellow Citizens, suspicions for which, had they been activated by the motives imparted to them, they would have found it easy, to have assigned a more malignant cause. Illustrious Warriors, in that moment of self government, the splendid triumphs of dignified condescension, were more glorious, than those fading, and diminished rays, which gild the Coronet or beam around the proudest Monarch who ever wore a crown — Doctor Smith believed no language could do higher justice, or more emphatically delineate the institution, than its own elegantly expressive articles of association, and he quoted the whole of a very animated paragraph, while at the affecting, and well known sounds, the tears of pleasure glistened in my eye — Doctor Smith introduced from a sermon of his own, delivered in [the] presence of our immortal Chief, long before the Order of the Cincinnati had a Being, a sublime, and beautiful allusion, which he modestly observed, if he might be allowed to assume so much, possibly originated the institution, or at least must claim the honour of a prediction — In the selection adduced by the Doctor, the Columbian Hero was hailed as another Cincinnatin — The Dictator to, and the Redeemer of his Country, and, the Orator added, if rightly I divine, as he approacheth the horizon of life, his setting beams will be still more conspicuously splendid — Doctor Smith, in the conclusion of his discourse, borne with divine enthusiasm upon wings prophetic, beheld the thirteen United States, now again entwined in the sweet bands of Union, increasing in population, civilization, industry, propriety of manners, and benvolently effacious laws — Nor were his ideas confined by these emancipated States still soaring in the aerial regions of boundless anticipation, he beheld, amid the untutored and savage wilds, of uncounted Realms, magnificent Cities bursting into life — Gathering myriads, of myriads, brightened upon him — Humanized indian Nations, forever burying the bloody hatchet, the murderous knife, adoring the salvation of our God, and mingling in their Orizons grateful remembrance of those heroes, who had so nobly founded, the broad base of wide spreading liberty — Doctor Smith is not often found in the Pulpit, he informed his audience, that he stood there upon that splendid era, by the honourable choice of the Cincinnati, and the acquiescing suffrage of the Right Reverend Bishop White — The matter of his discourses is, as I am told, always excellent, perhaps the manner is not quite an explainable, but appointed President of the University, he is generally engaged in the more particular duties, of his most important office — After the services of the day, the bells again sounded most harmoniously, and the decent manifestations of joy, were abundant and truly gratifying — On Monday every restraint being taken off, the ebullations of hilarity obtained their utmost latitude — The bells were clamorous, the colors displayed, and the Cannon discharged — The military of every description was concluded by a display of fire works from the State House, and a superb illumination of Schuylkill gardens — The Proprietor of that Elysium, had advertised a variety of additional exhibitions, such as an artificial Island, a [Tavern] house, garden etc to be represented in the evening, upon the River, splendidly illuminated — a number of heathen Deities rendered luminous, and distinguished by their insignia — Bridge dressed in shrubbery, and appropriate Colours for every state in the Union — The Arms of America and France entwined by Liberty — a rich display of Fire works, exhibited from the Lawn, in front of the Federal temple — Thirteen Boys, and an equal number of Girls, issuing from the Grove, habited as shepherds, and shepherdesses, and proceeding to the Federal Temple, chanting responsively, an Ode to Liberty, with a number of songs, Odes, and Choruses, in honour of the auspicious event, which the day commemorated. An advertisement of this kind, originated the highest expectations — It produced in the gardens a vast concourse of people, upwards of six thousand persons, Candidates for the pleasure of the scene — In an assembly so multifarious, characters of every description, you will not doubt, were collected — Urged by curiosity, my husband, supposing it would be unpleasant crossing the floating Bridge, took me in his Carriage to the middle of the ferry — never did I behold a scene more truly enchanting than Nature then presented, upon the Banks of the Schuylkill — The river was divinely serene, and the margin was ornamented by romantic, and beautifully variegated imagery — But crossing the stream we approached the scene of riot — Never did my Fancy in its most tumultuous, and capricious combinations, sketch a view so replete with wild disorder, and confused uproar — With much difficulty we obtained tickets of admission, and when we reached the grounds, the unlicensed Mirth, the prevalent anarchy, boisterous manifestations of unbridled joy, and rude elbowing of the promiscuous throng, was really distressing — In vain, in the midst of those sweetly rural, and enchanting recesses, where we had recently enjoyed so much, we sought the honeysuckle arbour, or embowering shade — upon every seat, and in every embosomed haunt, noisy frolick, with rude unmannered stare had taken its stand, and it was well if the thronged croud allowed us to keep our feet — All ranks of people were grouped together — The Orchestra, that beautiful seat of harmony, was taken by the Mob, and from the correct mind, every idea of enjoyment was of necessity banished — so great was the croud that to obtain the smallest refreshment, was out of the question, and our only remaining wish, was to gain a passage out of the gardens — To effect this was, however, impossible [—] Thick and lawless ranks lined the gates — all our addresses, and perseverance, proved abortive and I was nearly sinking upon the spot, when a friend taking compassion upon our sufferings, led us through a flight of rooms, into a subteraneous passage through which, winding our way, we once more found ourselves safely conducted into a spacious street — when instantly mounting our Carriage, and crossing the floating bridge at the risk of our lives, from the pressing horses, chaises, Coaches, and throngs of people, we very cheerfully left behind us illuminations, fire works, heathen Gods, and Goddesses etc etc most sincerely felicitating ourselves, upon our happy escape — By the depredations of the Mob, we are told the Paradise recently so beautiful, is greatly injured but time I hope will restore it to accustomed Order and neatness — Tuesday, we devoted to visiting an amiable, and substantial family, of the name of Sewall, from the individuals of which, we derived much pleasure — We passed Wednesday morning agreeably with Doctor Rush and a Mrs Elsington, by whose honest attention we have been greatly obliged — On Wednesday too, we once more availed ourselves of the marked politeness of our elegant friend, Mrs Mackie, by accepting an invitation to dine — I had expressed a desire, to devote at least one evening to the Theatre, but as it was apparently attended with many difficulties, and I had reason to believe, it would implant a wound, in the bosom of simplicity, my acquiescing mind, had yielded to the necessity of the times — Mr & Mrs Mackie, however, with most obliging, and correct address, laid a plan which produced me at the Theatre in coy — A large black bonnet completely enveloped my face, and a scarf thrown over my shoulders, as it was believed, sufficiently disguised me — Mr & Mrs Mackie, with their sister, and their Eliza, regaled us in the afternoon, by an enchanting ride along the winding, and beautifully variegated Banks of the Schuylkill, on to [P...ants], and we returned to the Suburbs, where, entering a neat recess, the Avenue to which was shaded by a row of well trimmed spruce trees we took a dish of tea, and having secured a side box at the Theatre, we parted from Mr Murray, and proceeded immediately thither — The Exterior of the Play house is not more than tolerable, but the inside is fitted up after the English Taste — The stage is considerably elevated — The side and front boxes commencing from the stage, form a semicircle — There is only one row of Galleries, the seats in which gradually ascend. The Pitt is upon an easy descent to the stage — The boxes are neatly finished, every box is pierced with a separate opening, which leads to a lobby, that conducts us out of the house, and, of course, egress, and regress are at pleasure — The first box upon the right hand of the stage, is elegantly decorated, and distinguished, and it is reserved for the Governor of the State and the two Chief Magistrates, without whose approbating sanction, no piece can be performed — Cold hams, Cakes, fruit, wine, etc etc for the refreshment of the company may be obtained, upon the out side of the Play House — The Theatre is handsomely lighted, by a number of Globular glasses, supplied with wax tapers — Lighted branches illumine the Stage, a row of candles are arranged in Front, and they have the English method, of throwing a profusion of light upon the stage, by means of little concealed Lamps, the effect only of which is visible — The scenery exceeds every thing of which I had formed an idea — The superb apartment, richly furnished, and decorated by fluted pillars, enwreathed with flowers, from the window of which, so perfect is the deception, we imagine we behold individuals passing, and repassing, is dexterously changed giving the place to a view in an open street, magnificent buildings rising round, to a rural walk, a returned recess, or, in short, to whatever arrangement, the Nature of the piece may require — Previous to the rising of the curtains the audience sufficiently attracts attention — Pleasing ideas of social refinement take possession of the mind — highly zested pleasures are afloat — while a Ventilator suspended from the ceiling, by its gently fanning breezes, gives us to enjoy, amid the heat of summer, the softest vernal airs. The front of the stage is pleasingly ornamented [—] The Pennsylvania arms are conspicuously displayed in the Centre — The Galaxies rest upon arches, supported by pillars — The Orchestra is arranged before the stage, and the musick is drawn from Violins, and Clarinets — For the rising of the curtains the gallery is horribly clamorous — hissing, hooping, stamping most outrageously — The piece performed on Monday evening, was a comedy of five acts called the Contrast, and written by a Citizen of the United States — This Essay is a species of composition, universally acknowledged arduous, [it] hath, in my opinion, much merit, and unless we pronounce one or two scenes rather too expressive may be considered as unexceptionable — The Contrast between a genteel Continental Officer, a Native of Boston, brave, intrepid, patriotic, manly, and humane — in short whose bosom seems replete with every sentiment, which can do honour to humanity, and a frivolous conceited Coxcomb, who had with infinite pains formed himself upon the Chesterfieldian system — This Contrast is supported with much spirit and most judiciously conducted — Colonel Manly's servant also, and Billy Dimple — Valet de Chambre, serve as Counterparts to their superiors, and admirably continue the Contrast — The New England Jonathan, constitutes the humour of the piece, and his...simplicity gives birth to some ludicrous scenes, the representation of which, gave me an opportunity of observing some anti Federal ideas, which, every regulation not with standing are yet but too prevalent — No sooner did Jonathan make his appearance, than the eyes of all our party were involuntarily turned upon me, and a supposition of the mortification it was imagined I endured, to see my poor Country thus ridiculed, gave rise to some remarks of an apologetical nature — The ridicule was however just, and I experienced no pain, but what originated in the unconstitutional disparation, which the applications of my friends evinced, while my heart spontaneously questioned — Is not then America our Common Country — Colonel Manly is exhibited in a variety of interesting, an amiable characters, as a duteous, and obliging son, and a tender, affectionate, and brave protector of a vivacious, and beautiful sister, as an honourably impassioned Lover, as a consistent Soldier, continuing to wear the bands of Amity with his fellow soldiers, whom he styles his family — and as a genuine Patriot venerating with noble enthusiasm his native Country, and seeking to reform rather than expose her errors — The Colonel is thrown into the most delicate situations, from which he extricates himself with unimpeached Rectitude — But as I intend possessing myself of this Play, I shall only add, that the Catastrophe produceth practical justice, that Colonel Manly is rewarded with the maid of his heart, who seems every [bit] worthy of her distinguished Lot — while Billy Dimple, makes his exit, with that contempt which he most richly merited — Mr Morris did ample justice to the character of Van Rough — Mr Wignall to that of Jonathan, and Mr Biddle to that of [...amy] — Mr Hallum played Manly, and notwithstanding the representation of this Comedian, perhaps, in a private letter, I may have the presumption to remark, without any great hazard — His manners appeared to me too stiff, formal, and constrained, — In one word, it was too apparent that he was indeed an Actor [—] Mr & Mrs Henry [bear] the palm upon the American Stage — this, however I am told, for I had not the pleasure of seeing either of those celebrated performers, except in a private room — Mrs Morris in the character of Charlotte Manly, was admirable, she appeared to me abundantly superior to the other females, although they too, possessed appropriate excellence — A humourous piece in the character of a drunken sailor succeeded the Comedy — it was spoken by a young gentleman, in his novitiate, from New York — This was followed by the agreeable Surprise — a farce in two Acts — It is a physical Entertainment — A Male and Female exchanged in their infancy, by their Parents, are reared up with erroneous ideas of their birth — In consequence of which, Laura, supposing her Mother would never allow her to unite herself to the humble fortunes of Eugene, of whom she is violently enamoured, is on the point of eloping, for the purpose of a Clandestine Union — from which she is preserved, by the honour of Eugene, when his real Father, who proves to be the person who had educated Laura, exultingly acknowledges his Son — Laura is claimed by him who had hitherto discharged the paternal duties to Eugene, and the result of this "Agreeable Surprise" is a marriage, which had already been designed by the Father of Eugene — Such is the Plot of the "The Agreeable Surprise" — Many laughable scenes are produced, by a Mistake relative to a widow, who seems an original character and a pedantic affectation of erudition, in an illiterate, conceited Brother, and it is impossible to help being diverted, at the ludicrous representation of these follies — The piece is enriched by some excellent songs — but the music was not of the first rate — A transparent scene from Nature, was next introduced — Of Nature beautifully adorned by Art — Chinese shades followed[,] these shades were highly characteristic — flitting across the scene, suddenly rising upon, and as suddenly sinking through the stage — A sea light, in all its variety of horrors, imposingly arrested our attention — The Ocean was out spread — two ships appeared in view — We saw them approach, we beheld the hostile signals displayed — They meet, The engagement commences, they exchange a broad side, the action grows more arduous, the blue waters become ensanguined, the vessels are enveloped in smoke — One of the masts is shivered — it tumbles — it falls — the ship is almost a wreck! but the intrepidity of her commander is undiminished — See another Mast is shot away — and look — she sinks!! — She is whelmed in the bosom of the waves, while her Antagonist triumphantly rides the ample Circle of the deep — I confess, that the certainty of this scene being so often dreadfully realized, agitated my bosom, with painful sensations, and my admiration of the art, which could, by the mere force of painting, and Machinery, thus animate its imagery, was hardly a balance to the glooms, which pervaded my soul. We were, however, relieved by a scene not quite so interesting — a hunting piece with a view of the sportsman, and his faithful dog, after which our feelings were again exercised, by an exhibition of a boat, completely manned, instantaneously swallowed up by a huge Whale — A Tavern, a Wind Mill, and a broken bridge, and a Traveller in vain assaying to pass it, with a carpenter insulting his embarrassment, next claimed our attention, and these were followed by the Miller and his Jack Ass, the Jolly Miller and his bottle — The Millers Maid, Cow, Goat etc etc and the evening concluded with Harlequin's Skeleton, a pantomimical Fete — which entertainment, although in dumb show, was so expressively represented, as to render it easy for the attentive observer, to understand — That the Nymph was the daughter of a white headed Man, that she was engaged in a Clandestine Correspondence with Harlequin, that the Clown had taken it upon him to resent, that he imagined he had ultimately effected the death of Harlequin, after which he supposed himself haunted by the skeleton — the address of which was so wonderful, as to produce the most happy termination — The old gentleman yielding his Collumbine, to the embraces of her Harlequin, these unaccountably restored to life — Thursday we attended at Commencement, a day sacred to the conferring [of] degrees in the University of Pennsylvania — The Order of Procession was respectable, it proceeded from the Hall of the University — and the exercises took place in the German reformed Church — This Church is a handsome building, elegantly finished, and the pulpit uncommonly neat — It is decorated by two branches of Candlesticks, highly wrought, and superb Chandeliers are suspended from the ceiling which are of cut glass, and exquisite workmanship — In this Church was assembled a numerous and brilliant Audience — The entertainment opened by a concert of vocal, and instrumental musick, when the President addressed the throne of grace — after which a salutory Oration was delivered — four other orations upon various subjects succeeded, which were followed by an interlude of musick. An Oration upon the education of children could not fail to interest — Mr William Bache — Grandson of Doctor Franklin pronounced an Oration upon the history, cultivation, and qualities of potatoes! The composition was humourous, and after giving the natural history of the plant, and enumerating its many properties, after attributing to the abundant use of the Irish potato the bravery, hospitality, and patriotism of the Irish Nation, after deducing from this source the beauty of its females, with the fascinating powers said to be peculiar to the Lancaster Fair Ones (a Town in England notorious for their successful cultivation of this [art]) — he produced a huge potato, which extended to the full length of his arm, he endeavoured with much seeming earnestness, and great force of language, to [introduce] his Countrymen, and particularly the Ladies of Philadelphia, to the extensive culture, and constant use of the Potatoes — its most potent root, which would undoubtedly originate in their bosoms every Virtue, and could not fail of adorning their exteriors with every beauty. The rhetorical harangue of Mr Bache, was received with uncommon applause, and the audience clapped him so long, and so loud, expressing their admiration by feet, hands[,] canes etc, and in a matter so exactly theatrical — to the great annoyance of the Clergy, who with countenances, every feature of which indicated distress, throw abroad their hands, thus properly assaying to hush the still augmenting Clamour which reprehending, and very potent appeal, produced its salutary effect, and the music — opportunity striking in, the decency of order was restored — With an Oration upon the feelings of Gratitude, we were greatly pleased, for although delivered in the German language, yet so expressive, and so appropriate was the action of the young Declaimer, that being apprized of the subject, we easily found words to cloath those ideas, which his energetic gestures, and interesting manner suggested — This little orator, is a German, educated by the philanthropic feelings of respectable Gentlemen, and young Endress, is become a prodigy of learning Esteeming himself the Child of benevolence — his emotioning[s] were strikingly visible — Repeatedly soft, and solemn musick, assayed to calm the transports of his grief — to which wiping his swimming eyes, he listened with wrapt attention — The Conclusion of his Oration was in English, when bidding adieu to his Class Mates, he pathetically, and severally, addressed the heads of the Seminary, particularly his venerable Benefactors, and, affectionately exclaimed — "Who now shall guide my youthful steps, or where shall the inexperienced Voyager, direct his cours? ["] Suddenly, however, by a beautiful, and animated Apostropher — toward heaven he raised his streaming gaze, and clasping his hands — in elevated, and supplicating strains, he besought the interposing goodness, and protecting arm, of the God, who had hitherto upheld him — In my eyes I confess the humid drops presented, and my heart spontaneously yielded to devotional Amens — Two other Orations with the intervention of musick preceded the conferring the degrees

The number of graduates was respectable — and the diplomas adorned with blue and purple ribbons, were bestowed with affectionate solemnity. An elegant Valedictory Oration succeeded — followed by vocal, and instrumental music when the President proceeded to give the charge, and the prayr and benediction with a repetition of vocal, and instrumental musick, concluded the whole — I confess I very highly enjoyed the day, but my satisfaction would have been still more complete, had not my attention been frequently arrested by a pretty Flatterer, assayed in all her charms, and fully conscious of her all conquering power, who, most unfortunately for me, was receiving homage directly before me — At the shrine of this Belle, a modern Beau delightfully performed, with milk white hand, and lily face, was audibly sacrificing — I regretted that his Orisons were not offered by the silent language of the eye, as the incessant volutility of his articulated devoirs, confused by the murmuring in my ear, combined with the Voices of the public speakers, and created such a confused jargon, as, occasionally totally distracted my ideas — Pity that the Frillers of the age, do not take into consideration, an[d] digest, a code of real good breeding — Friday Morning we part with a rurally sentimental friend, our party too was sentimental, and we enjoyed it most delightfully — In the afternoon we visited the hospital, and experienced while pacing its different apartments, a mixture of pain, and pleasure — The Hospital is a noble Brick Edifice, embosomed in tall rows of beautiful sycamore, surrounded by a substantial brick wall, not less than ten feet high, the ringing of a bell, at a well finished gate, neatly ornamented, summons the Porter when we are introduced into a spacious lawn, from which we pass into the house — ascending a flight of steps, and entering the Hall, we have a view of an ample apartment, provided with beds, and other necessaries for the sick — Upon the right we ascend a staircase, which leads to other rooms, appropriated to the scene of benevolent use, on the left we enter a parlour, finished in fine taste — the marble of the chimney richly veined, and highly polished — This parlour contains a grand Medical Library, pictures etc among which is an elegant Painting, of the good Samaritan — This picture is exhibited in various parts of the Hospital — We are shown paintings from the pencil of a self taught Genius, which may claim rank, with the productions of many, whose talents have been highly cultivated — All the apartments in the Hospital are lofty, and the view from the Cupola is paradisical — A decent family resides in, and has the care of the Hospital — Of this, had we not been previously informed, our own observation would have convinced us — For although we visited every cell, and were unexpected guests, we could not but admire the uniform order, which was preserved — Cleanliness abode in the Apartments of the sick, and the air was manifestly as pure, as in the most healthy dwelling — The Cells of those unhappy lunaticks, who are most outrageous, are ranged upon a line, under the ground floor, which are however sufficiently lighted, and aired — We penetrated with the eye of curiosity, these little recesses — Our observation did not appear to distress them and we entered into conversation with those, who were apparently the most rational — One female, whose countenance was truly prepossessing, I could not forbear distinguishing — She was young, and her eye was expressive of mild benignity — her features seemed fashioned by gentleness, and although the traces of misfortune have deeply marked her fine face, a pleasing kind of Resignation seemed to have triumphed over her sufferings — I observed that I thought her uncommonly handsome, and the sound vibrating sweetly upon her ear, seemed still to possess its charms, for it illumined her face, with a transient smile of pleasure — she complained that she wanted employment, and solicited a needle, and thread, which receiving, she appeared so perfectly engaged, as to be unconscious of a single spectator — I asked a Matron, who regar[d]ed us with an inquiring eye — how she found herself? — She replied she had been made disordered, but was upon the recovery — God I hope will restore you to perfect health, I rejoined — She raised her eyes to heaven, and clasping her hands, eagerly repeated — I hope so — Indeed I hope so — One unhappy body was sure she had seen me before — or if not me, some one exactly like me — in short they generally appeared solicitous to join in conversation — A white headed Man complained, that he had been seized by Recessions, and conveyed to that abode of misery, and when we wished to know if he were not well used, and what could be his objection to a residence in the Hospital? His shattered remains of reason, evinced its natural, an[d] unextinguished love of Liberty, by a declaration that he wished to be master of himself, to visit neighbor Jones, and go to Church — But this is the fair side of a deranged mind — other cells exhibited all the horrors of distraction — from the cell of a black Man, issues dreadful cries, and lamentations — and in one cell the Manic selecting his text, which he thus worded — "And Moses said unto Nathan Thou are the Man,["] preached universal damnation, to the world of Mankind, while kneeling at a little distance, another individual, with out stretched hands, vociferously imprecated curses, upon every created being, himself excepted — Among these intellectually disordered persons, is a very extraordinary Woman, whom I saw, and conversed with — She is a handsome Matron, apparently about sixty years of age, and she hath the finest hand[s], and arms, which, at her years, I ever saw — Disguised as a soldier — (this is an unquestionable fact) — she served two campaigns under the King of Prussia distinguishing herself as a Trooper, and receiving from that Prince, honourable testimony of her intrepidity — Many affecting circumstances are connected with her story — When she was first received into the Hospital in Philadelphia, she was shockingly outragious — but many, many years have since revolved, and now she is always peaceful, and at times rational — Every method is taken in the Hospital, to mitigate the calamities of the sufferer — The sick in Body, or Mind, are furnished with every thing necessary, and if judged salutary — with every delicacy life — Those whose derangement is supposed temporary, or slight, those whose frenzy is more confirmed, with the frantically raving, are severally disposed of, and provided for with the utmost tenderness, according to the exigencies of their several cases — being uniformly nursed, and supplied from the same source — Its funds are at this present, prodigious. The seal of the institution is benignly expressive — It delineates the Good Samaritan, binding up the wounds of the unfortunate, despoiled, and lacerated Traveller, and the inscription is thus worded — "Take care of him — and when I come I will repay you" —

Such is the philanthropic spirit, which pervades the Philadelphians — nor, with this well regulated and e[x]tensive Asylum for the neccessitous, although outspread upon an exceeding broad base are they satisfied, they have recently added a dispensary, resulting also from private exertions, which, from the date of its institution on April 6th one thousand, seven hundred and eighty six, to August 1st 1789 attended too, and relieved no less than five thousand two hundred, and forty two destitute persons — Blessed City, God Almighty will reward the benevolence of thy inhabitants — When He comes — He will indeed repay thy chil[dren] ten thousand times, ten thousand fold, and O may Peace, sweet peace, be ever found in thy borders — may thy sons and daughters be still crowned with plenty, and may they still be found in the strait and undeviating path of rectitude — Thus have I brought down my Week, to the present day — you will observe it hath been unusually crouded — but a few days will take me from this City, and then my subjects being neither so various, nor so copious, my recounts will not run to such an unconscionable length — Indeed I some times fear my proloxity will fatigue you, but you can take my letters up, and lay them down, at pleasure

This day I was most apprehensive I should have been necessitated to mark down to disappointment — The post came at noon, but no letters — The evening, however, crowned the day, by presenting a delightful close to the week, and putting me in possession of a letter from my dear Mrs Sargent, and of two letters from my honoured father — Accept, dearest parent, my most sincere thanks, Next mail shall present my responses for at this time, being rather weary, my replies must be general, and first, while I grieve at the sufferings of my dear, and tender Mother — I yet mingle therewith rejoicings — Forgive me dear honoured sufferer, I cannot but rejoice, that thou art still in existence, and that I can still say, to the inquiring stranger — while sensations the most delightful pervade my bosom — Yes, I have a Mother — Blessed be the God of life, my Father, and my Mother, are still alive — They still live to guide, to soothe, and to render luminous my added days — I had hoped that, e'er this, you would have been able to announce, that our dear Anna, had passed her hour of trial — but I will believe, this pleasing event, will shortly reach our ears — The misfortunes of my dear native place I must always deplore — Particularly those attendant upon Mr Ellery, and yourself — Give my love to the worthy Man, to Esther, Sally, my Orphan Girl etc etc and always believe, that you are ever in possession of my heart's best affections — Farewell — I am, with tender duty ever yours —

Letter 769 To Mrs Sargent Philadelphia Arch Street July 15 17[9]0

Judith is unwell, and has taken to her "chamber." This letter, then, is largely filled with responses to family news she received in her aunt's last letter, and with personal reflections. Writing, she tells her aunt Mary Turner Sargent, is her "favourite employment." Congress has chosen Philadelphia as its permanent site and, Judith reports, the Philadelphians are "elated." Judith and John are about to commence a "curcuitous" journey to New York — "out of the post road" — and she will not be able to send or receive letters for a couple of weeks. (Note: a "Grimalkin" is a kind of cat.)

I have, my sweet friend been really unwell — yet, compelled by the intreaties of a pleasing, and hospitable Circle of friends, I have been every day necessitated, to sacrifice a portion of my feelings, to civilities with which, in the present state of my health, I would gladly have dispensed ——— On Tuesday I came to a resolution, that submittting to the arbitrary dictates of indisposition, I would take refuge in my chamber, yet tuesday evening presented me at a promiscuous tea table, where were collected, the grave, the sentimental, the interested, the gay, the flatterer, and the insipidly affected Coquet — yesterday I was positive I must yield — yet I passed the day in company, and the evening produced me at the Oratorio, and this day feeling somewhat relieved, I seize the brightening moment, to mark with gratitude, and to respond with pleasure, to your last most interesting favour — If the language of my heart, which is the spontaneous result of sincerity be productive of pleasure to you, let not that pleasure know an alloy, by a supposition that my pen is dipped, in the adulterated stream, which issueth from a fountain so mixed, and equivocal, as adulatory complimenting. Perhaps there is no life wholly faultless — There are errors which originate in amiable benevolence, and if He, who organized the mental system, regardeth, as He undoubtedly doth, the motives of an action, surely they ought, in a finite view, to make a part of its estimation — I declare positively, I think an individual may be so circumstanced, as to render a step abstractedly reprehensible, not only justifiable but laudable — It must eternally be wrong, to form a judgment of any event, previous to a knowledge of the concurrent causes by which it was produced — A fault may be striped of its most unlovely properties, and it may only retain enough of its original texture, to preserve its human features [—] Any how, I would never be severe to mark, or to condemn, and I conceive it to be an irrefragable truth, that there is more wisdom, prudence, and direction, requisite to the extricating ourselves from difficulties, in which we have been unaccountably involved, in emerging from a cloud, which with obscuring influence, hath enveloped our reason, than if, in the entangled maze of a winding path, we had never been induced to wander — Doubtless those individuals are peculiarly happy, who have undeviatingly persevered in the flowery walks of pleasurable consciousness, but, as the sun breaks forth with added splendor, after a dark and tempestuous night — so the lovely wanderer, regaining her ascendency, is doubly armed with native worth, and that self possession which she hath once more attained. Officious, then, was the crimson blush, and humid eye, of your friend, and when again you are admitted into a confidential interview, with the heart of that charmingly susceptible Girl, I pray you to assure her, that the terms prudent, and discreet, were not from my pen unmeaning epithets, that I conceive they are attributes, to which she hath an undoubted claim, since she must possess them in a high degree to be able to say — Thus far I will go — and no farther —

Fear not my friend, Writing is my favourite employment, and my application is not so unremitted as you imagine — I could not forbear a smile at the experiment of Lucius Manlius, and I should have been fond of witnessing his pretty astonishment at the consequence — If the race of the Grimalkins in the habitation, to which you advert, are capable of gratitude, this young brood, will certainly esteem our little Cherub, as a very important benefactor, in thus emancipating them from the ten thousand kicks, and cuffs, to which, in their progress to maturity they must have been subjected — Fitz Winthrop's dream is pretty and I am fond of believing that this vision of his night of Innocence, is prophetic — May you still be able to transmit me the delightful assurance, that these dear children are well, that they are passing on to those attainments proper to their years, and that they retain in their bosoms a warm corner for their maternal friend — I anticipate much pleasure from the promised confidence of your young friend [—] I never yet saw a page of hers, which was not productive of much satisfaction — I respect her for the extract with which she hath favoured me, and I am pleased to learn, that she hath taken up the pen — For surely it is irrationally debasing the noblest, and most correct feelings of the soul, to suppose that Friendship, celestial friendship, cannot exist — without passions — which in the most candid estimation, cannot but take rank in the lowest order of those sensations, which are common to the human heart — From experience we obtain the act of self government, and a few years ending the conflict, we shall wing our flight to better Worlds, to an existence, where the emancipated spirit, raised to a higher class of Being, shall freely expand, indulging in all those refined enjoyments, a prelibation of which, now constitutes the prime felicity of the well regulated intellect — But whither am I led — I beg leave to declare the office of Dictatress to your young friend, I am too deeply interested to take upon me so important a trust, and you may assure that lovely, and most excellent Girl, that, from the observations I have made, I hesitate not to pronounce that her own judgment, in an exercise to which it is fully competent, will be the best talisman for her conduct — I am obliged by Mrs R—'s intended politeness, and I am pleased that the Gloucesterians enjoy themselves — The present is indeed a fluctuating state, and our party can scarcely be elevated, but upon the depression of another — Of the truth of this observation, two of our principal Cities now furnish an example — The removal of Congress elates the Philadelphians, and, I suppose, the Citizens of New York are proportionably chagrined — How happy that a permanent residence in deed awaits the sons and daughters of Men — I cannot obey your kind commands relative to announcing the time of our return — We calculate upon leaving this City next Monday, our design is to reach New York two weeks afterwards, and our arrangements do not extend beyond this — Our route for fourteen days after our departure from hence will be circuitous, and generally out of the post road, and the probability is, you will not hear from us, so religiously as heretofore — but wherever I may be, depend upon it, I cannot be other than your affectionately admiring Friend —

Letter 770 To my Father and Mother Philadelphia Arch Street July 17— 1790 — Saturday

Judith and John have attended a Catholic mass — her first — and she describes in great length the church and the service, which was celebrated in German and Latin. They have visited with more friends and attended a benefit concert at College Hall, the orchestra, vocalists, and program of which she details for her parents. They have visited the home and gallery of the late artist Robert Edge Pine which Judith describes. They have seen artist Charles Wilson Peale again and viewed his "transparent moving pictures." Peale's portrait of his wife and their stillborn infant were quite upsetting for Judith. The Murrays have been to Schuylkill Falls as the guests of Colonel and Mrs. Coates, where they were entertained by music and elegant refreshments. Many Philadelphians owned summer houses at the Falls, and Judith observed that the "spirit of equality," or republicanism, was indeed prevalent there — attributable, she felt, to Quakerism. She noted that people from all walks of life were able to earn a decent living and own a summer house, not just the wealthy. The Murrays have visited a new mill invented by Mr. Ramsay, and Judith is fascinated by how it works and what products the mill produces. They attended the commencement exercises at Philadelphia College, founded by the recently-deceased Benjamin Franklin, who was remembered on that day with great respect. Later in the week, 30 chiefs from the Creek Nation, on their way to the treaty signing in New York, arrived in Philadelphia to the welcoming sounds of bells and canon. A sermon denouncing John has been given and they will stay an extra day for John to respond. Finally, Judith repeats a favorite anecdote of the late Doctor Franklin.

I now set me down, and with superior pleasure, to perform my promise of one week standing. To confess obligations to you, my beloved parents, can never give to my bosom the shadow of regret — It is in course for children to receive benefits from the authors of their being, and they behold accumulating favours, with a sweet, and filial kind of satisfaction

The letter before me evidently dictated by paternal love, is one of the most pleasing instances of its effects, and my acknowledgments result from tender, and becoming gratitude. We have, my dear Sir, received from you, since we left home, four letters, if you have written a larger number, they have not yet come to hand, and for these you have our most sincere thanks — If the connexion between Mr— and Miss— should terminate in marriage Mrs— will find her mind sufficiently acquiescent — I cannot see any valuable purpose, to be answered, by implacable opposition. I fancy the report of my Brother's return to Marietta, is premature — St. Clair's movements are not without observation, and the intelligence would have reached this City, before it could have travelled so far Eastward, as the Town of Ipswich — We are obliged to inquiring friends, we wish them to accept our respectful regards, and we have to assure them, that we mean to reach Gloucester, so soon as the various claims, made and making, upon Mr Murray, will, with any degree of propriety, allow — That it is my fervant wish to behold once more my Father and my Mother, with all those who so largely share my affections, I flatter myself you will not doubt — I think the presence of so worthy a Man as General Lincoln, in your Town, must have been an agreeable circumstance — If Captain R— brings any tidings of Fitz William, you will have the goodness to transmit it, and you will, I trust, give me credit, for some of the finest feelings of which my nature is capable, when I trace, in characters most legibly expressive, the united benedictio[ns] of those revered persons from whom I know existence, benignly worded, over the signature of my ever honoured father — On the bended knee of gratitude I yield my thanks, supplicating for them, the richest blessings — To continue my cursory remarks, since they are thus productive of amusement, I cannot hesitate. Taking up, therefore, my account from saturday last, I proceed to say, that although service was performed in the Church of the Universalists, on sunday, yet, by the indulgence of my husband, I attended upon the morning of that day, in the new Romish Chapel — The religious ritual performed there was, to me, a novel scene, and it was believed just, that my curiosity should be gratified — of a religion consisting so much in show, I had formed no idea, and the ceremonies of Mass, were as new to me, as any that I could have witnessed in a Turkish Mosque — The Roman Chapel is a neat brick building, and on entering the principal avenue, we are presented with a view of a superb Atlas, directly opposite, with an elegant pulpit upon the left — The painting[s] of the Atlas are rich, and expressive — A view of the Redeemer, in his hour of agony, extended upon the Cross — a Magnificent portrait of God The Father, the serene majesty of whose countenance, is beyond description — An affecting view of God the son, triumphant[ly] presenting his pierced side, and perforated hands, the holy spirit descending as a Dove — Winged Cherubims surrounding the Altar — The Divinity conspicuous — None but lucid clouds apparent, and the whole handsomely decorated with branches of palm, and various other ornaments — The foliage of the palm tree lines the whole wainscoting of the house — Upon either side of the Altar are placed a large number of silver branched Candlesticks, adorned with evergreen and supplied with wax tapers — The scene altogether was strikingly pleasing — The Altar is raised by a neat pallisade, curtained by wrought muslin, and the ascent thereto is easy — Upon the left side of the Altar, is a small table, upon which stands a crucifix, with other requisites, of the characters and uses of which, I was ignorant — The Orchestre fronts the Altar, in which is a fine toned Organ, the Gallery of the Orchestre, is the only one in the church — Besides the branched Candlesticks upon the Altar, lights are advantageously disposed in various other parts of the Temple, and three beautiful glass Chandeliers, are suspended from the ceiling.

At the several Vestibules of the house, Marble basons present the holy water, and these consecrated vessels, are truly elegant — The Church service was in latin and the sermon in German — The music was enchanting, the softness of the Cadences, and the solemn sublimity of the deep toned sounds, responding from the Organ, with the rich, and mellow sweetness of the whole, was indeed truly wonderful — but not understanding the language, in which the exercises were performed, and being ignorant of their Order, or expression they, of course, appeared to me little better than a solemn pantomime — The congregation was decent, and apparently devout — The Priest was arrayed in a lawn Robe, adorned with needle work, and caped with black, and a narrow ornament of rich tissue, was thrown around his neck — He was evidently animated by his subject — his gestures were various — now apparently wrought up to the height of indignation, and now sinking to the supplicating, and pathetic — Having delivered his discourse, he disappeared, when an individual kneeling at the altar, light the tapers, and the Priest, in all his sacerdotal habiliments, again entered — His lawn vestments were exchanged for a linen habit, which was bordered with a deep lace — and over his shoulders he wore a mantle, edged with broad gold lace, and skirted with rich brocade; the centre of this mantle exhibited specimens of exquisite embroidery, he was attended by a number of boys, habited in white Robes, and bearing in their hands, tall white lighted tapers — Those boys performed a number of evolutions, which were to me enigmatical — suddenly they extinguished their tapers, and continued alternately passing to, and fro — and, with seeming devotion, occasionally supporting the mantle of the priest

A white sarcenet scarf was repeatedly thrown over his shoulders, and removed by consecrated hands — A number of ceremonies succeeded, incense was brought[,] the host was elevated, the Priest received the Eucharist etc etc — I am, free to own, the frequent kneeling, and clasping of hands, with the passing, and repassing, had to me a frivolous appearance — Yet, had I understood the order, and design of their ritual — it perhaps would have appeared appropriately significant — The Romish Religion thus evidently [rich] and external excitements, would, I should imagine, captivate the youthful, and inexperienced mind. For myself, my reflections, while a spectator of those devotional exercises were rather pleasing, and I could not forbear hailing the auspicious era, which had established a government, that like a tender, and judicious parent, as benignly indulgent to the unoffending and harmless caprices of its children — We passed Monday agreeably, with a genteel family in a neat little rural recess, in the Northern Liberties, or suburbs of this City — The seat of Colonel Coates is upon the banks of the Delaware, and he hath happily blended the City and the Country — his family are amiable, of a numerous progeny two daughters only remain — His eldest daughter, however, a beautiful Woman, being happily united to the Man of her heart, hath already given to the bosom of her parents, no less than five promising children who very naturally supply the places of their deceased offspring — The whole pretty group were collected on Monday, and we highly enjoyed the scene — Music in the best style contributed to the pleasures of our afternoon entertainment, and we returned home pleased, and grateful — Tuesday we took tea with Mrs Kipley — wednesday we dined with Mrs Wescott passing our evening at the College hall, where was performed a grand concert of sacred Musick, for the benefit of a distressed Clergyman, who possesses from Nature a delightful voice uniting all the powers of sound — In his youth he was some time Chorister in an english Cathedral — but taking holy orders, he became a pastor of a Church in Virginia — Previous to the Revolution, and during its Progress, his support was decent, but Peace, when established, leaving him only a stipend of forty pound per year to support a Wife, and nine children, and his Lady being far advanced in her tenth pregnancy, his circumstance had such a melancholy effect upon his feelings, as to destroy his health, and procure a temporary derangement — but recovering his reason, while no small measure of bodily indisposition remained, he was, by the advice of his friends, induced to make an excursion for the double purpose of reaping the salutary benefits of exercise, and change of air and possibly obtaining pecuniary relief — The countenance of the Rev. Mr Blagrove is a very powerful recommendation, it is venerably descriptive of wisdom, and the index of an informed and good Mind — years and misfortunes are, in legible characters, deeply impressed upon every feature of his face, and his head is bleached by time — His manners are mild, and his whole deportment remarkably prepossessing — He brought with him letters of address highly recommendatory, and he hath been generously patronized by Mr Bache and sundry others — In Baltimore a liberal donation was instantly raised and the humane Philadelphians, with their accustomed benevolence, have selected a very refined, and delicate mode of relief — A sacred Oratorio was planned, in which the venerable sufferer became a principal Performer, thus embracing the idea, of yielding to the Contributor, an adequate compensation. The audience collected upon this occasion was the most brilliant I have ever seen — The hall was handsomely illuminated, and the concert consisted of

Violins, bass Viola, clarinets, kettle drums, french horns, trumpets, bassoons, handboys, german flutes, and Piano Fortes — the Gentlemen of the band lent their assistance gratis, and even Mr Bache, for the purpose of promoting so benevolent an intention appeared upon the stage with his Violin — The entertainment was in two parts — It commenced with a grand Overture, which was succeeded by a solo from the Musical performed by the celebrated Mrs Henry — A Chorus — Te Deium etc by Mr Adgate's choir — After which, Mr Blagrove performed a divine solo Anthem, when a solemn Concerto, catching the sounds, elevated and charmed every individual capable of those animating sensations which the various modulations of sweet, and harmonious sounds, can bestow — [the] second solo from the Messiah chanted by Mrs Henry, with a chorus by Adgate's Choir concluded the first part [—] The Overture in the second part, was succeeded by pious Orgies and solemn airs constituting a heavenly solo — executed in a superior style, by Mr Blagrove. The Chorus again chanted "Arise Shine" etc when Mr Blagrove performed a second Anthem — "Acquaint thyself with God" etc etc [—] a solemn Concerto succeeded, when a third solo from the Messiah was admirably executed by Mrs Henry — A grand Hallelujah Chorus, also from the Messiah, in which Mr Blagrove was a principal performer, concluded the whole — The entertainment was undoubtedly of the highest kind, and when we remembered the design in which it originated, it became indeed divine — Tickets of admission were one dollar each, and about one thousand persons were assembled. The respectable subject of this well judged, and delicate munificence, appeared, during the evening, greatly affected — Often at the breaks, and solemn pauses of the musick, he wiped his eyes, then raised them to heaven — expressively lifted his hands evincing by a modest and becoming deportment, the decent and grateful sensations of his soul. May he return to his family crowned with health and peace. Tuesday morning we devoted to Mr Pine's Gallery of pictures [—] These paintings are of a higher kind than any thing which I have yet seen — the touches are bold, and masterly, and the speaking canvas seems indeed to live — Mr Pine and his Lady are natives of England — Mr Pine is no more, but his Lady still occupies his elegant Mansion house, devoting herself very successfully, to the pursuit of this fine art — Many of her own paintings were in exhibition, among which we particularly distinguished two Baltimore families, admirable performances, and, were it not arrogantly presuming, I would say, her touches seemed to possess a delicacy, and mellowness, which we in vain sought to discover in other pieces — This spark caught from heaven, illumines the bosoms of the descendants of Mr & Mrs Pine — their daughters paint with great taste, they have made wonderful proficiency, we saw pieces of their finishing, which were truly admirable, and Mrs Pine now presides, at a seminary, where young Ladies are taught this elegant art, in high perfection

The dwelling of these Votaries of Genius, and talent, is romantically pleasing — We enter under the shade of the weeping Willow, and other trees and the walk is adorned with a variety of flowers pleasingly arranged, as if by the indulgent hand of nature — The stair case is handsomely ornamented, with paintings, among which innocence, in the figure of a beautiful infant is personified, this piece is endearingly attractive — The Gallery or Hall of Exhibition, is spacious, and lined, with pictures, in the most animated style — The collection contains many fine portraits of illustrious personages, but it consists chiefly of historical pieces — Full in view, as we enter the Hall, an allegorical painting of our Country, greets the eye — It describes her after having suffered the depredations of war, and deplored her unhappy situation, after having lamented her Heroes slain, her desolate Towns, and expiring Commerce, kneeling in an extacy of gratitude to the God of battles, at the appearance of peace, which in the form of a celestial Messenger, extends, through an opening cloud, the auspicious olive branch — Liberty is led on by heroic Virtue — Concord attends — Industry is followed by plenty, and a smiling group expresses a gladdening view of augmenting population — returning Commerce is denoted by spreading sails, and the Cornucopia is conspicuously displayed — Garrick makes his appearance, in various parts of the Hall and Mr Murray assures me the resemblance is perfect — The countenance of this celebrated theatrical wonder, is animated by intelligent and — his eye is intelligent, beyond what I have ever conceived — He figures while speaking the Ode to Shakespeare, almost divinely — The most commanding characters of that immortal Bard, are grouped together — designed to express Garrick's various powers of representation. He is surrounded by the Muses, the loves, and the Graces, and the whole produces a most enchanting effect. Mr Pine hath embodied, if I may so express myself, many of Shakespeare's most celebrated scenes, among which is a view of the fourth act of Hamlet, where Ophelia, in her deranged state melodiously chants, and we almost hear her say "I would give you some violets, but they all whithered when my poor Father dyed — We were also shown a scene in King Lear, where, in her night of age, after having relinquished all to his barbarous daughters, the decorated Prince is seen, amid the war of contending elements — His white hair seems to stiffen in the wind — Melancholy distraction is deeply marked in every line of his farrowed face — every trail hath an appropriate expression — The faithful Kent is at his side — The Fool makes his appearance, Edgar advancing from the Hovel, is strikingly delineated, and the whole is unquestionably a masterly performance — We are presented in another view, with the good old King — he instructed upon the bed of death, his attendants weep around — Cordelia is of course the prominent figure, and the language of every feature is "Had you not been their Father these white flakes did challenge pity of them" [—] An interesting scene from Macbeth, with many other commanding views from Shakespeare are collected in this Gallery. Our admiration was greatly excited by a fine portrait of Mrs Siddons in the character of the Grecian daughter, and we were particularly pleased with the family of a flemish peasant. A fanciful representation of time clipping the wings of Cupid, the imagery of which was highly characteristic, arrested its share of attention — We did homage to the portraits of Rubens and Vandyke, and we viewed with great satisfaction, an original fruit piece, done by Michall Angelo — In Mr Pine's collection, is a view of Congress, voting for independence — The colours taken in the Capture of Lord Cornwallis — and General Washington resigning his commission to Congress. The Portraits in these pieces are all from life, and we regretted that the masterly Artist, did not have to complete his design — Madness is delineated in this Hall of exhibition, in a manner horribly just, while we are opportunely relieved by a view of contemplation, veneration, and adoration, designated by appropriate expression — Busts of Voltaire and Doctor Franklin, said to be exact resemblances, are found in this collection — but to ennumerate every Worthy individual who most forcibly demanded, and received admiration, is beyond my power [—] Harried from scene, to scene, sketches only are allowed me — and from an entertainment so copious, and so fruitful of pleasure, engagements too soon summoned us, we paid a variety of morning visits, some of them sufficiently frivolous, and at five O clock in the afternoon, attended Mr Peale's completion of his transparent moving paintings — To form an idea of this exhibition, you should have been present, it is really a wonderful effort, and attainment in art — A sketch of the falls near Schuylkill, I have already transmitted you, to which Mr Peale hath now added, a night piece, at the front view of which, darkness is so prevalent, that the trees and houses are scarcely visible — Gradually the dawn appears, the light advances by natural steps, the purple morning breaks, the gay horizon extends, the azure sky is brightened, the lucid clouds are fringed with gold, the pretty Warblers commence their notes — sun beams streak the blue Vault of heaven, they glitter upon the windows, a variegated landscape, an elegant Country seat, embossomed in trees, stands confest — the distant lowing of Cattle is heard, until at length the full blaze of a divine morning, completely beautifies the scene — producing the winged choir full in view, swelling every note, and melodiously chanting their early rukus [—] Mr Peale next exhibited a view of Market street — the night approaches, by almost imperceptible degrees, until undistinguishing darkness wrapped the whole — When instantly, as if by magic the lamps are lighted, and their reflection upon the houses, and pavements is wonderfully, and perfectly conspicuous, the market is in view, and we easily designate the adjacent buildings! The effect of these transparent pictures is beyond expression pleasing and we penetrated with wonder, and admiration. One painting in the Gallery of Mr Peale I cannot forbear marking — It was to me particularly interesting — It is a portrait of Mrs Peale — The breathless Corse of a beautiful Infant, prepared for sepulchral rites, is stretched before her — The lovely Matron, with eyes raised to heaven, and every feature descriptive of holy resignation, with folded hands, from which a milk white handkerchief is suspended — standing beside the clay cold little tenement, seems supplicating that unerring being, who but in paternal love chastizeth the creature whom His hands hath fashioned — My eyes were wet — Thus wrapped about by icy death, was my darling babe, in the only view, with which I was favoured of that form, for which I endured unutterable pangs — but enough of this — We will, if you please, pass on to friday — On Friday a party of kind friends took us in a Carriage to Schuylkill Falls, we were gratified upon our way, by a view of a number of elegant seats, scattered upon the banks of the Schuylkill, where, during the heat of summer, the opulent Citizen of Philadelphia repairs, to enjoy the freshness of the salutary rural breeze — Perhaps it may give an idea of the extent populosity, and wealth of Philadelphia, when I repeat a fact — It is no uncommon thing for the mechanic, such as shoe makers, tailors, etc to possess, in addition to their town houses, elegant Country retirements — A Barber, not far from Arch street, came in to Philadelphia in his youth — his puff and his bag made up his whole property — yet he is now the proprietor of a number of handsome dwellings in this City, and his rural Villa, about four miles from hence, is magnificently elegant — Thus every thing is upon a large scale, and the spirit of equality, or republicanism, seems remarkably prevalent — Every honest, industrious Man, be his calling what it may, obtains respect, and is considered reputable, and this also I regard as the result of quakerism — Even the burial grounds in this City, are distinguished by an ample spread, and if upon our journey, we were pained by that want of respect to the deceased, in many instances but too apparent, we are here proportionably pleased — Large, and convenient lots, are taken up and inclosed, by a handsome brick wall, of a decent height, and thickness — In these grave yards, however, a body can not be deposited, until a certain sum is paid to the society to which they belong, which sum is appropriated to the augmentation of a fund designed for general utility — But, that the Philadelphians may be in all things consistent, they have purchased a commodious square, which they have named the Potter's field, in which the poor and strangers who may not find it convenient to discharge sepulchral expenses, are intered. — Our yesterday mornings jaunt was for the purpose of viewing some mills of a new, and curious construction

— The invention, or rather the improvement of the invention, is by a native of Maryland, a Mr Ramsay, and, by the most simple cause, prodigious effects are produced — The house in which these mills are found, is of stone, beautifully shaded by tall Oaks, and Poplars, at the feet of which meanders a little edging of flowers — The stream which works these mills, is, in its apparent source, a small inconsiderable rill, but its issues are produced thirty one feet deep — To sketch these mills, I ought to hold the pen of an Artist — yet, untutored as I am, my journal must record them, and in my own manner — The stream is conducted horizontally, to the mouth of a tube, down which tube it is conveyed perbendicularly to a stationary trunk, through which it again pursues a direct course to a metalic Cylinder, which introduces it into a rotatory syphon, united to a shaft, where encountering a quantity of air, the water again presseth to its apertures, and this reaction produceth that amazing velocity, which sets every wheel in motion — From this simple machinery, a variety of manufactures are perfected — We saw the chocolate in the nut, the process which prepared it for the Baker, and we saw it disposed in the several pans from which it receives its texture, and deposited in the cooling room [—] We viewed the tobacco, in its natural state, and beheld the progress by which it takes the appearance of that elegant powder, which is to many a source of amusement — we saw mustard prepared from the seed, and wheat divested of its chaff, receiving the delicate hue, and figure, of the finest poland starch, hair powder etc — Barley of the most beautiful hue, and form is parted in these mills and the Proprietor observed with a laudable kind of pride the preference manifestly due to his barley over any imported from Europe. The whole of this complicated machinery is instantly set in motion by the pulling of a small line and by touching an opposite cord, its movements are as instantly suspended — We saw, we questioned, and we admired and after a morning spent in this high gratification, we joined a party upon the banks of the Schuylkill, where in a terrestrial Eden, we were engaged to pass the day [—] Our company was not small, it consisted of nineteen gentlemen, and sixteen ladies, our entertainment was elegant, collecting every thing proper to the season, and the desert was made up of a variety of fruits, sweet meats, floating Islands, Ice creams etc etc [—] Our repast over, we were most agreeably surprised by a sudden vibration of sweet sounds, truly harmonious — A concert of vocal, and instrumental musick struck up, in the next apartment, and a shower of rain enduring it inconvenient to enjoy by walking the rural beauties of the place, the afternoon was devoted to musick — Mrs Butler, daughter of Colonel Coates, was of our party[,] Mr Butler too was present, Mrs Butler sings enchantingly, and she very obligingly joined her voice to her husband's flute, thus mingling sense, and sounds, only not divine — Mrs Butler is a beautiful Woman — a stranger, whose tongue —

although he spoke tolerable english — proclaimed the foreigner — thus addressed her, upon her singing "Madam, had I the honour of your acquaintance, I would say many words to you — but, although a stranger not even having your name, your figure will ever be present to my imagination" — Passing the day thus pleasantly, you will judge we returned to Town much gratified, and experiencing for our polite entertainers Colonel Coates and Lady, the most pleasing sentiments

This day, saturday, we have concluded the week by enjoying the exercises of Commencement in the Philadelphia College — We were, you will recollect, recently present at the conferring of degrees in the Pennsylvania University, and we have this day received high satisfaction — The salutary Oration, was succeeded by a syllogitic dispute, in our Mother Tongue, and the question was critically examined, whether upon the supposition there was no future state of rewards, and punishments, the obligation to practice Virtue would not remain — The intrinsic beauties & advantages of rectitude, were clearly demonstrated — Virtue shown forth with inborn splendor, and the decision being referred to the President, he gave it in favour of the independent, and inherent superiority, of that celestial origin of every rational, and innate enjoyment upon this equitable award, two embittered Clergymen left the hall [—] Various other Orations — among which was a visible declaration, upon noses — were delivered, and the praises being supplied by Music, the students received the wreath of Academic honour, when with much spirit, action, and beauty of language, the Validictory Oration was pronounced, introducing an apparently reluctant Classmate, and exclaiming — "Peace with you fiddling there — it must be spoken" when endeavouring upon James to speak, who plead his awkwardness, and inability to deliver himself before such an audience, especially so brilliant an assembly of Ladies — he is however finally compelled and proceeding to ridicule, with much wit, the occurrences of the day, he seems totally to have relinquished his timidity, and running full tilt in the career of his volubility, he urges upon the pulpit when he is called to order by his companion and cut short in his harangue — who taking the matter up pronounces a masterly and Classical eulogy, upon the progress of science which naturally leading to Doctor Franklin, the venerable founder of the Seminary, his panageric properly succeeded, when a beautiful Ode, sacred to the Memory of the Doctor chanted in dirgful strains, to the tune of soft flowing Avon, was pathetically performed, and distinguished by the accompaniment of musick — The facitious Declaimer penetrated by the power of harmony, then joining issue, with his friend proceeded in animated numbers, and with a laudable kind of enthusiasm to hail the General of Science, to celebrate the peaceful influence, and salutary consequence of its wide spreading, and extensively progressing Empire — His Classmate, catching the glowing admiration, continued to expatiate — The youth, wrapt in futurity, exclaimed "Already for a Cincinnatin, we show a Washington, Already other Tallies, and other Virgils rise["] — But this is not enough, science shall explore the utmost limits of the Western World, upon the shores of Erie it shall meet the Tawny Chief, or trace his paths, among those embosomed Forests, which deep embrown the vast Ontarios side — yea until ignorance exists no more, until knowledge universally prevails, until in every untutored haunt of savage beast, or Man, the polished Villa, and towering City shall arise to gladden and to bless — This view produced a duet in honour of those celestial Beings — Peace, and Science — exquisitely performed by Mr Blagrove, accompanied as before, which, with an address to the audience, closed [with] a piece, that I cannot forbear styling an elegant dramatic sketch — The very respectable audience were dismissed with a prayr, Gloria Patris, and benediction, and we proceeded to dine with our polite friends, Mr & Mrs Mackie en famille [—] This afternoon hath been distinguished by a discharge of Cannon, and ringing of bells, designed to announce the arrival of thirty Indian Chiefs of the Creek Nation, who are on their way to New York to adjust a treaty with Congress. This evening a sermon hath been delivered in the College Hall, in opposition to the sentiments attributed to Mr Murray, and the responding to this sermon, appointed for Monday evening next, will detain us in this City, one day longer than we had intended — Thus have I brought down my account to nine O clock saturday evening, this seventeenth day of July, when no letters present either from Gloucester, or Boston! On Tuesday we purpose going into the Jersies, when departing from the post road, my tenderly anxious parents, will not expect to hear from me as regularly as they have hitherto done, but my letters will meet the favourable gale of opportunity, and I shall continue with all affection, duty and becoming tenderness ever sincerely yours ———

P.S. A Lady's Postscript is said to be the best part of her letter — I feel a kind of pleasure in strengthening a sentiment, which hath obtain[ed] the venerable rust of time — Accept, therefore, an anecdote of Doctor Franklin's [—] Agreeably to the providential care, to which he was accustomed, he had laid in his stock of firing, to light up his cheerful hearth, and philosophic haunts, during the continuance of an approaching inclement season — A neighbor, upon whose character blighting suspicion had never fastened, was by the Doctor's servant, frequently observed to help himself, from the ready wood pile. The man reported the matter to his master, but the Doctor was incredulous [—] Occular demonstrats was obtained, when rising early, he purchased a load of excellent wood, and ordered it to be deposited at the door of the Offender — The poor Culprit, greatly surprised, insisted that the wood was not for him — "I was ordered, Sir, to say, that Benjamin Franklin directed this wood to your door" [—] It is a mistake Sir[,] Doctor Franklin lives in yonder house — "Sir I am positive this is the place" — Stop Friend, I will make inquiry — The astonished Man proceeded to the Doctor for information — "Yes Sir" replied the facetious Philosopher — "I ordered the wood[,] I believed it too much trouble for you to fetch your firing from my pile, and to obviate the necessity for so much fatigue, I have taken this method." N.B. Did the Doctor recollect a similar conduct in our Governor Winthrop?

Eleven O clock — Saturday evening —
Within this hour, letters from Gloucester, but none from Boston have reached me — It is too late to reply by this mail, but I will shortly shape my grateful responses — Meantime my honoured Father, my obliging sister, my amiable Cousin, and my charming Niece, giving me credit for a proper share of sensibility, will accept my thanks — I rejoice to learn that you all possess a good measure of health, that you have commemorated the fourth of July so laudably, and that you seem disposed to enjoy the blessings which surround you — My next intelligence from home, will as I trust, complete my satisfaction, by apprizing me of the return of Fitz William, and the birth of his first born — Once more I repeat my request, to be remembered to every friend, and I pray you to accept, for yourselves, my tenderest salutations —

THE NEW JERSEY COAST AND INLAND RETREATS

**Letter 771 To the Same Jersies Mount Place
July 24th— 1790 — Saturday Morning —**

It seems Judith's parents are still unaware of their son, Winthrop's, whereabouts. Judith writes that she will ask General Henry Knox for his assistance in this matter when they reach New York. The Universalist convention has closed, and Judith has attended the final ceremonies over which John presided. These included a celebration of the holy Eucharist and she explains what this ceremony means to Universalists. The 30 chiefs of the Creek nation have entered Philadelphia, led by Colonel McGillivray whose mother and wife were "indian" although he was schooled in England by his English father. "Multitudes flocked to see them" — including Judith, who describes their dress and procession stating that they were "received with marks of high respect." Part of the chiefs' procession involved floating down the Delaware River on a newly invented boat designed by Mr. Ramsay (who had invented the new mill they had just seen).

John's doctrine of universal salvation has been challenged again, and he has had to answer the "charges" against him. The "Mr Relly" referred to here is James Relly, among the first promulgators of Universalism whose landmark book, Union, instigated a Universalist movement far beyond his native England. John Murray studied with him before emigrating to America, and considered Relly his mentor, teacher, and dear friend. It was Relly's book that first piqued Judith's father's interest in Universalism.

Eventually, the Murrays had to leave Philadelphia and many tears were shed. Their parting was indicative of how beloved Judith and John were and many of the women, in particular, would remain Judith's close friends and regular correspondents. But on they went — to Kensington on the Delaware River, and across the river to the Jersey shore where they reached Burlington by early tea time. They stayed with the Mayor of Burlington where John preached and they enjoyed a sumptuous meal. Leaving Burlington for their next destination, the Murrays encountered an old friend of John's from his first days in America (twenty years earlier). They visited with this friend — now blind — and John promised to return to preach. By moonlight, they continued on their way to Mount Place, home of Michael and Molly Mount, where John had resided years earlier. They were welcomed with great affection, and Judith describes the home, furnishings, grounds, farm, and household members of Mount Place. John preached here, and returned to the home of his blind friend to preach as well. In each case, he was attended by "throngs" of "listeners," many of whom remembered him from before.

But John's health was failing. Judith reports that "he is constantly engaged," and that "inclination and duty prompts him to reply" to almost every request. He is exhausted, and she is worried.

I confess, my beloved Parents, the highest obligation for your condescending attention to the several Commissions, which I so liberally imposed upon you — I hope my Mother will receive advantage from her frequent airings, nothing, beloved Mother, can be so conducive to your health and I do most earnestly entreat you, catching the fleeting moments, to improve every fine day serene as it rises upon you — My sister Anna, must wait the auspicious moment appointed by our common Father — I dare say her deportment manifests that becoming resignation, and gentle patience, which, as I believe, will ever mark for her character — When I reach New York, I will devise some expedient, to collect from General Knox, intelligence which you so naturally wish, although, from the difficulty of communication I rather suppose, that no particular information will be obtained, until my brother shall return to Marietta — I think, if my memory be correct that I took leave of you at eleven O clock on saturday evening last, and the succeeding sunday was happily serene — it was gilded by a tranquilizing reflection, upon the several favours, conveyed in your envelopment, from my dear native village, and it was distinguished by a memorable event. The Universalists in Philadelphia, having at length form[e]d themselves, agreeably to the articles of faith, and practice, transmitted in a late letter to you, into a regular church received from the hands of him who had been unto them a Messenger of Peace, the holy Eucharist — I took a seat among them, and catching a spark from the animated devotion of the Speaker who was uncommonly affected, I received the figurative bread and wine, my bosom glowed with love, gratitude, and reverence to the divine Author of this institution — You know, my revered Parents, that Mr Murray hath not taught us to conceive of the broken bread, as a symbol of the sufferings of the unbroken body of our Lord — The agonies of the Redeemer, he supposes were typified in the slain Lamb, a bone of which was not to be broken, and which was to be eaten with bitter herbs — while the bread and wine being a collection of the many, express the gathering of the people in the complex character of the God Man — Bread and wine will continue to show forth the death of Emmanuel — To exhibit the Saviour of sinners, as tasting death for every Man, until He comes, and when we thus discern the Lord's body, we can eat and drink without condemnation either to ourselves, or our fellow Men — considered in this view, it is certainly an endearing memento of a most important, interesting and glorious transaction — It leads our thoughts to the condescending Redeemer — It commemorates the Union and completion in Him, and destroying all invidious distinctions, it breaths a spirit of Philanthropy and teaches us to embrace in the arms of affectionate Amity, the wide spreading family of Man — The little Church in Philadelphia, beholding these emblems, in a proper view, received with sacred joy their combined testimony — Great unanimity, cordiality, and devotion were manifested — It was an animating scene and had its proper effect upon my bosom. The Commemoration succeeded the close of the afternoon service, as being more consonant with our ideas of supper, and those who remained as spectators of the solemnity, who were indeed almost the whole congregation seemed tacitly, by their devout, and correct attention, to approbate the communicants [—] I think I announced to you the arrival of our yellow brethren — The progress of the President could scarcely be marked with greater eclat — Numbers of respectable characters went out to meet them, and their approach was noted by the ringing of bells, and

discharge of Cannon, with every appropriate demonstration of joy —
They arrived on a saturday evening and on monday addresses were
presented them by the City Corporation, and many other societies —
If I remember correctly, I observed to you, that these indians are a
deputation from the Creek nation[,] that their company consists of about
thirty persons, among whom are their Sachems, or kings, and that they
are on their way to new York, for the purpose of adjusting a Treaty, with
Congress — They are conducted by a Colonel McGillivray, who is the
descendent of an Indian Woman, by a European Father — Great care
hath been bestowed upon his education, which he received in an
academy in Edinburgh — but, reaching maturity, he hath attached
himself to the family of his Mother, and was not long since united in
marriage to an Indian Girl, the daughter of one of the principal Sachems
— In the counsels of the savages Mr McGillivray constantly presides,
and he is said to be the main spring of all their investments — yet he is
not habited like his Countrymen — his garments are of scarlet cloath,
made after our manner, nor hath he adopted the strange whim of
lacerating his flesh, for the introduction of the suppostitious ornament.

The curiosity excited by the arrival of these Chiefs, was very
great — Multitudes of people flocked to see them — the streets were
crouded with spectators, and it was necessary to appoint a magistrate,
to attend their movements, in order to prevent the pressure of the
populace — The dress of these Indians was white — some thing like
the riffle Frock, which we have seen, they were highly painted, their
heads were ornamented with feathers, and they wore nose jewels, ear
rings etc [—] The Aboriginie is to me a great novelty, and upon the
morning of Monday last, I took a seat in the Balcony in Water street,
for the sole purpose of beholding these Kings, Chiefs, and Warriors, and
who were to advance down Arch street, to the new invented steam
boat, which, for their accommodation, was then to proceed down the
river — You would, my dear Sir, be amazed to see the rapid progress of
this boat — We are indebted for this discovery, to the ingenius
Mr Ramsey [—] It hath neither mast, nor sail, it makes its way against
both wind, and tide, and obtaineth the best, and most speedy passage,
in a perfect calm This prodigious effect, is produced by the compact of
fire, water, and air — the boat is propelled forward by the steam issuing
from these combined elements, and the velocity of its movements, and
singularity of its appearance, is really curious — It requires no hand to
work it, except the Man in the steerage — The warlike strangers were
received onboard of this vessel — instruments of musick harmoniously
combining to give interest, and enchantment to the scene — they
proceeded up the Delaware, after which excursions of pleasure and
curiosity, they were escorted to Grays gardens, attended by the Artillery,
and light infantry companies — An elegant entertainment was prepared

for them in the State House where, at the hour of five in the afternoon, they dined, and a discharge of fire works, planned for their amusement, was to have concluded the evening — But our gentlemen preferring seats in the Play House, this demonstration of respect, was deferred until their return — They left Philadelphia on Tuesday morning, and upon their way, at Trenton, etc etc were received with marks of high respect

It is said the Citizens of New York surpassed the Philadelphians in their manifestations of high wrought civilities — A packet was dispatched to meet the strangers at Elizabeth Town Point, where they embarked, and their passing the Battery was marked by a Federal salute, which was repeated on their landing — The Society of St [Fas...], the tutelar guardian of Columbia, in the habits of their order, together with detachments from other companies, escorted them to the secretary of war, who introduced them to the President of the United States — and the whole body of the Nobles now holding their grand council at New York — These extraordinary honours, are in consequence of a recommendation from the President, and are the result of sound Policy.

I informed you that a discourse was delivered by a Quaker on saturday evening in the College in opposition to the tenets held by Mr Murray. This of necessity delayed our departure, and my husband appointed Monday evening for making his defence — I will endeavour to divest my self of every idea, which adverts to my relationship to the Preacher, and assay in my proposed sketch of the evening, to render that justice, to which a stranger would be entitled — Well then — The hall is handsomely lighted — it is filled by a decent audience — range above range — in serious ranks, they rise, a silence the most solemn prevails, and attentive inquiry is sealed upon every countenance — The venerable objector, his head white as snow, is seated in a conspicuous part of the hall — The Preacher appears, he ascends the Pulpit stair, he opens the solemnities of the evening, by a poem, sacred to devotion, and he addresseth in manly, energetic, and pathetic strains, the God of his life — a second hymn is chanted, when he opens the book, and previous to wording his text, delivers an exordium, expressive of his regret, at the necessity of meeting, upon such ground, his respectable opponent — The portion from the sacred Oracles is next read — "Do we then void the Law through faith God forbid; yea, we establish the Law" — Mr Murray proceeded to ennumerate, so far as his memory would serve, the charges exhibited against him — he was conscious that he ran some risk here for although in the tumult of saturday evening, he earnestly requested a loan of the manuscript, for the present occasion, pledging his word that not a sentence should be transcribed, and that it should be returned on tuesday morning, he was peremptorily refused, and of course was reduced to the necessity of defending altogether upon his own recollection — Antinominanism, in its most pernicious view, was, as he believed, the base of [the] indightment — It was said that he denied the ability of Virtue!! That he conceived death levelled all distinctions, and that the soul, when departing from the body, however immersed in guilt, even although a stranger to the emphatick name of Jesus, would, notwithstanding, wing its instantaneous way, to realms of blessedness!! To these charges, with noble intrepidity, and holy confidence, stretching forth his Arms, in the presence of the empannelled public, he plead —— Not Guilty — "Do we then make void the Law God forbid — Nay we establish the Law, rendering it honourable" — The Redeemer of Sinners bowed the heavens, and came down to fulfill the law, in every point, and to bring everlasting righteousness, and we know, that He enjoined a life of purity, upon His Followers [—] It is true we do not make the efforts of the creature, the price of his Redemption but, with the apostle, endeavouring to stimulate him to every good work, we urge this tender motive [—] Because he is washed, because he is cleaned — because he is bought with a price.

We do not verily believe, that nothing which is impure can enter beatified presence — We do not imagine, that death can transform the mind — We conceive that no person can enter into spiritual rest, until he apprehendeth the glorious, and complex character of Emmanuel, and we believe, according to the scripture, that at the day of final retribution, many, even all those who lie down in sorrow, will arise to the resurrection of damnation — Yet, with reverential joy, and devout gratitude, we add — and this we have because the sanction of a — Thus saith the Lord for our assertion, that after the World are judged out of the books, according to their works — another book — the book of life, shall be opened, in which all the Members of Him, who was, who is the head of every Man, are written — Consequent upon which we find the innumerable company, who have then washed their robes, and made them white in the blood of the Lamb — consequent upon which all tears are wiped from all eyes, and the rebuke of the people taken away. We know that Jesus Christ is the saviour of all Men, and, in due time, we believe he will be manifested as such, to every human being. In the interim, we are truly ardently solicitous to promote virtue among the children of men — We know that the unbeliever is already condemned, or damned, and that he must thus continue, until the veil is taken from his heart, and we also believe, that the angel of death, can make no change upon the immortal mind —" But acquainted as you, my beloved Parents, have long been, with the sentiments of my husband, it is hardly necessary to proceed. Mr Relly had also been, on saturday evening, accused — Mr Murray introduced that able Writer, as speaking for himself, by reading some pages in his Saddnces detected, and, finally, he produced a letter, written some time since, to a friend in Philadelphia, which letter, had been shown to the venerable Objector, a circumstance which was candidly supported, must have slipped his memory, since and extract then read evinced the writer, a warm, and faithful Advocate for the utility, necessity, and propriety of the practice of every Virtue. — The objector requested the whole of the letter might be read — Mr Murray replied, it was a private letter, written to a private friend, a great length of time had lapsed since it was penned, and it contained many particulars unimportant to a publick audience — but, if any individual wished to see the letter, Major Moore, to whom it was addressed, would communicate the whole —

The introduction of Mr Relly, now doubtless in the paradise of his God, to answer in his writings, an accusation of heresy, and licentiousness was necessary, and proper, and could not fail of impressing a mind, rightly turned, with that solemnity, requisite to the interesting investigation. Mr Murray possessed himself throughout the whole, departing in no instance from that meekness which ought to characterize the follower of Jesus, and his discourse consisted of a complete chain of masterly reasoning, united, and embellished by a flow of energetic, elegant, and pathetic language — The whole was concluded by a prayr, a hymn of praise, and the Gloria Patris — A Mixture of pain, and pleasure, pervaded the bosoms of our friends — They were pained, even to agony, that we were on the Eve of departure, and they were transported that we were brought of[f] triumphantly — that we were able to render so God honouring a reason, for the hope which illumined our days — They crouded around us, some pressed my hands to their lips, to their hearts, others clasped me in their Arms, and females, to whose names I am a stranger, exclaimed — You Go Madam, and may the upholding presence of the Almighty go with you — But O! for Heaven's sake return unto us — urge your Murray — This City is large — and we shall not account any recompense too mighty — Mrs Mackie, the elegantly tender Mrs Mackie, begged leave to detain me a moment, after the croud had left the Hall — It was long before they departed, when sinking upon the seat, she threw her arms about me, repeatedly she pressed me to her bosom, kissing my cheek with fervour — Soft, and gentle were the effusions of her soul, and deep upon the tablets of my heart, they are inscribed — registered in the volume of friendship they can never be forgotten — Tuesday morning was devoted to adieus — and about eleven O clock, quitting a City, where we had received so many marks of hospitality we passed on to Kensington, where we dined with a friend, upon the banks of the Delaware, in a sweet rural recess, skirted by the river, and commanding a view of the City — The owner is wealthy, his acres are multiplied — his City, and Country houses are rapidly encreasing — May Peace environ his dwellings — We crossed the Delaware, some miles from the City, bidding adieu to Pennsylvania —

The view was picturesque, the River beautifully serene, inventing every prospect — A neat little stone farm house appeared upon its Banks which were ornamented by thick Groves, diversified by interjacent meadows, [fertile] lands, fields of grain, etc etc [—] Forgive me, my friends, if I acknowledge that my heart confessed a pang, and that the tear of regret trembled in my eye — Soon however we landed upon the Jersey shore, and proceeding rapidly on, reached Burlington at early tea time — The Mayor of the City of Burlington, had dispatched an express to the City of Philadelphia, to solicit Mr Murray's abode with him, during his stay in that place — This circumstance was the more extraordinary, as he was an entire stranger to his person — We however availed ourselves of his politeness, and tarried with him one night — The minds of the people of Burlington were replete with expectation — The Court House doors were thrown open, and the message of peace was, with animated devotion, delivered there — Mr Murray was opposed at Burlington by a Rev. Mr Heath, and Episcopalian Clergyman, whom he was enabled to answer — Burlington is a pretty little City chiefly built of brick, and washed on one side by the River Delaware — It is beautifully shaded with trees, which gives it a pleasing and a rural air — It is twenty two miles from Philadelphia, is in its turn the seat of the Jersey Government, and is, I fancy, a place of considerable trade — It has an Episcopalian Church, two or three dissenting Churches, and a market, which is a miniature of that in Philadelphia — We were received with great cordiality by the Mayour, who very politely handed me into the Court House — He is an agreeable man, a widower, about forty years of age, and he hath a promising family, growing up about him

A genteel supper was provided, consisting of cold ham, beef, with a desert of tarts, custards and floating Islands — his Niece headed his table, his parlour is elegant, and our lodging room was perfectly neat — We departed from Burlington on Wednesday morning — Mr Murray having engaged to deliver a sermon at eleven O clock, in a little Village, where a surprising number the place considered, were assembled — after which we were with all expedition pursuing our road, when upon the left hand, and aged Man almost impeded our course — My Friend looked at the stranger — he seemed lost in contemplation — my husband a second time cast a penetrating glance — "Certainly I have some where seen that furrowed face — No, it is not possible" — and he passed on When suddenly an exclamation arrested his progress _ "Stop, stop in the name of Friendship, stop" — This was enough — Mr Murray leaped from the Carriage, and it proved that this white headed Man had been one of my husbands first adherents in this younger World — since he had been favoured with an interview with the Promulgator of peace — years accompanied by their calamities, had revolved and a series of misfortunes wer[e] followed by a fever which totally deprived him of his sight — Hence his strange appearance and altered countenance — It was no wonderful he was scarcely recognized — He had heard it was expected Mr Murray would that day pass the little retreat, where he had chosen to finish his care worn existence, and he had placed him self by the way side, a few paces from his own gate, vainly imagining he could distinguish the wheels of his friend — It was, however, the Companion of his sorrows, who sounded the intelligence — She saw from her door the Carriage, she caught a glance — and, positive she could not be in error, she audibly pronounced — There, there, he is gone past[,] this moment speak, or in an instant he will be out of hearing — Thus produced the exclamation — and thus brought us back to his neat, although humble dwelling — With this faithful Couple we passed some pleasant hours, pleased to learn, that in this dark close of their lives, they yet possessed a competency — We were regaled with some excellent tea, and Mr Murray, promising to return in the course of a week and give them a sermon, they were more easily reconciled to our departure — We left them just as the setting sun, emitted his parting rays — we had seven long miles to this Place, but the mild beams of the moon, illumined the blue expanse, and we came on in tolerable safety, reaching this pleasant residence, about nine O clock in the evening — Of Michael, and Molly Mount, you have often heard — Their Mansion is the Mansion of peace – Integrity dwelleth here, and Order, with his hand made neatness, presides in every department — We enter the domain of this little Independent Community, by a gate many miles distant the house — The tenement is a pretty white box, in an airy situation, and decently rising the Village Pride — a palisade before the door, incloses a verdant airy, which exhibits some flourishing locusts, and pear trees, with a number of young shoots, which promise umbrageous perfection — Beyond the inclosure a fine extensive green, beautifully level, greets the eye, and the burden of the shorn meadows, being cut down, have received their pyramidical form — Upon the right is a little peach Orchard, verdantly flourishing, and further on, rich fields of corn and Rye, form a wide spreading Circle, replete with latent good — the back ground displays a kitchen garden, where the vegetable world, rises in useful, and regular succession, and the ground is bordered with a rich variety of flowers — Upon the left we have a view of a solemn Grove crowned hill, and beyond a chain of thick woods terminate an extensive horizon, and seem to embosom the fields, the meadows and the glade — Mr Mount[,] devoted to agriculture, and dependent only upon his God, seems to enjoy an ample Competency — Without is the bleating of Cattle [—] his luxuriant fields, meadows, and gardens, and within abideth friendship, and hospitality — The Companion of his life, by her cheerfullness, vivacity, and prompt attention affectionately lendeth him every needed aid — One is their hopes, and one their faith, and they literally come up from this Wilderness, leaning upon the beloved — The inroads of time begin to appear, and gray hairs, those venerable ornaments of added years, adorn the head of Mr Mount — yet they enjoy a good share of health and the evening of their days is serene — it is irradicated by the refulgent light of the sun of righteousness — They have been many years converts to the truth as it is in Jesus — yet they hang upon the lips of the Preacher with encreasing delight — and Mr Mount frequently exclaims — "O! It is just, it is true, it is clear as meridian day" — The tear drop trembles in his eye, and he is never satisfied with hearing — They have buried many children — Four, however, two sons, and two daughters, they have reard to maturity — These, like their parents, are truly amiable, Their eldest daughter is settled upon their right hand, she is happy in her connexion, and blessed with a promising Offspring, while her pecuniary circumstances are easy. Their eldest son pursues the steps of his Father[,] his dwelling rises upon the left hand, and he hath united himself to a agreeable Woman, of improved mind, and pleasing manners, his children also prattle around him — Their second daughter is well married, and established twenty miles from hence — the second son, who is the youngest branch of the Family, is still in the house of the father, he is I should imagine at least twenty years younger than his eldest sister — he is the very image of my brother Fitz William — and his manners also, frequently remind me of him — It is a family of love, and the most endearing, and affectionate familiarity is apparent — Jacob, and Betsy Hendrickson — Samuel, and Becky Foreman — Foreman, and Peggy Mount are the only distinction kept up, while they all salute the venerable pair, by the tender affectionate Daddy, and Mammy, and so equal are their regards to each other, and to their Parents, and so undistinguishing is the parental return that it would be difficult to determine, from their manner, which were the real Offspring and which the connexion formed by marriage line — Through the whole house the utmost harmony is apparent, — nine slaves make a part of the family, it is the present abode of the school Master, a grand Son, and a Niece also reside here, and these, with young Mr Mount, and his Father, and Mother, complete a circle, in which uniform complacency and good nature uninterruptedly reign — This family was, for a great length of time, the home of my husband [—] The home of which you have heard him say so much, and where I am received as a beloved daughter, and regarded with every demonstration of tenderness and affection — Did my honoured Parents know these worthy people, in the arms of honest amity, they would enfold them, and they would aid their child, in becomingly expressing the pleasing sense which she must ever retain of unreserved kindness, and parental regards, which have been so abundantly heaped upon her — upon thursday afternoon Mr Murray expatiated upon the words of life, to a large Concourse of people, who through every apartment, upon the first floor of this [building] nothing can surpass the demonstrations of joy, which many discover at seeing my husband, again among them — We met Mr Mount in Philadelphia, drawn thither by a hope of seeing once more the man, who had been unto him a Minister of peace, Mrs Mount was almost wild in her expressions of satisfaction — Is it not, she exclaimed a deception — do we in very deed behold your face again among us. Friday, agreeably to appointment Mr Murray returned to his blind friend — I did not accompany him, but the resort of people was, I am told, astonishing — Today we are to dine with Mr Mount's son, and tomorrow, those who wish to hear, are to collect in Du Wils Grove where, in former times Mr Murray hath frequently met his friends — you will wonder how the Promulgator supports such a constant succession of fatigue — I can only say, the Redeemer bears him up — and the ever lasting arms of his God, being underneath, he still continues the instrument, by which great joy, and much peace has been communicated to many — yet, his health declines, the weather is, occasionally, intensely hot, and he is in fact almost constantly engaged — for when not publicly employed, inquiring friends press around him, to whom both inclination, and duty prompts him to reply — Upon the consequences of his incessant labours, I dare not reflect — his spirits frequently sink, and the prospect before me is then most dreary — May God Almighty forever bless my beloved parents, and brush from their evening sky, every obtruding cloud.

Letter 772 To Mrs Mackie [of] Philadelphia — Jersies Mount Place July 26— 1790

Written to her new friend, Judith tells Mrs. Mackie how much she enjoyed meeting her, visiting with her, and establishing a friendship. She apprises Mrs. Mackie of their travel plans.

Will, my dear Mrs Mackie allow me to address her by the tender application Friend? or will she not rather condemn the hasty claim, and pronounce with the Post, the endearing term proper only to an attachment, which hath been the growth of twenty summers — Surely the curtailed date of our existence, is unpropitious to such sage deliberation — It might indeed have been well enough for the antedeluvian World, who after having lived a Century, were considered only in their Novitiate, and who generally first evinced their pretensions to love and friendship, at the early period of their three hundredth year — but for us, beings, I had almost said of a moment, to be so very profuse of ourselves, with all due deference to the very elegant Originator of this institution, is, I humbly conceive, absurdly extravagant — Be this, as it may, I am positive, let Poets soar ever so high, that I shall continue to remember Mrs Mackie with affectionate gratitude, and if these Worships, or their Reverences, insist that gratitude is no part of Friendship, why then, being impressed with a humiliating sense of my limited term of being, I shall not squander time, by contesting the matter but let them not irritate me too far — I would counsel them to take especial care — for I may come forth...and entering the lists I [may] adduce incontestible proofs, that tender, and grateful affection, absolutely bonafide, constitutes the very essence of Amity — Forgive the flippancy — First letters like first Visits, should, it is said, be short, and my design is merely to give vent to the effusions of my heart, by enquiries after the health of yourself, and family — May peace — sweet peace ever environ your dwelling, I am pleasingly affected as recollection presents the testimonies which I have received, of your regard — your favours, dear Lady, have been as unexpected, as unmerited — But duplicity dwelleth not in a form so fair, I read in your mild eye, and seriously impressed countenance, the source from whence your acts of kindness originate, and I very cheerfully acquiesce. I have passed in your hospitable Mansion many pleasurable hours, which, with the painfully delicious moment, snatched in the College Hall, upon the evening previous to my departure from your City, are registered in the fairest page of the Volume of my Amities — Hitherto, our journey hath proved agreeable, we are now forty miles from Philadelphia, and Mr Murray is in the midst of those Adherents, among whom he commenced his American Career — They are faithful, steadfast, and affectionate — We shall tarry here a few days, after which we shall proceed to New York with all possible dispatch — Please to present my very affectionate compliments to Mr Mackie, whom I shall ever remember with great esteem, and to Mrs Morgan, whom I tenderly respect, May she, after a voyage crowned by success, again meet the Man of her heart, whose departure she so deeply regretted — I pray you to remember me to inquiring friends, in your own manner, you will have the goodness to embrace your pretty Eliza, and your lovely boys, in my behalf, and you will, I flatter myself, always believe me, gratefully, affectionately, and respectfully yours ———

Letter 773 To Mrs Woodrow of Philadelphia — Jersies Mount Place July 26— 1790

Mrs. Woodrow (their hostess in Philadelphia) has asked Judith to inquire at Mount Place about her sister's failing health. Judith reports that the sister has passed away, but that she was well taken care of up to the end. She tells Mrs. Woodrow about John's many preaching engagements and expresses her deep concern for the declining state of his health. But, she maintains, the "Master will uphold him until he hath completed the work committed to his charge." Judith thanks Mrs. Woodrow for her hospitality and friendship, regretting that they had to leave while Mrs. Woodrow was unwell.

To have quitted our hospitable Mansion, in any situation, would my dear Mrs Woodrow, have given me pain, but to be necessitated to depart, when you were so suddenly — and your time of life considered, so alarmingly thrown upon a bed of agonizing sickness, was, I do assure you, truly distressing — But I trust you are, long e'er this, relieved — The journey through life is to every Traveller, more or less fruitful of disappointment — But you, my revered friend, seem to have encountered sufferings which, from their reitteration must be considered uncommon — Every sympathetic bosom will feel for you, and you are entitled too, and will receive, the tender pity of every commiserating heart — yes, I know the fortitude by which you are so conspicuously distinguished, has been repeatedly called into action and I highly honour the becoming resignation, with which you have bowed to the supreme disposer of events. The knowledge that there is a period, to all those tender Amities, to those natural ties, which made, upon opening reason, the first impression cannot be accompanied by a pang — Yet, considering the misfortunes generally attendant upon the present mode of existence, I imagine your reformed, and yielding mind, will not experience a permanent regret, for the demise, even of a beloved sister — She had my dear Madam filled up her measure of woes — She departed this life upon tuesday the 13th instant and was, upon the following thursday, committed to her parent Earth — She received from surrounding friends, every possible attention, and every alleviation, which her case would admit — Not being in possession of her reason, it was, to her, [a] matter of indifference who administered to her infirmities — such are the particulars which — agreeably to your wishes — I have been able to collect [—] Mr & Mrs Mount, with their family, attended her funeral obsequies, and now, resting from her labours, she doubtless occupies that part of universal space, which is, precisely the best calculated to promote her ultimate happiness — Do not, my honoured Friend, allow your heart to reluct, as recollection shall present my image — because our correspondence opens with a confirmation of your record of death — but rather endeavour to regard me, as an individual, who hath transmitted a certainty of the emancipation of the Companion of your youth, with whom you have taken sweet council, and whose enlightened, and enlarged spirit, will unquestionably, at some future period, meet you with a song of praise. Mr Murray will probably write to you, he is now engaged with a number of friends, assembled in the parlour —

In the midst of his first adherents, it is with difficulty they can think of parting with him, so soon as his exigencies will render necessary. Mr & Mrs Mount received us with utmost joy — Mr Mount, you know, I had before seen [—] Mrs Mount greatly surpasses my expectations — Mr Murray preached at Burlington upon the evening of the day on which we left Philadelphia — where a Reverend Mr Heath publicly opposed his testimony — wednesday morning, upon his way to this place, he delivered his message at a Village, called Black Horse, where a considerable audience attended — Thursday afternoon he met his assembled friends in the Hall below — friday he rode to Mr Chapmans, about seven miles from this place, where he again delivered a sermon, and yesterday was devoted to the Grove — How he will be able to obtain strength, to support these reiterated fatigues, his indifferent health considered — I know not — yet his Master will uphold him, until he hath completed the work committed to his charge — you will please to present my respectful Compliments to Captain Duncan, and say to him, that I shall ever remember him with gratitude — Be so obliging as to kiss your darling baby for me, and although, while I abode with you, she invariably shrunk from my embrace, yet, possibly, through the interposition of her good Mamma, she may, with a more yielding grace, receive my endearments — To Doctor Dunlap, and his amiable Lady — Mr & Mrs Jackson, and Mr and Mrs Binny, I do not offer compliments — My bosom swells for them, with sensations of a superiour kind. I honour, and admire their endearing qualities, I love their social Virtues — in the pleasing moments of retrospection memory will not fail to present them, and they will be led on by the venerable Matron, to whom I now do myself the honour of employing my pen — Ask Mrs Dunlap to word my adieu and to express my acknowledgements to her worthy Father and his obliging family — I trust Mrs Dunlap will be made happy by the returning health of that daughter for whom in her humid eye, the tear of apprehension, so often glistened — you will, my dear Madam, have the goodness to present us precisely as you shall think proper, to that numerous, and hospitable Circle of Friends to whom we are so largely indebted in your City and, I trust, you will always believe me to be most gratefully, respectfully, and affectionately yours —

Letter 774 To my sister Jersies Mount Place July 29th— 1790

Judith tells her sister, Esther, that she has met Mrs. Mount's granddaughter — an infant of the same age her son would have been had he lived. The baby, Margaretta, has mistaken Judith for her mother. She tries to breastfeed from Judith and, even after realizing her error, refuses to leave Judith's arms. They spend a great deal of time together, and Judith is again despondent over the loss of her own child. Esther has asked Judith whether or not she and John will leave Gloucester, to which Judith replies such a move would "fill [her] with extreme regret."

I have a retired moment, and I will indulge myself, in devoting it to my beloved sister — There is something very fatiguing, in this constant succession of objects, and in the necessity of tearing oneself from a Circle, just as the yielding heart, begins to take an interest in its hopes and fears — Doubtless there are pleasures attendant upon this kind of life, but it hath also its inquietudes, and its inconveniences, and I confess that possessing from Nature, a mind formed to reap enjoyment, from the select few, from the pleasures to be met in the domestic walk, I would very freely resign, to the soul of versatility, every flower which can flourish in the crouded, and ever varying scene — I declare I would prefer a single hour, such as I can imagine, to every tumultuous joy, which the round disipation hath to bestow, for it is the tender amities of life which can alone warm me to felicity.

you, my sister, are privileged to wear, the honoured name of Mother — your offspring rise before you, and the next habitation you are preparing, will probably descend a parental memento to your children — May no lacerating event cloud your smiling prospects — I too have, from many sources, encouraged hope — but the barbed arrow of disappointment, hath pierced my soul — Cast in a mould, exquisitely feminine, my bosom is capable of tasting the chaste, and highly zested sensations, which constitute the maternal feelings, and my heart, arrogantly questioning, often inquires — Why am I thus cruelly debared, every rational hope, of ever tasting those soft endearments, that nameless tenderness, which gladden, and expand a Mother's bosom? The pleasures I once experienced from the fair prospect before me, were beyond description — A tear blisters my paper — Ignorant Butcher — why was I sacrificed to thy absurd pretensions — Into what sufferings, hath any undue attachment to my family, precipitated me — But I had resolved to confine to my own bosom every agonizing reflection — yet an event, rather singular, hath awakened my feelings — upon my arrival in this seat of harmony — Mrs Mount informed me, that she wished to introduce her little granddaughter to me — always adding Margaretta is a sweet Baby — I know you will be pleased with her — I allowed for the fondness of a parent, and did not think much of her Margaretta — This infant entering her first stage of existence, was then in the novitiate of her sufferings — she is about the age that my Boy should have been, and her Mother, choosing to spare herself those perturbed emotions which I suppose every parent must feel, upon resigning the employment of a nurse, when they witness the lamentations of the sweet Creature, to whom they have for a delightful period, yielded delicious nourishment, had embraced the opportunity of performing a little journey — she had been three days absent, when Mrs Mount entered my chamber, bearing the little bereaved in her arms — she was dressed in white muslin, and I think I never beheld a more beautiful babe — I happened, on that morning, to wear a muslin headdress — similar to the caps in which her Mother usually appears — Her little snowy hands, were instantly stretched forth to embrace me — the child was particular by arms from strangers, and not immediately recurring to the reason of this endearing advance — I arose with great surprise, and upon taking her in my arms, her little head spontaneously sunk upon my bosom, deep sobs succeeded each other — for a moment she reclined, when lifting up her sweet face — her fine expressive dark eyes, shaded by long silken eye lashes, of the same hue, glittered with her tears, again she sunk upon my bosom, reiterating her sobs, when once more lifting her head, she proceeded to open my handkerchief, and to press my bosom, with a mouth and lips, than which nature never formed one more lovely — Of this uncommon occurrence, I speedily suspected the cause, and the lovely insinuating baby, continued, by every insinuating entreaty, of which she was capable, to solicit the grant, of what alas! it was not in my power to bestow — silent persuasions were, however, the only rhetoric which she employed. It is true her charming eyes were frequently humid, but her sorrow was of that kind, which most deeply affects, and which at all times challenges the deepest pity — Inessable were the sensations which shaded my soul — They were indeed unutterable — Margaretta — My sweet Margaretta, I exclaimed — Pretty Love, how endearing is thy mistake, and how great my regret, that I am not indeed thy Mother or that my own dear pledge of chaste affection, so soon inmingled with his Parent Earth — It was impossible to court the child from my arms, she clung to me with all the strength which her little form could command, and when her Father, and Mother returned, as in about three hours after they did, although, she smiled upon her Father of her Mother — who, contrary to her usual custom, was dressed in her own hair — and a riding habit — she did not appear to have the least knowledge — The Mother was affected, even to tears, but no person possessed sufficient charms, to dispossess me of the Infant, and, placed in a rocking chair, I hushed her to sleep, upon my bosom! Her predilection for me still continues, for my arms she will quit any member of the family, and I have taken her in a Carriage two miles from hence, her Mother not of the party — and I have kept her through the day happy upon my knee, she appears to have no other want, and what is still more remarkable, although she hath ceased her entreaties for refreshment from the bosom which hath nourished her, she still continues her tender supplications to me — Great heaven! why am I denied — but enough of this — Melancholy I am rendered by reflection, I still derive pleasure from the letters of my obliging, and affectionate sister, and although it is almost twelve o clock at night, and every creature in this happy Mansion, myself excepted, is, as I verily believe, fast locked in the arms of balmy sleep, I will yet pen my cursory responses — No, my Love, happiness is not in the gift of affluence [—] one real friend far outweighs its glittering endowments — a competency indeed is necessary and may this blessing always continue in the possession of my sister — To leave Gloucester for any other permanent abode, this side [of] heaven, would, in truth, fill me with extreme regret — yet I fear, much I fear — but why should I call in contingencies to torment me, rather let the dear Deceiver flatter still. Lament not the limited education of your daughter — it is liberal when compared to that which some females receive, who have yet performed the voyage of life, with honour to themselves, and to their connexions, and when sleeping sweetly in the grave, white handed fame hath preserved their memory — If Nature hath been bounteous, even should the aid of her hand sized Art have been scanty, the pretty flower perforce will open, and where talents are denied, no attention can supply the deficiency — you are happy that your children are distinguished by pleasing forms, amiable dispositions, and improving minds — I at all times deeply feel for my dear, suffering Mother, for the world I would not add to her distress — I could not therefore indulge the smallest wish to induce her to an exertion, which would be attended with inconvenience — The situation of our sister Anna, hath indeed been for some months, truly melancholy — but I trust, e'er this, the rosy morning hath more than dawned upon her Sweet Girl — and may she [be] bathed in true joy — God forever bless her feeling heart — Do embrace her for me, and present to your husband our fondest salutations [— give] him our affectionate regards, and I pray you to believe that both Mr Murray and myself are truly, and sensibly, with fraternal and sisterly affection, ever most cordially yours

Letter 775 To Miss S.S.E. Jersies Mount Place
July 30th 1790

Judith praises her niece, Sarah Sargent Ellery, for her letter writing and her intelligent mind. She then advises Sarah about preparing herself for the rest of her life. She tells her to consider that — God willing — she will be on this earth for almost a century, and that she should be able to look back on a life well prepared for and well lived — one of honour, virtue, and kindness to others. She counsels Sarah about the "Universal family" — that we are all connected under God. She tells her to accept God completely or she will not have peace, and that it is an insult to God not to do and be her best.

Thank you, my dearest Girl, for the prompt reply, which your feelings have induced you to make, to my letter you have written very prettily, you have expressed yourself most becomingly, and I do take it upon me to pronounce absolutely, that you would not have been surpassed, upon a like occasion, by any young Lady of your age, although educated in any of the Academies, in Philadelphia, or even in my favourite Seminary at Bethlehem — your manner partaketh much of that modest delicacy, concise frankness, and chastized freedom, which distinguishes the Bethlehem pupil, and I council your dear Mamma, to regard with complacency, the progress you have made, and to consider herself happy, in her Girl — I am pleased with your mind — I believe it to be mild, innocent, and good, and I conceive it cannot be too early impressed, with general, and important truths — Infants, occasionally reflect, and questions will issue, even from the lips of childhood, to which the longest life cannot furnish an answer. Long before I had attained your age, a future state of existence rose to my view, agitating my bosom, and exciting alternate hopes, and fears — Indeed I do not remember a period, when my spirit was not seriously impressed — The gay inconsiderate may smile at this assertion — but you my sweet Love, will as I trust, judge more deliberately, and you will consider it as highly consistant, that while we are forming plans, for a duration, which cannot be extended much beyond a Century, and which possibly an hour may terminate, we should be abundantly more solicitous, respecting arrangements, which will deeply interest us through the continued round of a brandless, and never ending state of being — I do not, my dear, mean to preach to you, but I would wish you to view yourself as a Candidate for a more elevated, and dignified scene of action. I am anxious you should learn to make just estimations, not even an idea debasing that etherial emanation, which is to make the Circuit of the sky, and to take its seat in the paradise of our God — We shall never, as I trust be divested of the power of recollecting the persons, and things which in the Routine of time have suceeded each other — Our identity will, as I believe, remain and how delightful will be the reflection that we have never intentionally injured a fellow creature, that our lives have been unoffending, that we have contributed to the utmost of our power, to the well being of those about us, and that we have seditiously persevered in the paths of peace, and honour [—] It is, my Girl, an incontrovertible truth that every effect must have a cause — hence, when toward heaven I raise my eye, when I behold the blue expanse, the lucid, or fleecy cloud, or the rich purple, embroidered with gold, and the genial orb of day, majestically sublimating and beautifying the whole — Anon when the changing scene presents the darkened Atmosphere, the forked lightning, and the rolling thunder, all evidently calculated to purify, and to render salubrious, the element in which we move, and to fertilize the earth, on which we tread when I turn toward that earth, and behold it conveniently apportioned, richly stored, and adorned with whatever can please the eye, when I examine its glossy carpet so variously enamated its embowering shades, its hills, its dales, its thick grown woods, and opening glades [—] When I reap from its bosom every support which my nature can require, and am gratified by every delicacy — when I taste the delicious fruit, and inhale the odiferous scent of the damask rose, when I reflect upon all these realities penetrated with gratitude, I devoutly acclaim every of these delightful effects, must have a Great, a Vast, and an incomprehensible Cause — yea, and of this Self Existent Cause, it is rational to suppose that I too am the offspring — Nor I alone, all the children of Man, with whom, however remote, being of my species I am either directly or indirectly connected — These were all formed by one Omnific hand — The sons and daughters of mortality are ushered into being precisely in one mode — We are all subjected to similar casualties and death with undistinguishing hand, closes the scene ———— If I admit that the God who made me, possesseth all power, all wisdom, all mercy, and all goodness — I cannot suppose he hath called me into being, to plunge me into irremediable, and comfortless despair — His purpose toward me must be like Himself — gracious — and, if I have sinned manifesting Himself, in the character of a Redeemer, he hath made for my transgressions a full, free, and complete atonement — yet it is His to Chastize — and if in the Career of life, virtue should not be my guide, I shall be pierced through with many sorrows — The Father, of my spirit will Correct, and although I cannot conceive His anger will forever burn against the Creature whom He hath made — yet He will I doubt not, mark the deliberate offender, and, in the course of His providence, He will pursue those methods however severely they may lacerate, which will be the most effectually calculated to reclaim the Wanderer [—] Mean time, we experience that virtue, or propriety of conduct is to the bosom, fruitful of renovating peace, while vice, or irregularity, is still the thorn in the flesh. If I do not seek to apprehend the complex character of the Saviour of Man — If I lie down upon the bed of death, unacquainted with the nature of His office, and the benign import of His errand, into this our World, which errand, was, to seek, and to save, those who were lost — I shall be a stranger to genuine peace, and, although Emmanuel hath died to purchase me, yet, ignorant of this emphatic truth, the probability is, that I shall rise, in the day of retribution, to the resurrection of condemnation, that the darkness of my spirit will originate inexpressible anguish, and that fear which hath torment [—] It is not unlikely, that I may be found with those, who seeking to hide themselves from Him, who filleth the throne, shall call upon the rocks, and mountains, to fall upon them, and to shelter them from His <u>wrath</u>!! It is possible I may continue in pangful, and agonizing incertitude, until after the sealed are taken up — Until the Angel, flying through the midst of heaven, shall preach the everlasting Gospel; until all tears shall be wiped from every eye, and even the remnant of His people shall be saved [—] Here then is a sufficient reason why I should be solicitous, in this my day, to acquaint myself with the things that belong to my peace, why I should be careful, by a life of innocence, usefulness, and integrity sustaining in the sight of Men, a blameless character, to adorn that doctrine, which I verily believe originated in the bosom of Deity — Why I should liken to Heaven's Vicegerent, placed as an alusive in my bosom — Persuaded, as I am, that my fellow mortals are equally interested with myself (—although this consolatory truth is veiled from their eyes—) Persuaded also, that the due time shall come, in which this shall be testified, and in which every thing that is hid shall be made manifest — Persuaded that One is our Creator, Preserver, and Redeemer, I cannot so far declare the image of my Maker, as to subject it to undue humiliation — Providence, it is true, permits a degree of subordination — but I will always render the yoke of those dependent upon me, as easy as possible — I will with reverential gratitude, and holy joy, and love, adore my God, and I will contribute, so far as my power extends to the felicity of every human being, well knowing the period hastens, which shall produce the Universal family, upon more equal terms ———— This, my sweet Love, is not the kind of letter which I had intended to write you — My pen hath involuntarily taken this course — and probably it may be as well — Let me know how you like my creed, and if any objection arises in your mind, suggest it I pray you — and I will attempt an answer — I have offered to my beloved Niece, the [ideal] which I myself wish to reduce to practice, and as she is very dear to me, I have, thrown upon paper these views, which are most precious to my soul — they will render her, as I believe more amiable and more uniform — that is suppose they reach the heart and they will serve to elevate, expand, and tranquilize her bosom — I most fervantly wish you my beloved child, the first of blessings, for I am truly your maternal Friend —

Letter 776 To Miss Allen — Jersies Mount Place
July 30th. 1790

Mary Sargent Allen (1773-1846), Judith's 17-year-old niece, has written that her mother, Sarah Sargent Allen is very ill and has asked after Judith. Judith tells Mary how much she loves her, and how important her role as a daughter is. She asks Mary to contact Anna, and have her return to Gloucester in advance of their arrival. She urges Mary to tell her everything she can about goings-on in Gloucester. The

"Mr and Mrs E.S." referred to are the Epes Sargents of Gloucester Judith is close to; "Catherine" is their daughter. "Mrs Saunders" is an aunt on the maternal side of Judith's family.

I had, my Love, a presentiment, that a line from me, addressed to your dear Mamma, would give her pleasure, and I am conscious of acting, precisely as I ought, when assaying to augment, in ever so small a degree, her stock of amusements — Had I known your Mamma, I should have loved her, although I could not boast my descent from the same revered line — but exclusive of her own particular merit, she is entitled, as the sister of my Father, to every thing from me, that is in my power to yield. If we value, as they merit, the Authors of our being, our affections will proportionably extend, to every branch of the same stock and surely there must be some radical fault, in that mind, which is conscious of marked, of not glaring deficiency, in those respectful and duteous feelings, which is due to the parental character — If we do but reflect upon the many anxieties, and sufferings, which agitate the maternal bosom, and exercise the feelings of a Mother, even before our existence becomes visible — If we can imagine the pangs, by which we are ushered into being — If we retrospect the watchful tenderness, with which our helpless dawn of being was attended — if we can imagine how often, and with what exquisite care, we have been lulled upon the soft bosom of repose — If we recollect the reiterated instances of kindness, which hath encircled our advancing life, we shall be constrained to acknowledge, that we can hardly be too affectionate, too assiduous to please, too duteous, or too grateful — I have, my lovely girl, from the moment which gave you birth experienced for you a lively, and most sincere affection — I clasped to my bosom your infant form, and I said, this sweet child shall be unto me as a sister, and I have, from that period continued, to view your every action, with that partiality, which is the growth of fond attachment, you have often appeared very amiable in my eyes, but I freely confess you never figured to my admiring gaze, half as lovely as when the tear glittering in your soft eye, unequivocally expressed your apprehension, on account of the declining health of your Mother — A daughter, while she is only a daughter, is never so much in her proper sphere, as when she is respectfully contributing to the happiness, or endeavouring to alleviate the misfortunes of the Man, and Woman, to whom she owes her existence — and if she is deprived of one Parent, her duties to the survivour, doubles upon her — I am pleased with the becoming manner in which you express yourself of your Mother, in the letter before me — and I do assure you, my sweet young Friend, that I am, not a little obliged to you, for speaking for her in this way — It was very pretty of you, it was proper, it was descriptive of sweetness of temper, and gentleness of heart,

or, to say all in one word, it was acting like your own charming self —
Most certainly — My dear, I should have responded to her,
my engagements not allowing me to address you severally, had I not
known that the strength of her maternal tenderness, will always induce
her to regard, with redoubled pleasure, whatever can be considered as
gratification to her daughter — I regret that your Mamma still continues
in an ill state of health — or rather did, when your letter was written —
I trust she is now convalescent — and I wish you to assure the dear
Lady, that I give her full credit, for every benign sentiment, and that I
entertain not the smallest doubt of her partiality — you will please to
remember me affectionately to her, and to your brothers, for whom I
shall ever retain due sentiments of Amity — I have written to Mr and
Mrs E.S. — When you see them say to them, that the warm place which
they have long filled in my bosom, will never be unoccupied by their
pleasing images — Poor Catherine — I grieve for her early sufferings —
do inform every one of that little interesting knot, of which she is the
head, that they are very dear to my heart — remember me to
Mrs Saunders, whom I always recollect with tenderness — but there
would be no end to my Commissions, were I to proceed, I stop therefore,
at the very commencement of my requests, only desiring you to express
in my name, proper regards to all inquiring friends — To my dear Anna,
I have frequently written, and I cannot but regret the untoward
circumstances, which must have prevented her replies, I understand
she corresponds regularly with you — with which I am greatly pleased
— When you next write to the dear Girl, I would thank you to let her
know I wish her to return to Gloucester, if she conveniently can, the
first of September — I had rather she be there some time before we
reach home — The style of your letter was good, it was correct, and
pleasingly familiar, it was just what letter writing should be — I am of
cours highly gratified by your avowed preference for me — With regard
to your acknowledgement of favours — consequent obligations etc etc
— O! dear — O! dear [—] But possibly they exist only in your little
romantic pericranium, and as it might perhaps be worse occupied, I will
not assay to route the visionary phalans — Bewitched — Indeed — but
if my letters have had for you pretty flights, I shall not, the Cause
considered, be so severe in my remarks, as you seem to apprehend —
I protest, you are an Artful Hussey — how admirably you have contrived
to hurry your letter to a close, and when I was absolutely starving for
every anecdote that could be collected — for every thing that hath
taken place, or that possibly may take place, during my absence from
Gloucester, how ever trifling such intelligence may appear to you —
Conjecture forsooth steps into your aid, & you quaintly say — "I guess
Ma'am by the time you have read thus far, you will wish for a conclusion
of my nonsense" Mighty pretty truly — Oh Mary, Mary — but, with all

your demure finessing, I must love you — bidding you — saucy baggage as you are — reluctantly Adieu — Seriously, Accept, I pray you, my tender salutations, and believe me ever yours ——————

Letter 777 To my Father and Mother — Jersies Mount Place July 31 1790 Saturday

This letter, more than any other, gives us a real sense of John Murray's charisma and powerful oratory skills. He has preached at "Du Will's Grove" before over 1,000 people who have journeyed many miles to hear him. Many who came were his "earliest adherents" since he first left England for the colonies, landing on the Jersey shore in 1770. During his talk it began to rain, yet not one of the "admiring throngs" left. Instead, "every countenance confessed the most solemn attention." And soon, the sun reemerged. Watching him, listening to comments from the audience, Judith was "beyond expression affected." She tells her parents "language must ever be inadequate" to describe how proud she was to be John's wife.

Although exhausted, Judith and John found "rest impossible" at Mount Place. They received "accumulating invitations" and Judith had to stay up very late to write home. John was asked to preach at Burdentown, and they made their way there through Allentown and Crosswicks to the home of Colonel Cirkbride whose furnishings, garden, and property Judith describes in detail. In Burdentown, John preached to another large crowd and, again, "scarce a breath moved the leaves." Judith writes about her feelings of inner complacency, knowing that she and John "are in the path of duty."

I apprized you, my beloved Parents, that we were to meet on Sunday, at Du Will's Grove — but I had no idea of the grandeur of the scene, which was to be exhibited — The Grove is about one mile from Mount Place — It is thrown by Nature upon a spacious Green and it is formed by rows of tall, and umbrageous Oaks — The Concourse of people was prodigious — I do not believe there is more than half a dozen houses in view from this dwelling, in any direction, yet, upwards of a thousand persons were collected in the Grove — among whom were, as I am told three hundred Quakers — The Congregation was gathered from more than twenty miles round the Country — They have in this State, much in use, a kind of Carriage, which runs upon four wheels, and is drawn by two horses — its top is solid, and it hath curtains which can be let down at pleasure — it is neatly painted, and lined, and it can accommodate many individuals with great convenience — I think it is called a Jersey Wagon — These Carriages formed a wall round the Preacher —

The Circle was widely extended — it appeared to me, there were, in number, at least one hundred — Many attended in their one horse chaises and the horses being taken therefrom, every one kept their seats — which seats on either hand were also placed in this consecrated Grove, and an open eminence, was prepared for the Messenger of peace — Rain is now much wanted in this part of the Country, and just as this vast assembly — the place considered — were quietly disposed, and preparing themselves to listen most attentively, the distant thunder began to roll and the fertilizing shower to descend — I looked, that this circumstance would disperse the people, for the gathering of clouds, appearing through the foliage of the thick, and solemn Grove, wore a most portentous aspect, and there was every reason to expect, heavy, and repeated showers — The Preacher, however arose, and a benevolent smile brightened upon his countenance (—while a handsome Lad, benignity expressed in every feature of his youthful face, held over his head a large umbrella—) and stretching forth his arms to the multitude, thus expressed himself "How seasonable, my beloved friends, is this shower — from the want of a blessing, it is said we learn to estimate its value — how expressive then, must this figure now be rendered — "My doctrine shall descend as the rain, as the fine rain upon the tender grass etc etc["] — The calmness which apparently possessed the bosom of the Preacher, doubtless produced its proper effect, and not a single person left the Grove. The serious attention, in such a place, and from such a throng, made up of people of all descriptions, and in such circumstances, was indeed surprising — The clouds soon broke, the azure sky appeared [,] sun beams began to play, and the birds chanted melodiously — A hymn of praise opened the service, The throne of Grace was addressed — "Although Abraham be ignorant of us, and Israel acknowledge us not — yet doubtless thou art our Father — Thou art the God of the spirits, whom thou hast breathed into these clay built tenements" — The book was opened, the text was worded "The Grace of God which bringeth salvation unto all men, hath appeared — leading us that denying ungodliness, we should live soberly, righteously, and Godly in this present world" [—] In his own animated, energetic, and devout manner, the Preacher proceeded, and every countenance confessed the most solemn attention — The rustling of the leaves, the singing of the birds, were not heard, or heard only as adding to the beauty of the scene — During the intermission of the services of the day, scarce a person quitted the romantically enchanting spot — and the Preacher having stepped aside I listened in enraptured silence, to the various Comments — Serious investigation was now abroad[,] light seemed more than dawning upon the assembly, and I was particularly happy to hear an old Man, utterly deprived of his natural sight, evince by his remarks, that he clearly saw the things which made for his peace — One aged black man, in the midst of the discourse, softly exclaimed to a Bystander, "Blessed God — is there then redemption for a poor slave, as well as for his more happy Master?—" The afternoon service commenced, and the importantly interesting, and divinely affecting subject, was continued — The multitude augmented, but decency, and Order still presided, and, amid admiring throngs, the day was concluded — Mr Murray, in appointing a meeting at the Grove for the following sunday, thus expressed himself — "We will once more assemble in this house of God — yes, my serious hearers, in this house of God — For surely one God is every where, surely the Lord is in this place — He is with us, and will keep us, whither so ever we go — Jacob journeying to Padanarain, resting on his way, in a place where collected stones formed his pillow — where the heavens were his canopy, and the earth his Carpet — yet there counteracted by Jehovah — He said this is now other than the house of God, and this is the gate of heaven" — The scene appeared to me truly august — The solemnly energetic speaker, the surrounding multitude, moved apparently by one spirit — the animated, and correct gladness of their souls standing confessed, and swelling every feature [—] For myself, I repeat, I was beyond expression affected — Tears of transport often trembled in my eye, and I seemed to enjoy a prelibation of that heaven, which is reserved for us — indeed, language must ever be inadequate to delineate, the sensations of a chaste, and tender Wife, as she takes her seat amid the admiring croud, and hangs with the enlightened multitude, upon the hallowed lips of the revered, and beloved Lord of her wishes — May the Almighty be grateful — We had anticipated in this rural spot, a season of repose, but thus we have found rest impossible — we have every day been reduced to the necessity of accepting the accumulating invitations, which have been pressed upon us, and hardly a leisure hour hath been allowed us — Even the moments which I devote to my kindred I steal from my pillow, and consequently, they will acknowledge my indifferent writing, entitled to every allowance — To the family of Mr Mount our first attention was due, and, of course, we have visited them, in their respective dwellings — With a very hospitable Mr Holms, we have past a pleasant day, and, on wednesday last, the Preacher again held forth the words of life, in a little Village, about five miles from this place — Thursday, visiting Imley Town, we passed the day in the family of that Mr Imley, whom you once saw, a sufferer in Gloucester — His Mother is now a widowed Matron — but she is supported by a numerous, and promising family, no less than six sons, and six daughters — their situation is rural, and pleasing, a pretty water piece is in view, and Lawns, and interjacent Groves, regale the eye — we were received with obliging kindness, entertained by some delightful musick, and returned home, admiring the beauties of a most enchanting evening — Friday, too, was devoted to visiting, we passed the day with a numerous, and respectable family, of dutch extract, by the name of [Covenhaven] — Their dwelling commands a fine extensive prospect — they are obliging in their manners, and know how to appreciate that enviable independence, which the Farmer may justly boast [—] The younger part of the family have attained a degree of elegance, not often met in what we name unpolished life, thus minds are in a measure formed, and the whole group exhibit as much native politeness as I have seen — This day — Saturday — we have passed most pleasingly it hath been a white day — A Gentleman Colonel Cirkbride — one of the principal characters in Burdentown, had earnestly pressed Mr Murray to visit him, in that Place, and to deliver his message there — Agreeably to his reitterated request, this day, was appointed for his gratification — Burdentown is 13 miles from hence, and early in the morning, we commenced our little tour, accompanied by the Mounts, and a Mrs and Miss Edwards, sister, and sister in law to young Mr Mount who are very agreeable Women — Many natural, and picturesque scenes arrested our attention — and our eye was frequently attracted by all the beauty of indicious cultivation — We passed Allentown a handsome Village, upon the right hand which exhibits an Episcopal church, and a neat brick dissenting meeting house, with a smooth Green extended before it, which green, handsomely enclosed, and shaded, contains the Sepulchers of their dead — We proceeded through Crosswicks, which is also quite compact, and we reached Burdentown, about half past ten — With Burdentown I am not a little pleased — We entered a street, in which the dwellings, in regular succession, form a range upon either hand, and are terminated by the Banks of the Delaware, which in this place are verdant, and lofty — This street is ornamented by a fine growth of trees, which give it an enchanting appearance and it is distinguished by a decent Academy in good repute. Burdentown also exhibits two houses, sacred to publick Worship — We visited the family from which the Village takes its name, and were charmed with the apparent fortitude, with which its present head, supports accumulated misfortunes — But it is Colonel Cirkbride, our genius host, who must upon this occasion bear the palm — His house is an elegant white Mansion, and rises modestly aspiring, and spaciously descriptive of the ample benevolence which designates the bosom of its Master — The area before the door is neatly flagged, and shaded by a tall row of beautifully flourishing locusts, and weeping willows. on the left of this Area, which is commodiously furnished with seats, is a handsome view of the Delaware, the town of Lamberton, in perspective at which place Congress, once contemplated their permanent residence — with a number of romantic little Islands, beyond which is stretched the Pennsylvania shore, and upon the right is the street down which we came. We were met at the entrance of the great

Hall, by Colonel Cirkbride, who with genuine politeness, and expressions of his sincerest pleasure, leading me in, introduced me to Mrs Cirkbride — Colonel Cirkbride enjoys a fine old Age — he is a handsome Man, his countenance is prepossessing, and his figure is commanding — upon his cheek is the ruddy glow of youth, while his head is ornamented by the silver honours of time — His Lady is amiable, and hospitably good — They are opulent, and have no children — The furniture of the house is answerable to the elegance of the Master's ideas, who is a Man of taste, and of extensive information — A variety of cool liquors were tendered us, and I had the good fortune, to obtain what I have never before seen, since I left home — a glass of small beer, served up with precisely such a white cap, as that excellent spruce beverage exhibits with which my Mother regales her friends — Conducted to the Garden, we walked there until the hour of dining — The garden is an ample spot, intersected exactly in the middle, by a long smooth gravel walk, leading in a direct course to the verge of the banks of the Delaware, which serve at this extremity, as an inclosure — The walk is bordered by flowers, shrubery etc etc[,] winding grass walks present, and the garden abounds with every thing useful — Upon the right of the gravel walk, a romantically enchanting little Arbour arrests the view — It is formed by a wild vine, whose umbrageous foliage is surprisingly extensive — seats are fixed in this bower, and it is a delightful recess — Before us the River — perhaps one of the finest in the world, winds its course, and it abounds with shad, sturgeons, etc which fish often leap the surface of the water, pursuing their cheerful gambols, to the no small amusement of the spectator, who is seated much at this case in the arbour — An interjacent Island greets the eye, and the Pennsylvania shore terminates the view — upon this shore is erected an elegant seat, the property of Colonel Cirkbride, viewing it through a telescope, we were charmed by its appearance, by its Lawns, its meadows, and its intersecting Groves — Here, with the feast of reason, and the flow of souls, Colonel Cirkbride frequently regales his friends, and, blest with a mind attuned to harmony, a Concert of vocal, and instrumental music often constitutes an essential part of his entertainment — we left these charming scenes with regret, but dinner being announced, we took our places at the hospitable board — At two O clock, precisely, the meeting was appointed, and rising from the table we were conducted to a charming retreat, on an extensive Green, upon which rose the friendly shade — a white awning was judiciously contrived under which awning, a number of seats were arranged, and an elevated stand was erected for the Preacher — Colonel Cirkbride, as if to evince himself the approving friend, and Patron of the stranger, assiduously assisted in accommodating the hearers — and when this was accomplished, folding his arms, while a pleasurably kind of solemnity took possession of his features he prepared himself to listen, and with remarkable attention — The animated Speaker proceeded in his accustomed manner —— "<u>Our God is a consuming Fire</u>["] — This was his soul interesting subject — you have heard him expatiate upon this text, and, he forgot not his usual perspicuous energy, his illustrations were opposite, and striking agreeably to the sacred Oracles, he exhibited the Deity, setting upon the people as a refiner's fire — he showed Him as having His fan in His hand, thoroughly purging His floor, burning up the Chaft with unquenchable fire, and gathering His wheel into His Garner, he pointed to that symbolic view, where every grain of wheat encircled by its tares, growing together until the Harvest — when carefully separated, not a single grain is willingly lost, but the tares bound in bundles, are committed to the devouring flames, and lastly he referred to that memorable section of the divine writings, where we are assured that if we build upon the only [foundals] wood, hay, stubble, silver, gold or precious things — The day shall try every Man's works — If they abuse he shall challenge the reward — Nevertheless he himself shall be saved, so as by fire. The Audience was numerous, decent, and respectable — scarce a breath moved the leaves, and many took seats in the branches of adjacent trees — Tea was prepared for us at Colonel Cirkbride's, and we returned home with that kind of conscious complacency which must ever result from an idea that we are in the path of duty — The evening was crowned by the arrival of Mrs R— who had met Mr Murray at Burlington, who had been necessitated to depart home, and of whom we had began to despair [—] she was accompanied by her daughter, a young woman of a prepossessing appearance but I ought first to have observed that Mrs R— was one of Mr Murray's earliest adherents in America, that she hath continued steadfast and unwavering, and that she is a good, and respectable character — Tomorrow meeting is appointed at the Grove, and on Monday we expect to leave this place — At New York you will hear from us again — If my brother Fitz William be arrived assure him that our hearts affections are his — to our dear Anna, we offer tender love, and I wish you to embrace for me, the little stranger, who doubtless, e'er this, makes a part of your family — It will be insensible of the endearment, nevertheless it hath brought into the World with it, a title to my affection, and I assure you on my return, I will not resign this privilege to another — God bless you all — we beseech you to know us for the sincerest, and most respectful of your friends ———

NEW YORK, GEORGE WASHINGTON AND CONGRESS

Letter 778 To Mrs Sargent —— New York Chapel street August 5— 1790

Judith finds New York hot, "crouded," the "tumult greatly annoying." But upon arriving in the city, she finally receives letters from home. Among them, was one that announced the birth of her brother Fitz William's daughter, Anna Maria, who was born on July 11. Ironically, Judith received this news exactly one year after her own baby had died. Still, she was delighted for Fitz William and his wife, Anna.

Among subjects discussed in this letter to her aunt, Mary Turner Sargent, are the value of a vegetarian diet, the Bethlehem Academy, and family news including the fact that a mutual friend has committed suicide. She explains her plan to acquire news of her long-absent brother, Winthrop, by writing to General Henry Knox. But, in the meantime, John has met the General at President Washington's home and they finally have news of Winthrop's health and travel plans. Judith has not written to Winthrop during this journey, she explains to her aunt. Apparently, Winthrop did not want Judith to leave Gloucester — probably out of concern for their aging parents. Judith did not want her brother to think she was ignoring his wishes. They would resolve their differences in later years, and Winthrop and Judith would always remain close friends and regular correspondents.

The weather is intensely hot, and we were, ten moments since, sat down in Chapel street, at private Lodgings in this crouded City, not a breath of air can we obtain, and the noise, and tumult is greatly annoying — What a scene doth this anniversary recall to my remembrance — at close of day after pangs unutterable, I was only allowed to embrace a clay cold form — why was this — Can you, my Love, determine? — How is my heart formed to taste all those nameless tendernesses, those big emotions, which stock a Mother's bosom — my expectations were highly raised, and hope blossomed upon every opening thought — but alas! this returning fifth of August, will ever, as I believe, at least while my present mode of existence is continued, rise upon my soul, fruitful of attendant glooms — It is a day ever to be registered in the page of sorrow, ever to be marked with regretting tears [—] Hath not your sympathy led you to recur too, and to retrospect its horrors — Fancy lifts the eye of inquiry — you are gloomy, and alone, and you drop over my disappointment, the reiterated tear — But why is that — how ill doth my practice conform to that theory, which alone consists with the Christian Creed! Well, if I can reach no higher attainment, I will assay to continue my sorrows to my own labouring bosom — Mr Murray is gone to wait on Mr Goodhue, in the hope of letters, that Gentleman's covers have been of great advantage to us — for scribling so largely as I have done, and the demands of postage being most exorbitant, our expenses, but for Mr Goodhue, would have amounted to a little fortune — But the recess of Congress will, I have [been told], take Mr Goodhue hence early in the ensuing week, neither shall we abide long in this City — The journal I shall inclose, will render to my lovely friend, an account of our departure from Philadelphia, and subsequent events, during the past week — But [this] morning caters a little Cargo of letters — No less than 12! Well, I have read — and I am soothed, pleased, pained, agitated[,] charmed and penetrated with the most lively gratitude — Is it not a little strange, that this very fifth day of August I should receive an account of the birth of a daughter to my brother! Excuse me my Friend — a tear will blister the paper — yet God, is my witness, I rejoice, greatly rejoice, in the happiness of Fitz William and his beloved Anna — May the Protector of innocence have the little stranger in his keeping — I attend, with a melancholy kind of pleasure, to the pages of my friend [—] She is, indeed she is, very good, and I wish not for my own soul, a happiness more highly zested than that with which I would, were it in my power invest my friend — Fatigued as I am, and accumulated as are the calls upon my time, she will forgive the cursory manner, in which I am necessitated to skim the surface, of such precious pledges of friendship, upon which, in other circumstances, I could expatiate through many an added sheet — I have already acknowledged your prolific fancy — It hath augmented to me the pleasures of our route, and meeting you in every romantick spot, while warmed by your lively imagination, the scene brightens upon me, and my enjoyments are doubled by participation. I yield a soberly attentive ear to your remarks, and I am pleased, and instructed. your objections to taking the life of an animal, are familiar to my mind — I have made similar efforts to abstain from partaking the guilt, and the effects have been the same — yet, I believe, if we had never dipped our tongues in blood, if we had never tasted the once animated food, the necessity so to do, would not have existed [—] Nay, I have thought, we should enjoy a much less interrupted state of health, and that being more alert, the functions of the soul would be more easily performed — in short that we should more clearly evince the immortal, becoming more etherial, and abundant less gross — but I am aware, that upon this disputed subject, I am incompetent to judge

Perhaps Franklin might have been better satisfied, with his economical plan, by a consideration of the eligibility of a vegetable diet, but, be this as it may, I suppose the authenticity of the anecdote in question, rests upon his own veracity, as the Lady, from whose mouth it was taken, had repeatedly received it from the lips of the venerable Relator — I knew that my Bethlehem tour would add to your pleasures — your mild eye, I assured myself would delightfully trace the lovely Group, at the sepulchral rites [—] I was persuaded you would attend and in the emblematic Grave Yard I believed you would mournfully wander — deriving thence from your well turned imagination, abundant exercise — Yes my sweet Friend the doctrine of the restitution of all things, was originally one of the fundamental principles of Count Zinzendorff, who was the Founder of the Moravian persuasion, and whose contract is still exhibited, and with high veneration, at Bethlehem — It is possible he might be received at Nazareth, whether Boys are transferred for the completion of their education — but of this I am not certain — nor should I be anxious in this respect — the mode of education, adopted by the Moravians, is as I believe, better calculated for the meridian of female delicacy, than for those active scenes which usually engage the other sex — The proofs of love which your frequent attentions exemplify, are very dear to my soul — and I think I cannot too often repeat, that I never will cease to be grateful [—] your fifth of July strongly excites my [soul] — It is delivered in your own fascinating style, a style which hath a thousand times chased from my bosom, the corroding sigh — Let no fears for me, disturb your peace — It will not be long before I shall bid adieu to this tenement, when the painful ravages of anguish, or of ignorance, will be felt no more — Opian figures, in your page, with added beauties, and as he laments his Malvinia, in the character of the younger Bards, these falling tears seem to comingle with those of their venerable original — Lucius Manlius is a sweet fellow — he almost seems to contest with his brother the superiority in my bosom — but it ends, as all fraternal contensions should, they unite hands in amity, and undo the banners of sweet equalities, take their seats in my heart — Poor Mrs D— How often are we necessitated to repeat — The ways of heaven are indeed inexplicable — These frequent instances of suicide are truly shocking — May God continue us in the exercise of reason, and endow us with that holy resignation, which is so requisite for dependent beings — I am pained to hear you express so much contempt for your letters — suffer me to say that such paragraphs strike me, as very exceptionable — Excuse me, I cannot bear to see you thus delineating with the pen of indifference, testimonies which do honour to friendship — We will certainly visit your Miss E— never doubt it — The view as you have given it, is enchanting — The passage written in your summer house, places you full before me — Charming Woman — May you live to possess your wishes —

Friday Morning Early

Last evening's post handed me a further addition to testimonies of amity, which will never cease to be most dear to my soul — No, my lovely friend, you are not in debt, for you still repay ah — and with a most liberal hand — and, upon the faith of friendship a proper sense of your bountiful, and indefatigable exertion, will ever live in my devoted bosom — I have not during my journey addressed my brother — you will recollect the request he once made relative to my continuance in Gloucester, I have not been — I am not unmindful of this request, and should I now date a letter, from any of the Towns or Villages, through which I pass, will it not look like an avowed intention to disoblige? It is true, I neither expect, nor wish my movement to be concealed from him, but if I myself make a parade of arrangements, retrograde to his wishes, may it not wear the appearance of a carelessness with regard to him, which is in fact foreign from my heart — My Father, and Mother, have enjoined it upon me, to make inquiries, relative to my brother, of General Knox — I shall obey them, and I contemplate the following method [—] The day before I quit this City I will thus address the general "A kinswoman of Major Sargent is deeply interested in his welfare, and commissioned by his parents — takes leave to inquire of General Knox, whether he hath had any late accounts of the Major, if he knows his present circumstances, and place of abode — It is long since any tidings hath reached his friends, and they request the General to inform them whether there is any way of communicating intelligence, and what mode of conveyance will be most expeditious — An answer to these inquiries, highly interesting to the Writer, directed to A.B. and left at Mr Robinson's Merchant in William Street, will be received, and acknowledged as a peculiar favour —" I shall not fail to transmit to my several friends, the result of this application — May my sister experience much happiness in her new dwelling, Once I hoped, but no more of complaining — I join with you wishing you had been favoured with the presence of Mrs Rosea — but Mrs R— acted herself — We shall, with high satisfaction accompany you to your rural retreats, wherever, and whenever your elegant taste shall conduct us — Sweet susceptible friend, I kiss the blistered paper, and with the indelible signet of friendship, I mark the circumstance — How proper is your method with your children — Go on — your tract is sanctioned by wisdom, and I am gratified, truly gratified, by the rapidity of their progress — I deplore your intellectual depression — Cheer up, beauteous Mourner — the voyage of life will soon be over — The Port of never ending felicity is full in view, and we shall be everlastingly anchored, in the Haven of rest — you are right, my Love — by all means endeavour to suppress ideas, the hydra suggestions of which, will have the most baleful influence upon your peace — Summon your utmost fortitude, and let us, my friend, remember, that He wh[o] sitteth in the Heavens ruleth with unerring propriety, and it is certain, that we ourselves, know not what is but One thing we, however know, that with the God of wisdom, who is also sovereign in goodness, and in mercy, all knowledge is found — No, I will never assay to hang with icicles the sunny beams of friendship — Tell that dear Girl, of whom you so affectingly speak, and while I make the avowal, my heart is upon my lips, that if I have seemed to declare the part, which her partial love assigned me, by the purest amity to her, I have been urged to the decision — Conscious of my inborn attachment to her, I was fearful that attachment, would hoodwink my judgment — would obtain over my easy faith, an influence too extensive — thus betraying her dearest interests — but you may add — if she will trust me enervated, and impassioned as I am, my utmost aid shall never be withheld — yes, the light of my enfeebled Reason shall beam its fairest radiance, and may its humble glimmerings, bequeath sweet consolation, to the bosom of the affectingly conscious sufferer — As I listen to her melting complaints, my very soul seems to die within me — Certainly, certainly, if her little bark is within my grasp, at the mercy of either wind, or tide, it shall never float — for as far as I may, however fraught with temerity the attempts may seem, I will assay to point its course — O! May the commanding voice of heaven, calm the impending tempest — guard this charming Votary of Virtue, and give to the perturbed bosom, the rich blessings of peace — upon your intelligence from Martinco, I sincerely congratulate you — May God restore in safety, your absent son [—] What a family hath that of the H— proved — who but must pity the poor deluded Girl —

Mr Murray hath this moment made me a communication, relative to General Knox, which entirely supersedes my plan of operation — Accidentally meeting the General at the President's — the necessary inquiries were brought on, the result of which is — Mr Knox says, one week since, he sent forward a packet from my brother, to New England, addressed to my Father — that he himself received a letter from my brother, dated May 7th. he was then in health, and the General is positive, he will be in this City in one Month — but, he adds, he will not visit New England. Whether General Knox is authorized to pronounce this decisively, I know not — It is probable the packet forwarded by the General, contained a letter for you, which will no doubt give you the fullest information — Farewell, my sweet Friend, excuse haste — and, with your accustomed goodness, imagine every thing tender — believe me you cannot draw too largely upon the affection of your devoted Friend ———

Letter 779— To Mrs E. S. New York — Chapel Street August 6th 1790

Dorcas Babson Sargent (Mrs. Epes Sargent) has apparently written to Judith about how much she is missed in Gloucester. Judith's response reveals how deeply she values love, esteem, and friendship, and that she and John will "hasten to the dear spot, which contains the choicest of [their] treasures."

you say right my dear Lady — Love is indeed a divine emanation and hence we are proportionably happy, as we are conformed to its genuine principles — I declare, upon the faith of my veracity, that my pleasures have ever been augmented, in an exact ratio, as they have approached that celestial emanation — Love hath still been the talisman of my enjoyments, and, as its sweet, and benign influence hath aquired strength or faded in my bosom, just so, the finer feelings of my soul have been set afloat, or chilled by indifference, withered by contempt or blasted perhaps by anger — Every sweet, and complacent hour — and what are those but the offspring of Love? — especially if any circumstance hath rendered them memorable, possesseth the power as often as reflection presents them, of clustering a train of harmonious ideas — of ideas becoming a Candidate for an existence which we pleasingly believe will be productive of all those refinements, which result from communicative and social happiness — But the moments usurped by Murderous contention rise up as assasians of my peace, and I could wish them ingulphed in oblivion — yes, my dear Mrs E.S. — Friendship, esteem, and Love, I do most cordially embrace, and I devoutly wish, nothing may ever disunite the charming Trio —

I am truly pleased at the effect produced by my letter — It corresponds exactly with my wishes, and I am happy that I obeyed the impulse, which prompted me to write — May the continuing cord never be loosed, nor a haughty passion be found, hardly enough to cut the Gordian knot — By the intention of Charles, although not executed, I am gratified, and flattered — I love that integrity which, as I believe, moulds his heart, and I supplicate for him a maturing of worth — your expected solicitude for our return, is truly pleasing — and we shall, with no common aim, hasten to the dear spot, which contains the choicest of our treasures — Mr Murray returns acknowledgements, and regards, and I, dear Lady, am indeed, and in truth, your very affectionate, and grateful Kinswoman —

Letter 780 To Miss C.S. New York Chapel Street August 6th. 1790

Sixteen-year-old Catherine Sargent, daughter of Dorcas Babson and Epes Sargent, has written to Judith about how much she and her brothers and sisters miss their older cousin. Judith is delighted with the letter, and pleased with the progress in Catherine's education. Apparently, Catherine has been very ill and Judith regrets that she is so "early taught by sufferings." However, she believes her cousin has been "made wise by experience."

It will, my sweet Girl, always constitute one of my principal felicities, to be regarded with confiding affection, by those whose opening minds, are just bursting into the rosy morning of existence— youth is exhibited to every candid construction and surely it ought not to be deemed an exertion to yield unto the charming proficients, an alleviance so indisputably their due — Whatever your susceptible timidity, may induce you to apprehend — justice impels me to say, that although the few years you may have numbered, ascertain your claim to all those indulgences which the right hand of experience, should delight to proffer — yet, it is true that your attainments obviate the necessity of that candour to which you appeal — your letter produced in my bosom, sensations truly pleasant — could you have taken a peep into my heart, your native benevolence, would have acknowledged ample recompense, for any effort which you may have called into requisition, and with a pleasure, all your own, you would have traced its soothing, and truly gratifying effects.

your name my Dear — Catharine Sargent — hath ever been hallowed in my ear and I was not so long the bosom friend, of the revered Lady, who bore it, without learning to appreciate those endearing qualities, which, at a very early period, her discerning eye beheld, opening in the mind of her Girl — May she, with her name, transmit to you, those accomplishments, intrinsic, and ornamental, the inherent seeds of which, ripened in her life, and so consistently graced her own amiable character — It is with inexpressible pleasure, I persuade myself, that the friendship with which she honoured me, inherited by her charming descendants, and early implanted in their lovely bosoms, will take such deep root, as not to leave me, in the evening of life, destitute of the rising prop where on to rest my declining days — Bethlehem, my dear, is indeed a spot, where education hath become a business, and the student, no doubt, derives many advantages from the regular, and consistent plans, so uniformly observed — But, that justness of reflection, which at so early a period, you remarkably possess, hath no doubt taught you, very properly, to estimate your own privileges — Genius, seems to have descended to you, in an hereditary line — your parents are abundantly capable of supplying you, with every requisite, which can inform, or embellish, your understanding — In the dawn of being you have entered upon the flowing path of knowledge — and I do most sincerely congratulate my young friend, that she possesseth talents, designed by Nature — under such forming auspices — gradually to unfold and to obtain a complete growth of loveliness — That you have cast a thought upon me, is truly flattering, your expressed impatience for my return, is exactly what I would ask, and still more endears the smiling circle to my heart — you say we and of course I connect that sweetly blushing sister, who is the mild Companion of your fairest heart [—] Arria too, with pretty archness points her wishes — Charles, and John James, produce unequivocal proof, that they accord with their sisters — Anna too, if she may be allowed to keep close to Mamma's elbow, will have no objection to see me, once more take my seat in the happy parlour — See how [evident] is the growth of Vanity — But I am pleased with your letter, with the testimonies of your regards, which it contains, and I am doubly so, as it stands as an undisputed Voucher, of your returning health, for I trace, on every line, that ease, and animation, which could never be the offspring of a mind, debilitated by sickness — you are, my dear, early taught by sufferings, a due appreciation of health and your ordeal, commencing in the first stage of your existence, you are thus made wise by experience, but, as I trust, the laughter loving days of youth, still await you and I do most confidingly hope, that sickness, with its hydra evils, may, for a very long season, stand aloof from your pretty tenement. I deplore the alarming complaints of our Aunts, Allen and Saunders — the loss of either of those valuable friends would make a mournful chasm in our already curtailed enjoyments — but, my Love, as you advance in Life, you will frequently be constrained to say with the Poet, "String after string is severed from the heart —" you are the eldest of a numerous, and encreasing family, your avenues to pain, as well as pleasure, are multiplied — May you have fortitude to support the one and equality to dignify the other [—] Mr Murray unites with me in tender salutations — We are, with growing esteem, your admiring and affectionate Friends —

Letter 781 To Mr E.S. New York Chapel Street
August 6 1790

This letter is typical of many written to her cousin, Epes Sargent, in which Judith discusses her thoughts on duty to God and the "late transaction at Stratsburg" she wishes she could have witnessed. She is pleased that Epes's crops in Gloucester are doing well. Farmers in Pennsylvania, New Jersey, and New York are presently experiencing drought conditions.

Your favours, my dear Sir, by reason of slow progress through the Jersies, having so lately reached us, and Mr Goodhue's departure being accelerated beyond our expectations, reduceth us to the necessity, of replying more concisely than our feelings would otherwise have prompted. Great as are our obligations to Mr Goodhue, we would gladly augment them, and I for my heart would keep Congress sitting at least until we were ready to quit New York! So well it is, that we have not the power to bend large bodies, agreeably to our Capries

In the face of a Chesterfieldian prohibition, I risk an adage, or proverb "They well should practice, who so well can teach —" Is there [one] who can more delicately administer the delicious draught of praise, than my obliging Animadverter? Nature, from your hand the incense is highly refined [—] In the Laboratory of Ingenuity, the proper particles fly off, but the rich essence remains, and is not the sweet perfume thus furnished with more subtle, and penetrating potency? I remember when you were a student in the University at Cambridge, you expressed, in one of the letters you had the goodness to address to me, the following statement — It made, at the time, being originated by a son of Harvard, a very strong impression upon my mind, it hath gone through life with me, and although my memory is, by no means tenacious — yet, I believe, I can, at this moment, give it verbatim — "Praise, if well applied, hath a good effect, it stimulates us to Virtue, and raiseth us to actions almost divine —" Its present application should be general, and I am bold enough to risk the repetition of a truth when I declare, my letter to you, contained the genuine sentiments of my soul — Again, I say, I could amply retort, but having a natural aversion from recrimination, I forbear the attempt [—] My pleasures have always been augmented by communication, and if you or yours, have derived the smallest gratification, from the various scenes which I have assayed to sketch, it cannot fail of being [a] matter of satisfaction to me, My sister, I dare say, was pleased with your remarks, but who shall combat the force of habit or war against the impressions of ease, or who shall account for engagements so retrograde to reason, into which we are too often precipitated — Better judgment would dictate the social hour the sweet intercourse of minds — it would point out the comparative frivolity of every thing which can only affect a state of being so extremely circumscribed — but the phantoms press, we imagine a necessity and in a hurricane of mighty nothings we are borne away — and this also is ordered in wisdom for did not these fleeting scenes so deeply interest[ed] to fill the Circle marked by heaven, would be producive of sensations, still more strongly marked — you do me justice when you say — I cannot if I would eradicate from my bosom the feelings of amity — yes, by very tender attachments my heart is warmed, and around your peaceful dwelling, my fond affections will not forget to hover. What ever a flippant fancy, in some playful hour, may have suggested, I have not the least objection to the word Obedience — It never grated harshly upon my ear — I love to be dictated to and that assured confidence, which becomes a prop to my mind, that sweet complacency, which attunes my soul to peace, when, with becoming acquiescence, I have submitted to a proposition, or yielded, without murmuring to an exigency, convinceth me, that formed for obedience, submission will ever constitute my happiness: To the Will of Heaven, in every dispensation I would be constantly resigned — nor, if I could avoid it, should even a refractory thought rise in opposition — The Tyranny of passions is indeed dreadful — and shocking as may be the idea, it is yet true, that they frequently, and impiously arraign the attributes of the Most High [—] Certainly the character of the Redeemer, exhibits the brightest example of calm, and dignified patience — the precepts of the holy Religion, which He taught, abound with lessons proper to humanity — Its morals are like its divine Author, and if its spirit were universally imbibed, a blissful era would most unquestionably commence — The progress of philanthropy must interest, and charm — I should have witnessed the late transaction at Stratsburg, with an elevated kind of pleasure — Indeed my imagination hath placed me in the hallowed Fame, I have seen the polished shafts of reason, piercing the very vitals of gloomy bigotry — A Calvinistical Church allowed in a Roman Catholic Country — Nor only so — consecrated with great solemnity — Magistrates of all descriptions with the Clergy of the Roman, Lutheran, and Calvinistical persuasion, while their voices blend in the Te Deum — I listen attentively, I mingle in the procession, I enter the Cathedral, the occasional sermon seizeth every faculty of my soul — my bosom catches the extatic glow, I bless the powers of the animating Orator, and I behold with divine rapture, the God honouring effect — Amazing, the zealous sectarians, animated by an emanation of Divinity, in one and the same moment embrace each other — yea doubtless, their adherents follow this example, and their audibly expressed resolution, of never ending, and fraternal amity, is but the offspring of that truth, which, with irresistable energy, shall one day mould every obdurate spirit — The scene must have been truly august — Religion with her beauteous daughters — Reason, and humanity, triumphing over the unyielding, and rebellious passions, which, abated by ignorance, and prejudice, have hitherto usurped her fair domain — Glorious, and happy Crisus, no wonder that every eye gushed, and that each subdued heart, so divinely penetrated, ratified the bond of extensive, and permanent union — I make no apology for this reference to a recent fact, which news papers and Magazines, have doubtless presented you — for your heart, possessing as I believe, feelings correspondent to those which have produced this uncommon event, will not retreat from hearing it expatiated upon. That your prospects of a plenteous Harvest are so good, cannot but interest, and please — you will gather from my journal, that the fields of grain in this part of the Country do not smile so luxuriantly — Those pleasures which a Rush, and a Rittenhouse, have afforded us, we have endeavoured to sketch for you, your society and that of your amiable Lady, would indeed have pointed every enjoyment — but what is there in this world which is complete? — My Father's health, and spirits, always as often as they come to my knowledge, exhilarate my soul — It is unnecessary to add, I rejoice in the welfare of my family, and that I feel my obligations to you, for the pleasing account you so obligingly transmitted — May your Catharine, and every other pledge of your...happiness still augment your pleasures — My heart thanks your children, for their united regards — Mr Murray, writing at the same table thus accosts me "Do tell me to what part of that elegant address, to which we have an equal claim — you have responded?" He takes up the paper and her really — Oh! barbarous! yet I have laughed very heartily, and so I doubt not will you — The good Man hath however left me little to say, only our feelings, around the solitary Mansion are Correspondent, and will not need to be told that Friend Murray seldom drops his tear alone — I do not know when I have been so charmed, as with your sketch from Doctor Watson — Pray may I not read him, or is his work beyond my depth? — His anecdote of the Dutchman is natural, and the conclusion of his Majesty of Siam easy to be imagined. I am pleased when I find those relations which I know to be facts, called in question by individuals who are ignorant of them, and that from the apparent absurdity, or impossibility of the record — The reason is obvious I am confirmed in the credence which I yield to events, striking my reason, as equally fabulous, they may have been brought about by unknown Causes — and produced in a natural, and consistent chain — How admirably doth the Doctor point our reflections — Will the deluge be henceforth a subject of ridicule —? The union of Religion, and Philosophy is indeed happy — your youngest son — Ah! how many images doth this Cherub child cluster in my bosom — Oh! May he be every thing which the fondest, and most sanguine parents can hope, or wish — May God bless you all, and may you continue to love, and to be assured, of the affectionate regards of your sincerely attached kinswoman —

Letter 782 To my Father and Mother New York Chapel Street August 7th. 1790 Saturday

Judith traces the journey to New York, including their tearful departure from Mount Place. Numerous friends had gathered to say goodbye to "their revered Murray," probably seeing John for the last time. Judith wonders how, 20 years ago, he could have left a place where he is so openly loved. But off they went, to the home of Dr. Stiles in Cranbury, to Brunswick, Woodbridge, Elizabeth, Newark and, finally, New York City. Along the way, Judith describes the effects of the drought and how slaves are treated in New Jersey. She imagines the recent birthing scene that took place in her parents' home, anxious to meet her new niece. John has been presented to President Washington and will deliver an address on behalf of the Universalist convention. "General Greene" is General Nathanael Greene, a leading military strategist who served with distinction under General Washington.

I have now to inform my indulgent Parents, that we reached this City — but we will, if you please, proceed agreeably to the order of time — I am, as you know, an admirer of method — Well then — Sunday last Mr Murray once more met, in the hallowed Grove, his assembled hearers — the multitude was encreased, and no less than fifteen hundred persons surrounded him — The portion of scripture which he adduced, his address to the people, and his concluding adieus were equally apposite, interesting, and affecting, and I do not believe, that in this promiscuous Assembly, a dry eye was to be found — several Carriages accompanied us to Mount Place, and the residue of the day was devoted to serious investigation of select portions of sacred writ — Mr Mount's second daughter, with her husband, had joined us from their distant abode — and our Circle was now complete — I had not intended to have presented you with any more parting scenes, but I must again tax the patience of my friends — for a place in my journal must positively be sacred, to the morning which separated us from the Mounts — I described the stair case — no less than fifteen females, decent and elegant in their appearance, but clad in the sad livery of grief, lined the Hall — Male Friends, in a much larger proportion, were passing to, and from, the various apartments — I was abashed, and involuntarily receded a few paces — but recollecting myself, I assumed a cheerful countenance, and came forward with my...salutations — Mr Murray too, serenely smiled — which smile was too much for the venerable head, of the little Village of Amity — and he affectingly exclaimed — I cannot bear this — you should not smile — Consider they are your Old your first American friends whom you are about to leave — perhaps forever — Indeed it is not right — and waving his aged hand — his expressive silence seemed to add, surely I would, upon this occasion dress the world in tears, and not a laughing feature should presume to meet my gaze. When the day of departure hath arrived, painful are the hours which intervene, until the final farewell is pronounced — yet, on Monday last, from six O clock in the morning, till twelve at noon, we were doomed to struggle with the failings attendant upon such a situation — We had received every testimony of affection, and we must have possessed that equanimity, which makes up part of our characters, could we have witnessed the scene without strong emotions — But the parting moment, is at length announced — the Carriage is at the door — one half an hour since, the less interested, leaving these united benedictions, have retired — The Mounts gather round — The sons and daughters lift their hands, in tremulous and speechless agony — Their revered Murray — they cannot pronounce his name — they embrace my hands, my lips, and resign me to their honoured parents — Mrs Mount throws around me her maternal arms — Farewell, Oh Farewell forever — I approach the old gentleman — his venerable countenance expresses all the Father — Features impressed by paternal kindness, I can never behold without mingling reverence, and extending my hand, I bent my knee with duteous affection — and you will go then sobbed out the poor old Man — "Say not Sir I will — Say rather necessity impels["]— he caught me in his arms, and in a fervant ejaculation, commended me to the direction and preservation of the prayr hearing God — you will judge of the attachment of these worthy people to Mr Murray, by the genial warmth of those rays, which, although but reflected therefrom, so pointedly beam on me — Indeed, considering the exquisitely tender feelings which warm the heart of Mr Murray, I am induced to wonder, how he ever brought himself to quit this rural abode, and its peaceful environs — Well, but we are seated in the Chaise — the whole family are drawn out — blessings, blessings without measure or number, are heaped upon us — With streaming eyes, and uplifted hands, the solemn benedictions are repeated — and they add — tell your Father, tell your Mother, that although personally unknown to them, our hearts, by the softening influence of tender love, are drawn toward them, and that in the kingdom of our common Lord, we trust we shall meet and become familiar with their honoured countenances — One child of the family was absent from the scene, it was — she said — too much for her feelings — and upon a slip of paper, she penned her adieus — "Excuse dear Sir — Excuse dear Lady, your afflicted Margaretta — The task of bidding you adieu, in any other manner, is too painful for me — May God bless you both, and grant you through the journey of life, every thing which is essential to your happiness["] — At length we have quitted the hospitable door, and we call upon the Villagers as we proceed — The white headed Men, wring the hands of our Murray — their sons approach with a more equal, but affecting composure, and the females exclaim — if we lose sight of you now, we shall never more behold you — Thus we pass those tranquil abodes, which might have figured in the golden Age, and the fervant and grateful orisons of our spirits, were spontaneously uttered, in their behalf — O! may the dear Redeemer, still lift up the light of his countenance upon them, and may his upholding truth, still continue a wall of Amity round about them — Monday Evening we reached Cranbury, and were received by Doctor Stiles, whose residence is fourteen miles from Mount Place, with much kindness — The Doctor with his Lady, are also Old Friends and our reception was proportionably warm — Their dwelling is neat, and shaded by Woodbines, and a number of flowering shrubs, in which the humming bird holds unmolested its luxuriant residence — The circumstances of the Doctor are easy — and having no children, he is the better able to gratify the inborn hospitality which is manifest in his own, and his lady's truly pleasing manners — Mrs Stiles has discovered the art of rendering her black people truly serviceable, and on tuesday they prepared for us an entertainment, without the least assistance from their mistress, which would have done honour to any table, in the United States — The African is still enslaved in the Jersies, but he is treated with the utmost humanity, and were it not for ideas, which certain magical sounds, never fail to agitate, I should believe him altogether as happy as his Master — At the dwelling of Doctor Stiles, we did not continue a sufficient time, to reiterate a scene, similar to that which we had witnessed at Mount Place — for resisting, very heroically, the most pressing remembrances, we left them, on tuesday...taking a cup of tea on our way, with another <u>Old Friend</u>, and reaching Brunswick, just as the setting sun had [extinguished] his last parting beams — The road from Mount Place, to Brunswick, is remarkably fine, it is nearly level, and aboundeth with picturesque scenes, tall thick woods rise upon either hand — cultivated Nature every where appears, and the [eye rests] upon a constant succession of beautifully pleasing views, our pleasures were however checked, as we observed the stunted growth of those fields upon which but for the [absence] of the fertilizing shower and succeeding heats, would have been now well nigh ripe for harvest. No doubt, many a sighing heart, will mourn through the wintry months, the curtailed crops which it is feared this Autumn, unless a sudden spring should be given to vegetation, will return — At Brunswick we brightened the chain, which that kind of merit personified by my dear Mrs Dunham and which carries its credentials upon its face, had contrived to rivet, and on Wednesday morning, crossing the Rariton, we came on through Woodbridge, and the handsome Town of Elizabeth, where we dined agreeably, at an Inn, in company with a stranger from whom we received many obliging civilities — After which we proceeded to the beautiful Village of Newark, taking up our lodgings, agreeably to invitation, at that Mr Smith's where we informed you we passed a morning so delightfully — Thursday, crossing the three Rivers, which in the space of ten miles from Newark, to New York, impede the course of the Traveller, we quitted the Jersey shore, and were once more landed in the tumultuous City where every inferior consideration, was absorbed by the inexpressible pleasures which were deduced from the multiplied packets of our New England Friends, which in unexpected numbers, surprised our souls with the sincerest joy — The birth of the little stranger we devoutly hail — auspicious to the hour, which hath introduced her into being — Her accession to existence was announced to me, upon the fifth of August — upon the first anniversary of that fifth of August, which was so fatal to my hopes, which gave to my bosom a clay cold form — may my friends, all of them, taste those highly zested joys, which are, no doubt for wise and paternal reasons, denied to me — I wish me thinks, you could have transmitted me the name of my brother's daughter — May Angels guard the pretty Voyager — May every shield, which matured wisdom can furnish, form a bulwark for the little innocent — By a Father's arms, may she soon be encircled, and reard by parental tenderness, may she repay with duteous attention, every anxious effort — I rejoice that her gentle Mother hath so happily surmounted the perils, attendant upon the pangful hour — and that her reward is so great [—] I long to embrace, and to confess to her, our added obligations, and I sigh to clasp the charming Baby to my bosom. you was, my dear Sir, in your circumstantial account, particularly obliging — With you I impatiently waited the approach of the skillful Physician — as a Woman, as a sister, I felt for the patient sufferer, and the footsteps of the Doctor, vibrated upon the ear of my imagination — At nine O clock sunday morning — was it not? I echo the joyful tidings, and the beauteous infant is right welcoming to my soul — The image of her Father you say — If Fitz William were with you, the scene would indeed be complete — Once more — May God restore him to domestic happiness [—] I grieve that my Mother doth not possess that health, so requisite to give a zest to every enjoyment — May the Redeemer enable her to possess her soul in patience — you wish for a variety of subjects — nothing, my dear Sir, can be uninteresting from the pen of a Father, and have you not forwarded me the most delightful intelligence — I grieve for my Aunt D— and I wish for my Aunt B— every thing she ought to derive — I love her children, I do not care how fortunate Doctor Babbit is, but

I must confess, I never hear him mentioned without a pang — this may be unjust — perhaps it is so, and I will endeavour to combat my feelings — To strike an old Man, was certainly wrong but I am happy I do not set as judge — For every particular from my native spot I again thank you, remote as I am, nothing can be uninteresting — My letters are indeed long, I have been fearful they would fatigue you, but you must accept my old apology — they constitute my journal — I am fearful it will be a long season before I shall again hear from you — we shall soon leave this City [—] Mr Goodhue is hastening Eastward, many are our obligations to this worthy Gentleman — It is impossible to say where we shall be, or to whom to request you to direct — We shall however determine as we go on, and we shall be careful to apprize you of the result — Mr Murray only waits to present an address to the President — and we are gone —

The necessary inquiries have been made — Mr Murray met General Knox at the President's who informed him, he had, one week since, sent on a packet from my brother — God grant it may have come safe to hand, that it may convey pleasing intelligence, speaking peace to your revered bosoms, respecting the principal branch of your family — Mr Murray was introduced at the President's to the famous Colonel McGillivray — The Leader of the Creek Indians, General Knox then announced the Promulgator of glad tidings "Mr Murray, Sir, a gentleman of a very singular character — who, while almost every other Clergyman, are generously giving the Majority of Mankind to his satanic Majesty — he, viewing the matter in an opposite direction, beholds them all restored to the fountain from whence they originated — So that you will observe, Sir, according to his creed, your Indian tribes are upon a level with our most enlightened Boasters—" McGillivray, I have already informed you, is a man of liberal education, and it is said he possesseth a good natural understanding, upon this occasion he looked pleasure, as he replied — "If the Gentleman merits this character, he is the first Christian Divine whom I have known — Certainly that Being cannot be consistent, who doth not protect, and preserve the work of His hands["] — The widow of General Greene is now in this City — Mr Murray hath seen her, and she received him with her wonted kindness — On Monday I am to be introduced to this Lady — but this, with many Etceteras will make a proper part of my next letter — If any thing relative to either of my brothers, reacheth you, your feelings will prompt you to hasten it to me — you will please to remember us particularly to every inquiring friend — May God protect my Parents, and long preserve them, rich blessings to their grateful children

*"My eyes had never before beheld him — but it was
not necessary he should be announced — that
dignified benignity, by which he is distinguished,
could not belong to another...." (from Letter 783)*

George Washington by James Peale, after Charles Wilson Peale, ca. 1787-90.
Courtesy of the Independence National Historic Park Collection.

Letter 783 To the Same New Rochelle
August 14th 1790 Saturday

Judith has met President and Mrs. Washington — the "Lady Presidentess" — and their granddaughter, Eleanor Custis. Judith and John dined at the president's residence (which she describes here in detail), and even though Judith had never met Washington before, she wrote, "it was not necessary he should be introduced." She was moved by his presence and his greatness. "[T]o speak truth of the President is impossible, No Painter will ever be able to do him justice," she wrote. With Martha Washington Judith was impressed as well, and the two women became friends and lifelong correspondents. Martha confided in Judith her fears for her husband's health, only recently restored after a serious illness. Nine-year-old "Miss Custus," who lived with her grandparents since her parents were deceased, took an immediate liking to Judith and would also become a regular correspondent. Before leaving New York, Eleanor presented Judith with a painting of flowers she had finished just for her. Judith wrote her a poem of thanks which she copied in this letter.

*Judith and John also visited with Vice President and Mrs. Adams, with whom they were already acquainted. John had first met the them in 1788, on his return voyage from England. They became friends and, later that same year, John took his new bride — Judith — to meet them in Braintree. In New York, Judith found that John Adams was still "the man of sense, and the Patriot," and that both John and Abigail were "the same kind, and hospitable individuals" they had always been. Years later, in 1798, Judith dedicated her book, *The Gleaner, to John Adams. Their copy of the book, signed by Abigail, is still housed at the Adams family library in Quincy, Massachusetts.*

This letter also describes the signing of the treaty between Congress and the Creek Nation. Judith and John witnessed the occasion in Federal Hall, presided over by President Washington in his purple satin robes. Judith describes the dress of the Creek leaders, the ceremony, and terms of the treaty which everyone agreed was "mutually beneficial." She hoped that, "perhaps succeeding Centuries may not repeat" the necessity of such agreements. The treaty being signed, everyone joined hands or linked arms and sang a song of peace.

Judith and John have visited John Trumball's studio where his painting of George Washington was almost complete, and the letter concludes with a recounting of the hot journey to New Rochelle. "Col Humphrys" is David Humphreys, Washington's aid and adviser. "Mr McGillivray" is Alexander McGillivray, whose half "indian" heritage gave him a unique ability to arrange treaties.

You will, my dear Parents, judge that we are moving quite in the Court Circle, when I shall inform you that we have taken tea at the President's, passed a day at the Vice President's, and visited at the Secretary's — and, further, that we have taken Coach with the Widow of General Greene etc etc — But lest you should imagine us so much elated, by those honours, as to become absolutely giddy — I will pursue my narrations with my accustomed method — Sunday, being rather indisposed, I indulged myself through the day in my chamber — The Churches in New York are all shut against Mr Murray, but he met his friends, among whom are some of the most respectable characters, both forenoon and afternoon, in the Assembly room, and the evening produced many Ladies, who did me the honour of calling upon me — On Monday, Mr Murray as the Minister of the Universal Gospel, presented the address of the Churches, professing Universalism to the President of the United States, and was most graciously received — The form of the address, with the answer, will no doubt reach you, in the line of publick intelligence, long before the period, in which this letter is destined [to reach] your hands — While Mr Murray visited at the President's Mrs Washington dispatched a Messenger from her apartments, importing that she should be pleased with a visit from Mrs Murray, that if she — Mrs Murray — preferred enjoyment to ceremony, she need not wait for a Levee day — for Mrs Washington would certainly be at home, whenever it should suit Mrs Murray's convenience, and the President too, deigned to enquire, if my journey had bestowed upon me the blessings of health — all this, you will believe, was highly flattering — ...About Six O-clock we took a coach for the presence, and at the door of the great Hall we were met by a well looking, and well dressed Man — I however recollected myself, and neither bowed, nor curtsyed

At the bottom of the stair case Colonel Humphry's, offering his hand, ushered us into the drawing room, a number of Ladies were with Mrs Washington, and her matronlike appearance, and Lady like condescension, soon dissipated every painful idea of distance — taking my hand she seated me by her side, and addressing herself particularly to me, as the only stranger present, she engaged me in the most familiar, and agreeable Chat — she interrogated me respecting my journey, asked if my acquaintance in New York was extensive, and in what part of the City I abode — She informed me she had the pleasure of being acquainted with my brother, and she spoke of his late marriage, and the death of his Companion, as events which had interested her feelings — I cast my eyes round the room, and I read in the countenances of the Ladies, a pleasing kind of respect — Mr Murray was engaged with Colonel Humphrys, who occasionally regarded me with flattering attention — Thus were we disposed of when General Washington

*"Mrs Washington's face is an index of a good heart,
and those Virtues which I am told she eminently possesseth,
are impressed upon every feature...." (from Letter 783)*

Martha Washington by Charles Wilson Peale, c. 1795.
Courtesy of the Independence National Historical Park Collection.

entered the drawing room — My eyes had never before beheld him — but it was not necessary he should be announced — that dignified benignity, by which he is distinguished, could not belong to another — Mrs Washington introduced me[,] I arose, and with a countenance that spoke not my heart, if it were not impressed with affectionate respect, and the highest degree of veneration[, s]lowly bending, in a marked, and expressive manner, I performed my duteous salutations — a smile of pleasure illumined the features of the President, he requested me to be seated, and taking a place by my side, proceeded, with peculiar affability to question me relative to my health, to my brother, to Philadelphia etc etc [—] To discant upon the Virtues of General Washington, however [interesting] the theme, frequently as they have been capatiated upon, and inadequate as I am, I assay not —

Yet I will so far indulge my feelings, as to say, that his figure is elegant beyond what I have ever seen, that his countenance is benignly good, and that there is a kind of venerable gravity inscribed upon every feature — as I sat by his side, Homer's Nestor frequently occurred to my imagination, and, of this I am certain, no Grecian Dame, could have beheld the hoary sage, with greater admiration — my heart, my exalting heart, highly appreciated the uniform Hero, acknowledging a kind of homage only not divine — The vestments of the President were of purple satin, but his figure and not the aid of this regal dye, to inspire those sentiments, which are deemed the tribute of royalty majestically commanding, his appearance will ever, insure the love, and reverence of every unprejudiced beholder — To speak truth of the President is impossible — No Painter will ever be able to do him justice — for that which he possessed beyond every other man, the Art of the Linner or language of the panegyrist, however glowing, can never reach — It is a grace in every movement, a manner, an address, an inimitable expression, especially when the sedate dignity of his countenance, is irradicated by a serene smile — in short a nameless something, in the tout ensemble, which no skill can delineate, no art can catch and which of course no portrait will ever transmit — Mrs Washington's face is an index of a good heart, and those Virtues which I am told she eminently possesseth, are impressed upon every feature — need I add, that her countenance is irresistably prepossessing [—] The residence of General Washington is in Broad Way, and the edifice which he occupies, presents a superb Front — The drawing room, and the apartments of which we had a view are lofty, and magnificently spacious — the Furniture is rich, but it doth not surpass what I have before seen — The upper end of the drawing room is pierced, with three glass doors, which open into a handsome Balcony commanding an extensive view of the Hudson interspersed with beautiful Islands, and washing, at the opposite point, the Jersey shore — In this Balcony Mr Murray was honoured by a tete a tete with our illustrious Chief, in this Balcony, after we had taken tea, Mrs Washington requested we would walk, and in this Balcony, Mrs Greene, taking her leave, thus addressed your daughter — "Early in the morning I shall leave this City for Hartford, my stay there will be short, I shall proceed to Rhode Island, where having made my visit, I shall return to this City — I then propose passing some time with my Girls in Bethlehem, from whence I shall proceed to Georgia — at the idea of Georgia, I feel a pang, for which I cannot account — Possibly I may never see you more, but should you ever hear that I am again fixed to any one spot — remember I early knew your husband, that I no sooner knew than I loved him — Remember my claim hath the privilege of priority, I am among the first of his friends, and as such, I urge my pretensions to your regards — Remember then, I say that I am entitled to some portion of your time, and when I am again a housekeeper I shall expect you, among the most familiar footing —" In the course of the two hours passed at the President's various topics of conversation were introduced — Mrs Washington, as I said was condescendingly attentive to me, as a stranger I was constantly by her side, and addressing me in a low voice, she spoke of her family — she hath been a happy mother, one son, and one daughter, by a former marriage, they now, however, both sleep in the narrow house — One grand Son, and three granddaughters survive — I know, said Mrs Washington, that my daughter in law would soon enter into new engagements, and I urged her to yield her two youngest children to my care — this she obligingly did, and consequently a grandson, and granddaughter, reside constantly at the President's — Mrs Washington hath educated a Niece, now united in marriage, to a favourite Nephew of the General and the young couple reside upon, and have the care of that fine Estate, of which we have heard so much, at Mount Vernon — To which elegant seat, the President and his Lady, will during the recess of Congress, rapidly bend their steps — The family, thus circumstanced, it is hardly to be regretted, that the General hath no son, to whom to transmit his honours, and his Virtue, for he cannot but be immortal — his Lady is universally beloved, and the sons of Columbia are their children — Mrs Washington's Grandson, is about nine years of age — we saw him but a moment — her granddaughter is hardly eleven — she is a fine sprightly Girl — The President and his Lady complained that she was not sufficiently industrious but she played and sung for us, at the first word, and her performance evinced, that she must have had her hours of application She is, I am told a child of an extraordinary capacity — attention only being requisite, to her acquiring attainments judged beyond her years, and she assures her Preceptors, if they will but allow her frivolity, until she hath completed her twelfth year, she will yield the rest of her life to their direction — some pieces of her drawing were exhibited — They had great merit, and were, you will not doubt, highly applauded — The Ladies severally solicited her to execute for them, some pretty flowers which might serve as a memorial of her opening Genius, and the sweet pliability of her disposition rendering refusals painful, she fled to my elbow, apparently for shelter — In a whisper she thus accosted me "only thank you Ma'am, how solicitous every Body is, and Mrs Greene too absolutely insists upon my finishing a piece for her, although she leaves New York early to morrow morning"! My pretty Love, I returned — your paintings are so excellent, it is hardly to be wondered, the Ladies are earnest to possess specimens — I do assure you, had I an equal claim, I should be equally urgent — but, stranger as I am, I presume not to petition["] — Whether it was my manner, or what, it was I pretend not to say, but she appeared amazingly struck, and even affected and, seizing my hand, she tenderly questioned "Pray when do you leave Town?" We expect to depart on saturday, or monday at farthest — "Well Ma'am," she rejoined, if it be possible I will sketch for you a flower piece, before that period," I was most agreeably surprised, and pressing her forehead with my lips, I returned, "Thank you my little Charmer — very sincerely I thank you, and even should you not find time to execute an intention so flattering to me, this sweet, this spontaneous expression, will ever live in my memory["] — Turning to her grandmamma, I related our little Confab — the President listened, and they both smiled their approbation, while Mrs Washington observed, that Miss Custus had made me as absolute a promise as she was ever allowed to make, that considering unavoidable accidents, might intervene to arrest the accomplishment of any purpose, it was always best to introduce a saving clause [—] Thus passed our afternoon — never did I see less of restraint — The Common Tea parties in the Country Village, hath more of ceremony, and we took leave penetrated with a proper sense of the honour which had been done us — Mrs Washington in our aside conversation, spoke of the General's later alarming illness, and while she expressed her happiness in his present restoration, a tear of apprehension for futurity, was in her eye — I embraced this opportunity, of expressing the emotions of my bosom and while I adverted to the common interest, which every American held in a life so precious, I allowed the superiority of her tender, and sacred claims — Our invitation to the Vice President's was for wednesday — and thus it was worded — "If Mr & Mrs Murray are disposed to confer an obligation, they will make their appearance as early in the day as possible — " Such a summons, from such a character, you will judge we easily disposed ourselves to obey, and accordingly half past twelve, produced us at the gate — The seat of the Vice President is just two miles from Federal Hall — It is situated upon the Banks of the Hudson, and commands a variety of the most beautiful and picturesque views — The house is a

"...the Vice President still continues the Man of sense,
and the Patriot...he is still benignly good, and
dignifyedly affable...." (from Lettter 783)

John Adams by Charles Wilson Peale, ca. 1791-94.
Courtesy of the Independence National Historical Park Collection.

"[the Vice President's] Lady is not unduly elevated,
nor spoiled by the adulatory incense of
surrounding flatterers...." (from Letter 783)

Abigail Adams, unfinished portrait by Gilbert Stuart, 1800.
Courtesy of the Massachusetts Historical Society, Boston.

spaciously elegant structure — its Architecture of a light and pleasing kind — and it is highly finished — Its hue is a rich white, and its front consists an upper, and lower Balcony, supported by ample pillars, handsomely flutted ornamented by a pyramid, and decorated by various carvings — the apartments are roomy and lofty and the ceilings display specimens of fine stucco work — The furniture is in fine taste, and the drawing room is graced by portraits of the President and Mrs Washington — original paintings which preserve admirable likenesses — From the great doors, in the hall the most enchant[ing] views are displayed — In front the waters of the Hudson pursuing their wandering course to the right, on their way to Albany, several little islands are interspersed — Here trees fancifully sit, intercept the prospect of the river, which yet breaks upon us through the openings, romantically beautiful — and there, at the foot of the descent, which slopes the lawn before the house, a pond susceptible of high improvement spreads its glassy surface — The Horizon describes a view of the Jersey shore crowned with rich, and variegated Verdure — upon the right is the Country charmingly rural, and upon the left a very advantageous sketch of the City of New York — The interjacent road, widely spreading — is an agreeable addition and in the back ground is thrown a garden embosomed by the Cataphin, and various other forest trees, with a number of flowering shrubs and plants, beyond which rolls the East river, and woods and plains, Groves, and meadows, hills, and dales, are luxuriantly displayed — at a little distance from this elegant Mansion is a beautiful natural terrace — The Valleys on either hand are gradually sunk, and richly verdant — the meadows are enchantingly out spread — a willow grove is in view — The City and the River mingle their respective beauties, and the celebrated orangery, and gardens of Mr [B...non] are distantly seen — In short exhibited in every view perhaps the united States cannot furnish a more charming retreat — Nay Mrs Adams, who may be said almost to have completed the tour of Europe, declares she hath never observed a spot, uniting so many advantages — and it is with no small regret, she submits to the necessity of relinquishing so pleasing a residence [—] Congress however hath decreed, and even Mrs Adams must obey — Having already introduced to you the present Possessors of this terrestrial paradise, I forbear even upon subjects so copious, to enlarge, and I have only to add, that the Vice President still continues the Man of sense, and the Patriot, that he is still benignly good, and dignifyedly affable, that his Lady is not unduly elevated, nor spoiled by the adulatory incense of surrounding flatterers — In one word, that Mr & Mrs Adams, are the same kind, and hospitable individuals, who some months since, while they cultivated their inheritance at Braintree received us with most affectionate and amicable condescension — Our reception on wednesday was equally flattering and we were honoured by the most marked and distinguished attention.

    We set down to dinner at half past four, convivial smiles, and sweet hilarity prevailing, and our entertainment was various and pleasing — Lady Ann Grifith, and her daughter, joined us at the tea table of Mrs Adams, and we chatted most familiarly — Upon taking leave we were obligingly requested to reiterate our visits and this day — saturday was named, but almost certain of leaving Town, we necessarily declined an invitation, by which we confessed ourselves honoured — Thursday, very unexpectedly opened another scene — I was sitting in my little apartment, alone, and buried in thought — strange that I possessed not the smallest presentiment, of the distinction which awaited me — but so it was — a loud rap at the door roused my attention, I cast my eye toward the passage, where a powdered figure, plentifully adorned with gold lace, etc presented himself — "Is Mr Murray at home?" I was on the point of answering he had the advantage of me, as I did not recollect meeting him before but fortunately extending my view — a gay equisage elegant beyond what I had ever imagined caught my eye, and the inquirer proved to be a gentlemanly attendant — I was at home you will not doubt, and Mrs Washington, and Mrs Lear were immediately ushered in If any thing could exceed my surprise, it was the charming freedom with which Mrs Washington took her seat — The unmeaning fopperies of ceremony seem to make no part of this Lady's Character, inborn benevolence, beams upon her countenance, points her address, and dictates the most pleasing expressions to her lips — one whole hour she condescendingly devoted to me, and so much of friendship did her salutations connect, so interesting and animated was our conversation, that a bystander would not have entertained an idea of the distance between us, would hardly have supposed, that we met but for the second time, thus benignly good, and thus adorned with social virtues is our Lady Presidentess, and I confess that in a way perfectly correspondent with my feelings, I have been most highly gratified — Mrs Greene obligingly sketched for me the manner of a Levee — The apartments are always greatly crouded — The Lady is introduced by some gentleman in waiting — she courtsies low to Mrs Washington, who returns the ceremony — but not a single word is exchanged — the Lady then steps back[,] mixes in the rooms, takes her share of tea, Coffee, and Cakes, in their variety — fruits, ices, Lemonade, wines etc etc and at the close of the visit, she is again led up, makes her silent obeisance as before, and departs [—] The Levee of the President is upon a tuesday and is continued from three to four in the afternoon — The President himself then stands, and of course no one else takes a seat nor is the smallest refreshment offered — It is in addition to my former account of the ceremony of the Levee, that I detail these circumstances, as every thing relative to such personages becomes of importance — and my authority cannot be doubted — Mrs Washington informed me in the course of her visit, that her granddaughter was busily employed, that she indulged a hope she should be able to accomplish the promised flower piece, and of this attention I could not fail of expressing a becoming sense — Early accustomed as is Miss Custus to the sweet incense of flattery, many persons expecting to make their Court by pointedly distinguishing this opening bud of worth, it would not be strange to find her affected and capricious, but the reverse of this is the truth — Easy and unassuming — her manners are beautifully simple, and she prepossesses every beholder in her favour [—] Thursday afternoon presented the Chariot of Mrs Adams, but after the event of the morning, I was not to be elated by such a circumstance — We took tea with Doctor Smith, and family — the afternoon was solemnly sentimental — The Doctor, as I said, is a Man of sense, and information — he is a religious Man — and his Lady hath a mind formed for social, and for mental pleasures — I can enjoy, said the Doctor, conversation or a sermon, even although it should not be, in every particular exactly to my taste — What appears to me agreeable to the truth, I can extract, and I can be silent upon its supposed errors, looking with assured expectation for a brighter day. Some observations relative to this afternoon, which will be to me ever memorable, I had purposed to transmit — but my design is frustrated — Friday morning we paid a visit to Mr Trumball, who is engaged in painting a full portrait of the President — the Piece is at least seven foot long, and Trumball hath nearly succeeded in catching the soul, as well as figure of the President — It is an admirable likeness — his character seems more than sketched upon every feature, and on the point of retracting a recent opinion, I am almost ready to say the very air, the manners, the moving soul, of our illustrious Chief is here more, abundantly more, than attempted — This noble painting, at the request of the City corporation, is done from life, and, it is to constitute the principal ornament of their Federal building — Mr Trumball's room was, as much crouded, as if the President himself had personally presided at the Levee — It was pleasant to observe the strong emotions of the croud — a murmur of applause ran through the whole assembly which was composed of both Males, and Females, "Look it is the President Himself — Trumball hath fortunately hit him off — See what dignified fortitude is stamped upon every feature — What a noble figure, how graceful is that attitude — Oh! Mr Trumball you have made New York infinitely happy — Was ever any thing so martial — The whole of his military career, his sedateness, his predigious resources, his self command, his efforts, and his successes, all, all stand confest, in that assemblage of strong lines, which are so justly, and in a manner so masterly delineated —" Such were the remarks from a hundred tongues, while many, with folded arms, contemplated the nearly finished piece —

Trumball hath indeed described the General, the horse you know, is, to a military Commander in Chief, always an appendage, and in all the portraits, which I have hitherto seen of our Hero, the horse, as if conscious of his importance, with head erect, hath seemed to be the most prominent figure — Trumball hath judiciously escaped this absurdity — Upon the fore leg of the horse, a fly hath fastened, and this brings down the head of the indignant animal, to revenge the temerity of the insect, and thus the General is left unrivalled, and although ample justice is done to the parts, and proportions of the horse yet he presumes not to arrest the principal attention — We proceeded from this scene to another of more radical, and general importance — The illustrious object of our veneration was to take part in a most interesting transaction — The Indian treaty was to be publickly ratified, and we took our seats in that superb Hall, where the delegates of the United States, so lately convened in council — Behold then the galleries filled by a respectable, various, and highly gratified populace — Males, and Females, are indiscriminately seated — Gentlemen of the first rank, are ranged in the body of the room, appropriated to the representatives of the people — The handsome and commodious seats without the pales, are occupied by a brilliant circle of Ladies, richly habited, and displaying some of the most beautiful faces, which nature when bounteously indulgent, hath to bestow — Mrs Washington, with dignified ease takes her seat — elegant Women compose her train, and, upon either hand, are seated her grandson, and daughter — The Chair of State is empty — a number of chairs upon the left, are also vacant, and the Vice President takes his seat upon the right — Suddenly rude, and tumultuous sounds are heard — frightfully terrific they vibrate tremendously upon the ear [—] Now the most dreadful shrieks wear the semblance of horrid yells, and now they characterize ceaseless riot, and unlicensed mirth — "What sounds are these?" — Every eye seems to ask — It is the song of praise as sung by the Kings, Chiefs, and Warriors, of the Creek Nation, and now having entered the edifice [sounding] their untutored joy — They fill the vacant seats — They are in a complete uniform of blue, laced with red, and McGillivray takes the lead — The beads are bound about by a handkerchief, others are ornamented with feathers —wreaths, etc etc and all are fancifully painted, and decorated with earrings, and Nose jewels. Thus is the assembly disposed, when the Illustrious President of the United States appears, He is followed by his sate — he is habited in Vestments of rich purple satin — Every eye is upon him, while his benign regards, equally distributed, he bends with inimicable grace to surrounding spectators — He ascends the Chair, a reverential silence pervades, and the articles of the treaty are distinctly read by the Secretary — They are fourteen and they commence with a stipulation of perpetual peace, and amity! They acknowledge the Sovereignty and protection of the United States; they demand the emancipation of prisoners, they describe the boundaries of the two Nations — they guarantee possessions, they proceed to the adjustment of a variety of particulars, they grant to the Creeks, an annual subsidy, of one thousand, five hundred dollars, they stipulate many other immunities, they promise an oblivion of resentments, and, upon the whole they look with a very benign aspect upon the interests of Concord — The treaty being read, our august Leader, rising from his seat of eminence, delivers, in his accustomed elegant, energetic and animated style, his sentiments to the assembled Citizens, and to the Kings, Chiefs, and Warriors of the Creek Nation — He observed, that as far as he was capable of judging, the Treaty was mutually beneficial, he recommended a spirit of Amity, and he added, that a studious cultivation of unanimity was expected — He enjoined it upon the Indians to interpose with their good offices, so far as their power extended, to endeavour to annihilate annimosities, and to conciliate the Nations, with which they might stand connected — and he supplicated the great Spirit, the Master of breath, to forbid an infringement of a Contract, formed under such happy auspices

The address was solemn, and proper, and it was delivered in sentences, which thus detached, were communicated by a sworn Interpreter to the Indians. The Creeks, in their own manner, audibly assented to each proposition, and the signing of the treaty succeeded — The President presented to Col McGillivray — as a token of perpetual peace a string of beads, with a paper of tobacca, to supply the Calumet of friendship — McGillivray, who is invested with the Indian Sovereignty, received the tokens, returned a short speech, and compliments to the President with the Wampum — and now the Kings, Chiefs, and Warriors one by one advance — They approach Majestically, with native elevation, and they join hands in peace, and with unusual warmth, McGillivray follows the accustomed Mode, a few indians are influenced by his example but the majority, seizing the President by the elbow entwined their arms with his, thus ardently expressing their satisfaction, and a second song of peace, by the indians concluded this affecting, important, and dignified transaction — Thus I have endeavoured to sketch for my beloved parents, as concisely as possible, a scene of which I was a spectator, which highly interested my feelings — and which, perhaps, succeeding Centuries may not repeat — We devoted the remainder of Friday to calls of ceremony — visiting upon Mrs Lear, Mrs Pintard, Mrs Robinson etc etc [—] Friday also presented the drawing from Miss Eleanor Custus — It was a flower piece, of which, a beautiful moss Rose fully blown, with its buds, and appropriated foliage, elegantly painted, are the most conspicuous — We were upon the wing, visits to make and baggage to put up — yet detesting even the semblance of insensibility, I had the temerity by way of expressing my thanks to hazard the following reply —

To paint the feelings which spontaneously flow,
Effusions soft, on sudden thought which grow,
Which on your cheek in mantling blushes play'd,
And the face promise voluntary made,
Or to delineate the glow I felt,
When on your lips the sweet appearance dwelt,
To give a form to gratitude divine,
Expansive passion, which I feel is mine,
I should possess — Dear Maid, your happy art,
The kindling ardours of your youthful heart,
Thanks are inadequate — my charming friend —
All emulous my breathing wishes are!
But while sensations in my bosom live,
The wreath of worth your merit shall receive
     Soft are your touches — Nature stands confest
Of all the power to designate possest
New beauties spring beneath your forming hand
And genius buds as the fair leaves expand.
     Borne to my fav'rite haunt — the pretty knot
Shall grace my parlour in some hallow'd spot.
Secured from injury — and neatly glazed,
To my pleas'd eye a fair memento rais'd,
The little tale full oft I shall repeat,
While clustering round the gathering Circle meet
     And O! dear Girl permit a fervid prayr,
May you of hovering angels be the care,
Sweet as the rose may your young fame arise,
On the rapt senses seal with glad surprise,
May radiant Virtue lend its damask hue,
As you the mazy path of life pursue,
Perfume your actions — all your movements grace,
And doubly arm the beauties of your face,
With white rob'd innocence supremely crown'd,
Experience, spreading all her guards around,
In wisdom's flowery walks progressing far,
The stores of knowledge resolute to share,
The voyage of life may you securely make,
Nor o'er the glassy stream of peace forsake —
     Full well I know the skillful hands which guide,
Which wait to bear you o'er the swelling tide,
Train'd as you are — warm'd by so bright a sun,
Under such Vigil your career begun,

Almost superfluous, every wish may seem,
Yet, little rills to the Vast Ocean stream,
And cheer'd by the same animating ray,
Which yields augustly the pervading day,
The humble songster warbles in the Grove,
And chants away his grateful heart to prove.

Miss Eleanor Custus   New York August 18— 1790

      Leaving Town this morning, I gave the lines for Miss Custus to the care of the President's secretary, and bidding adieu to Doctor Smith, and Lady, who with a number of other friends, obligingly called upon me at our lodgings, we came on rapidly, as the intense heat would allow — One mile from the City, we met the President and Lady in their Coach of State, from both of whom we were honoured by repeated, and smilingly benign salutations — Upon the skirts of Harlem — nine miles from York, fatigued, and tranquil, and only not sinking under the piercing rays of a potent, and vertical sun, we were slowly proceeding, when, from a rural and sweetly shaded retreat, two gentlemen accosted us — Mr Murray did not recollect that he had ever seen them — they were, however, among the number of his friends — "Pray Sir, do us the favour to stop — to pursue your journey in the middle of this day is surely wrong — Here is cool punch and Lemonade, and we prepare the turtle feast, at which, if you will preside, we shall never be unmindful of the honour, which you will thus confer — many persuasions were not requisite, and we alighted with our hearts truly grateful — A respectable Circle from New York, had devoted the day to decadent hilarity, many of our Philadelphia friends were also present, the turtle was rich — Various other dishes were prepared, and the desert was handsome — But you my dear Mother, will judge that my feelings have been of the most pleasant kind, when I heard one of the gentlemen, who first addressed us in the Carriage, designated by the name of your honoured Father — Captain Thomas Saunders — Indeed the figure, and manners of this hospitable son of Neptune — bore a strong resemblance to those of my Uncle Bradbury Saunders — We passed some white hours with our convivial friends and leaving with the politely social party, our united benedictions, we pursued our road to the hospitable abode — The New Rochellers have been introduced to you, and I have only to say we were received as before — We regretted we were not in time to witness the vows of Mr Byard, and a Miss Pinsard to whose nuptials we had been summoned — despairing of our arrival, this night, one hour before we reached this place, the ceremony was performed — Thus one more week of our various Journey hath elapsed and I trust the hour approaches when I shall again behold the faces of my honoured parents — again I say, I almost flush at the length of my letters, but if they be fati[gu]ing to you, a single hint shall confine my papers to my letter box, when my testimonials of attention to you shall be less diffuse — Every week I have said would be less fruitful of events — but, contrary to expectation my subjects still grow upon my hands, and I am unwilling to omit any circumstance, which, at the time, gave me pleasure — But there is no necessity of my thus burdening you — Well, and if it be really an inconvenience, let me know, and as I said, I will, withhold, or curtail my accounts — I am impatient to hear from home — yet we shall be for many weeks consistently changing the scene, and any letters you might forward would probably be lost — But if you will be so obliging as to inclose, in a blank cover, to John Carter Esquire of Providence, we shall certainly meet your letters upon our arrival in that place — You will be kind enough to remember us particularly to every inquiring Friend, and do pray kiss my newborn Niece in my behalf — The time, I again repeat, will as I trust shortly come when I shall be able to perform this pleasing duty for myself — I wish I knew her name, I have heard you balanced between Julianna, and Anna Maria — Do my dear Sir let me know, by what appellation I am to give this little stranger her seat in my bosom — Accept, dear Parents our united salutations, and continue to love, and to bless your children —

A RETURN VISIT TO CONNECTICUT

Letter 784— To the Same New Haven August 21st 1790 Saturday Evening

This letter begins in New Rochelle, where the Murrays attended the wedding festivities of Mr. Pintard's daughter and where they met Elias Boudinot, a past president of the Continental Congress. In a conversation at one of the wedding parties, John engages people in a discussion about the "equality of the male and female mind." From New Rochelle, Judith and John travelled to Stamford where they were the guests of Mr. and Mrs. Jarvis, and John preached to another large gathering. From there, they travelled through Fairfield to Hartford. Judith notes that the drought had not affected Connecticut's crops, and she is cheered to see the "Parent Waters" of the ocean again. "For Boston, for Gloucester my heart frequently sighs — I wish for home," she writes, but they still have many more stops to make despite John's deteriorating health. She wishes her family well, especially her

sister, Esther, and Esther's husband, John Stevens Ellery, who are
building a new house. "Jack" is their son, also named John Stevens
Ellery (1773-1843). "Ignatius" is Judith's cousin, Major Ignatius
Sargent (1765-1821,) whose father is her uncle, Daniel Sargent.
"Miss Parsons" is Mary Parsons (1771-1792) who married Ignatius
in 1791. Sadly, Mary died the following year, not long after the birth
of their only child.

    Lognacious as you, my honoured parents, may pronounce me,
I yet omit many descriptions, and circumstances, which had I the leisure
to sketch — I am confident, interested as you are, would contribute to
your amusement — My last letter sat us down in New Rochelle —
Sequestered amid those peaceful shades, you no doubt expected the
pleasures of retirement, and contemplation would be ours — The various
scenes and picturesque views, which distinguish New Rochelle, must
forever remain unmarked by the traveller, who merely passeth its skirts
— amid such rural, and enchanting abodes, after the crouded Circles
which we had witnessed you had a right to imagine us solacing, and
enjoying rationally, all the blessings of reflection ——— But nothing
of all this in reality took place — Mr Pintard is a gentleman of a family
and fortune and the marriage of his daughter, which I mentioned, to
which we were summoned, had collected from Philadelphia, Brunswick,
and New York, his numerous connexions — Mr Pintard hath long been
the avowed friend of Murray, and although we were not in time for the
ceremony, we could not avoid accepting the most pressing invitations
to join their large, and genteel parties — The young Lady is well married
to a Mr Byard of Brunswick — she is modest, delicate, and sentimental,
and, the Lord of her wishes, adds to an elegant figure, and a fine animated
countenance, a mind extremely improved, and the parents being capable
of distinguishing real merit — you will conclude their joy was complete
— Our entertainment was liberal, in the best style, and perfectly
appropriate — The seat of Mr Pintard, and his adjoining grounds are
judiciously, and tastefully disposed, they exhibit an assemblage of rural
beauties, while an intensive view of the water of the sound, skirts the
borders of the fields, of the Groves, and of the meadows. The guests, as
I said, were very happy, They lined a spacious hall, and the informed,
the improved and the refined were collected — Mr Boudinot whose
name so frequently occurs in the account of the debates in Congress
with his amiable Lady, were of the Party [—] Mr Boudinot apparently
unites the gentleman, and the Man of sense, and information, and the
higher character of a Christian — His moral, as his political life, is truly
respectable, and every observer hails him, as an elegant, and entertaining
Companion — Various subjects were candidly and pleasingly discussed,
many religious tenets were examined, and the veneration due to the

sacred Oracles becomingly preserved — Mr Murray, being earnestly requested upon his favourite theme after which the utility of Novels was questioned and defended — the Nature of spirit, and the equality of the male, and female mind — Nature claimed her share, and a variety of her productions were introduced — Plants, flowers and fruit were descanted upon, and I cannot deny myself the pleasure of recording, under this head, an extraordinary circumstance — Mr Boudinot informed us, that the President had shown him no less than nine different colours all produced from a dye, extracted from a single species of Indian Corn, in the state of Connecticut — The stock, the leaves etc, all possessed their peculiar hues, every color was strong, and beautiful, and the powers of this remarkable vegetable, extended from the deepest crimson, to the lightest brown — Mr Bondinot had examined the colours, and the President assured him, the fact was within his own knowledge! and that every thing was fast, and permanent — The breaks of conversation were filled up by airs enchantingly harmonious, by musick, which, perhaps hath not often been exceeded, and all the charmingly social affections seemed afloat — Sunday, after divine service, and Monday, were devoted to these Pintards, and their Connexions, and on tuesday we obeyed the summons of a gentleman, who possesseth another of those delightful retreats, with which New Rochelle abounds, and, enjoying an easy competency, he devotes the evening of his life to a sister, who possessing a congenial soul, returns with equal warmth, the fraternal affection of her brother — In addition to the agreeable objects which I have heretofore met in the family of Mr Bartow, was a young Lady upon a visit from New York — Sweet Girl — beautiful and innocent, thy image can never be erased from retention, and while I admire the justice, which thou so amply and so becomingly renderest to the talents, to the merit, to the unquestioned worth of thy sainted Mother — thy own exquisite lines will never fade from my memory — yes female excellence, female claims, female genius, as often as they rise to my view, will always collect among their most pleasing imagery, the fair form of Miss Bleacher, and my admiring mind — with honest joy, will never omit to render the tribute of applause — Writing thus, journal wise, and addressing friends so uniformly indulgent — Apostrophes, digressions, and a number of irregularities drop from my pen — while I seldom have leisure to apologize — Well having advanced thus far, a reformation would now be an effort, which I should find it difficult, if not impossible to make [—] confirmed habits are rarely conquered, and it may be as well to proceed, with all my faults upon my head, or rather upon my pen — Wednesday morning we left New Rochelle, and calling on our way on our benevolent friend, Mr Bush we came on moderately to Stamford — Stamford, although a small Town yet imported a variety of commercial articles, long before this enterprizing spirit obtained among the Yorkers — It is, you may remember the residence of that Mr Jarvis, who received a promise from Mr Murray, while on his way to Philadelphia, that he would visit him on his return — Much of singularity usually attends, the manner in which Mr Murray forms his connexions — At Stamford for example — while his horse was feeding, he amused himself by a walk through one of the principal streets in the Village — Mr Jarvis met, and distinguished him — he requested his name, Fame had before wafted to Stamford, reports of the Messenger of peace — he requested him to tarry, at least one night — he could not, his appointments were made — but an assurance of a future opportunity was obtained, and in consequence of this apparently casual circumstance, behold, on wednesday evening, the doors of the house appropriated to the Presbyterian worship are thrown open — a large audience is collected — The Messenger of peace ascends the Pulpit, and the pearl of Great Price is handled, much to the satisfaction of the people — Thus the dawn of truth pervades, inquiry is originated, and who shall say what peaceful consequences may result — General Waterbury, formerly an acquaintance of my brother's, was among the admiring hearers of Mr Murray, we were hospitably entertained by this Gentleman, he spoke of my brother with high respect — Mr & Mrs Jarvis are a worthy and agreeable couple — they have no son, but they have three daughters, who constitute the happiness of their parents — They have educated their eldest daughter at a Seminary in a Town the name of which hath escaped my memory — Their second daughter, is at Bethlehem Academy, and their little Harriet, is impatient to number her years sufficient, to take her place in that peaceful recess — We were shown a number of letters from the young Lady at Bethlehem — they were charmingly descriptive, and we were of course highly gratified — We abode with this pleasing family until Thursday morning, when we resumed our journey, dining at Fairfield, and reaching Hartford in the evening — Verging upon New England we perceived with pleasure, that the season had been abundantly propitious to its vegetation — Connecticut is indeed a rich state — Its Vallies stand thick with corn, and its meadows gladden, by their encreasing burdens, the cultivating swain — Equality, I must repeat, pregnant with substantial good, smiles upon the inhabitants of Connecticut, and they are undoubtedly a wealthy, and a happy people — Perhaps you will remember that Stratford is the Town, where a Doctor Poor accosted, and would have detained us on our way — agreeably to a promise then made, Mr Murray had apprized the Doctor that we should pass through his Town on thursday, we were delayed beyond our expectations — The sun was just setting as we entered Stratford the people were assembled, and their anxiety, in fear of disappointment, was great — The Promulgator of glad tidings, however appeared, and before we had quitted our carriage, the ringing of the bell for church, commenced, and announced to the Villagers, the certainty of his arrival — Hearers from every quarter flocked together — a prodigious concourse of people were collected, and my husband proceeded immediately to church — By the pressing instances of many, Mr Murray was prevailed upon to tarry in Stratford through Friday, when the word of life was again held up to the people — The head of the Presbyterian Church in Stratford, a second time made part of the audience — he waited upon us at our lodgings, urging us to visit him — from what source these attentions originated, I attempt not to decide — Stratford hath two religious societies, an episcopalian, and a presbyterian — and these societies are in apparent Amity — The handsomely ornamented, and milk white fanes rise upon adjacent, and beautifully verdant plains, and every thing wears the appearance of harmony — The assembly at Stratford appeared decent, and even elegant — Their attention to the Preacher was marked, and truly solemn, and by propriety of deportment we are naturally charmed — We left Stratford about nine O clock this morning — It is just fifteen miles from this City, which we reached at One O clock — The refreshing breezes now abroad, are, after the intense heat which hath indeed been extreme, doubly agreeable — and the spires of New Haven, its verdant heights, its rich meadows, its interjacent Groves, its opening harbour, and all its variety of enchanting views, we once more, and with peculiar pleasure recognized — We mark with animated satisfaction, every sketch of the Ocean — so long separated from these Parent Waters — We hail with becoming joy, their vast encircling flow — Our friends in this Place received us with unequivocal demonstrations of joy — They had expected us — until they began to fear for our health and their manifestations of complacency, were in exact proportion to their anxiety — We have passed the afternoon with a large circle of Ladies, and the time of night, potently reminds me, of the necessity of rest — For Boston, for Gloucester my heart frequently sighs — I wish for home — but the accomplishment of this wish is, as I fear, yet remote — Our distance is still great — and it is impossible entirely to resist the entreaties of the many — I lament that the uncertainty of our movements, denies me the alleviation of letters from my friends, and I can confidently hope, I shall not fail of receiving intelligence at Providence — I trust Fitz William is returned, that my sister Anna is restored to perfect health, and that the little dark eyed Maiden smiles upon you, with all her Mother's softness [—] That my dear father and Mother enjoy as much of tranquility as is consistent with mortality, In one word I trust that domestic happiness still presideth in the dwelling of my Parents. My wishes frequent take flight, and descending the well known, and long loved declivity, they hover round the peaceful Circle collected in the little neat breakfast parlour — Mr Ellery, Esther, Jack, and Sally — God bless you all — May no cloud with malignant aspect, ever dash from you, the cup of mutual affection, mutual endearments, and mutual confidence — May your joys be matured, may the dwelling you have so nearly completed, witness your contentment [—] May you continue its proprietors, as long as life shall be lent — Its undivided Possessors, and may you transmit it, a pledge of parental care to those you so greatly love, and who so much deserve your tenderness — I pray you, my dear Parents, to present my regards to all those whom I have so repeatedly enumerated, and to all inquiring friends — For Mrs Forbes, my heart acknowledges a very sincere respect — Doubtless you will have many opportunities of presenting my very respectful regards to that Lady — Ignatius and Miss Parsons are dear to my heart — Do tell them so — Mr Murray is at present very unwell — I impute his illness to the sudden change of the weather — a Night's rest, with the return of that perspiration which he is endeavouring to promote, may restore his health — I will hope for the best — May all good Angels have you in their keeping — I am, and shall be, while my consciousness continues with all duty, your truly affectionate daughter —

Letter 785 To Mrs Sargent New Haven August 22d 1790 Sunday Evening

In New Haven, Judith and John are the guests of Colonel Drake, she tells her aunt. They have witnessed an Episcopal baptismal service, which was a new experience for Judith. Later that day, John preached about universal salvation to a large crowd and Judith repeats many of his words here.

Your taste, my beloved friend, unfashionably impelling you to have for your favourite Correspondent — Am I too vain? The Wife of a Parson, a Critic upon your preferences, will tell you, that you are to esteem yourself fortunate, that she is so rarely seized with the spirit of sermonizing [—] For once, however, let me appear in character — Judging of your feelings, and inclinations by my own — writing upon the evening of this day, and being highly pleased with the instruction it hath afforded I indulge the impulse of the moment, by sketching for you the outlines of subjects, in themselves interesting and important, and to which I have, with unfeigned devotion, attended — A vacant Church in this City, supplies Mr Murray with a convenient place, in which to speak to the many, who are solicitous to hear — but wishing to avoid interference with the several religious societies, he appointed service there at five O clock this afternoon, a full hour after the close of the public worship of the day, which is statedly observed — Colonel

Drake our hospitable Host, with his family, are attendants upon Mr Hubbard, an episcopalian Clergyman stationed here — We accompanied our friends to Church, the usual ceremonies were observed, when a beautiful female infant was devoted to her Creator [—] It hath so happened, that I have never before witnessed the baptismal rites of the Episcopalian church — It may be my mind is naturally fond of show, and should it ever ascertain that frivolity is in fact an ingredient in my composition, I must however confess, that I was pleased with the apparent solemnity of the transaction, and when the white robed Priest, came forward presenting the pretty Creature, who having already sojourned a few months in the abodes of mortality seemed to have intelligence inscribed upon her features — when he exhibited her to the people, and pronounced her dedication — I could scarcely forbear an audible exclamation, for the future well being of the little innocent while my eyes failed not to confess the tender emotions of my soul — at length the good Divine mounted the pulpit — He opened the book — He read — "Be still and know that I am God" How proper the command, viewed in its connexion — I was charmed with the method observed by Mr Hubbard — With his text — Many solemn and consolatory truths were uttered — To the afflicted spirit — and who hath not tasted the bitter Cup — they must indeed have been balmy, and salutary, and effacious — most admirably calculated to heal the wounds of every probationer in the school of adversity — Mr Hubbard proved from a variety of reasons, the propriety of resignation and he adduced his examples from scripture — The illustrious Sufferer of Old was heard to exclaim "The Lord gave — The Lord taketh away — and blessed be the name of The Lord" — "It is the Lord, saith the Man of God, and let him do what seemeth him good" — Mr Hubbard assured us that God was the Father of every creature — that he made us for happiness, and designed not the final misery of any of his children, that nothing happened by chance — That although Almighty God worked by second causes — Yet He Himself was the first Originating Cause the prime source of every event — that He did not willingly afflict the children of Men — that He followed them, with paternal care, through every calamity — See yonder Infant — It is seized by excrutiating agonies — its little form writhes in anguish — Its sufferings are exquisite — and soul piercing are the sighs which seem to rend its bursting heart — Mark the [hand of] the fond Father, with what commiseration it hangs over the pangful scene — Mark and remember, That as a Father pitieth his children, even so, our God pitieth us — Here, a natural question presents — Why then doth he not relieve and the answer is equally ready — God is all Wise, all just, all gracious, all merciful, and all powerful He cannot therefore err, He cannot wrong his Creatures — His goodness, His mercy, and His power, will preserve them — and hence we rationally conclude, that every Chastisement will eventually effectuate their happiness — Reason teaches acquiescence, and Resignation — and we have abundant cause — The whole economy of events is in the hands of a benign, and Omnipotent Being, and that Being is no other than the paternal Deity — It is true He will employ means adequate to His purposes, both the will and the power to produce the felicity of His Creatures is His, and He will no doubt accomplish all His plans [—] Present sufferings and disappointments may bend the most incorrigible —— May meliorate the yielding heart, and, at any rate, they will enhance our future enjoyments — Here is a consisten[t] plan — The Sovereign of the Universe acting according to His own good pleasure, in the armies of heaven, and among the sojourners in this lower World — disposing events exactly agreeable to His own predestination [—] Creating Beings, Candidates for an opening [in] Heaven, zesting the joys which await them, in their Elysium, by the distressing contingencies of time, and finally educing from the whole, an uninterrupted state of bliss — When keeping in view the grand Catastrophe — who, my friend but may support with fortitude the ills of life — Will not you, will not our suffering friend, and shall not I be still as well knowing that the disposition of time and eternity, is in the hands of our all wise Creator, God, and Father — Blessed redeemer — hush, I entreat thee, every tumult in my perturbed bosom, and give me to regard more uniformly, that brightening period, which every eye shall most assuredly behold — In no instance through the whole of his discourse, did Mr Hubbard depart from this God honouring and most consistent view — Whether the features of his sermons are always alike uniformly harmonious I know not, but from his character I should deduce the most pleasing conclusions [—] his benevolence, and humanity, are said to be extreme, and a friend of this good Divine assured me, that Mr Hubbard cannot even to this day read an account of the replenishing [of] the Widow's well near exhausted stores, as recorded in the 17 chapter of the first book of Kings, without tears — One hours intervention produced us in the vacant Church — The hall is large, and it was crouded — The congregation was respectable elegant and remarkably attentive — Prayr and reiterated singing succeeded, in the accustomed routine and Mr Murray named the portion of sacred writ, to which he proposed particularly to attend — "If the righteous scarcely are saved, where shall the ungodly, and the Sinner appear?" To have formed an adequate idea of the expression of surprise, which immediately pervaded the features of the audience, you should have made one of the assembly — The Preacher proceeded to inquire — and from scripture and from observation, it was clear, that among the sons of Men, there was none righteous no not one — An Apostle, putting the matter beyond a doubt, had declared — That he who offended in one point, was guilty of all, and the venerable synod, composing the shorter catechism, hath pronounced, that no mere Man, since the fall, hath been able to keep the Commandments of God — but that the children of Men daily do break them, both in thought, in word, and in deed — Reason, and observation, hourly evinceth that frailty is deeply inscribed upon every human action — and that, if an immaculate thought would purchase interminable felicity, we have it not in our power to produce it — Thus were the children of Men circumstanced, when the holy Saviour bowed the heavens, and came down — He was not mere Man — therefore He could fulfill all righteousness, and this righteousness, thus wrought out by the Head of every Man, is unto all, and upon all them who believe, for there is no difference — Now, it is eternal truth, that redemption, is the finished work of Emmanuel, is completed for every son and daughter of Adam — but although this righteousness be unto all — yet it is not upon all, at least not upon those, who have not in their own apprehension put on the Lord Jesus — Those who believe possess a consciousness of an existence in their head — of their relation to the Redeemer, as members of His body, which relationship, ascertain their claim, to all that is His, and which, consequently constitutes them Righteous — yet even these Righteous are scarcely saved, for, notwithstanding their eternal life is secure, is the person of the Redeemer, yet, in this distemped state of things, the imbecility of their nature often, originates doubts, and he who doubteth, saith an Apostle, is damned. Here it evidently becomes necessary, to distinguish between the salvation dependent upon Jehovah, which is firm as the everlasting hills, and that salvation which may be regarded as a talisman of our concessions of the truth — the one is as durable, and unchanging, as its Author, and the other takes its hue from the impulse of minds which are constantly fluctuating — Thus Righteous therefore, from a variety of contingent evils, are scarcely saved, and the peace in their bosoms, while in this abode of sorrow, is subject to almost every exigency — from the clouds of uncertainty enviously arriving to envelop, and from the darkness which is a concommitant, they are scarcely saved — This then, being an incontrovertible truth, the question is natural — Where shall the ungodly, and the sinner appear? — May not those be characterized as ungodly, who never having received an idea of the God Man of the complex character of Emmanuel, God with us, of necessity live, as respects their apprehension of Deity, without God in the World, and are not the sinners, to which the text refers, those who having received the word of life, have, by turning therefrom, done despite to the Son of God? Thus, grossly sinning against light, and knowledge, and pouring contempt upon the testimony of the grace of God, they become ashamed of that sacred truth by which they are redeemed, and therefore saith the son of God, I will be ashamed of them, in the day when surrounded by the holy Angels, and shrouded in refulgent light, I shall descend — But where then shall these ungodly — and these sinners appear? Perhaps there is little hazard in pronouncing decisively — They can appear no where, but in the presence of Him — Who made them — Reason teaches us that from an omnipotent Being, pervading all space, there can be no spot so remote, as to be excluded from observance, and the language of Revelation is "If I take the wings of morning, and ascend up into heaven, behold thou art there — If I make my bed in Hell, even there thy right hand shall lead me["] — yes, undoubtedly, these ungodly, and these sinners, not obtaining a consciousness of the righteousness of the Saviour, or, turning with impious pride therefrom — Will, in the day of the Lord, appear in the presence of their Redeemer [—] they will unquestionably arise, to the resurrection of condemnation, or if you like it better, of damnation — unquestionably they will upon rocks, and Mountains, to fall upon them, and to hide them from the wrath of the Lamb — But is there Wrath in the Saviour of the World? — Certainly not — indignation dwelleth in their imagination only — It is they who are the vessels of wrath filled for destruction — but they shall be emptied of this wrath — They shall be broken, or slain — but He who woundeth can Heal, He who killeth can also make alive — A grand Catastrophe awaits — it was prefigured in the history of Joseph, and his brethren of these unhappy Beings the Judge is the Brother — He will manifest Himself as such, and all tears will be wiped from every eye — I trust I have not fatigued my lovely hearer I flatter myself she will indulge the freedom of my pen, and that she will allow me to commend her, with the sincerest affection, to our Common Redeemer —

Letter 786 To Anna New Haven August 23d 1790

Judith is writing to Anna, her "sweet Orphan" and the "child of [her] care." Most of this letter contains Judith's advice about friendship, trust, and marriage — that Anna should "revere herself," a frequent theme in Judith's published essays. Judith reminisces with Anna about a trip they took together to New Haven in 1786. She describes for her the home and gardens of Colonel Drake, their host.

That I take my full share in your pleasures, I would not, my dear Girl, have you, for a single moment doubt — I am only solicitous that they should be, of a nature to bear reflection, that they should always be correct pleasures, never involving a necessity of regret — A young Woman should indeed "<u>revere herself</u>" for upon the propriety, and decency of her deportment, the fairest hopes which her present career can furnish, frequently rest, and it will generally be found true, that the confidence, which she lavishes, will be <u>lightly esteemed</u> — Reserve — unminded however with prudery — becomes her character, and although she may be circumspectly familiar yet in her intercourse with the other sex, she can hardly be too guarded — Neither am I fond of young Girls, reposing unlimited confidence in their female associates — I have often told you, and I take this opportunity again to declare, that the only proper confident for a Woman, is her Mother, or some individual invested with the character of a parent, and if in the bosom of a husband, she can repose her every thought — I do not condemn select parties, or even tete a tete conversations — I do not condemn epistolary Correspondences — far from it — my whole heart, and my best judgment applaud such pleasing avenues of enjoyment, and instruction, but let your subjects be sentimental, improving, and general, while the inmost recesses of your bosom, are reserved for a maternal friend — So great, my Love, is the ingeneous frankness of your mind, that I am often induced to tremble for the communicative disposition it connects — yet I do not wish you to be unduly mysterious, or suspicious — but I would have you always remember, that instances of duplicity are frequent, and that there is more truth, than Poetry, in that line which tells us "friends grow not as thick on every bough" — Young Ladies have their own hopes, their own wishes, and their own fears to consult, and it is rare they will sacrifice their own interest to a foreign claim — Hath your spirit been wounded I am happy that modest, sincere, virtuous and unblemished, in these respects, even Envy hath not where of to accuse you, and, I add, in the name of discretion — In your own chaste bosom, let your dearest secrets remain fast locked up — Since I parted with you — you have written, frequently written, but not to me! If my caution be unnecessary — It is well — It will not however injure you — but if, an unguarded expression, hath escaped you, allow me to hope, that it may in future enshield my lovely Girl, from many evils — your letter, but recently received, hath contributed much to my satisfaction — I wondered at its delay — and I received it with a degree of complacnecy, proportioned to my anxiety — It is impossible I should ever forget you — accustomed to regard you, entwined as you are, with my best affections, you must always continue the child of my care — that I have not of late written, particularly to you, should be imputed to my ignorance of your destination — you know the plan was that you should abide in Gloucester — Duty and inclination combined to impel my address to my Parents — I imagined that this gave you every necessary information — for I concluded that to interested friends, communications would be made, and my time being much occupied, I contented myself with this persuasion [—] One or two packets — however, I severally commissioned, and these wafted my good wishes to my sweet Orphan, which I am happy to learn hath reached her, and augmented her enjoyments — A knowledge of your remote situation would have produced another mode of conduct — but as you so soon propose returning to Gloucester you will consequently be in the way of intelligence, and of course I shall pursue my accustomed plan — you were quite right in availing yourself of the goodness of your Aunt Sayward — Nay, I do not see how you could have acted otherwise — Be assured that you are placed perfectly agreeably to my wishes, while you continue in York, and I am right happy that your regular manner of living, hath produced such salutary effects — If this line should meet you in York, offer to the good Deacon, and his Lady, my respectful salutations, and say to them, I am truly grateful for every favour they have conferred upon you — Give my love to your sister Mary, my respects to your Uncle, and Aunt Lyman, and my affectionate regards to Mr & Mrs Barrell, Mr Keaton, and every other individual of that truly amiable family — As it is rather uncertain when we shall reach home, I should be glad you would return to Gloucester, so soon as you conveniently can, Letters included in a blank cover, and directed to Mr Carter of Providence, will meet us there, free of all charges, and, I persuade myself, you will not omit to write. We are now at New Haven, you doubtless recollect this beautiful City, and the pleasing hours we passed here, in the summer of 86 — Do you not remember the prodigious fine strawberries, and Cherries, by which we were regaled — Colonel Drake hath quitted that charmingly rural situation for a stand more favourable to business, which is quite in the bosom of the City — His present Mansion is upon a larger scale, and equally as elegant, as his former abode — A neat palisade before the door incloses a verdant area, we enter by a walk flagged with stone, and the opposite door of the hall commands a view of a fine fruit, and flower garden, beyond which a productive kitchen garden, and Orchard, are skillfully disposed — Competency still resides in the dwelling of Colonel Drake, and we are received even with augmenting friendship — The face of the family, however, is in some measure changed — Mr Brush is far away, and the amiable young Man, whose absence these worthy people once mourned, is now returned, his figure is good, his countenance is pleasing, and Nature hath liberally endowed his mind, nor hath his education been neglected — yet although so considerably cultivated — being much attached to mercantile pursuits, and more apparently engaged in pecuniary views, he is not altogether so pleasing, as a transient companion, as was Mr Brush — he is, however, perfectly obliging, sensible, and manly, and the Woman he shall love, and who returns his passion, will have no cause to murmur at her Lot — I have met here a gentleman, of whom I have not the smallest recollection — yet it seems he was conversant with us, when we were last in New Haven — He says you will ever live in his memory, that you assured him, when here, you were in sentiment a devoted Royalist, and, upon expressing some surprise that you could, at such a period, risk so daring a declaration, he replied, you had with amiable address, stolen from him the secret of his political creed, after which, you fairly considered yourself safe in your subsequent confession! — Are you not a shy baggage? — He wished to know if you had not an inclination to connect yourself in the bands of Wedlock — adding, that he supposed your years would admit of such a transaction — I replied that a worthy friend, and Protector, was a desirable object, to any young Woman, but that twenty was not an age which asked precipitatency of choice, that a single life was preferable to an important selection, and that if esteem, friendship, and meliorating love, fashioned not the knot, improbable as it was, it would be better it was never tied — That you were delicate in your ideas — generally deciding justly — That in compliance with my wishes, you had endeavoured to bend your heart, to a connexion with a kinswoman of mine, but — finding your efforts [in] vain — you had wisely declared taking upon you vows difficult, if not impossible to perform, and that you were now entirely disengaged — We shall tarry in New Haven a few days — when we shall proceed on our journey — Mr Murray unites with me, in tender love — Adieu my dear, always consider me as your sincerely attached maternal Friend

Letter 787 To My Father and Mother Wallingford
August 28 — 1790 Saturday Evening —

John's preaching engagements in New Haven were well attended and successful thanks, in part, to their hosts, Colonel and Mrs. Drake. The Drakes planned numerous "social parties" for them as well, introducing them to the "polite Circles, which are the boast of New Haven." A group of friends took Judith and John to a "pleasure house" outside of New Haven, where they feasted on the largest musk melons Judith had ever seen. Judith writes that the gardens of New Haven were particularly impressive, especially those filled with unusual flowers which she calls "children of Nature." They visited a famous hideout cave, and Judith tells her parents about the exceptional quality of New Haven's silk industry. Now in Wallingford, they are staying with Doctor Potter. Judith writes that she does not expect to be home until late October. She misses her family terribly, but more and more people want to hear John preach.

Thus passeth the time — and thus, however slowly, we approacheth the spot which contains the dearest of our friends —

We reached this Village about sunset, and it is a most divine evening — the heavy rains of yesterday, have purified the air, and every breeze is salubrious. We have passed this week at New Haven, Mr Murray hath been frequently called upon to hold forth unto the people, the words of life — On sunday he published glad tidings in a Vacant Church, and on monday reiterated his testimony in the same place — but in conformity to very earnest solicitations, he hath since made his interesting report, in the brick church, in which a Doctor Dana statedly officiates, and he entered these pulpits by the unanimous suffrages of the Proprietors — a spirit of affecting, and earnest inquiry is abroad, and the efforts of our friend, generally diffuse pleasurable satisfaction — He closed his commission in New Haven, by a subject drawn from the following sacred affirmation "The Grace of God which bringeth salvation unto all Men, hath appeared, teaching us that denying ungodliness, and all worldly lusts we should live soberly, righteously, and Godly, in this present World" [—] The text and the doctrine, rationally deduced therefrom, were gratefully received, lighting up in the features of the Audience, unmixed complacency, and their ready tongues, as they passed from church, coupled the gladness of their hearts — You are acquainted with our hospitable friends in New Haven — They are now made happy by the presence, and Virtues of that son, whose absence and declining health, when we visited them four years since, they unfeignedly mourned. Duteous affection, proper application to business and unimpeached integrity in his dealings, are conspicuous traits in his character — I have grateful expatiated upon the honest attachment of Colonel Drake to my husband — his son is not behind, and, he adds to the sincerity of his friendship, all the warmth, and ardour of youthful affection — Mrs D— is in union with those she loves, and you will hence conclude, that our family party must have been pleasing — We parted with them with pain, but our regrets were softened, by an assurance, voluntarily given, that as Mr Murray was to assemble the people in Wallingford, on the morrow, although Wallingford is thirteen miles from New Haven, they would nevertheless join us at Church and we accordingly expect them en famille — Mrs Drake possessing a large share of natural gentility — with apparent ease — hath been studious to contribute to our enjoyments — Social parties have been every day collected, and we have had the honour of an introduction to these polite Circles, which are the boast of New Haven — They are unquestionably a pleasing, and a hospitable people — On Tuesday last the scene was varied by a jaunt into the Country, a select number of friends joined us, our route extended six miles, and we passed the day in a rural retreat — The effort to oblige, proved very pleasant, the Country is delightful, and the day presented a sky charmingly serene — while the scene of our amusement was sufficiently attractive — Before the door of the pleasure house, a finely shown Green, on the left a winding river seems to lose itself among thick woods — on the right tower the forest trees, an Orchard is behind, the sound rolls its waters before, and the view is terminated by the grounds upon Long Island — We have feasted upon prodigious fine melons, of an extraordinary size, and quality, and I have seen a single musk melon, supply a large company, not sparingly — but in such plenty that a considerable quantity hath been left — Indeed said musk melon, weighed no less than twelve good pound, and a half. I cannot deny myself the pleasure of noting the variety, and beautiful order, of the flowers with which the gardens of New Haven abound, and the Ladies universally evince the delicacy of their taste, by the careful cultivation which they bestow, upon these odiferous children of Nature — They regard a new blow as an important acquisition [—] They industriously collect, and transplant, and perhaps, by their assiduous attention, and studious variation of soil, they may in fact create a less variously motled, and of new, and uncommon beauty — I was informed by Mrs Edwards, the Lady of a celebrated Barrister, that she had the last spring, blown in her garden, at one time, upwards of eight hundred tulips, among which the variety of hues, streaks, and shades she essayed in vain to enumerate — The Ladies in New Haven live in perfect Amity, they are fond of promoting each other — and, during the flowery months, their leisure hours, are commonly devoted to observations, made upon the progress of their respective parteres and the Gentlemen are generally engaged in pecuniary pursuits —

Having already, when upon a former tour sketched for you the out lines of New Haven, I will not hazard a repetition — A Cave is found in the environs of of New Haven, rendered famous, for having afforded for many years a shelter to two of the judges Gonff and Dixwell, who audaciously presumed to assist at the trial, and condemnation of Charles the first of England — This Cave is the resort of every curious stranger — New Haven is a pleasing, and a growing City [—] its situation hath a thousand charms, and, as is common in this state, much equality prevails among its citizens — Connecticut is laying the foundation of a manufactory which if she can establish, will undoubtedly become a source of opulence to her sons, — I mean the extensive propagation of the silk worm — almost every little Town produceth its share of silk — Forty yards is generally made in a single family, in the course of one year and I am told they have obtained the art of colouring, from a European, who accidentally passed through their state — The daughter of a wealthy Farmer, in a Town a few miles from New Haven, hath astonishingly excelled — her bridal vestments, were indeed her own production — she attended upon the worm, she received the curiously constructed little sepulchres — The whole of the process, until her web was prepared for the loom was her own, nor was this all [—] her fair hands directed the shuttle, and under the eye of the charming Weaver, the beautiful texture compactly grew — Not having the same [motive] with Penelope, you will judge that she aimed not to unravel her work, and the shy Lady just after her nuptials she made her appearance in a light straw coloured lutestring — her record exhibition was in a suit of changable[,] the warp of which was azure blue, shot, or woofed with a bright pink — Who can deny this industrious damsels title to silken [excellence]? Not I, I am sure Connecticut hath long raised, and manufactured its own consumption of sewing silk, and black satin of a superior beauty, and quality, is made in this state.

You are acquainted with the place of our present residence — at Wallingford, in the house of Doctor Potter, we have been repeatedly entertained, and we are not accustomed to be niggard of our pleasures — you will, I take it for granted, conceive that we are with an assured friend, surrounded by prospects verdantly rural, and receiving every attention, which sincerity urged by Amity, can bestow — Of our health we should be ungrateful to complain, we are in general indulged with freedom from pain, we have fine appetites, and zest most delightfully, the luxuries with which the Country abounds — Our regrets originate, at this present, in sources foreign from our individual selves — we are impatient to hear from our yet far distant friends — We number the days yet to revolve, previous to our return, and we number them with sensations of regret, and we are unhappy that we are denied even the alleviation of letters — We trust, however, that tuesday next, will produce us again upon our journey homeward, and we hope to meet at Providence, the ready Packets — I am fearful we shall not reach Gloucester until late in October — Believe me I grieve at the necessity which impels this assurance, but it is impossible to pass through intreating crouds, with the rapidity which we too earnestly wish — The eager inquiries, and solemn attention of the people, are really affecting — In many places a wish to understand, and ascertain the great truths of Christianity, makes, as it undoubtedly ought, the prime, and most important business of the inhabitants — They ask with anxious solicitude — who will show us any good? and they exclaim "How beautiful upon the mountains are the feet of him, who bringeth good tidings of good things — Who publisheth Peace, and who saith unto Zion — Thy God liveth["] — I persuade myself it is unnecessary to reiterate expressions of affection to my several friends — they cannot, as I believe, question the strength of my attachment — they must jointly, and severally know, that I am ever firmly, and devotedly, the affectionate kinswoman, sister, and daughter of my family —

Letter 788 To Mrs Sargent Wallingford August 30 1790

The weather is hot, and Judith misses her family, she tells her aunt, Mary Turner Sargent. But she is enjoying her visit at the Potter home, and she describes here the house, grounds, garden, and distant landscape. She was particularly delighted with the ability to pluck a ripe peach from a tree just outside her window. Describing such scenes, she writes, makes her feel less lonely — as if her aunt were there with her, sharing her experiences.

How fares my charming Friend — This heart of mine sickens to embrace you, and those lovely children, who are deeply interested in every Orison which, from the inmost recesses of my soul, ascends her throne of grace — It is natural to love them, it is natural to be attached to innocence so interesting — I feel that it is, and added days will but augment my affection — This is a season which, asketh a sequestered abode, among the embowering shades of some sylvan scenes — The heat hath been intense, and the rural breeze is particularly sweet — I wish I could, at this moment, place you, in propria personne, in my window seat, the prospect is truly enchanting, and full well I know, that in the dwelling of benevolence, you would be a pleased, and pleasing guest — Doctor Potter is a philanthropist, I do not pretend to judge of his medical abilities, but he will never do an intentional injury — The grounds of this Village are remarkably rich, and a few genteel buildings are thinly scattered — This house is a pretty tenement, and the surrounding views are picturesque — it is pleasingly shaded — a little flower garden, in which the sun flower is most conspicuous, and where a number of odiferous, and party coloured plants, nevertheless flourish is behind — a peach tree, of the delicious growth of which I can, by stretching forth my hand, possess myself, was ornamentally before my window — A little onward, extends the great eastern Post road, which is, perhaps for miles, embowered by full grown trees rising in a direct line on either hand — A large luminous ball, seems at this distance, as if it were suspended upon the verdant branches, by which it is in part enveloped, but on our approach we find it erected, an appearance to the weary traveller, that the decent Inn is at hand — Hills, and Vallies, Woods, and plains, fields and meadows, are richly, and variously displayed — upon the right, in the back ground, a little rill murmurs along throu the glade, high lands, forming a chain of hills, ascend at a distance, and the horizon seems as if it were resting thereon — The grounds, however, are broken and we have a distinct view of the several eminences — A Grove beautifully detached, this moment strikes my eye as uncommonly, and pleasurably romantick — It crowns the most lofty activity, its hue is deep, and rich, its foliage [lush] and so regularly fashioned, that we are ready to pronounce it shaped by the hand of art, rather than the wild, and an uncultivated growth of luxuriant nature — I am fond of sketching for you, my sweet friend, as far as I may, the situations in to which I am thrown, it gives me the better to realize your charming presence, and when separated from those we love, it is unquestionably justifiable to illude, by the aid of fancy, the pain of absence — It will, I am fearful, be quite in the month of October, before we are allowed to return, and of course we have many weeks yet to number — Do not, I beseech you, my beloved friend, fail of meeting us by letter in Providence — I am chagrined that I have no means of forwarding my letters — Their bulk prevents my committing them to the post — I proceed, however, to make them up, that they may be in readiness for the favourable gale of opportunity — Salute my friends, my real friends, for me, and believe me most seriously, tenderly, and unalterably yours ——

Letter 789 to My Father and Mother Hartford September 4th 1790 — Saturday

John preached in Wallingford where he "gave much satisfaction." One of his hearers, Mr. Lyman, urged them to dine with him in Middletown. While they were there, General Sage "accosted" John, asking him to prolong his stay in Middletown, preach in the Presbyterian church, and accept his hospitality. He agreed. Meanwhile, Judith had seen a young man who looked remarkably like her sister-in-law, Anna Parsons Sargent. Eventually, she discovered that this man and his companion were Anna's cousins. What's more, the two men had news that her brother Fitz William, Anna's husband, had returned safely to Gloucester from his voyage, and that her brother Winthrop had returned safely from his journey to the Ohio Territory. Judith was tremendously relieved, and better able to enjoy their visit with General Sage whose gracious home she describes in detail. She also describes 80-year-old Mr. Mortimer, a widower, whose benevolence toward young orphaned girls she found quite moving. She describes the grandeur of his "mansion" as well. When John preached in Middletown, the response was a "universal burst of joy," and the minister even took up a collection for John. Leaving Middletown, Judith tells her parents, they arrived at the home of Mrs. Webb in Weathersfield by early tea time.

Agreeably to promise our New Haven Friends rejoined us at Wallingford, and they were accompanied by a Doctor Beardsley in whose composition, the milk of human kindness, is apparently the prevalent ingredient — A Mr Bishop was also in their train, a promising young gentleman, who is a Candidate for orders in the Episcopalian church — The service of sunday was performed by Mr Murray, both morning and afternoon, in the presbyterian Church I have reason to believe he gave much satisfaction — Upon the evening of that day, the New Haveners departed, while both our lips, our hearts, petitioned our God to bless them — Monday we continued at Wallingford, it produced many inquiries, and we passed, the day agreeably — A Mr Lyman, of Middlefield, eight miles from Wallingford, came forward with a request, that Mr Murray would dine with him on Tuesday, on his way to Hartford, and afterwards deliver in their house of worship, his message of Peace — accordingly tuesday morning produced us on our way, escorted by Doctor and Mrs Potter — The dwelling of Mr Lyman is about twelve miles distant from Wallingford, his situation is truly rural — a white house embosomed by woods, arrests the attention and its master is as far independent, as an agricultural competency can render him — He is hospitably good, he possesseth an informed mind, and his countenance is open, and prepossessing — Mr Lyman traces his origins, to the same stock from which the Lymans with whom we are acquainted descend — Three brothers Richard, Robert, and John, quitting England, fixed down in North Hampton, casting in their lot with the sons of Columbia, and from thence the various branches of the family have spread — General Lyman, when in England, although he made [a] diligent search, inquiring at the heraldry office & found no traces of the name remaining there — The family of Mr Lyman is pleasing, we dined agreeably, and passed on to Church — A large concourse of people were collected from the neighbouring Towns [—] curiosity was strikingly expressed in every countenance, and Mr Murray proceeded in his accustomed manner — Astonishment gradually took place — The subject opened, parallel scriptures were introduced, and a burst of solemn satisfaction, and sublime joy, ultimately triumphed in every face — As I passed into Church, I observed a handsome Carriage at the door. I noted it to Mr Murray, and my heart beat with unusual emotion — I wondered at the sensation — if it were not too fanciful, I would say subsequent hours explained it — Two young gentlemen, dressed in genteel mourning issued from the carriage — The face of one, was the exact resemblance of my sister Anna, he exhibited her air, her character, cast however in a manly mould — He appeared about twenty years of age — I started, I gazed, and a mixture of surprise and pleasure pervaded my bosom — The croud soon hid him from my view, but a train of ideas were roused, Retrospection was busy, and my family stood before me — uncertain in regard to their present circumstances, suspense sickened my soul, and I silently, and spontaneously breathed the fondest wishes for their felicity — The service over we parted with the Doctor, and Mrs Potter, and with Mr and Mrs Lyman the only individuals among this vast croud of whom we had the smallest knowledge — The sun was nearly setting, and we had five miles to Middletown — We had not either acquaintance with, or introduction to, any individual in that place, and our plan was to pass the night in an Inn —

While our carriage was making ready, we accepted the civilities of a solitary stranger and took seats in his parlour — The apartment soon filled, a promiscuous assembly thronged the room — numbers crouded round my husband — but reflection rendered me a solitary and melancholy spectator of the scene — When lifting my eyes the countenance of the young gentleman again presented the face of my sister Anna — Once more I started, and most earnestly did wish for an introduction to the pleasing vision — I fixed upon him my inquiring gaze, and he answered me with a silent, gentle, and benign kind of expression — Exactly the manner of my sister, said my heart — Just at this juncture — the voice of benevolence pervaded the assembly — "Will any one be kind enough to introduce me to Mr Murray["] — the croud gave way, and a middle aged gentleman portly, and well made, handsome and prepossessing benignity beaming in every feature, rapidly advanced — Many tongues were now ready — "General Sage of Middletown Sir —" "Yes Sir" added the stranger "My name is Sage — I have this afternoon attended your labours, and I accost you, Sir, as a petitioner, I come with the united requests of my respectable brethren of Middletown, that you would sojourn, at least a few days, with us, the doors of our churches are open, and my house is prepared for your reception — honour it, respected Sir, by accepting a residence therein" — so courtly a request, and urged with unquestionable sincerity, you will not doubt was yieldingly, and gratefully accepted — General Sage is Collector at Middletown, and hence, having obtained a promise of the preacher, he was necessitated to add "Being the servant of the public, it is, Sir, requisite that I hasten home, I have depositions to take, to which I must attend — but here Sir is one" — presenting the young gentleman in whose face I had taken so deep an interest — "who will gladly be your Escort —" The youth bowed, looked everything that was kind, and obliging, and the General departed — The person at whose [mansion] we were — insisting upon our taking tea, we were again seated, and my eyes, as far as decency would allow incesently wandered over the countenance of the young stranger — something, but to this hour I cannot ascertain what, introduced the name of General Parsons, and, Mr Murray expressing himself, with that kind of warmth, which normally distinguishes him, when speaking of his friends, produced an [exclamation] — two young gentlemen arose from their seats, one of them you may be sure the person who had so thoroughly arrested my attention — we, Sir are the sons of General Parsons, and we rejoice to meet in Mr Murray, the friend of our deceased Parent — My heart leaped, the resemblance was accounted for, and, separated as I am from every natural connexion, with these young gentlemen my heart instantaneously claimed kindred — But this was not all — listen, and you shall hear — Mr Enoch Parsons, who exhibits in his face, every gesture, so exact a likeness of my sister, Anna, hath never seen her, nor any individual of his Uncle Thomas' family — but Mr Walter Parsons, his brother passing some time at Newbury Port, had obtained a knowledge of, and affection for, his amiable relations — As yet they knew not the connexion in which I stood, but learning that I was a native of Gloucester Mr Walter Parsons approached me — Mrs Forbes Madam was a favourite sister of my Father's — I trust she is well — I trust she enjoys herself among you — her second daughter, my Cousin Anna, when I was last in Newbury Port, was apprehended in a decline — can you tell me, Madam how she is? Yes Sir that sweet, and amiable girl, verging as was supposed upon the very borders of her future Elysium, is now a pretty little married Woman, and a joyful Mother of a charming Girl — Pleasure lighted up his countenance — and he exclaimed "Is it, can it be possible? In deed I was told she was married, and to a Sargent, but I hardly credited the report, her health, when last I saw her, was so extremely delicate — Pray can you tell me what family she is connected with? Her husband Sir, I have the happiness to inform you, is my brother — "Indeed Madam, one question more, Is he related to Major Sargent? — That Gentleman, Sir, is also my brother — Well then, my brother is recently from the Western World [—] Possibly he may give you some intelligence of the Major — Again my heart leaped, and I turned to the mildly intelligent young Man, who was seated on my right hand — Dear Sir, Is Governor St Clair returned from his late Voyage? The Governour, Madam, is in New York, they all returned in health — the Major continues in Marietta, for Government having attached the duties of Governor, to the office of secretary, the Major is consequently obliged to tarry there, during the absence of the Governor — To hear that my eldest Brother was returned from a most hazardous expedition — to learn that he was in health — but language is insufficient to a delineation of my feelings — I pass them, therefore, in silence — yet, neither was this all — Mr Enoch Parsons proceeded, and still in the very accent of our dear Anna, Have you a brother lately arrived from Europe Madam? The tears started in my eye — I cannot tell — I sighed deeply — a long period hath elapsed since I have received any intelligence from home — I saw, Madam, in the papers an account of the arrival of a Captain Sargent in Boston from London — Did you Sir — and my heart bounded — but there are more Sargents than one — Pray Sir can you recollect the Christian name of that Captain? It was not given — but he brought with him a number of passengers [—] my heart sank —

and I almost panted for breath — Again I interrogated — Do you remember Sir, whether he commanded a ship, or a brig — A ship Ma'am, bearing the name of the Marietta — Gracious God! — It is enough — I am satisfied Thou everlasting father, art abundantly better to me than my fears — My spirits thus exhilerated, you will conclude that my ride to Middletown was enchanting — It was — and the elegant Carriage I had marked on my entering the Church conveyed the young gentlemen, who led the way — they regretted they had promised General Sage to accompany to his house their Mother, they said, would have had particular pleasure, in receiving us in her Mansion house in Middletown [—] To the dwelling of General Sage we however came, and we were welcomed in a manner, which would have done honour to a friendship, of ancient growth — General Sage is the head of a numerous and respectable family, his own immediate descendants form around him, a protecting Circle, his children have all, one daughter excepted, united themselves in wedlock, and multiplied themselves in children — The young Lady who continueth with them, is pleasing in her lovely manners, and of a sweet, and amiable disposition — Mrs Sage is a good matronly kind of woman [—] their dwelling bears the marks of antiquity — It is upon the borders of Connecticut river, and commands a variety of charmingly rural prospects — We behold from the window the approach of distant masts, as if moving through the woods, until the opening River presents a full view of the white sails, and of the richly freighted Bark — The mind of General Sage is in some manner improved, and his observations are extensive — He entertained us with a variety of anecdotes relative to the late war, among which he could not but do homage to his deliniation of the gray haired Volunteer — When upwards of seventy, influenced by motives truly patriotic he had taken arms — He possessed seventy good acres of wheat, yet, bearing his fire lock, he resolutely appeared in the ranks, submitting very cheerfully, to the exercise, and discipline of the youngest, or meanest soldier! General Sage informed us, that the Connecticut Farmer is making large strides to affluence, and consequent independence, that he entertains proper ideas of frugality, and industry, and the present most fruitful season, will add incredibly to his opulence — wednesday morning presented Mr Enoch Parsons, he came with his Mother's request that we would take tea with her family, and, he added that his Mother took the liberty to join the public wish that Mr Murray would gratify them, by his scriptural investigations — The Reverend Mr Huntington dined with us at our lodgings, and General Sage introducing Mr Murray, expressed himself to the following purpose — I was Sir, Commissioned to solicit Mr Murray to visit us, and I am happy to learn, by a billet received from you this morning that I have acted in perfect unison with your wishes — Mr Huntington replied, I am indeed pleased with an opportunity of seeing Mr Murray, and were it in my power, I should in this age of free inquiry, consider myself most reprehensible, to interpose a barrier! Our dinner party was highly social — The bell rang for church, and Mr Huntington waited upon Mr Murray, Escorted him to the pulpit[,] held open the door, and followed him in!! The Church is spacious, the audience was numerous, respectable, and genteel — The subject was the rich man in the parable taken in its connexion — The attention of the people was solemn, and unremitted, and it was affecting to observe, by what gentle gradations, an expression of conviction, and approbation, took place of that eager wonder, and curiosity, which had swelled every feature — A lecture, preparatory to the reception of the Eucharist, had been previously appointed for this day, and after the service of wednesday, Mr Huntington requested Mr Murray to tarry and preach for him upon the occasion! Mr Murray consented, and we proceeded to the dwelling of Mrs Parsons — I am charmed with our family connexion at Middletown — Mrs Parsons, the widow of the General is a sensible, and Pleasing Woman — her manners are not unlike those of Mrs Forbes — she hath three sons, and four daughters, Her eldest daughter is disposed of in marriage, to a genteel young barrister, of the name of Hosmer [—] he is accomplished, and promising — Her eldest son is also married, and they are both advantageously settled in Middletown — The family character, and manners, like those of their connexions, whom we know, are engaging — they are rather handsome — Mr Enoch Parsons hath the eye of my sister, and a dark soft eye armed with an expression unconsciously pleasing is the eye of the family — We were much urged to bide with them, during our stay at Middletown, but respect to General Sage would not allow it — they, however, insisted on a promise of our Company at dinner, on Thursday, and I was at home in their hospitable dwelling — Mr Enoch Parsons gave me many anecdotes of my eldest brother — his garden at Marietta he say[s] is a matter of astonishment to every observer and he declares he never tasted melons, so richly flavoured, as those produced there — The whole family have conceived a strong predilection for Mr Murray, and his doctrines, and they unitedly join in a wish that my brother, Fitz William, and my sister Anna — may find it convenient to visit them

The benevolence of Mr Parsons in becoming bondsman for a debtor, hath cruelly involved his widow, and her orphan children — Middletown presented a family of faithful adherents, who were early and warmly attached to Mr Murray — a Major Otis and his daughter, who had removed from Newport, but my husband was ignorant of the place of their present residence, With Mr Otis, we were solicited to take up our abode, and invitations from all quarters multiplied upon us — We devoted thursday morning to a number of visits En passant — Mr Mortimer, an old gentleman of a singular character, had solicited our attendance — To Mr Mortimer much is due [—] allow me to bestow a few moments upon the Man, and his place of residence — Mr Mortimer is a native of Hibernia, he hath by industry, accumulated an abundant fortune — he hath grown old in the exercises of benevolence — eighteen years since he buried the Wife of his youth, and although she left him no [binding] pledge of love — yet he hath still continued wedded to her memory — The Orphan, and the destitute, hath in him a ready, and indulgent Protector — he hath educated many young Ladies, and they have not, left his tranquil abode, but to take command of a dwelling of their own — One instance I will give — a female child who is unconnected by ties of blood, and no more than three years of age, was carried by her Mother to visit Mr Mortimer — She immediately became strongly attached to him — it was impossible to relieve her from his arms! and when forcibly convened away her [sobs] knew no suspension...Mr Mortimer received the pretty Creature, into his family, he watched the growth of the opening flower, he reared it with all a Father's tenderness, and his genial influence continued until he surrendered her to the protecting arms of a worthy Man — Even to this day she spends one portion of every week, at the seat of this worthy old gentleman — Mr Mortimer lives a life of the utmost regularity, rising every morning before the sun, when if the weather be propitious, he indulges in the salutary exercise of walking, and, precisely at eight o-clock, in the evening after taking his bowl of milk, he retires, and this custom, although he is now upwards of eighty years of age, he is never known to vary — His setting life is calmly serene, and although his family now consists only of servants, yet his own reflections are a rich fund, upon which he draws, and no marks of solitude, or gloom, are ever traced upon him — One thing only was wanting — a view of the complete character of the Redeemer — an eye of faith, to behold every evil, finally eradicated from the works of deity — He had heard of the Promulgator of peace — he sighed for his presence — he hath seen him — he hath repeatedly heard him, he believes, and his prospects are without a cloud — The situation of this aged sojourner in mortality, is beyond expression charming — Passing the high street, a venerable shade presents — We have not the most distant idea of a dwelling — opening a Chinese gate neatly finished, and painted white, adjoining to which is a curious stone, upon which, in capital letters, the name Hibernia is engraved — We have now entered the Middletown Mall[,] Mortimer's Grove, or, more properly speaking, an extensive, and beautiful Vista — The Tall sycamores rise to a prodigious height, and uniting over our heads, form an umbrageous, and most enchanting shade — The walk is continued many feet, and as we advance the Mansion house of Mr Mortimer presents — convenient seats are placed at the bend of the walk — upon the left, a direct angle is formed, which leads in a straight course to the house, the embosoming trees still enfolding their verdant branches — The avenue from the point of the angle, is flagged with large square stones, and the dwelling is capacious and elegant — It exhibits in front a kind of Alcove, round which sweet Woodbines are romantically trained, and over the door, and on either hand, in bass relief is a shepherdess, with her crook, and attendant sheep, with the bard of Wisdom handsomely sculptored — The house is genteelly finished, and furnished — decorated by a collection of well chosen pictures, and from different directions, a variety of picturesque prospects are traced — An intensive view of the great River, and its navigation winds its glassy course — Columns of trees, meadows, corn fields, and spreading lawns, form the interjacent scene, a richly prolific Orchard, and level greens, are methodically arranged — a pigeon house in delightful security, is erected upon the shorn grass, and, at a little distance the gray stone arises sacred to the memory of the deceased — This hallowed burial ground, is shaded by the tall, and unbrageous elm, and beyond is the great road, which leads the traveller on to Hartford — Thus this pleasant retreat, in the heart of the Town, steps a little on one side, and is embosomed in all the sequestering solitude of rural beauty — We passed some agreeable moments with Mr Mortimer but being, as I said engaged to dine with Mrs Parsons, we quitted, sooner than we wished, the variegated scene — The afternoon again collected the congregating multitude — The respectability, decency, and attention of the audience, could not but animate the Preacher — The subject was particularly interesting — "Whose fan is in his hand, and He shall thoroughly purge His floor, and gathering His wheat into his garner, He shall burn up the Chaf with unquenchable fire — Tears were in many eyes during the investigation of the text, and they beheld the purification of the nature at large, agreeably to scriptural testimony —

The universal burst of joy, which was indisputably expressed, is beyond my power to paint [—] The singing in Middletown is charming, and the voices of the Choristers seemed as if softened and mellowed by a bright sense of redeeming, and of pardoning love — Mr Huntington, accompanied by another Clergyman, again attended Mr Murray to the pulpit taking their seats with him, a number of Clergymen were collected from neighbouring Towns, and you will judge of our astonishment when, at the close of the service — Mr Huntington — the Reverend Mr Huntington — himself, advancing to the front of the desk, informed the audience, that it was but just they considered the gentleman labouring among them, that he merited much, and he doubted not they would be proportionably liberal! The people were unprepared for this request, it produced however about eleven dollars, and this singular occurrence, I record with an equal measure of pain, pleasure, and surprise — We closed our day on thursday with Mr & Mrs Phillips, in the family of Major Otis, where too, we were joined by a large number of inquirers and Major Otis, as a Citizen of Middletown, expressed in the name, and behalf of that City, his grateful thanks to Mr Murray, for what he termed his well timed, pleasing, and instructive Visit — yesterday we took an early dinner with Mr and Mrs Phillips, and, accompanied by General Sage, Mr and Mrs Phillips and a Mr Warner, who escorted us five miles on our way, we took leave of Middletown — we were urged to prolong our stay, but unavoidable engagements pressed us on, and a tear was upon the cheek of the good Mrs Sage and her amiable daughter — We reached Weathersfield at early tea time, where we were regaled with an excellent dish of hyson, by Mrs Webb — of Mr Webb you have heard my brother speak, he is brother to the General of that name — Poor Gentleman, a dark cloud envelops his once brightening prospects — He is now a close prisoner in Hartford — yet his Lady although faithfully affectionate, and tender, supports herself with an amiable equanimity, and her deportment is honourable to her character — you have heretofore heard me express my self of Weathersfield, and in terms dictated by my feelings, but I ought to have informed you, that Middletown abounds with delightful situations, that its dwellings are descriptive of elegance and competency, and that the whole town wears a thrifty and pleasing appearance — and above all, I should have remarked that the Rev. Mr Huntington invited Mr Murray to his home, that he met him with an open bible in his hand, that they had much, and most interesting conversation which resulted in apparently mutual satisfaction — These Religious Societies amicably flourish in Middletown and if we may trust our own experience, the people are hospitable, social, and good — We reached Hartford just at dark last evening — We are in the midst of an agreeable family, but my letter having thus unexpectedly grown under my hands, this family must obtain a place in some future page. Thus having closed another Week of my long, long journey, allow me to congratulate you on the return of your Fitz William — May God long continue to you so rich a blessing — The mild countenance of my sister Anna, seems at this moment to meet my eye, it beams unutterable pleasure — With what complacency, if this good be yet in store for me, shall I contemplate this young Father, and Mother, bestowing their fond endearments upon the first pledge of their early, their mutual love — The felicity of my sister Esther too, is, as I trust, once more complete — Again she views her little family entire, and again I supplicate — May no cloud obscure the blissful scene — Give I beseach you, my hearts love to them all [—] The last of October I hope to join them — until, when, and while memory shall last, I continue respectfully, affectionately, and dutifully yours ———

Letter 790 To the Same Norwich September 11th 1790
Saturday Evening

In Hartford, Judith and John stayed with the Ball family, who she introduces to her parents. She also met Mrs. Webb, a relative of the Ball family, whose husband was in debtors prison. Judith writes of the "agonies" Mrs. Webb felt when her husband was arrested. A year later, her husband is still incarcerated and Judith and John visited him with her. Mr. Webb asked John to preach at the prison, and he obliged finding that "the opportunity was affecting." Judith considers the treatment of debtors outrageous, remembering her first husband's fatal escape to the West Indies to avoid debtors prison. Leaving Hartford, they travelled along a stretch of particularly rough road and Judith had an accident. She cut and bruised her face, but she tells her parents she is all right. Finally reaching the Norwich home of Dr. Turner, a cousin, John collapsed from exhaustion.

In Hartford we received much kindness, and in compliance with the earnest solicitations of a Mr Ball, a respectable merchant in this City, we tarried at his house — His family are truly hospitable, truly obliging, and he himself is warmly attached to the Religion of the Redeemer — Mrs Ball is sister to General Webb — She is a step Mother, and discharges the duties of her truly arduous character, in a manner which confers upon her the highest honour — Miss Ball, the eldest daughter of the family, is an accomplished, and agreeable Girl, she hath a correct ear for musick, and plays elegantly upon the guitar, and, of her talents in this line, you will conclude we gladly availed ourselves — Mr Murray, in compliance with the most earnest importunity, repeatedly congregated the people in one of their Churches — The Rev Mr Strong was seated in the pulpit, and with apparent gladness, and solemn joy, the necessary peace was received. By Mr Webb, as I hinted in my last, our feelings were much interested — from the vindictive and undue resentment of a single Creditor, confined in the prison at Hartford, he is wearing out the prime of his days, in a situation that is truly melancholy [—] his sufferings have already continued upwards of a year — peculiar hardships attend his case, and render the sanction of law he hath to complain of much injustice – Were he liberated, the means of extricating himself, and of rendering service to his Creditors are within his reach, but to ill nature, and to obstinacy, who shall prescribe bounds. His family reside at Weathersfield, four miles from Hartford — his Lady is, as I said amiable — Since the imprisonment of Mr Webb, they have buried a fine son — the heart of the Father was particularly agonized, but he was denied the relief of attending upon the bed of death!! Such is the ferocity of our jurisprudence, that the honest Debtor, to whom no fault can be justly attributed, whose exursions have been proper and unremitted, and who is sinking under the pressure of a series of mighty, and unavoidable misfortunes, is in many particulars upon a level with the most attrocious offenders! Mrs Webb is now able to give daily attendance upon the Prison, although as her residence being four miles distance, it is no inconsiderable inconvenience — but the time is rapidly approaching, when she is to expect inevitable sickness, and should her hour of peril prove particularly hazardous, tenderly attached as are these unfortunate sufferers, how will they be able to support an augmentation of their distress, so exceedingly aggravated — When Mr Webb was first arrested, the agonies, the heart affecting agonies, of Mrs Webb were beyond description! More dead than alive she was supported to the goal — and in the sorrow of her heart, she mournfully exclaimed — she should never more know peace — But how lenient are the operations of time — Upwards of a year is elapsed, and she now trips into Mr Webbs lodgings, as she terms the prison, with as much vivacity as she would enter the most elegant drawing room — Repeatedly, agreeably to her request, I accompanied her to the prison, and I observed with pleasure, that even in circumstances so truly distressing the mind is tranquilized by habit — Mr Webb requested Mr Murray to indulge him — and the rest of his companions in adversity, by speaking to them of the things of the Kingdom — and as this wish earnestly, and repeatedly urged, was so consonant with the duty and what ought ever to be the inclination of an ambassador of that Sovereign, whose dominion is universal, you will conclude that the prison walls at Hartford echoed the glad tidings of salvation — They did so — The prisoners assembled in the long Room — Many respectible persons, whose circumstances were more eligible, also joined us, and the opportunity was affecting, and, as I trust, happy — Having in former letters, said so much of Hartford, I have now little to add — Its beautiful meadows I can never retrace, unattended by a pleasurable glow — They are at this season particularly pleasing, for, although the approaches of Autumn are now so generally visible, they are as gaily clad, as mildly verdant, as in the promise giving Month of May — Our stay in Hartford was short — circumstances prevented us from availing our selves of the civilities of Colonel Wadsworth, and we left Town on thursday morning — Crossing the River, we proceeded through East Hartford making all prudent dispatch to Lebanon — The road from Hartford to Lebanon is not the most pleasing in the World — it should seem that in our progress from thence, to this place, we are destined to misfortune — you will recollect that it was on this very route, four years since, at an hour extremely mal apropos — we were overtaken by the accident to Mr Murray's Sulkey — our late disaster should not, at this time, have the honour of being recorded by me, were I not fearful, that as circumstances are often aggravated by distance, in an exact ratio, to the number of miles which they travel [—] some very formidable account may, most unceremoniously assault the ears of my anxiously affectionate Parents, and others of our interested connexions — here then follows the tale verbatim, and I pray you take notice, I do not knowingly or wittingly either add or diminish — It was on the thursday evening of September the ninth — one hundred seven hundred and ninety, on or about as I can determine seven O clock, the shades of evening began to prevail, when we were proceeding with all due caution, and much gravity upon the great road to Lebanon, being solicitous to reach a house of entertainment, in that Village, where we had reason to expect tolerable accommodations. When, behold, suddenly, unexpectedly, and as I have strong reason to believe accidentally[,] our horse — and let them who think they stand henceforward take heed lest they fall — for better, gentler and more sure footed beast I take upon me to pronounce never yet served a careful, and well deserving Master — yet even this beast, I say, when, not dreaming of such an event, we were in no sort upon our guard, instantly, and at a moments warning, measured his whole length upon the ground — This action of his — so very uncivil, without ever consulting propriety, or my conveniences, precipitated me rather roughly, I must confess, from my seat in the Chaise, to the front of the Carriage, and my nose, who would have conceived that my nose could possibly have ever stood in the way — It was nevertheless truly, and humble as it is, upon this occasion, the prominent figure, and in consort with my lips, it received a contusion, which it resented by issuing a sanguine stream, not however very copious — but sufficiently unpleasant — Thus you have the whole of the matter, and if any report should make the accident better, or worse, I again positively declare, I have neither extenuated, nor exaggerated, It is true, that both my nose, and lips bear conspicuous marks of my late recounter, but as these hospitable Norwichers have seen me, when my pretensions to face were better founded, I am not quite overwhelmed by this misfortune — The horse was soon in stato quo, and we came on without further difficulty — About noon yesterday we reached this dwelling, and when I say it is the Mansion of Doctor Turner, in which we are now lodged, it will hardly be necessary to add that we are received with every demonstration of friendship — No indeed, this amiable family are in no sort cooled in their regards, and, in their pleasing dwelling, we are still at home — But you are surprised at the flippancy of my style, and your astonishment will encrease, when I tell you that Mr Murray was yesterday so ill as to be necessitated to retire immediately to bed, upon his reaching this house, that at four O clock this afternoon he had not quitted it, and that I had every reason to expect a confirmed fever — To his friends who crouded to see him, we were necessitated to deny him, and his illness every moment encreased — Had you seen me this morning you would have beheld me bathed in tears — separated as I am from my natural connexions — not a ray of light, but from worlds beyond the sky visited my soul — I however endeavoured to stay myself upon my God, and to possess my soul in patience, But Mr Murray is better, and the lightness of my heart is thus accounted for — He has sat up two full hours this evening, giving to Mr Tyler, and to many others heartfelt pleasure — and, as it is now late at night, you will allow me adieu — My heart's affection, as is duty bound, are ever yours, and my tenderest wishes attend the beloved Circle —

Letter 791 To Mrs Sargent — Norwich September 12th 1790

John is very ill. He has developed "symptoms that are truly alarming" and Judith's "mind is...very much depressed." She tells her aunt, Mary Turner Sargent, that "crouds fill the house," waiting for news of his restored health. (Note: a "Sulkey" is a kind of carriage.)

I have yet many revolving days to number — e'er I can rationally flatter myself, with the prospect of beholding the mild image of friendship, gently beaming in the expressive countenance of my beloved Correspondent — Our journey hath been protracted much beyond my expectations — and although our delay is, of necessity, yet I am at times peevishly impatient, and I would most gladly accelerate the hour of our return —

You will be much surprised at the alteration in my person — Writing opposite a large mirror, and accidentally lifting my eyes, my figure most officiously obtrudes — I cannot account — yet my glass shall not arbitrarily impose upon you a subject so selfish — My mind is at this moment very much depressed — your gentle spirit will, I dare believe swell a sigh, for in the bosom which goodness bosoms over, the angel pity loves to dwell — Mr Murray is ill — very ill [—] when I closed my journal of yesterday, I indulged a hope that his complaints would pass off — but they are this morning returned, with some symptoms that are truly alarming — you will find in my account of yesterday, that immediately upon his reaching this place, he retired to his bed, continuing there until the evening, when he was enabled to present himself to his expecting friends — I was elated, and upon the wings of buoyant hope I was serenely borne — but this morning the clouds gather — It is really affecting — crouds fill the house, The church doors are thrown open, and they were assured that those hallowed walls, would this day echo the glad tidings of redemption — But, for us, our circumstances might have been much worse. We are in the hospitable

Mansion of Doctor Turner — Connecticut doth not produce a more eminent Physician — his benevolence is unquestionable — His Lady and family are precisely what I would wish them — Well then I will essay to pierce the dun obscure, and once more endeavour to bask beneath the sunny beams of genial hope

Letter 792 To the Same New London September 15. 1790

The medicine Doctor Turner gave John seems to have worked, and John has declared himself well enough to preach. However, this is not the first time, Judith tells her aunt, that John has left his bed to preach only to return to it immediately after. Concerned for his constant state of fatigue she has, nevertheless, "learned not to remonstrate." Since his illness delayed their journey, John has written ahead to his friend in Rhode Island to have letters from Judith's family forwarded to the Turner home. Judith was delighted that he was so "obligingly attentive to [her] feelings," as John often was. Apparently, divorce was quite commonplace in Connecticut and Judith tells her aunt an amusing anecdote on the subject. She also tells her aunt that a letter of hers, written months ago, had been lost, sent to New York, then New England, and only recently received by Judith!

Preceding evils, do indeed most delightfully zest present enjoyments: the vivid tincts most commandingly glow, when judiciously displayed upon the darkest ground, and, it should seem, that our general Mother could hardly estimate the good, until she had learned to compare it with opposing evil — Quitting you last sunday, I endeavoured in vain to tranquilize my bosom — That balmy Hope, which I had presumed to arrogate, became regardless of my advances, and pervading glooms continued to enwrap my soul — Until twelve O clock every appearance was against me, when a medicine skillfully administered, began its salutary operation — Mr Murray declared himself better, much better, and avowed a resolution to answer the expectations of the people, by meeting them in the afternoon — I have often known him to pass from his bed to the church, and to return to it again immediately after the close of the service, and I have learned not to remonstrate — The effort last sunday, was manifestly advantageous; the spirits, and the health of my husband, were surprisingly restored — and my satisfaction was proportioned to my previous inquietude — But this was not all, that I might inhale — unmixed — the draught of pleasure [—] a large packet of letters was put into my hands by Mr Murray — obligingly attentive to my feelings, he had written to Mr Carter requesting him to forward any parcels, which he might have for us, in consequence of which I am put in possession of at least three weeks earlier than I had hoped, of your sweet favour of August 26th — your friendship is truly soothing to my soul, and these testimonials most pleasingly corroborate what, although I cannot doubt, yet, nevertheless, vibrates so charmingly upon my ear, as to render it impossible to reiterate it too frequently [—] I shudder as I read the midnight complaint of the Son of my Love — Oh! my friend was not your maternal caution of its guard, when you suffered your gentle Boy, to encounter, during a long, long walk, the intense rays of a piercing sun — Forgive me if I stretch too far the privileges of Amity, or if you are inclined to censure, let the sweet smiles, of my dark eyes Cherub, make my peace — But he is restored to health, and I unite with you in offering, at the throne of grace, the glad orisons of a grateful heart — I only wonder, that in such a situation, you could write at all, but I bless the stimulous which thus impels your kind attentions, and again I repeat, that your tender affections, are as How natural, thus it will ever be — Friendship glowing and tender, will beautify my warmest wishes, will sigh for the songs of the morning, that it may hasten to...the bosom which possesseth its...Love... — If you have received my last letters, they will give you an account of the manner in which the intelligence of Fitz William's arrival reached me, and I assure myself that you experienced, while perusing that part of my journal, sensations which corresponded with those of the Writer. To your charming pen I am obliged for a circumstantial account — Much indeed am I indebted to you, your last communication has given me inexplicable pleasure, and I greatly rejoice to learn, that our young adventurer hath received, even in the Commencement of his Career, such ample encouragement. How often do dreams mock our wishes, yet there is a sense, in which they may be said to be pictures of life — Well, by and by, we shall awake to substantial good.

your early attention to Fitz William, was like yourself — you, what an honour to know — The marriage of Mr— with Miss— and D's account distresses me, otherwise — but no matter, and, really you say — well, upon my word it is astonishing — however, I do assure you, I shall not regret to learn that Mr— hath actually taken the vow matrimonial, may his nuptial bands be silken, I say — Mr A.B. strange to tell — well God bless them all and give them that quantum of discretion, requisite in a voyage so important, precarious, and interesting — Mentioning this — to the inhabitant of Massachusetts — indisposable knot — reminds me of a peculiarity, admitted in the jurisprudence in this good state of Connecticut, The marriage contract, it should seem, ought to be differently worded in this State — The parties should not be required to say until death do us part [—] Divorces are frequent, and the difficulties attendant upon obtaining a bill are trivial — almost any pretense is sufficient — Those who become disgusted, have only to engage a Lawyer, who steps forth, pleads his Cause, and the Legislature signs the necessary releases — A single instance of an unsuccessful Application to authority, hath, I am told never yet been known — if the wedded Pair are unhappy it is enough — They have only to state their grievances, go through a form of Law, and the marriage is dissolved! — Neither is this transaction considered as disreputable, it frequently occurs in the best families, the sister of General Webb is married to a gentleman in this predicament — Infidelity which you know is, with us, the only admissible plea, was not even presumed — and in the small Circle of my acquaintance in New Haven, I visited two Ladies, who mix in the best company there, who have each of them two husbands living at the same time, in that City — Nay, I assure you, I have myself been asked, by a Connecticut gentleman, whether my first Connexion was deceased, or whether I had obtained a bill!! Nor did the interrogator believe his question involved the least indelicacy, much less of offence! you smile incredulous, but the theory is absolutely so common in this State, as to not call up a blush, or even to be considered as a subject of wonder! I render my account from unquestionable authority — It is notable, it is a serious, irrefragable, and unexaggerated fact — I thought my Rose Bud would please, and I know my elegant friend, would not fail to pronounce Miss Custus a charming girl — I regard your having taken a copy of the lines, in a flattering point of view, and it is then you truly oblige me, when you consider me, and my papers, as devotedly at your disposal — The art of Manlius, to draw your attention, was admirable [—] how plainly doth this trait evince his origin — I absolutely long to clasp him to my bosom, and, sure I am, that were I even elevated to those mansions of bliss in which he insinuated he had heard me Carol, I should not cease to regard with marked attention, so fair a flower

My heart swells at the subsequent passage — yes indeed the days which you so anxiously name her[e] will expire — I am coming and every feature of my face shall announce that gratitude, which upon the tablets of my heart is indelibly inscribed — The first paragraph of my last letter will convince you that the report of Mrs D— was without foundation [—] I cannot account for Mr Murray's manner of writing, and I can only say — This Man, the best of them have their whimsical moments — Certainly, an event of such a nature, would not have been concealed from you — Accustomed to believe you interested in all my hopes, and fears, and the inmost recesses of my soul, having been disclosed to you, I could not have avoided communicating what would have lighted upon my bosom — I am free to own, the sincerest pleasure — Thank you most amiable and indulgent of Women, most sincerely do I thank you for an assurance which in the same moment that it essentially gratifies my feelings confers upon me the highest honour —

I am happy that you approve the resolution expressed in my last letter — It is then we become in a good degree sure of our parts when they are sanctioned by the better judgment of those, we both love, and esteem — such a pleasant confirmation of our arrangements, operates upon the mental plan, like the presence of a guide before us, in a road which is too intricate for the foot of a stranger — Our beloved Girl hath not offended me, delicate in her expressions, and gentle in her disposition, she can never intentionally wound — An odd circumstance hath taken place relative to one of your letter designed for me — Being without a date I cannot say exactly when it was written — it is however short, and it was penned when my Father was an inmate in your hospitable Mansion — it contains an expression of pleasure at perusing the vision of Mr Jay — your approbation of my journal, an extract from a letter written by your Maria, including her tender regards, with those of your son Ignatius — and it concludes with wonted expressions of affection — This letter was inclosed to Mr Goodhue during his continuance in York — It found its way to that City in safety — but preferring, as it should seem, it abode with a member of Congress, to taking its place among the sweet mementos of amity, it contrived to conceal itself among that gentleman's papers, and being conveyed therewith to the state of Massachusetts, its retreat was not discovered until it reached the good town of Salem — Mr Goodhue being at a loss to determine its Writer and ignorant of my address, very naturally inclosed it to my Father, who agreeably to his accustomed goodness, seizing the dear fugitive clapped it under additional bonds, and dispatched it forthwith to me, so that after all its peregrinations, it hath at length reached me safe, and sound, and I, receiving it in stato quo thus acknowledge, to its lovely Authoress an additional debt of gratitude — I trust you will not fail to address my grateful regards to Ignatius, and Maria, who I do assure you possess a very warm place in my heart — To my Uncle also, to the young gentlemen, and to our beloved children — My feelings relative to yourself, deign not to submit to language — they are, I must repeat, energetic as amity, tender as love, and unfeigned as sincerity —

Letter 793 To my brother Fitz William New London September 17— 1790

Judith congratulates her youngest brother on his safe journey home and the birth of his daughter, Anna Maria. As with any voyage at sea her brother (a merchant) would take, Judith was "fearful for [his] safety and...proportionably happy in [his] return." She wishes him well carrying out the new "trust reposed in [him]" by God — being a parent.

God bless you, my dearest brother, you could not have hit upon an expedient more effectively calculated to oblige me, than by forwarding to me a letter, so truly fraternal, yes indeed, your welfare, and your pleasures, will ever constitute a very large proportion of my happiness — Previous to the receipt of your kind address, I had rejoiced in your happy restoration to our maternal friends — The place where, the time when, and the manner how, you will find if I mistake not, recorded in the seventeenth week, of my peregrinations — That section of my journal, forwarded to our Parents, I hope they have received — It was a part truly interesting to me written warm from my heart, and very circumstantially, and amply narrated — Some accounts relative to your ship, had made a deep impression upon my heart, I was fearful for your safety, and I am proportionably happy in your return — I think, my dear, that your career in life has commenced under the most pleasing auspices — may its meridian, and termination be equally propitious — I have many things upon which to felicitate you — your successful voyage, the birth of your daughter — how affectingly interesting this sounds — with many less brilliant events — But were I to toast the affections of my heart, in their fullest expansion, a long, a very long letter would be the irresistable consequence and, apprized as I am, of your sentiments in this respect, I dare not trust my pen — your Anna is extremely dear to my soul — She is truly deserving in her own character, as your Wife she possesseth an indubitable claim to my affection, and as the Mother of your daughter, her consequence to me, is, in no small degree augmented — I am impatient to see, and embrace her — and I ardently long to clasp the little Anna Maria to my bosom — I am told that your expressive eyes, and the whole cast of your countenance is hers — Sweet Cherub — Strange that thou should be so long in existence, and the eldest, and most venerable of thy Aunts never once blessed with a sight of thy pretty form! I do assure you that this protraction of our journey is, in many instances, very painful to me, but it is a necessity which cannot be avoided — Do tell me, what are your sensations? Were I to conjecture, I should suppose, the character Father would elate you, quite as much as any attentions which I have received, can contribute to my Vanity — I do assure you I would freely exchange situations with you, in this particular at least, and yet I do not see but you are quite affectionate, as in any part of your life — But seriously, an important change hath devolved upon you, and my wishes, that you may execute the trust reposed in you, by our common Father, with honour to yourself, and advantage to the sweet Innocent committed into your guardianship — Do you indeed wish to see me, and doth your Anna unite with you in this wish? — My sensations, as I trace the balmy assurance, are inexpressible — It is indeed as the sweetest musick to my ears — Assure the dear Girl of my tenderest regards, and may neither she, nor you, ever doubt my affection [—] Mr Murray unites with me in every expression of esteem, and love, to you, and yours — Kiss the sweet infant for me, and believe me ever, and most sincerely your truly attached sister

Letter 794 To my Sister New London September 17— 1790

Judith has just received a letter from her sister, Esther, and she tells Esther how fortunate she feels that they are so close. She shares some thoughts on why this is so often not the case with siblings. Missing her family and Gloucester terribly, she imagines what it must have been like when the family first saw Fitz William's "white sails" come into view. Judith's mother is still very ill, and Judith feels anxious and helpless being so far away.

your wish my Love is natural, and proper, and if we cannot ingraft friendship upon the stock of affection, of an affection implanted by affinity, something must be strongly wrong — and yet, it too frequently happens, that we do not find that apparent cordiality, surviving between the children of the same parents, which is evident in the branches more remote, or in adventitious connexions — To what shall we impute our arrangement so untoward, and unpleasant? Will you, my sweet sister, give me leave to hazard a conjecture? we are too apt to appear undressed before those with whom we have been from infancy in habits of intimacy — We become unguarded, we are not solicitous to please, we too incautiously wound, and scars do not easily give place to that smooth polish of tender love, which early years behold, damasked over by the soft bloom of young affection — By degrees the tenderness cultivated in childhood, blunted, and reserve, or indifference takes place — But it will be said must we be always acting a part, are no moments of our lives to be unstudied, must we never indulge the freedom of familiarity, and with what can we so properly unbend, as well those of our own blood? — That is, in other words — It is necessary we should occasionally be cautious, petulant, and peevish, we will not always rein in our feelings, and those we are most consistently with, shall submit to all the inequalities of our disposition — In answer to this, I take leave to observe, I conceive no real disadvantage would...a constant practice of all those delicate refinements, so ornamental to social life and to which we attend with great exactitude, in our more general intercourse with those whose esteem we wish to cultivate — Nay I conceive we should derive the most beneficial effects, from being accustomed to an elegance of expression, and manners thus rendering the obliging and endearing civilities or amities of deportment, as a second nature — This is perhaps a mental adornment, a becoming and decent habiliment, without which the mind never ought to make its appearance, of which it should never be divested, and in which we should as carefully enwrap it, as we cloath the exterior of our forms, e'er we present ourselves to the domestic Circle — That too much familiarity produceth contempt, is a proverb, which is not more homely than true, and I declare, had I children, I would accustom them, from the first dawn of their reason, to acquit themselves to each other, precisely in the way that I would require them to address their holy day associates — But whither hath your wish to enfold in your arms a friend, as well as a sister led me — For give me, my dear, my pen frequently runs away with my judgment — For myself, I received your sweet favour, with feelings which evince the spontaneous glow of affection, which evinced the sincerest amity, and my wishes, once more to embrace my beloved sister, are equally fervid with her own — your charmingly animated and beautiful description, hath placed me at the well known board — I look around — the infirmities of my dear, and tender Mother, command the scarcely suppressed tear — The anxious brow of my Father harrows up my soul — Every child, one only excepted, is removed — The table looks solitary — The hospitable board, so long, upon this day, devoted to domestic enjoyment, is unusually desolate — It is not like the saturdays, which you, and I, have seen [—] The healthful viands are hardly tasted, and melancholy forebodings seem to brood around [—] How suddenly is the scene changed — A Ship — A ship — God bless me, where, when — Every tumultuous passion is affloat — Suspense, Hope, Fear, joy, and Expectation are struggling on each perturbed bosom — But, the ascertaining voice of my Father is heard — I undoubtedly behold the white sails of my Son — and, to complete our joy, see, dear daughter how gaily yonder streamers proclaim, that rosy health still braceth the nerves, of those we so much love — my enraptured spirit attends the burst of joy, and every faculty of my soul, demands an ample share — I listen, and the orders for the Carriage seem to vibrate upon my ear, our dear Anna, and the lovely stranger are conducted to the parental Mansion, there to receive a husband, and a Father, and all those undefined tendernesses, and those big emotions which virtuous love, and innocent affection may conceive, but never can delineate — all these are in [evidence] — I rejoice — most sincerely I rejoice — I write my felicitations, and I mingle the glad tears of honest joy — But ah! My dear Mother! Confined and pangful thy hours still arise — How must even this white moment, have been clouded, by the consideration that it was not in thy power to meet the returning foot steps of thy darling Boy, to hasten to enfold to thy maternal bosom, this youngest prop, which remains to thee, of all the late born smiling group, to prop thy wintry life — Much do I grieve, dearest and most tender of women, for thy accumulated infirmities — but alas! it is not in my power to relieve. I can only say, may God support thee, giving thy bosom sweet hope, and patient resignation — I think, my Love, your happiness must have been complete — your son, your youthful voyager, hath, I trust, answered all your wishes — He is a good Lad, and I both esteem, and love this nephew of mine — In what ever situation he may be placed — I doubt not he will do honour, both to himself and his family [—] I expect great amusement, from an account in his own manner, of the persons whom he has seen, and the things which he hath observed — I am told he expresses himself in high terms, of the various life of a seaman!! My kind brother, Fitz William, hath been so obliging as to write me a truly affectionate, and fraternal letter, for which my heart is grateful [—] I shall write to Sally by the earliest opportunity — My wishes for the dear Girl are replete with tenderness — For Mr Ellery I cherish a true, sisterly regard — give my love to him, remember me to all inquiring friends and believe me ever, most truly, most affectionately yours —

Letter 795 To my Father and Mother New London September 18th— 1790 Saturday Morning —

Missing her parents, fearful about her mother's health, Judith writes about her love for them and thanks her parents for their "studious solicitude to support, protect, and render tranquil the life [they] have bestowed." She hopes they all pass together into the next world, not wanting to live in this one without them.

Taking up her narration, Judith describes the journey to New London where she hears stories about the exorbitant taxes levied to pay for the Revolution. The man with whom they are staying has not seen his daughter in five years. Judith cannot imagine such a long separation from her own father. Reaching New London, they take up residence in the home of three widowed sisters, what Judith calls a "female retreat." Norwich reminds Judith of Gloucester, and she describes for her parents its buildings, harbor, and countryside. They meet more interesting people, including General and Lady Huntington, the Winthrop family, and the family of Roswell Saltonstall (1741-?), a descendent of Sir Richard Saltonstall who sailed to Boston in 1630 on the Arbella and helped found the "city upon a hill." Judith describes the impressive Saltonstall home, gardens, and modern kitchen. John's preaching was well received in Norwich.

Norwich, my ever honoured Parents, seems destined the scene of my enjoyments — It is true a cloud hung over me, upon my first approach, but it soon dispersed, and the kindly influence of the brightening sun, was but the more gratefully, and potently felt — In consequence of Mr Murray's attention to my wishes, he had written to Mr Carter of Providence, to forward to Norwich, any letters he might have for us — In Norwich therefore, I received a large Packet from my friends [—] In Norwich the letters of my dear, and tender father, reached my hand, and administered heartfelt consolation to my bosom — Can there be a more proper, or rational source of enjoyment, to a [daughter] who hath originated from a worthy, and respectable stock, than a consideration of the capability which is possessed, of contributing to the enjoyment of those parents, from whom existence is directed? To you Sir, to you Madam, under our common Father, I owe every thing that I am — yes dear, and most revered sources of my life — indulgent origin of a career, which, to the utmost of your power, you have assayed to bless — To you it is owing that I have a heart to beat, a hand to receive, or a tongue to acknowledge the multiplied blessings with which the God of Nature hath surrounded me — Ushered into the World by you, I am thus invested with claims to immortality — I esteem existence itself, as a rich, a very rich blessing, and the good which I have in reversion, swells my soul with all the sacred rapture of devotion — What, although the present life be environed with evil — My Redeemer meets me at the close, and unfading pleasures bloom in his presence — How great then are my obligations to you, dearest best of Men, dearest best of Women, Accept therefore worthy, and ever revered Pair, accept my hearts best thanks, for the being you have given, for your studious solicitude to support, protect, and render tranquil the life you have bestowed — Can I, as I said, experience from any affections, feelings more delightful, than those which expand my bosom, when I have proof positive, that I have beamed a ray of cheerfulness, over an hour, which would perhaps have otherwise passed heavily in that apartment which too often witnesseth the pangful scene [—] If the benign features of my Father confesseth, at any time, the smile of pleasure, at my exertions — if I can illume any of those melancholy moments, so painfully restorated by my dear, sorrowing Mother — If I can be thus blessed, the Searcher of all hearts, knoweth, I have never yet tasted a felicity, more unmixed, or which hath been more highly zested — An approving Father, an acknowledging and Eulogizing Mother — surely the plauds of heaven, can alone surpass the blessings thus bestowed — Such my ideas, you will, my dear Sir, judge of my sensations, as I trace that sweet complacence, which you so affectionately avow in your daughter — Approbating Parents — It is enough — and I proceed with animated, and augmenting pleasure — That I grieve for the continued suffering of my Mother, I need not repeat — Full many a sigh, full many a tearful, supplication, to the God of our lives, to the Preserver of Men, doth my sympathizing heart wing to heaven on her behalf — but, unerring wisdom is exact in its economy, and the elucidating morning, will produce an ecclarcessment, of every seeming event — I wonder if your lameness proceeds from the same cause of my [brother's] — Would it were in my power to shield you both, from every pang — I think the Nausea upon the stomach of my Mother, is abundantly more alarming than her swelled feet — For God's sake endeavour to guard that seat of life — Air, and Exercise — Let me beseech you to embrace to the utmost of your power, those salutary vehicles of health — Let me conjure you to consult some approved, experienced, and able physician — I shudder at the approach of a Catastrophe, which may be awfully near! — I cannot bear the idea of a separation, a final of separation, from my parents — I have no children to supply the void which will then remain in my bosom — May they be continued in the present state of existence, until I also bid adieu to mortality — nor is there any thing so very irrational in this wish — The daughter of their youth, our years are nearly the same — Well then, I will hope the best — I have already congratulated you upon the return of our dear Fitz William — His letter to me was a very high gratification — It was an unexpected favour, and my pleasurable feelings are proportionated to the value, which I annex to his fraternal love, I am happy that his passage, and his passengers proved so agreeable — yes indeed, my dear Sir — you will undoubtedly know me, and right glad am I and much doth my spirit rejoice, in the assurance, that my image is too deeply imprinted upon the bosom of my Father even to be effaced — My parents will never be forgetful of me, they will continue to regard how dutiful the claims of their first born — I expected that my visit at the President's, and the attendant circumstances, would please and I am right happy that my utmost views in this respect, are answered — you supposition, that I shall not be unduly [pleased with the] honour, and I proudly add — it does me also justice — I can dispense with the duty of your Anna Maria — If she will only give me love, I shall be content — If Mr— be really married it may be as well to hope the best — agreeable consequences sometimes result from connexions which boded nothing but confusion — A youth of folly, may produce a maturity of reflection, and of that ripened wisdom, which is the growth of experience — at least, I think the parties connected, should endeavour to calm, and to accommodate their minds, since, although they cannot recall, armed with patient discretion, it may be in their power to reclaim, to appease, and to meliorate — you will please make our united compliments to Doctor P— and to express our thanks for his obliging remembrance — And now, having marked the most prominent features of your condescending, and affectionate favours, I again take up my narration — My husband, as I observed in my last, was greatly indisposed, he continued alarmingly ill the whole of sunday Morning, but the prescriptions of Doctor Turner, were so remarkably efficatious, as to produce him in the pulpit in the afternoon — The scene was uncommonly affecting, but having tarried in Norwich but a short time, and being to return thither early in the ensuing week every occurrence relative to that place, I refer to the commited detail which my next letter will probably present — On Monday morning we commenced our journey to this City [—] the distance is no more than fourteen miles, but the road being exceedingly rough, although the day was fine, we did not receive a superabundance of pleasure from our drive — We dined at a halfway house at a small Inn, the master of which possesseth terra firma sufficient, with other conveniences of life, to induce a degree of inquietude, at the augmentation of of taxes — He apprised us that for the same property for which previous to the revolution, only a single dollar was demanded, he is now annually called upon for no less than forty good spanish rex dollars! a like testimony is found upon the lips of almost every free holder [—] But the whispers of discontent, are yet in embryo and for my own part I am free to confess a wish, that they may be crushed there, the exertions requisite to support a separate government, will doubtless encrease exactions, but the new married pair might as rationally regret, that they had not continued in the home of their parents, when family expenses accumulate, as the Denizen of a free state deplore, the era which witnessed their subjection — The Landlord was an old acquaintance of my husbands, and inquiries after his family were of course — He informed us he supposed he had five [grand]children, he was not however certain — his eldest daughter had married a foreigner — she had followed the fortune of her husband — five years since he had received a letter from her, and from that period he had been ignorant of her fate — This he said, and communicated with an attendance of indifference! My own father rose to my view — what would have been his feelings upon such an occasion? — reduced to the necessity of rendering a similar account, how would his quivering lip and faltering voice, have evinced the reality of his paternal affection — His revered image, as I said, stood confessed before me — Fancy in vivid colours presented his manly struggles — The starting tear he would fain suppress, he would preserve that equanimity for which he is so remarkable — but it is in vain — the humid drop will find its way, and with an inimitably affecting expression of resignation, he continues silently submissive, or introduces a subject foreign to the matter which agitates his soul — Forgive this whim of the moment, may you never be called to realize it — We reached New London about four in the afternoon and proceeded directly to that female retreat, which four years since, afforded us so agreeable an asylum — Two more sisters are added to the gentle band — It seems a kind of Nunnery in miniature and received with accustomed Friendship, we were once more domesticated in their hospitable Mansion —

They recounted to me, last evening, a circumstance which pleased me — you recollect their early predilection for the Moravian tenets, and, with the brethren of that persuasion, they have kept up a constant Correspondence — Fourteen years since, Mr Murray, after visiting Newport made his first appearance in New London — The brethren from the capital of Rhode Island, and elsewhere, immediately came forward, with their addresses to this family, The matter of which were thus expressed "Receive the Preacher, we charge thee — Receive him in love, Receive him, for although he be not within the pale of our Church his doctrines are truly evangelical and he is undoubtedly an ambassador of Christ["] — I think I have already observed to you, the resemblance which this City bears to my native Town — The harbour [—] the disposition of its grounds, its inequalities, its soil, its situation, prospects, and the roughness of its environs — The Episcopalian Church which had reared its head when we were last here, is now elegantly completed — The Court house too is finished, and the old Presbyterian place of worship, is exchanged for a handsome building of a light, and pleasing Order[,] neatly constructed, uniformly designed, and adorned with a pretty spire — It is seated upon an eminence, hath received the last hand, and is furnished with crimson curtains, and Cushions — Some addition to our partial favourers in this City, hath been produced by this visit — Mr Learned, a genteel Man, who is a widower, and, hath a promising young family growing up about him — A daughter of General Sage's of Middle Town, by the name of Hallum, we have also met here, and another daughter, by that of Saltonstall, and after I have said, that they apparently inherit the hospitable disposition, which so conspicuously distinguishes the Authors of their Being, it will be unnecessary to add, that we received from them the most pleasing civilities — Mr Roswell Saltonstall was before [us] in the number of our friends — He hath since we were last here, erected a neat Mansion house, the views from which are picturesque and pleasing — His dwelling is rather convenient, than superb[,] it is genteelly furnished, and an original painting done on wood of his celebrated ancestor Sir Richard Saltonstall attracts the eye of the curious — His kitchen will please every domestic female — He is accommodated with many conveniences, and the drawing of a plug conveys the water even into the boiler, or, wherever else it is wished, and when it becomes unfit for use, within doors, it is reconducted by canals in various directions where it answers valuable purposes — The garden is in beautiful taste, it abounds with every wholesome viand — an arbour is placed neatly in the Centre — and the pretty spot even at this season, is beautifully verdant, and exhibits a various growth of flowers [—] The arrangements of the knots, the Circles, the fanciful disposition of the odiferous Compartments, and the deep green borders, most enchantingly varied, are all the

Offspring of Miss Saltonstall's imagination — The young Lady is the eldest daughter of the family, she is truly amiable and ingenious — The plan of the parterre, is, as I said, from an original drawing of her own, and it does her no small honour — Mr & Mrs Saltonstall are very worthy characters, they have a numerous family of sons, and daughters, some of them have attained maturity [—] we had the pleasure of seeing them all collected together, and I declare I hardly know a more agreeable family. The Lady of General Huntington also — we deal in Generals you know — hath done me the honour to call upon me, but I believe she was rather induced to this visit by a desire to receive a particular account of Bethlehem, to which place she is sending her daughters for their education, we have past an afternoon agreeably at her house, she is a native of New York, and has in her manner, an apparent frankness which renders her a very pleasing Woman — The General is a good character, he served with reputation during the late War — He is now Collector for this Port and being the only Port of entry, appointed for the Connecticut River, his engagements are sufficiently multifarious, he, however, devoted an hour to us, and if it were allowable to make up a judgment, from the observations so short an interview, we should pronounce that General Hunting[ton] possesses a good understanding and a cultivated mind — There is some foundation for the fear, that the name of Winthrop, as a family, will be extinct in New London [—] One only Male of that name remains here, and he fast advancing into the Vale of Bachelorhood, evinces no violent desire, to try the comforts of matrimony — Mr Frank Winthrop, after beautifying the Mansion house, and giving to that family a situated seat, and air of magnificent elegance hath removed with his new married Lady, and family, to New York — We have accepted an invitation to tea with Madam Winthrop, and met at her Levee, some friends of the family — The meeting house doors have been open to Mr Murray — his Congregations have been large and respectable, and our visit, upon the whole, hath been hitherto agreeable — Tomorrow, and on Monday afternoon, divine service is again to be performed — We are likewise engaged to dine on board a Jamaica ship on Monday, and on tuesday we propose returning to Norwich — My heart beats with accustomed tenderness for my friends and I can never cease to be duteously, and affectionately your truly grateful daughter —

Letter 796 To Miss S. S. E. New London
September 18— 1790

Judith is pleased with her niece's recent letter, finding it a "pleasing specimen of [her] abilities." Judith admires her frankness, and encourages Sally's (Sarah Sargent Ellery) learning and letter writing which Judith considers a "desirable...genteel, and necessary accomplishment." Sally's brother, Jack, has returned safely from a voyage at sea and Judith is pleased. In this letter, we learn that neither John nor Judith was fond of large "suppers" — the evening meal. Instead, they preferred breakfast, dinner (the midday meal), tea, and a very light evening meal. They have spent the evening at the Saltonstall home where Judith enjoyed a lovely table setting and floral arrangement designed by Abigail Saltonstall, Roswell's oldest daughter. Judith describes the scene for Sally, knowing her fondness for flowers.

you need not blush, my Love, at being necessitated to acknowledge the assistance of your Mamma — It is, at your time of life, natural to receive aid, and information — The present season is your seed time, and it is now you are to constitute a fund, which ought daily to accumulate, and from which you may, in future draw an interest, sufficient for your mental support — In youth it is easy to require, but in the evening of life, it is most eligible to subsist upon the ripened fruits of early efforts. The experience of years is a treasury upon which the claims of young people, are founded in Nature, and in justice — Application, a course of application, must ever be essential to the attainment of any considerable degree of perfection, in any valuable accomplishment, and I should as soon censure you, for not having obtained your full growth, as for not being able to write as good a letter as your Mother — I pronounce that the pain which you experienced, in being necessitated to acknowledge the hand of your maternal auxiliary, proceeded from a reprehensible source, and, that after all, you are a little proud baggage — I beg your pardon, my sweet Girl — Looking over [your] charming favour a second time, in order to shape my responses, I discover that I had totally mistaken the complexion of the first paragraph — your chagrin proceeded not from the necessity of avowing the direction you had received, but from a supposition that a paragyrick had been bestowed, to which you were not entitled — Now indeed, the affair wears quite another face and I have to give you full credit for an innocent, an upright, and an uncommonly ingeneous Mind — These qualities, my lovely Girl, will do you abundantly more honour, than if you had produced a Volume, of the finest composition, which ever graced the annals of the belles lettres, and were destitute of these superior treasures — To the bosom of which Virtue is the Regent, there is indeed a most painful consciousness, as the voice of undue commendation vibrates upon the ear, and upon those occasions, the hue of sincerity will not fail to tinge the cheek of the Votary of truth — I admire you, my dear child, for your frankness — Praise, upon a Mind like yours, will produce a legitimate effect, and if it should not happen to be exactly just, it will operate as a stimulus to future efforts — your last letter is a pleasing specimen of your abilities, and practice will no doubt render you an elegant Proficient in this desirable, in this genteel, and necessary accomplishment — I thank you for your attention to my plants — for your information relative to Mr and Mrs P— , Miss P— and the lovely little stranger, and for your wishes for my return — you must be very happy in the restored society of your brother — he hath been absent just long enough to teach you the value of his presence, and fraternal tenderness — My wish is that no circumstance of your lives may ever, for a single moment, interrupt that affection, now mutually submitted between you — I am, my dear, solicitous to produce a letter worthy your acceptance — Let me pause — What shall I tell you — I have often thought that you have evinced the delicacy of your mind, by a pretty taste for flowers — Well then I will present you with a view of a petit souper which cannot fail of pleasing you — I take it for granted you read all my journals, I should be exceedingly mortified, could I believe you did not think them of sufficient consequence, for a very minute perusal — This point thus ascertained, it follows of course, that you are well acquainted with the names of Mr and Mrs Saltonstall of this City — But I must first premise that it is established among our connexions as an absolute fact, that neither Mr nor Mrs Murray are fond of suppers — but it is well known that we are delighted with the production of the flowery World — Mr Saltonstall is, you know, in possession of a most beautiful flower garden — We have passed this evening at his house — Mrs Saltonstall is unwell and of late generally confined to her room — We have chatted away some hours most agreeably — she hath a number of charming daughters who like yourself, are the sweet buds of expectation, and just opening into all the full blown ripened charms of Womanhood — about nine O clock one of the young Ladies entered — "you are fond of flowers Ma'am, will you gratify us by taking a view of a display of your favourites, in the parlour?" Certainly, my dear, and tripping across the Hall, we entered the adjourning supper room — The view which had been presented was indeed beautifully fanciful — A table was spread, bordered by neat covers. In the Centre was placed a handsome glass Vase, enchantingly decorated — asparagus foliage, exactly set, was the ground work and it was variegated by a number of the most beautiful, and rare flowers, which the Goddess Flora hath to bestow — Round this Vase was a Circle of glasses, of the most beautiful texture, half filled with preserved strawberries, which retained a surprising share of their natural form, and delicious flavour, heaped to the rim with rich cream — At the head of the table a plate of small [biscuits], prettily arranged, and decorated with flowers, at the bottom a honey comb, from the regular compartments of which, as if implanted by the hand of nature, the sweet pea blossom lifted its head — the sweet pea blossom, is a wild flower, which resembles the lily of the Valley, than which perhaps there is not a more delicate blow — a small species of the Chinese Astrea, was judiciously intermixed — One side presented damson Puffs, which were answered by Puffs composed of peach marmalade on the other — and these were also variously ornamented, by the odiferous productions of the parterre — the breaks were supplied by...strained honey, rasped cheese, and printed butter — the four corners produced the richest wines, and elegant candlesticks lighted by handsome wax tapers created an artificial day — Among the furniture of the sideboard, was a musk melon of exquisite flavours — you can have no idea of the beauty and elegance of the view — It seemed, altogether a repast fitted for a superior order of beings, and it was produced by the pretty taste of the eldest Flora, who graces the house of Saltonstall — When I recollected your attachment to flowers I breathed a fervid wish for your presence, but by reason of a little collection of groser particles which surrounds your heaven born Mind — and a large proportion which yet clogs the operations of my spirit, not being able to accomplish my wish, I have assayed to sketch for your mental eye this petit souper — Tell your honoured grand Parents that I am coming, and that I would it were in my power to chase from their beloved bosoms all sickness and sorrow — Give to your Father and Mother, and to your brother, my hearts love, and accept for yourself a large portion from your maternal Aunt —

Letter 797 To Anna New London September 20th 1790

Judith reprimands Anna (her young charge) for not writing, telling her she is "provoked" by the long silence. She is interested in everything Anna is doing and with whom she is visiting. She hopes Anna is "comporting" herself appropriately and, since she is now in Gloucester with Judith's parents, directs her to look after her mother. Judith and John are presently visiting Doctor Turner's family in New London.

you have acted like a good girl, with propriety and I, of course, am much disposed to approve of your conduct — your Aunt Sayward hath been very obliging, and I trust you have not been wanting in proper acknowledgements — I should be greatly mortified to find you subjecting yourself to the accusation of ingratitude, or even to the smallest deficiency, in a just sensibility of the favours conferred upon you — I am pleased that your conveyance in the stage proved so much to your satisfaction, but I am induced to wonder that you did not contrive to fill a page by sketching for me, the portraits of the good people who formed your party — Were I, my Girl, to let every circumstance pass so slightly off, how could I possibly answer the expectations which are formed of me? — you cannot say that I have not furnished you with examples as well as precept — Were it incumbent upon me to write a letter, and were I not furnished with any particular topic, I would arrest the first occurence which presented, and moulding it into the best possible form, I would render it as a testimony, that I had at least been studious to oblige, and if nothing more promising offered, if the resources of fancy were frigid, or exhausted — I would peruse the gardens, the meadows, the fields, and the Groves — a flower, a tree, and...post, should be pressed into my service, and dressing it up as an offering at the shrine of epistolary intercourse, I would come forward with my tribute, rather than I would remain indebted for copious epistles, answering the close filled sheet, by a few lines upon every small paper, with difficulty extended to the second page — Why, my dear you have passed many weeks abroad, you have no doubt met with a variety of persons — you know I take a great deal of interest in your York friends — particularly in your Uncle Lyman's family, and in that of Mr Barrell — you stopped of course at least for a night at Mrs Parker's in Portsmouth — To Mrs Parker, and those under her care, you know I am strongly attached — and not, strange to tell, like some dignified visitant from the World of spirits, you are as mute as silence — Waiting as [it] should seem, until by the Voice of interrogation your Ladyship's lips are unsealed — I declare, in the sincerity of my heart I am sufficiently provoked with you — nay it is absolutely fact — to wish you at this moment seated in the vacant chair just beside me, when I would take my revenge, by pouring upon you, such a redundancy of questions, as would puzzle even the tongue of lognacity to shape its answers, but, distant as you are, you are perfectly safe, and I am to believe you will continue quite inattentive to my solicitude respecting your journey, leaving me to range in the wilds of conjecture for every occurrence, which might, or might not have taken place — Hath it never been suggested to you, that you are a little impolite in your plan — imagination permitted so wide a field without the smallest clue for its guide, how are you certain what spectres it may conjure up?

For example, suppose I should take it into my head to believe you have formed improper connexions — that you will not so far debase yourself, as to render an account, which will not correspond with truth, and that as you have nothing pleasing to relate, you are resolved to preserve an obstinate to eternity! — or — but why should I enumerate — a thousand suspicions may arise, and your ill judged reserve, may furnish a pretense for them all — It is true I have learned from second, or third hand, that your common tea parties have consisted of no less than fifteen beans, and as many belles — but what of this — it only serves to confirm my apprehensions — But seriously, your subjects my dear must have been copious, and you have not acquitted yourself, quite like yourself, exactly as I could wish, in not preserving for me at least the outlines of your little tour — yet, it is no matter if your time hath been filled up more advantageously, than in cultivating that epistolary talent, which I am confident you possess [—] I shall not, in reality, or with any great degree of censure, complain — The manner in which you speak of my letters, is very pleasing — I am happy if they amuse my friends, and that you, with the rest of my connexions, are waiting with impatience for our return — Were those I love, indifferent in this respect — Gloucester should be the last place which I would approach [—] I trust, my dear child, you will study to please those with whom you at present abide — especially my Mother — Right glad shall I be if you can render yourself of consequence to her — Her accumulated infirmities, ought to insure her marked attention, she hath a right to the most uniform observance, and a good, and susceptible mind, will become interested to execute if possible, her every wish — There is a kind of independence, which a useful individual may always command, and the reflection is pleasing, which assures that we in some measure yield an equivalent for the benefits we receive — I am fearful, that as our journey has been so unexpectedly protracted, you may have been subjected to some...pecuniary wants — Should this be the case, my Mother will have the goodness to supply you, and when we come, we will gratefully repay her — We have only just looked in upon the Norwichers — but we are to return thither again — The same regularity and uniform benevolence are still conspicuous in the family of Doctor Turner [—] The Girls, it is true, have attained a maturity of loveliness — Miss Lucy is on the point of marriage with a young gentleman of great hopes, who hath been trained to knowledge, under the benign auspices of her worthy Father — Nancy hath attained to Womanhood, and her every charm is sweetly meliorated, Eliza is absent on a trip to Boston, and Sophia is just what Nancy was when we were last here — The eldest son of the family hath been some time married to a beautiful Woman, whose sweet, and amiable disposition, augments the general felicity and Pitt still enjoys himself in his own way — They were all affectionately obliging in their inquiries after you — and they regretted much, especially the Girls, that you did not accompany us —

The change in the family we are at present with, is rather more striking — Mr Tabor hath left it — He hath commenced a sober married

Man, and the woman of his heart, as I am told possesses much merit —
Two sisters, and a Niece, have joined the female Circle — but the
cheerful vivacity, which once triumphed here, is now fled! Repeated
Misfortunes hath banished it — and the laugh of pleasure, by which
these worthy people were distinguished, hath given place to the gentle
smile of resignation [—] The Circle of our acquaintance in this City is
augmenting — I have passed a singular afternoon, nine young Ladies,
and not a single presiding Matron — yet I assure you the Girls did not
appear unhappy — I wish you, my dear, to take the first opportunity of
calling upon Mr E. Sargent, presenting our united regards, To every
individual of that interesting, and amiable family — Wait also upon my
Aunt Allen, with our respectful, and tender remembrance to her, and
hers — I have written to Mary — but have received no answer —
Accept, my Love, our united and parental regards — and believe us
ever your guardian Friends —

Note to Miss Abby Saltonstall
Morning of the 21 of September 1790 New London

*An avowed "admirer of Nature," Judith is delighted with the "flower
knot" Abigail Saltonstall has painted for her and thanks her in this
very affectionate letter. Judith calls herself "Constantia," one of the
pen names she used when publishing her poetry and essays. Occasionally, with intimate friends, Judith used this name in her letters as well.*

Constantia breaths for the pensive Flowerist, the warmest
wishes, her heart is truly grateful — The flower knot is elegant, and
beautiful — It is more, abundantly more, than a representation —
The whole charming view seems in sweet and vivid colouring to stand
confest, and while Constantia continues an admirer of Nature, or has
power to trace the pleasing efforts of fancy, the lovely Abby, and her
very ingenious essay will produce in her bosom the most glowing
sensations. Miss Custus would deem herself honoured by a comparison
— To the aspiring Fair, the various walks of Genious are alike open,
and from a laudable competition the highest finishing may result —
Miss Saltonstall possess the esteem, and tender regards of
Constantia, and the sweet sensibilities of the lovely Mourner, thus early
existed, hath extorted from her sympathetic bosom, the regretting sigh
— Constantia, and her Companion, feel themselves enriched by
Miss Saltonstall's endearing wishes, and they will supplicate Heaven,
that the charming Fair, may possess whatever eligibles life can bestow
— Whatever may place the wreath of propriety upon her brow, whatever
may give sweet Discretion to her bosom, thus insuring that consequent

fame, most honourable, most ornamental, most dear to female pretensions — In one word — Well knowing that her rectified arrangements may be trusted, they will solicit for the lovely Abby the completion of her fondest wishes

Letter 798 to Miss Eliza Saltonstall New London Morning of the 21 of September 1790

Judith did not have time to bid "adieu" in person to young Eliza (Elizabeth), but she does so in writing, with great affection. Eliza's mother is about to give birth, and Judith wishes them well. Eliza became a regular correspondent of Judith's, and in 1798 became an early subscriber to Judith's book, The Gleaner.

Thank you, my sweet Eliza your well written and charming billet seems to breathe the very spirit of Sterne — It possesseth all the delicacy and painstaking softness, which attended the feelings, and meliorated the page of the factious Bard, after he had enwreathed a garland for the Eastern Fair — yes, for me also the pretty floweret shall blow, I will assay to initiate the parterre of my Eliza, and the opening blossom, embosoming ten thousand sweets, and advancing forward to ripening perfection, shall stand to my admiring eyes, emblematic of the intrinsic charm, and decent form of the lovely maiden, from whom I consider myself as deriving so rational, and elegant a gratification — I had intended calling upon you this morning but when my heart is affected my tongue never utters the trembling Adieu, but my bosom acknowledgeth a Correspondent pang — My charming young Friend, will excuse me, and presenting my respectful regards to her amiable family, which will ever be imaged with the most pleasing remembrances in my bosom, she will have the goodness to accept for their united felicity, my very sincerest wishes — May your dear Mamma, rising superior to her approaching pangs, soon present to her human blossoms a sweet addition, and may every circumstance augment the pleasures of the charming group, I flatter myself that some individuals of the little Circle will not fail to remember with complacency, their affectionately admiring friend

Letter 799 To my Father and Mother Norwich
September 25th 1790

Judith is very ill, and fortunate to be staying in the home of Doctor Turner. Before reaching Norwich, Judith tells her parents that John was requested to preach in Groton. Later, they visited a British owned ship, the Hebe, *that was part of "the Jamaica trade," and Judith describes its cabin where they dined "luxuriantly." The road to Norwich was "extremely rough." Along the way, they passed through "an indian town" before reaching their present destination. In Norwich, they met William Pitt whose dedication to scripture and publishing Judith found noble.*

Since I last wrote I have, my dear Parents, been much indisposed — My confinement however hath not been long — yet I am fearful that a degree of remaining weakness may retard, beyond my wishes, my return to friends, whom my tedious separation, hath served still more to endear to my heart — It hath been happy for me that my illness hath taken place in this family — Under the humane, and experienced Doctor Turner — Happy had I never known a less skillful Physician — To the tender attention of Doctor Turner, with the care of his amiable Lady, under the benign Author of every good, I may impute my speedy and complete restoration, and I still hope that the last of October may yield me once more to your embraces — Did I tell you in my last letter, that in compliance with the request of a number of the inhabitants of this town of Grotton, Mr Murray passed the Thames River and delivered to them a sermon in their house of Worship? Monday last, agreeably to expectation, produced us on board the Goddess of youth, or in other words, the good ship Hebe — Captain Corse Commander — where we may be said to have partook the feast in the British dominions, or at least we were entertained under the auspices of the British standard — The ship is english property, in the Jamaica trade, and of three hundred tours burden — the cabin is elegant, handsomely painted, and ornamented with glasses and pictures — It is roomy and neatly furnished — A handsome brass stove, finely polished, China in the genteelest taste — Plate etc etc [—] The ship was moored along side the quay [—] a select party of Ladies were bidden, and, placed in an elbow chair, decently enfolded in english streamers, up the steep sides of the Hebe, we made our aerial ascent — The manners of Captain Corse, are descriptive of every pleasing trait, which can adorn the son of Neptune, his table was liberally spread — a rich turtle, or tortoise, deliciously prepared, made the first course, a large round of beef, which would have done honour to a real Albion feast succeeded, which was followed by roasted partridges, chickens, fish and vegetables of many kinds — Pickles in their varieties, among which you will not doubt that I did ample justice, to the large english wall nut, which was served up in high perfection and great abundance — The desert consisted of pears, excellent rare ripes, and musk melons [—] Wines of the first quality, punch, and Lemonade, were generously urged upon me, and every exertion to please, was evidently the result of genuine politeness — Our party, as I said, was select — It consisted of the Millar and Saltonstall families — and while on board the Hebe, I was introduced to Mrs Tillar — the Lady who is familiar to you by the name of Polly Millar the prospect there once was, of her taking the name of Sargent, and the near connexion with her, which we were taught to expect, naturally induced an interest in her person, and manners [—] she is rather pretty and her deportment is easy, and engaging — she is advantageously married, and hath marriageable daughters — We dined, as you will suppose, luxuriantly — chatted most agreeably, and descended from our exaltation, in the same balloon like manner, in which we had made our ascent — At four in the afternoon Mr Murray preached his farewell sermon, the whole party attended, and we afterwards took a cup of tea with a Mrs Millar, a pleasing Woman, at whose house I had the good fortune to see, and to make my respectful compliments to that ancient Maiden Lady, Mrs Anna Winthrop — The evening presented me with elegant billets, and flower pieces, from the Miss Saltonstalls, and on tuesday morning we quitted the New Londoners taking a peep on our way at Hallum's elegant little Villa, and garden [—] The road from New London to this place, is, as I have heretofore observed, intensely rough — In a few little spots Nature has assayed to beautify, but it is generally frigid, and inhospitable — The Indians possess, in the state of Connecticut, a large tract of land, which, according to laws still extant they can not alienate — We passed through an indian town, which makes a part of this appropriate ground and every object seemed to mark the continued ferocity of its Possessors — About two miles from town, we were met by Doctor Turner, and his Lady, who are in every instance polite, in every instance attentive — My indisposition hath since nearly filled my mind — but, as I said I am recovering — Let not the fears of my beloved Mother exaggerate — I have made the matter neither better, nor worse — I have ever thought it best to hold fast my veracity, and in the present instance whatever reports may reach your ears, let my sincerity bannish apprehension — More than a score of engagements are now upon my list, to which the ensuing week will enable me to pay proper attention — since we visited this family in 1786, a valuable addition hath been made to its domestic happiness — Doctor John Turner is united in marriage to a female of the family of Huntington, a young Lady whose form, and features are nearly faultless — she is beautiful as youth, and charming as innocence, and the little

India Marionet, to whom she hath given birth, in the pride and joy of this whole interesting family — Mr William Pitt hath recently, for so young a gentleman, taken a very uncommon turn [—] From accustoming himself to a very large range of reading he hath, for many months read no other book than the bible declaring all other writings totally unworthy his attention — Mistake me not, he is not seized with a religious melancholy, he is as [charming] and agreeable as conscious integrity can render him — He devotes whole nights to the study of the sacred Volume — Many excellent manuscripts predicated from that book, he hath already produced, and the probability is, he will one day commence a promulgator of the glad tidings of redemption — By the way, there is a Mr John Sargent now in America, a native of the United States, who was an established minister of great reputation in the presbyterian line, who hath some years since embraced the Rellyan plan, and is become an able Writer, and Preacher in its defense — He is, I am told, zealously engaged — powerful as an advocate, and an unwearied Labourer in the ministry of reconciliation — The tidings of this supposed error, reaching an aged Father, who although residing at a great distance sat out — with much grief, and real sincerity, to reclaim a beloved Wanderer —

Letter 800 To the same Norwich
Sunday morning of the 26 of September 1790

Her mother was well enough to write, and Judith is greatly relieved. Her father, too, is better and well enough to travel to Boston where Judith will meet him the following month. Her health is returning, Judith tells them, and she is off to church to hear John preach.

Of one more letter from my honoured Father, I was, half an hour since, put in possession and my heart again acknowledges, the pleasing glow of duteous gratitude — I am happy that my letters have reached my beloved Mother, and right happy that she was able with her own dear hand, to write you that she had received them — The line which informed me that her feelings, and the state of her health, allowed her to hold a pen, hath given me sensible pleasure, and my whole soul blesseth the revered hand, which transmitted a piece of intelligence so importantly interesting — I rejoice also, that your disposition, had so far yielded, as to admit of your Boston tour — To hear of the well Being of my honoured, and indulgent parents, will always communicate to my bosom, the sincerest joy — Much do I wish it were in my power, to accelerate the period of my return, but, from a combination of circumstances, I am fearful it will be impossible — Pray Heaven Fitz William may not have commenced his voyage — such an event will indeed be a great alloy to my promised pleasures, it will render me essentially unhappy, and it is necessary I persuade myself, that his arrangements, if for so early a departure, will be retarded — you will please to give unto him, and his charming Wife, my heart's love [—] I repeat that I am impatient to behold their little Girl, and I am sure, when she is within my grasp, I shall embrace her in the arms of true affection [—] My brother and sister Ellery, with their son and daughter, I also remember with accustomed tenderness — I have repeatedly written to many of my friends, and I trust my letters have come safe to hand — This twenty sixth of September is a fine day, I enjoy it most charmingly — Health is returning, and I am very much disposed to reiterate to my Father, and Mother, effusions of obligation to them, for my mortal existence...and most of all to the high Creating Power, who formed my Being, and breathed into my bosom the dignifying, and brightening hope of a happy immortality — Farewell my Friends — I go to join the assembling multitude — The Bell this moment summons me away — From a heart glowing with devotion to Nature's God — I shall offer up my glad orisons — I shall ascend with sacred joy, to His holy word and well as I can, I shall attempt to hymn the praises of Religious...Love —

Letter 801 To the Same Norwich October 2d — 1790 Saturday Morning

Judith has sent a packet of letters by sea which she regrets, given the likelihood of their becoming lost. She and John are doing their best to fulfill the increasing number of social obligations, and John has preached in Chelsea, Preston, and Lisbon. Judith is intrigued with a kind of floor matting she has seen only in Norwich. She is equally impressed with the flower arrangements and needlework of the "Norwich females." In Norwich, she finds more evidence of the "equality" so prevalent in Connecticut. Since America was founded on the natural and inalienable rights of Mankind, she writes, "I confess the rationality and consistency" of practiced republicanism.

It is storied of a celebrated Ancient, that when on his death bed, a review of the whole course of his life, presented him with only two circumstances, which, at that period, gave him the smallest regret, and one of those, I remember, was that he had made a journey by water when he might with equal convenience, and much greater eligibility, have performed it by land — Without the most distant idea of emulating this fortunate Worthy, I declare I am at this moment really suffering, in consequence of committing a very large packet to the conveyance of the winds, than which at this season, nothing can be more precarious

[—] when a single hour after I had thus imprudently relinquished my papers, the most respectable safe, and expeditious opportunity presented — Entrusting them to the care of the British Consul, the gentleman who took passage from London with my brother, and who hath passed through this good City of Norwich on his way to Boston [—] Committing them [as] I say to the Consul — lodged in his Portmanteau, a fleet pair of post horses would have transported them, with all speed, over terra firma, and a few days would have deposited them safe in the custody of the several very dear, and honoured friends, for whom they are designed — But now, alas! they are literally embarked upon a Cruise — Capes are to be doubled, a coast wise direction is to be pursued — the danger of the wide Ocean is to be tempted — they are to be borne upon the bosom of the fluctuating waves, and a thousand accidents may retard — while my anxious Connexions, are subjected to all the unpleasant sensations, which grow out of suspense [—] a whole week hath elapsed since the commencement of their voyage, during which period, their course hath been constantly impeded by adverse winds! — But I will hope that in pity to my feelings, Polses will manifest enough of the gallant, and real fine gentlemen, to harness a pair of his best steads, who can skillfully trace the several windings, and turnings bending the obsequious gale, and taking advantage of every breeze, to accelerate the passage — I had not the pleasure of seeing either the Count, or his Lady, Mr Murray met them accidentally on their return from New York, they were just entering the stage coach, and, on the wing for Boston — Well our week in this hospitable City, hath been passed in evincing our sensibility of the favours which we have received — Time will not allow of our discharging every obligation but we make the most of every day, and my state of convalescence allowing me to economize, I am industriously assiduous in my arrangements, exactly appropriating every hour and answering, according to my ability, demands which accumulate upon me — The most pleasing exertions are made to oblige — dining, tea drinking, and suppers — every one is solicitous to take a part — and riding, and walking variegate our pleasures — Activities, by an easy ascent, we have mounted tracing from their airy summits the most beautifully extensive prospects — To give a list of our Norwich friends is unnecessary — to letters heretofore written we must refer you, and I have only to add, that neither their numbers nor affectionate regards, are diminished — Mr Murray, agreeably to earnest solicitations hath repeatedly visited Chelsea, Preston and Lisbon, in each of which places, he hath laboured to convince the people of their interest in the Redeemer — Light seems brightening with more than its accustomed brilliancy and the christianized mind, will rejoice in its lustre — If my observations on the people of Norwich are just, they are frugal[,] industrious, and persevering — The houses in general are decent, and

entering a dwelling, everything is more than answerable to its exterior
— One piece of economy is perfectly new to me, the floors of the
Norwichers, are in many instances, carpeted by a cloath, the warp of
which is composed of the coarse hair of Cattle — This hair is mixed
with a small proportion of tow, just sufficient to procure a Consistence,
when being carded, spun and died, it is crosed by a woof of shreds, of
various quality and hue, and it furnished, I do assure you, a very durable
and tolerable covering — Norwich is the residence of many genteel
families — The Mansion house of the former Governor of this State is
in this City, and it was until recently the abode of General Huntington
— I have already expatiated upon the hospitality of the inhabitants of
Norwich, and, if our repeated experience be allowed to decide, we can
hardly appreciate it too highly — speaking of hospitality, I am reminded
of the many eulogies, which I have heard pronounced upon the
Metropolis of our Native State — Boston is famed in every Town which
we have visited, for possessing in a superior degree, a Virtue, which is to
strangers most pleasant — most important — I believe the panegyric to
be in a great measure just — I have heard it pronounced with conscious
pleasure, and my wishes, and my partiality, would render hospitality a
trail, which I should conspicuously adorn the character of every son,
and daughter of Massachusetts. This Town, like every other place in
Connecticut, to which our observation hath extended preserves among
its inhabitants, a great share of equality — The Lady of Governor
Huntington is visited by, and visits in her turn, the spruce Wife of the
decent mechanic — The best, and mildest effects of genuine
republicanism, seem prevalent in this State — Doctors, Lawyers,
Ministers, Officers of Government, Merchants, and handicraftsmen of
every description associate familiarly — The Tailor takes his seat at the
same board with the gentleman, whose person he hath contributed to
ornament, and the hatter, and shoe maker, after having accommodated
the head and foot of the Minister whom he venerates, unite hands in
amity and partake with him the feast, invidious distinctions are
unknown, and the only means by which a housekeper in Norwich, can
forfeit his right to the best company, is by an irregular or reprehensible
conduct — I confess the rationality and consistency of such regulations
— it is highly proper and truly descriptive of that liberality, and equality,
which America boasts, and it must I think be eternally true, that in a
government founded in a genuine knowledge of the natural and
unalienable rights of Mankind, merit will, and ought, unquestionably
to be regarded as the only road to preferment — The Ladies in Norwich,
like those In New Haven, are great admirers of the flowery World, not
satisfied with the blossoming Parterre, or handsomely adorned Chimney,
the various blow, in many a fanciful direction is trained along the
wainscot, perfumes the toilet, encircles the looking glass, and flourishes

upon almost every table — The taste which the Norwich females evince for Needle work is truly exquisite — their beautifully wrought muslins, would do honour to the Bethlehem scholar, and it is rare to meet with a Lady, who is not furnished with some elegant specimen of her ingenuity in this line — upon the musical abilities of the Norwich Choir[,] especially bands consecrated [to] public worship, I leave Mr Murray to descant — his ear is attuned to the softest sounds and the fine voices, and correct judgment of the performers, particularly by the female part, are to him truly captivating — Norwich is the native place of the Rev. Mr Lathrop, and many branches of his family, living in the genteelest style, now reside here — To the Universalism which it is supposed that gentleman hath embraced, they are however generally opposed which circumstance is I am told a considerable drawback upon the pleasures which his occasional visits, would otherwise produce — We expect to quit this place in the course of the coming week, my next letter will, as I trust, be written in Providence — May God forever bless the Circle of my friends, and may they continue to remember me with pleasure ———

ON TO RHODE ISLAND, THE NEWEST STATE

Letter 802 To Mrs Sargent Providence State o[f] Rhode Island October 9— 1790

Judith expects to arrive at the home of her aunt, Mary Turner Sargent, and uncle, Daniel Sargent, on Long Wharf, Boston by the 21st of October. Since they are so close to home, this letter is largely conversational, responding to news of family and friends, discussing how much she appreciates good writing, and that she is afraid of large gray spiders!

At length we are thus on our way, and if our unexpected detention, by over fatiguing, hath not abated that flattering impatience, for our return, which my sweet friend hath so obligingly expressed, she may now indeed number the days which yet remain, with a degree of precision which to a mind accurate, as that which irradicates her charming bosom, cannot fail of yielding a degree of pleasure — The 21st of this month, should no unforeseen accident intervene, and if the weather upon that day, should prove propitious, will produce once more, in the parlour of Amity perhaps at early tea time, one whose heart is so deeply impressed with your charming image, and who is so accustomed to admire you, that were it necessary, she honestly declares, she would apply to your virtues the microscopic eye, while your faults, if you had any, she would regard as specks in some gently beaming luminary, which were calculated to enhance the lustre of surrounding beauties — Last evening we arrived here — a few moments after your charming favours of the 13 and 21d altimo were put into my hand — by the way both these dates were on one sheet, and only one letter was sent on to Norwich — yet previous to forwarding these last dates, you supposed you must have two, if not three packets, lodged with Mr Carter — I trust I have not lost any of your pleasing favours; I have been careful to acknowledge the receipt, and to note the contents of every letter which hath reached me — your eulogy upon the Quill is excellent — I would have it recorded in letters of gold — yes, writing is indeed a substitute of mighty potency, and, although there are sensations which will not submit to delineation — although its own most comprehensive characters, can never fully reach its value, yet will my bosom never forget to do homage to its worth[,] to render high tribute to its elevated powers — I cannot, my lovely friend, say from whence the idea of fortunate, and unfortunate days originated, but I rejoice that the hitherto ill omened Friday hath proved a white era — whither can I account for the absurdity which connecteth with certain insects, the character of auspicious, while it rendereth others dreadfully portentous; but is I believe, that the influence of such whimsical fancies, obtaining in the yielding infantile mind, often tyrannizes over riper years — I declare that to this hour the large gray spider, independent of its uncomely appearance, merely from an apprehension of the ill fortune which it is said to prognosticate, chills my spirit, while by a small black spider, I am mightily exhilarated, and the meeting a bumble Bee, in my walks, or more especially if said Bee, before I am aware, finds its way into the window of my apartment — the seeing a new Moon over my right shoulder — with too many etceteras to be enumerated, most ridiculously soothe, and harmonize my Mind — Now I charge you, by the fealty which, at the shrine of friendship, we have mutually vowed, that you expose not this my weakness, for in the opinion of many, it would unquestionably entirely ruin me, and I know a certain very nice Lady, of our acquaintance, who upon a knowledge of the above declaration, would find her pericranium, and the whole concavity which it contains, seeking a resting place upon her bosom, and suddenly admiring the beauties of your Carpet — the thumb, and fore finger of her right hand, placed upon her forehead, and violently pressed there, would scarcely conceal the significantly closed lips, which she would sagely forbear to open — the probability is I might never regain her good opinion, and what consequences would result from such a deprivation, I have yet to determine — I do not pretend to account for, nor to defend these preposterous whimsicalities, I have only related a fact, which in the face of better judgment, and radical conviction, hath occasionally obtained in my bosom — and should a confession so derogating to my understanding, by any means transpire, I have only to shield myself under the banners of the...inquiring Greeks, and Romans — But, to be serious, I think any day, which presented your daughter elect, must have been esteemed fortunate — she is indeed a worthy Girl, and will no doubt greatly augment your domestic pleasures — I am much obliged by her remembrances, and by the kind inquiries of her admiring swain — The particulars you have transmitted from Gloucester, are highly pleasing, and your attention in this respect, is truly characteristic — But there are two sweet Cherubs, whom you have left out in the letter before me — The individual characters, which compose their names, figure so gracefully when arranged by your fair hand, as to forbid my receiving any other combination, as an equivalent — Give, however, unto the sweet fellows, my heart's love, they do indeed possess my very tender affection — I had a presentiment that various, as hath been your life, and often as your heart hath been lacerated, the command of the benign Father of your spirit, could not but strike you with imposing power — No doubt, said my objecting bosom, this command hath repeatedly vibrated upon her ear — but introduced, and disposed, as it was by Mr Hubbard, I believed you might experience sensations corresponding with those which as I listened to the humane speaker, calmed the surface of my own bosom — I obeyed the impulse of the moment, and the event hath met my wishes — you know my dear there are no Episcopalians in Gloucester, and that almost the whole of my life hath been passed in that Town — Once or twice only when in Boston — Curiosity hath produced us in an Episcopalian Church — When you recollect these circumstances, they will account for my not having, until lately, in New Haven, an opportunity of attending the Episcopalian celebration of the rites of baptism — How many generous actions would four thousand a year, put it into your power, and mine to perform, and yet this extravagant Blade, found it insufficient for his exigencies, upon the Albion shore — How strangely unconscionable some people are — No wonder thus Companioned, that his royal Master found it necessary to take out a state of Bankruptcy — Well — Let him pass, the World is wide enough for him, and me, and I only take leave to breathe a prayr, that the American Career, of this doughty Hero, may arrest no step of innocence — May swell no Virgin heart, with the corroding sigh of deep felt regret — Our pleasures at Wallingford were the[re] indeed mutual — O! The sweet Cement of connecting Minds [—] O! the inessable pleasures resulting from congeniality — How often have I too, like my susceptible friend, placed the well known garment in full view, while my imagination like that of Shakespeare's Countess, hath spread the folds, swelled every plait, filled each void, and almost given to the Vestment, the individual person, or the friend for whom my tears have copiously flowed — Our beloved Girl hath determined according to her accustomed discretion, and, influenced by her example, all observation upon the manner, and matter of her letter, shall be referred to some retired hour, when sequestered from the World, and sitting beside us, in the social parlour, she shall freely unbosom herself — Then, chatting unrestrainedly, we can compare, conjecture, and aim at just conclusions — I have lately written you, if I remember well, rather copiously — But as my packet was committed to the precarious winds — it is possible they may not have wafted to you — I was going to request you would write to me if it came to hand, but as we expect to leave Providence on thursday next, your answer would not reach us here — should any of your favours come to hand, after our departure — We shall request Mr Carter to forward them to Boston — We wish proper regards to every friend — Mr Murray unites in tender remembrances — If Maria is still with you, we hope she will accept our regards [—] To the children we breathe a kiss of soft affection — Adieu — your image can never be erased from my heart —

Letter 803 To my Father and Mother State of Rhode Island Providence October 9— 1790 Saturday

Judith apologizes for their continued delay in returning, but the "strong cords of duty" compel John to respond. Judith gives her parents an example of the kind of entreaty he received throughout their journey — a letter from the citizens of Preston, Connecticut, requesting the presence of "one of the greatest...instruments which God...hath been pleased to send forth." The "Church doors are thrown open" everywhere for John, and the "crouds daily increase." Along with preaching, she writes, John has worked hard to build a sense of common purpose and cooperation among Universalist societies. On October 6, Judith and John celebrated their second wedding anniversary. That same day they attended a "regimental review" of the Norwich troops. Making their tearful goodbyes to the Turner family, they proceeded up the "rough and unpleasing" road to Volenton and then to Providence. Along the way, their trunk was lost and they found themselves in Providence, in heavy rains, without a change of clothing!

Immediately upon reaching this Place, last evening, Mr Murray set forward to the Post office — It produced us one letter from my honoured Father, one from Mrs Sargent, and a third from Anna — for all of which we are, as is rational to suppose, very grateful — I am happy that my friends enjoy the[ir] accustomed share of health, and right happy, that my beloved Parents, are still, by the Preserver of Men, supported in that state of being, in which they can assure me of their continued tenderness, and unabating affection — the healing hand and all gracious, all commanding fiat, which rebuked the indisposition of my only not worshiped Father, my full soul penetrated by a high sense of Almighty goodness, must devoutly bless and, if I might be allowed to hope, the infirmities of my Mother, were in any degree lessened, the joy which grows in my bosom, would be immeasurable — you wonder at my delay — but you do not witness the arrangements and obligations, which throw around us the strong cords of duty — Alas! the conflict is truly severe, when inclination from whatever source, is compelled to combat the decision of rectitude — Were you a spectator of the supplicating thousands, who arrest our steps, you would rather be induced to an expression of surprise, that we have made such dispatch — One petition I copy verbatim as a specimen of the rest —

"West Society Preston September 17— 1790
"Rev. Sir
"We the Subscribers — Inhabitants of the Town of Preston, beg leave to embrace the opportunity with which Heaven hath been pleased to favour us, of testifying our respect, esteem, and veneration, for a person whom we consider as one of the greatest, and most happy instruments which God in his mercy hath been pleased to send forth, to explain, and unfold the sacred mysteries of the blessed gospel. We beg leave, Sir, to congratulate you upon the present flourishing state of the Universalist Church, in this rising Empire, firmly believing that happy period to be fast advancing, when the knowledge of the Lord, shall cover the Earth as the waters do the sea, when Jesus shall see of the travail of His soul and be satisfied — If Sir, your health (which may Heaven restore) will permit you, and you can otherwise make it convenient, to visit this place, we shall consider it as a fresh instance of that condescension, which forms so amiable a part of your character _ Although but very few of us, have ever had the pleasure of your acquaintance, yet we presume you will bend an ear to our united entreaties, and accept our respect for one, whom God hath so greatly honoured — We are, Reverend Sir, your great Admirers etc etc"

This request was signed by a large proportion of the most respectable inhabitants of the Town of Preston, and it is but a faint sketch of the pressing solicitations which are verbally presented. Inquiries proceed from every quarter, and shall an Ambassador of the

Prince of Heaven, refuse to deliver his message? The Church doors are thrown open in every Town, and Village through which we pass — Multitudes flock to hear, and the crouds daily encrease — Our Norwich visit ended, as it began, and we received every testimony of Friendship — Wednesday was our last day in that pleasing recess, of social enjoyments — It was the sixth of October, and the anniversary, the second anniversary of our wedding day — It was devoted to the family of Doctor Turner — it was marked by friendship, and celebrated by festal joy — Mrs Turner obligingly summoned various branches of her family, her children particularly, all except her Eliza, were present upon this occasion — Miss Eliza is absent on a visit to her friends in Boston, and I flatter myself that she will accompany us to Gloucester, and pass with us the coming winter — Wednesday too was distinguished in a public line by the Norwichers [—] It was appointed by authority for a regimental review, and the several companies when paraded upon the Green made, I do assure you, a very respectable, and regular appearance — the numbers were surprising, and they performed the several evolutions, to universal acceptance — The officers were in a genteel uniform of blue, faced with red — hats etc en militare — The soldiers were distinguished by a neat white rifle pack, handsomely fringed, and hats adorned with red feathers, as they stood in long ranks upon a beautiful Green, their snow white garments formed a contrast, which produced a prodigious fine effect — They appeared a set of brave fellows, tall and well made, and the probability is that many a female heart blessed them — the musick was martial and animating, and its powers were no doubt fully confest [—] The Governor and his suite, honoured the day, by presenting themselves upon elegant horses finely caparisoned, and the whole was concluded by a convivial entertainment — The evening crouded the parlours of Doctor Turner with males and females, anxious to breathe their affectionately respectful adieus — Mr Murray, as I heretofore informed you, has been labouring to accommodate, the different sentiments, which have obtruded among the Professors of universalism — To unite them in one common, and glorious Cause, hath been the wish of his soul — but, although they requested and with much affection accepted, his interposition, although they venerate in a high degree his judgment, yet it is to be regretted, that his success has by no means been proportioned to the integrity of his heart, to his unwearied endeavours, or to the warm expectations which have perhaps been too sanguine — To be over solicitous is undoubtedly wrong, for that God who formed the Creature Man, and breathed into him the breath of life, must, unquestionably be affectionately disposed toward the work of His hands; and possessing unerring wisdom, His economy can never be deficient —

Thursday morning opened a scene truly affecting — I forbear to describe it — To the feelings which it agitated language can never do justice, and, my efforts in this line perpetually mock my wishes — yes, the streaming eye, the wavering hand, with every mournfully expressive movement, which are familiar to sincere affection, as they illude the pencil of the Painter, so, disdaining to submit to the most energetic efforts of words, their fine spirit evaporates, when, by the help of characters, sentences, or paragraphs, we would designate them — Let me then only say, that we took leave of the hospitable family with sensations worthy the tenderness, by which we have been distinguished, worthy that cementing faith which mutually binds our spirits, in bands indisposable — Doctor Turner, with his Lady, and some other friends, accompanied us many miles on our way, and quitting our Carriages, the parting, and expressive embraces, were ardently, and repeatedly reitterated — But, again I say — of parting scenes no more — we are hastening forward to our Eastern friends, and truth to say, the full weight of this consideration was, upon thursday morning, abundantly necessary to dissipate the glooms which obtruded upon my soul — Amiable, polite, and humane pair — Amiable Family, farewell [—] I will not say forever — for at least in Worlds beyond the sky we shall meet again.

And now the Month of October is advancing on, and, e'er its close, I trust I shall rejoin Connexions in Boston, and in Gloucester who will not yield to any individuals, in continued, and indulgent affection — The road from Norwich to Providence, is rather rough, and unpleasing, and the various indications of winter, which we conceive taking place prematurely, did not contribute to the pleasures of the way. We reached Volenton at sunset, where we wore away the night, our accommodations serving as a contrast to those which we had so recently quitted [—] yesterday morning produced us again in the Carriage, when we soon bid adieu to the quondam dominion of the great Sachem Connecticut rejoicing most sincerely, that but the state of Rhode Island, lay between us and the government, whither our warmest aspirations tended [—] With regard to a voyage across the Atlantic, which you, my beloved Father conceive we may have in contemplation — I will only say that it makes no part of our present plan, and that should such a tour be ever meditated it shall not meet with my concurrence — While I am happy enough to boast that I have parents this side [of that] Elysium, except indeed, such voyage should receive the sanction of their approbation — you will please to remember me affectionately to our friends and tell my sister Anna, that I had the pleasure of meeting at Norwich an uncle of hers, who resides at Lime — he entrusted me with a letter to Madam Forbes, which as he wished me to deliver with my own hands, I forbear to inclose — To the sweet Anna [I] breathe a kiss of warm affection — This day hath been particularly gloomy, the rain hath continued without cessation, and my situation at present, is rather awkward [—] I have not a single article of apparel, not even a pair of hose, save what I have now on — This side of Norwich, near fifty miles from hence, [where] with the greater celerity, we made up the whole of our baggage in a large trunk [delivering] it to the stage which was to have left Norwich on Thursday but the stage is not in and what is worse, by intelligence this hour received, we have no reason to expect it at all! The Man whose property it is, hath given up passing any more, until some particulars can be adjusted, which will consume many weeks to accommodate so that you will judge of our perplexity [—] Mr Murray is this moment writing letters to Norwich, to entreat the interference of his friends [—] O! dear — May God forever bless my honoured Parents ——

Letter 804 To Anna Providence State of Rhode Island October 11th 1790

Judith acknowledges a recent letter from Anna, her young charge. She admires her poetry, but also chastises her for not relating news of family and friends. She discusses her thoughts on marriage with Anna, and gives her an updated account of her schedule. She expects to be in Boston soon, where John will "congregate his friends" and preach for a couple of days. They will then leave for Salem, and for Gloucester the following day, weather permitting. She expects to "breathe [her] native air" on the 26th.

Being engaged to pass the afternoon in a Circle of strangers, I have but a moment at my command — yet, hearing of an opportunity for Boston, my feelings impel me to snatch the pen, just to acknowledge the receipt of your last very pleasing, and handsomely written letter — To yield you my entire approbation will, my dear Girl, upon every occasion afford me sensible pleasure — the task of censuring is painful, and although the reproved, must always suffer, yet it is indubitably true, if the person who is under the necessity of pointing out an error, possesseth an ingeneous mind, he, or she, will always come in for their full share of unpleasant sensations — I hope, and I pleasingly believe, that discretion hath been your guide through the past summer — I trust your conduct hath been irreproachable — Indeed I fear nothing so much as your inexperience, communicative disposition, and a kind of pliability, which under proper direction, will form an ornamental, and useful trait in your character — The poetical part of your letter hath much merit — it is descriptive of a mind at ease, and while it excites a smile it finds its way to my heart, as a positive proof, that you are in possession of tranquility [—] you are perfectly right, my dear, it is much more eligible to perform the voyage of life without a partner, than to connect yourself unworthily — Death only dissolves the marriage vow, and much to be depricated is the situation of that unhappy body, who is reduced to the necessity of supplicating for such an event, as a release from hand worn bonds — The ardent, and susceptible Mind can hardly, in the marriage state, know a medium — In that most intimate of all connexions, if the parties possess feeling hearts, it cannot rationally be expected, they will ever know indifference, and, if all potent Love doth not deign to strew their path with flowers, the probability is, that hatred will be busy in souring the most obnoxious minds — Neither Reason, nor good Sense will ever consider the single life as dishonourable, and propriety of conduct will dignify any character, or any situation — If you can contribute to the pleasure or convenience of my Mother, I shall be doubly pleased, as I shall, in that case, be confident your advantage, and your satisfaction will be mutual — I grieve that the delay of our return hath been productive of so much pain to her revered, and tender bosom — but it hath been unavoidable, and I trust that the period is now at hand, when we shall once more rejoin her — I persuade myself, that at least a transient suspension of her pangful complaints, will allow her maternal countenance, to beam upon me with every sweet, and benign expression — My Father too, my brothers, my sisters, and the little knot of children, so sweetly augmented [—] What a charming group — Why, my dear, were you not more particular — Do you not know that I have been nearly six months absent from my home — Can you tell me why my Cousin Mary hath not answered my letter, but it will now be too late to forward any account to me further than Boston, which place we expect to reach the last of next week — Mr Murray will be necessitated to congregate his friends in that place, upon the following sunday, and the ensuing Monday, we shall commence our journey homeward — We do not purpose to pass through in a day, at this season it would be inconvenient, and ill judged — But tuesday we will be upon the [wing] — Let me see — upon the 26 of October, should the weather on said Monday, and tuesday prove propitious, I trust I shall once more breathe my native air — Mr S— at a Ball — upon my word — What strange revolutions six months have produced — However, I acknowledge this to be a very pleasant effect, of the fluctuations to which the minds of Men, as well as women are subjected — I feel very much obliged to Mr and Mrs S— for their attention to you — remember them en famille, very affectionately Farewell — the letters addressed to my Father and Mother, will transmit every particular of consequence, to your Parental friends —

HOME TO MASSACHUSETTS:
"THE LAST AND MOST PLEASING STAGE"

Letter 805 to my Father and Mother, State of Massachusetts
Taunton October 16 1790 Saturday Evening

Their trunk still has not arrived and Judith, in a "peevish mood," has taken to her chamber. There, she hears music which, she confesses, "possesseth over [her] soul the most potent influence." Thinking they would leave the next day, she does not seek out the source of the music. But the rain continued, and their stay was prolonged. They were invited to take tea with their host's tenants (who their host was forced to take in because of the "fraudulent currency" problem in Rhode Island) and there she met Mrs. Butler and her daughter. The trunk was returned in time for Judith and John to dress appropriately, they took tea, and Judith learned that Miss Butler was the musical artist she had heard the previous evening.

President Washington had made a recent visit to Providence. Rhode Island had just ratified the Constitution, and Washington went to welcome them into "the Federal Compact." Judith relates the popular response to his visit, and the kindness of the "humane Chief" to a wounded former body guard he spotted in the crowd. John preached in Providence, and they journeyed the following day to the home of Mr. and Mrs. Cobb in Taunton, Massachusetts. Having read the journal of Governor John Winthrop (the first governor of Massachusetts) Judith recounts the founding of Taunton by Elizabeth Poole — her flight from England because of religious persecution, and her purchase of land from the "indians." Judith also tells a story about Governor Winthrop signing a treaty with another tribe. Delighted to be back in her home state, Judith tells her parents she will "commence the last, and most pleasing stage of their journey" very soon — home to Gloucester.

My last address to my dear Parents, concluded rather in the ill Penseroso style — Our prospects continued to wear a gloomy aspect — The clouds still poured forth their inundating showers — Saturday night — and No Trunk — Strangers, according to custom gathered round — Riding had rendered a change of apparel absolutely necessary but of so pleasant a luxury I had not the smallest expectation at least not until our letters could reach Norwich, which might induce our friends to concent measures to forward our baggage — I retired to my chamber, my mind sufficiently impressed by the ineligibles of my situation —

The fluctuating arrangements of the inhabitants of the state of Rhode Island and the prevalence of the fraudulent paper currency, hath divested our host in Providence of so large a proportion of his property, that having a family of children to provide for, prudence hath impelled him to receive into the chambers of the right wing of his house a tenant, from whom he is separated only by a small entry —

Of a family satisfied with accommodations so small, and inconvenient, it was not in pride to think much, and, besides, I was not in a humour to form very sanguine hopes, and, as I said, I seated myself in my chamber — even my pen had lost its charms, and I was quite disposed to indulge a thousand little particulars which officiously obtruded — There is, it should seem, some thing very uncommon in the organization of my ear, for although I could never in my whole life, attain the exact modulation of the most simply constructed tune, yet Notes grave, sprightly, pathetic, or sublime are perfectly arranged in my ideas, nor can I, even to this day be convinced but by trial that I can articulate them — Musick possesseth over my soul the most potent influence [—] it elates, it soothes, or harmonizes my spirit, and I experienced in the moment to which I advert its fullest power — Suddenly, while I sat in peevish mood, my head reclining on my hand[,] sounds the most imposing, drawn from the Piano Forte, vibrated on my ear — sweetly soothing, and plaintively pathetic, they were regulated by the finger of judgment, and they indisputably issued from the adjacent apartment, while my feelings, as if touched by a magick wand, were instantaneously tranquilized, my glooms were dissipated, my chagrin was no more, and I involuntarily moved towards the door of my apartment — To commence an acquaintance with the Performer — for I took it for granted, such strains could result only from female efforts — became the height of my ambition, but as our stay in Providence was to be momentary, I condemned the wish as the offspring of that romantic fancy, in which my hopes, and fears, have been said to receive their contour — the music ceased — and the company in the parlour, the manners of whom forming a contrast — so said imagination — to those of our neighbours, summoned me to the tea table — The evening passed heavily enough, and sunday morning produced a repetition of the scene — Winds, and rain, tumultuously contending, and we seemed prematurely enwrapped in all the horrors of the wintry months — But the breakfast apparatus being removed, a genteel figure presented — she literally descended from above, and she came fraught with apologies from her superior, the substance of which was that confined by ill health to her chamber, she could not tender her personal compliments, and she was commissioned to request, that we would do her dear Mamma the honour, to take a cup of tea with her in the evening [—] The young Lady appeared about sixteen, her countenance was pleasing, and her manners would do honour to a Court — I would have excused myself, pleading my embarrassment from the detention of my baggage — but, with inimitable grace she observed "Travellers, my dear Lady, are entitled to every allowance — Permit me to hope, you will not mortify my Mamma by a refusal["] — I was irresistably impelled to acquiescence, and I shaped my reply accordingly — The young Lady, apparently well pleased at the success of her embassy, took her leave — It drew toward Noon [—] The clouds began to disperse — Twelve O clock restored a serene sky, and about one O clock — Heaven bless the benign spirit which so abundantly pervades the bosom of every inhabitant of Norwich — of whom I have the smallest knowledge — about One O clock I say, came our trunk — our situation was considered, the feelings of benevolence were engaged, and, through all the severity of the weather, over rough, and heavy roads, upwards of forty miles, it was hastened on and our previous anxiety, did but enhance our subsequent satisfaction — so true it is, that even in the most trivial circumstances, experienced disappointment, does but augment the good, which may await — Decently accoutred, we made our evening visit, and were surprised by an uncommon degree of elegance in furniture, disposition, and manners — We were attended by a livery servant, and every thing was in a style, which announced a general acquaintance with the World — To keep you no longer in suspense, allow me, my beloved Parents, to introduce you to a granddaughter of Governor Wentworth's — affiancing herself, unsanctioned by parental authority, to a British Officer, a Major Butler with whom she hath long worn the marriage chain — She hath repeatedly crossed the Atlantic — In Portsmouth, New York, and London, her children have been born [—] Her career in life was commenced with much eclat — only the wreck of her fortunes now remains — It is said Major Butler hath been distressed by a series of calamities [—] Mrs Butler is spoken of as the daughter of Misfortune — yet she appears tranquil and even cheerful — her deportment is descriptive of the polite, and thoroughly well bred Woman, and her manners were evidently the result of experience, and an extensive acquaintance with what is called good company — her figure is genteel, and her countenance rather agreeable — Her eldest daughter, the young Lady who paid her compliments in the morning, hath received her education in the City of London — Her eldest son, a youth of seventeen, is a midshipman in the British Navy, and she hath a son, and daughter but just in the dawn of being — Her abode in Providence will be transient — Major Butler is absent, in pursuit of some establishment for his little family, and their future destination is truly precarious — During our abode in Providence we received from Mrs Butler, many civilities, and at our departure — by way of regale upon the road, she pressed upon us some prodigious fine Oranges — In Providence we have many valuable friends — In the family of Mr Brown an opulent Merchant, we have visited and we received from Mr Henry Ward, and his Connexions, than which is difficult to conceive a more amiable, or more improved Circle, a continuation of good offices —

The last visit of our illustrious President, to the State of Rhode Island, was productive of inessable satisfaction — Indeed it was perfectly well timed, perfectly in character, and perfectly consistent with the conciliatory plans of that celebrious, and all accomplished Hero, and it hath unquestionably done much toward completing the Federal Compact — Such a glow of satisfaction seems at this period universally diffused, that we are ready to ask whither hath the disaffected fled? — The inhabitants of Providence [think] of the progress of the benignant Chief as of the descent of a celestial Being among them, and they can hardly command themselves, while recounting the particulars — Upon the day on which, for the gratification of the people, the President, and his suite, paraded the streets[,] a person, who had formerly been deranged in his mind, found the joys of his heart, too great for his but recently established reason — he hastened to his garden, and plucking from them a large Musk Melon, rushed out of his house, declaring that he would deliver it into his own hands — he proceeded with the utmost velocity, in pursuit of the General, passing through lanes, and streets, bearing in triumph his intended compliment — In vain the inconvenience of receiving such an offering in the street was represented to him — In vain he was urged to send it to his Hero's quarters — No, he disdained such clandestine proceedings — The World should witness his allegiance — It was a tender worthy the acceptance of a Prince, and he himself would be the Bearer — Thus he went on and hardly was he restrained by force from executing his purpose — Among the crouds of admiring, and delighted spectators, which, upon that day, lined the streets of Providence, was a poor industrious Man — He had in the course of the War been one of General Washington's life guards, and he had lost a leg in the service — but [through] hard labour, and honest industry he scarcely obtained the scanty means of supporting a number of children, and he hath constantly eaten the bread of carefulness — among the grateful, and only not adoring spectators this Brave Veteran, as I said, presented himself when his General saw and immediately recognized him — With an expression of surprise the humane Chief selected him from among the throng — On his wooden stump the soldier approached — The General reached forth his hand, grasping his fellow Citizen with great condescension, and apparent satisfaction — "How are you my brother [—] What say you — Should our Country again require your aid, will you once more join her standard — Can you yet fight her battles" — "Assuredly Sir," replied the old Man "assuredly I can — While Heaven still continueth a Washington to command["] — The Hero smiled complacent — Could he do otherwise — and he presented the brave Old Man, upon the spot, with five Johannes — We left Providence yesterday Morning — where I ought to have observed — Mr Murray repeatedly addressed a large, and respectable audience, who assembled in their commodious presbyterian house of worship, which hath recently been finished, and beautified — The evening preceeding our departure, the congregation was prodigious, and they listened with marked, and solemn attention, while the Preacher expatiated upon the sacred text "Thy King cometh to thee just, and bringing salvation" — Our road, owing to the heavy rains which have recently fallen in such abundance, was tedious and heavy, and three miles distant from this place, we were surprised by a sudden, and very copious shower — we were not, however materially incommoded, and the setting sun saw us pleasingly accommodated — With Mr & Mrs Cobb, our hospitable Host and hostess, and with Taunton you are well acquainted, and I have only to say, our reception was in no sort inferior, to what it hath heretofore been — Reading lately Governor Winthrop's journal, I have learned that an english Maiden Lady a Mrs Elizabeth Poole, was the Foundress of Tecticut, or Taunton — a Monument erected to her memory, by Mr Borland who was [her] kinsman I have this afternoon, and with no small degree of veneration, visited — It is now however going to decay — It is placed upon a beautiful, and extensive green —which contains no other Grave — She was of a respectable family, and [possessed] pleasing prospects in England, but she was not tolerated in the peaceable exercise of the Religion of her election — Persecution reared its hydra head against her, and she fled from her native Land — most heroically bidding adieu to a situation in every other respect truly eligible — She came into this country, then the abode of ferocious, and savage men — and purchased of the Indians the whole ground upon which Taunton now stands — It was then of course a Wilderness, but she immediately began to clear the Land — to plant, and to cultivate, and being solo Proprietor, she disposed of her grounds in a manner which she judged most advantageous to her infant plantation — she still preferred a single life, and employed herself wholly in acts of benevolence — Her conduct was, in every respect, truly exemplary, and the sanctity of her manners was remarkable — she was beloved, and venerated by all parties, and in the year 1654 having attained the 65th year of her age she paid the great debt of Nature long, and universally lamented — The Governor's journal contains many curious anecdotes, but I do not recollect a single passage that affected me more agreeably than the address of Okaco, the Mohegan Sachem, to the Governor of Massachusetts, upon the ratification of a treaty of peace — I will give it to you in his own words "This heart" laying his hand upon his breast "is not mine, but yours — I have no Men, They are all yours — Command me any difficult thing

— I will do it, I will not believe any Indian words against the English —
If any Man shall kill an Englishman, I will put him to death were he
ever so dear to me —" How gravely sententious, how richly
comprehensive — but it asks not the aid of a comment — And now my
best, my parental friends we have attained the bounds of our native
state — I speak, you will observe in the plural — for Mr Murray obligingly
tender, unites so effectually in my hopes, my fears, and my wishes, as to
render it hardly possibl[e] to recur to the circumstance of his not being
a native of that remote spot, which gave me birth — We expect to
reach Boston the last of next week — The ensuing sunday must of
necessity be devoted to the congregation in that Metropolis — but upon
the following Monday, with hearts beating with expectation, we shall
commence the last, and most pleasing stage of our journey, and if the
weather corresponds with our wishes, tuesday noon, will produce us
once more in Gloucester — I forbear, upon this occasion, to enumerate
my several friends — their respective claims are fully admitted, and
they all retain a due share of my hearts best affection — The sweet
Anna Maria, as being the only stranger in the circle of my connexions,
may perhaps be entitled to my particular attention, you will therefore
breathe into the ear, of that guileless young Lady, my fondest wishes —
Press her, for me, to your parental bosom, and know that I am prepared
to love, and to receive her into the inmost recesses of my heart —
Farewell — I am at all times duteously, and affectionately yours —

"We expect to reach Boston the last of next week...."
(from Letter 805)

Boston from Breed's Hill, from the *Massachusetts Magazine,* January 1791.
Courtesy of The Bostonian Society/Old State House.

Letter 806 To the Same — Boston October 23 — 1790
Saturday Morning Early

This is the last week of Judith's journal and the last letter, well aware, she writes, of the "sweet consciousness that I am verging toward my native home." Before leaving Taunton, John preached three times. They proceeded next to Stoughton, to the home of Colonel Gridley. Sadly, his wife had passed away only days before, and Judith and John stayed to help bury her — John officiating at one of the ceremonies "to do justice to the departed, and to administer consolation to [the] survivors." From Stoughton, they traveled to Milton and enjoyed a sumptuous dinner planned for them at a public house. Finally, they arrived in Boston, and Judith found herself "in the arms of [her] honoured Father." They will stay at her Uncle Daniel's home on Long Wharf before travelling to Salem and Gloucester. John is expected to preach for the Boston congregation. Three years later, in 1793, the Boston Universalists installed John as their minister. Finding it increasingly difficult to divide his time between the congregation in Gloucester and his new one in Boston, John decided to move his family to Boston in 1794 and make "the Metropolis" their permanent home. Although she can now recount her recent movements to her father in person, Judith writes this letter to conclude the journal she began six months ago. Soon, she will be home.

One more letter, my honoured Parents, and I close, for the present a correspondence which hath been to me, during our long, long absence, a most pleasing alleviation of those regrets, which a separation from such tender, and revered friends necessarily originates — I resign the pen with much pleasure — With superior pleasure I assure myself, that e'er the revolution of another saturday, I shall have tasted those virtuous joys, which result from the embraces that blest parental fondness will with indulgent condescension so liberally bestow, and with anticipated satisfaction upon the appropriated day, I have already in imagination, taken my seat at the well known hospitable board, inhaling all those sensations which are in the gift of parental affection, and, domestic happiness to bestow — Buoyed up by an expedition so animating, I proceed to bring forward the last week of my journal, which although less various than many other divisions of my time, hath nevertheless been zested by the sweet consciousness that I am verging toward my native home — Three times on sunday last, Mr Murray met a number of seriously attentive hearers, in the Court house of Taunton — Our visit to that place ended as it began, and we received various proofs of kindness — The weather on Monday was remarkably fine, and we commenced our journey to Stoughton — We had dwelt much upon the serene enjoyments which awaited us in the family of Colonel Gridley, and it was only in the dwelling of our parents, we expected more unequivocal marks of friendship — upon how many contingencies doth subliminary bliss depend — surely we ought never to promise ourselves the possessio[n] of any terrestrial good. We posted forward with much rapidity — for the convivial smiles of hospitality we were prepared — But alas! for us, the venerable Mistress of Stoughton Village had the day before our arrival, breathed her last! Her family[,] her bereaved family met us in tears, but her clay cold tenement shrouded in its burial dress, unconscious of our approach, preserved, with dignified tranquility, its sweet and expressive composure — Often had her arms with even maternal tenderness, been extended to receive us, while the tumultuous joy of her bosom, was delineated in every feature of her face — but her heart had now forgotten to beat — To the glad sensations of affection, it no longer awakened, and for the presence of the Messenger of peace, the sigh of her perturbed bosom will no longer ascend — she hath lingered out many years of pain, and her agonies for weeks past, have been exquisite — Ought we then to lament her exit — especially as she departed strong in faith and giving glory to God — yet, for me, I confess, I am selfish — considerably selfish, and while I stood gazing upon her breathless Corse, the agonized breathings of my spirit, to the Preserver of Men, were that I might never be called to view my beloved Parents, thus stretched upon the bed of death — The life of Mrs Gridley hath been amiable — she hath departed full of days and her connexions will retain the sister, the friend, the Wife, and the Parent, the sweetest remembrance — We had intended to have reached town earlier in the week — but it was not in Friendship to leave unburied, a connexion so venerable, or to resist the pressing importunities of her aged Companion, and the earnestly soliciting children — we continued at Stoughton from Monday noon, until Friday morning, yielding such consolation as an old, and unbroken, amity had a right to claim — On thursday afternoon the sepulchral rites were performed — her only surviving brother, a white haired old gentleman, with his Lady, and a number of other connexions, arrived about noon from Boston, for the purpose of attending the funeral obsequies of the deceased, thus sympathizing with the living, and paying the last honours to the dead — Mr Murray, previous to the commencement of the procession, delivered an affecting exhortation, and addressed the common Father of our spirits, in a well adapted prayr — He made suitable observations at the Grove which were calculated to do justice to the departed, and to administer consolation to survivors

A large number assembled at Colonel Gridley's on thursday evening, and we passed it like those, who entertained a sure and certain hope of meeting again, the beloved connexion who had so recently taken her flight — The weather yesterday morning proved most propitious to our wishes, and after a night of refreshing slumber we departed from Stoughton enriched by the fervant benediction of our dear friends — At Milton we were met by Mr J. Russell, and a number of our congratulating Connexions, who had ordered a superb dinner for us at a public house, said dinner consisted of boiled fowls, and their appendages, a loin of roasted veal, a pair of prodigious fine ducks, with the sauces of gravy, and cellery, a brace of Partridges, and a dish of Quails, these with tarts of a most excellent quality, a desert of fruit — Lemonade Punch, and super fine Maderia, procured for the occasion by the cellar of Mrs Jeffries compiled the groser part of our entertainment — The gentlemen expressed great exultation at the return of Mr Murray [—] But all description must [wait] — for we soon reached Boston and soon enjoyed the superior pleasure of meeting and indulging the fondest

"...upon the following Monday, with hearts beating
with expectation, we shall commence the last,
and most pleasing stage of our journey...."
[through Salem, to Gloucester]
(from Letter 806)

Fireboard: *View of Court House Square, Salem, Massachusetts, 1810-1820,* by George Washington Felt. Courtesy of the Peabody Essex Museum, Salem, MA.

feelings of affection, in the arms of my honoured Father — joining this revered Parent so happily, and unexpectedly, in this Place, it may be asked why do I continue my scribbling, for I can certainly transmit by him, without the aid of pen, and ink, every communication which I am so soon to return, can now be necessary — But, my beloved Mother is not present — and I hope my dear Sir, that both she, and you, will indulge me in the whim, of concluding my journal, precisely as it commenced — I regret much that my brother, and sister, departed home before I reached Boston — could they not have tarried one day longer — I am mortified that neither Esther, nor Fitz William, my sister Anna, nor Sally, found it convenient to respond to my letters — I would thank you to inform my dear Orphan Girl, and my Cousin Mary, that I have received their favours, but that my stay in Boston will be so short, as to put it out of my power to respond — I have been welcomed to this house, with accustomed kindness [—] I have received a letter from my eldest brother, which I would inclose were I not solicitous to give it an early answer — He expresses himself of the Authors of his being, with all respect and affection — I suppose he will soon be in Gloucester — If the weather should continue fine, you will expect us on the promised day — you will please to give to the domestic, the interesting Circle, my hearts love — My Father is on the wing — May God forever Bless you —

"I hope...you will indulge me in the whim, of concluding my journal, precisely as it commenced...."
(from Letter 806)

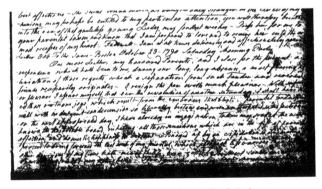

Fragment of the page from Letter Book 8 showing the beginning of Letter 806, the last letter about the 1790 journey.

Epilogue
∽

J udith Sargent Murray's story continues. We have much more to learn about this remarkable woman, and much more to learn about people, places, and events in American history from her perspective. Judith Sargent Murray's account, left behind in her letters, will make the American story more complete.

The letters contained in this book are merely a beginning — excerpts from a full length book, *The Letters of Judith Sargent Murray*, which will include edited transcriptions of all the letters (almost 2,000), more biographical information, and dozens of portraits, drawings, and photographs of the people, places, and belongings in her life. Meanwhile, the Judith Sargent Murray Society will continue its efforts to bring Judith's life and legacy to public attention through publishing, speaking engagements, school programs, and our web site. Through these and other efforts, we will continue to weave Judith's place in American and feminist history back into our national story.

As for John Murray, he, too, remains under-appreciated for his determining role in religious freedom in America. In 1837, his remains were moved from Boston to Mount Auburn Cemetery in Cambridge where an elegant monument was erected by the United States General Convention of Universalists. They saw fit to honor and esteem their early leader, as have later generations of Unitarian Universalists, but he deserves a wider audience — a more universal remembrance of his courage and faith.

As we piece together the puzzle of Judith Sargent Murray's life, we welcome any information you might have about the people and places described in this book. We gladly accept your ideas for collaborative programs and your financial support.

Please contact:

Bonnie Smith, Director
Judith Sargent Murray Society
15 Cameron Avenue
Cambridge, MA 02140

617-576-3869
Fax: 617-876-1038
bmhsmith@shore.net
Web site:
www.hurdsmith.com/judith

(To join the Society, please send a check for $25, payable to the Judith Sargent Murray Society, to the above address.)

Selected Bibliography

Primary/18th-Century
The Judith Sargent Murray Papers (microfilm, original documents housed at the
Mississippi Department of Archives)
The Gleaner: A Miscellaneous Production by Constantia (Judith Sargent Murray)
(orig. publication: I. Thomas and E.T. Andrews, Boston, 1798; reissued by
Union College Press, 1994)
The Life of Rev. John Murray, written by himself (orig. publication: by Francis
and Munroe, Boston, 1816; reissued by Marsh, Capen and Lyon, 1832)
1789 Letter from John Murray to Paul Dudley Sargent, transcribed from
The Dolphin,newsletter of the Sargent-Murray-Gilman-Hough House
Association, Spring 1994
A Vindication of the Rights of Woman by Mary Wollstonecraft (orig. publication:
1792, reissued by W.W. Norton in 1975)
History of the Rise, Progress and Termination of the American Revolution
by Mrs. Mercy [Otis] Warren (orig. publication: 1805;
reissued by AMS Press, 1970)
Boston Weekly Magazine (various, 1802-1805)
The Columbian Centinel, Thomas Paine, ed. (various, 1793-1803)
The Federal Orrery (various, 1794)
Gentleman and Lady's Town and Country Magazine (1784)
The Massachusetts Magazine (various, 1790-1794)
Julia, and the Illuminated Baron by A Lady of Massachusets [Sally Sayward
Barrell Keating Wood], (Oracle Press, 1800)
The Oriental Philanthropist by Henry Sherburne (Wm. Treadwell & Co., 1800)

Judith Sargent Murray, Family, and Friends
Dykeman, Therese Boos, *American Women Philosophers 1650-1930:
Six Exemplary Thinkers* (Edwin Mellon Press, 1993)
Gibson, Rev. Gordon J., *The Rediscovery of Judith Sargent Murray*
(Murray Grove Association, 1993)
Harris, Sharon M., *The Selected Writings of Judith Sargent Murray*
(Oxford University Press, 1995)
Low, Willa, *Winthrop Sargent: Soldier and Statesman*
(Sargent-Murray-Gilman-Hough House Association, 1976)
Smith, Caroline Turner, *Caroline Augusta Turner Sargent*
(privately published, Chatham, New Jersey, 1995)
Withey, Lynne, *Dearest Friend: A Life of Abigail Adams*
(The Free Press, 1981)
Gleanings (newsletter of the Judith Sargent Murray Society,
Spring, Summer, Fall, 1997; Winter 1998)

American History: Political/Women
Billias, George Athan, ed., *George Washington's Generals and Opponents*
(Da Capo Press, 1994)
Blum, Morgan, Rose, Schledinger, Stammp, and Woodward, *The National
Experience, Part One* (Harcourt Brace Jovanovich, 1981)
Cott, Nancy, *The Bonds of Womanhood* (Yale University Press, 1977)

Duby, Georges, and Perrot, Michelle, eds., *A History of Women: Emerging Feminism from Revolution to World War* (Belknap Press, 1993)

Evans, Sara M., *Born for Liberty* (The Free Press, 1989)

Ferris, Robert G. and Morris, Richard E., National Park Service, *The Signers of the Declaration of Independence* (Interpretive Publications, 1982)

Ferris Robert G. and Charleton, James H., National Park Service, *The Signers of the Constitution* (Interpretive Publications, 1986)

Kerber, Linda K., *Women of the Republic* (U. North Carolina Press, 1988)

Kerber, Linda K. and Dehart, Jane Sherron, *Women's America: Refocusing the Past* (Oxford University Press, 1991)

Morgan, Edmund S., *The Birth of the Republic* (University of Chicago Press, reissued 1992)

Moynihan, Ruth Barnes, Russett, Cynthia, and Crumpacker, Laurie, eds., *Second to None: A Documentary History of American Women* (The University of Nebraska Press, 1993)

Norton, Mary Beth, *Liberty's Daughters: The Revolutionary Experience of American Women, 1750-1800* (Little, Brown and Company, 1980)

Randall, Willard Sterne, *George Washington* (Henry Holt and Company, 1997)

Rebora, Staiti, Hirshler, Stebbins, and Troyen, *John Singleton Copley in America* (Metropolitan Museum of Art, New York, 1995)

Rossi, Alice, ed., *The Feminist Papers* (Northeastern University Press, 1973)

Tuchman, Barbara W., *The First Salute: A View of the American Revolution* (Alfred A. Knopf, 1988)

American History: Daily Life

Kay, Jane Holtz, *Lost Boston* (Houghton Mifflin Company, 1980)

Leighton, Ann, *American Gardens in the Eighteenth Century* (The University of Massachusetts Press, 1976)

Nylander, Jane C., *Our Own Snug Fireside: Images of the New England Home 1760-1860* (Alfred A. Knopf, 1994)

Taylor, Dale, *The Writer's Guide to Everyday Life in Colonial America* (Writer's Digest Books, 1997)

Wilbur, C. Keith, M.D., *Revolutionary Medicine* (Chelsea House Publishers, 1980)

American History: Gloucester and Essex County

Babson, John J., *History of the Town of Gloucester, Cape Ann* (orig. publication: 1860; reissued by Peter Smith, 1972)

Garland, Joseph E., *Guns Off Gloucester* (Essex County Newspapers, 1975)

Hurd, D. Hamilton, *History of Essex County, Massachusetts* (J.W. Lewis & Co., 1888)

Pringle, James R., *History of the Town of Gloucester, Cape Ann, Massachusetts* (orig. publication: 1892; reissued by Gloucester City Archives, 1997)

American History: Universalism

Eddy, Richard, *Universalism in Gloucester, Mass.* (Proctor Brothers, 1892)

Howe, Charles A., *The Larger Faith: A History of Universalism in America* (Unitarian Universalist Association/Skinner House Books, 1993)

About the Author

Bonnie (Marjorie Hurd) Smith first began her academic work on Judith Sargent Murray in 1982 at Simmons College in Boston. There, she received a B.A. in History and Communications, focusing on early American women's history. A few years later, she joined the board of directors of The Sargent House Museum in Gloucester, Judith Sargent Murray's home from 1782-1794. In 1993, Smith received her Master of Science degree from Simmons in Communications Management. Her thesis was a marketing plan to launch a "product" — Judith Sargent Murray — into mainstream American history. A public relations and fundraising professional, Smith was soon asked to chair the external relations committee at The Sargent House Museum and became its President in 1992. There, she developed programs, exhibits, and publications, worked with local schools and the media, presided over events and published articles — all to bring Judith Sargent Murray into the public eye and use the museum as a living history classroom. In 1997 Smith founded the Judith Sargent Murray Society, dedicated to promoting Judith's life, work, and legacy. The Society publishes a regular newsletter, maintains a web site, plans events, develops educational programs, collaborates and supports organizations, researchers, or students interested in Judith Sargent Murray. Smith speaks regularly on Judith Sargent Murray at venues from Gloucester, to Boston, to the Chautauqua Institution in New York. She is currently writing a book titled *The Letters of Judith Sargent Murray*. Bonnie Smith is Judith Sargent Murray's second cousin seven times removed. She resides in Cambridge, Massachusetts.